BLOODY SKIES

THOMAS McKELVEY CLEAVER

BLOODY SKIES

XV Fighter Command Against all Odds

OSPREY PUBLISHING
Bloomsbury Publishing Plc
Kemp House, Chawley Park, Cumnor Hill, Oxford OX2 9PH, UK
Bloomsbury Publishing Ireland Limited,
29 Earlsfort Terrace, Dublin 2, D02 AY28, Ireland
Bloomsbury Publishing Inc.
1359 Broadway, 12th Floor, New York, NY 10018, USA
E-mail: info@ospreypublishing.com
www.ospreypublishing.com

OSPREY is a trademark of Osprey Publishing Ltd

First published in Great Britain in 2026

© Thomas McKelvey Cleaver, 2026

Thomas McKelvey Cleaver has asserted his right under the Copyright,
Designs and Patents Act, 1988, to be identified as Author of this work.

All rights reserved. No part of this publication may be: i) reproduced or transmitted in any form, electronic or mechanical, including photocopying, recording or by means of any information storage or retrieval system without prior permission in writing from the publishers; or ii) used or reproduced in any way for the training, development or operation of artificial intelligence (AI) technologies, including generative AI technologies. The rights holders expressly reserve this publication from the text and data mining exception as per Article 4(3) of the Digital Single Market Directive (EU) 2019/790

A catalog record for this book is available from the British Library.

ISBN: HB 9781472865625; PB 9781472865663; eBook 9781472865670; ePDF 9781472865656;
XML 9781472865632; Audio 9781472865649

26 27 28 29 30 10 9 8 7 6 5 4 3 2 1

The quotations from Second Lieutenant Maceo Harris, Captain Wendell Pruitt, First Lieutenant Roscoe Brown, First Lieutenant Robert Williams, and First Lieutenant Leon "Woodie" Spears are from Chris Bucholz, *332nd Fighter Group: Tuskegee Airmen* (Oxford: Osprey Publishing, 2007). The quotations from Second Lieutenant Don Foley, Clyde Jones, Lieutenant Paul Mass, and Captain Jim Stitt are from John W. Lambert, *The 14th Fighter Group in World War II* (Atglen, PA: Schiffer Military History, 2008)

Maps by www.bounford.com
Index by Fionbar Lyons

Typeset by Lumina Datamatics Ltd
Printed and bound in Great Britain by Clays Ltd, Elcograf S.p.A.

Osprey Publishing supports the Woodland Trust, the UK's leading woodland conservation charity.

To find out more about our authors and books visit www.ospreypublishing.com. Here you will find extracts, author interviews, details of forthcoming events and the option to sign up for our newsletter.

For product safety related questions contact productsafety@bloomsbury.com

CONTENTS

List of Illustrations and Maps	6
Foreword by Captain USN (Ret.) Roy Cash Jr.	9
Author Preface	11
CHAPTER ONE: Black Sunday	15
CHAPTER TWO: The Fifteenth Air Force Takes Shape	38
CHAPTER THREE: The Fifteenth is Blooded	59
CHAPTER FOUR: The Fifteenth Air Force Comes of Age	76
CHAPTER FIVE: Target Ploeşti	93
CHAPTER SIX: Shuttle to Russia	114
CHAPTER SEVEN: Red Tails	150
CHAPTER EIGHT: July 1944 – High Point of the Campaign	169
CHAPTER NINE: August Crescendo	202
CHAPTER TEN: Where is the Luftwaffe?	235
CHAPTER ELEVEN: The Final Battles	270
Bibliography	301
Glossary	304
Index	306

LIST OF ILLUSTRATIONS AND MAPS

ILLUSTRATIONS

B-24 Liberators drop their bomb loads on the Concordia Vega refinery at Ploești during Operation *Tidal Wave*, August 1, 1943. (USAF Official)
P-38s of the 14th Fighter Group provided escort for the Ploești missions. (De Luan/Alamy Stock Photo)
B-24 "Sandman" flies away after a run on the Astra Română refinery in Ploești, as photographed by the automatic camera aboard "Sneezy," during Operation *Tidal Wave*. (USAF Official)
A B-24 Liberator flies over the Otopeni airfield in Romania during an attack on the airfield on August 26, 1944. (USAF Official)
Chetnik commander Draža Mihailović organized the rescue of American air crews shot down over Serbia in Yugoslavia and their return to Italy in 1944. (USAF Official)
In August 1944, Romanian Air Force leading ace Prince Constantin "Bâzu" Cantacuzino flew Lieutenant Colonel James Gunn, the senior American prisoner of war, to Foggia in Italy in his Bf-109G to arrange the evacuation of US and Allied prisoners of war as Romania prepared to surrender to the Soviets. (USAF Official)
The Bf-109G flown by Prince Constantin Cantacuzino of the Romanian Air Force to take Lieutenant Colonel James Gunn to Italy. (USAF Official)
Ground crews of the 1st Fighter Group work on a P-38J Lightning. (piemags/Alamy Stock Photo)
A P-38J of the 1st Fighter Group flying over Italy. (piemags/Alamy Stock Photo)

LIST OF ILLUSTRATIONS AND MAPS

31st Fighter Group commander Colonel Charles M. McCorkle briefs group pilots. His P-51B "Betty Jane" – named for his wife – sports 11 of his final total of 12 victories. (USAF Official)

The 31st Fighter Group's Captain John J. Voll was the top-ranked USAAF fighter ace in the Fifteenth Air Force with 21 victories. His last Mustang was P-51D "American Beauty." (USAF Official)

A formation of P-51D Mustangs of the 31st Fighter Group's 508th Fighter Squadron fly formation for the photographer in October 1944. (USAF Official)

A P-51B Mustang of the 5th Fighter Squadron shows the distinctive yellow tail section adopted in October 1944 as identification of the 52nd Fighter Group. (USAF Official)

P-38J Lightnings of the 82nd Fighter Group fly formation for the photographer. The 82nd Group was the top-scoring P-38 group in the MTO. (ART Collection/Alamy Stock Photo)

Colonel Benjamin O. Davis, commander of the 332nd Fighter Group. He fought both the enemy and USAAF commander General Henry H. "Hap" Arnold to keep the 332nd on operations when those opposed to an African American unit in the Air Force accused the pilots of "not measuring up" in the spring of 1944. (USAF Official)

Major George "Spanky" Roberts, commander of the 332nd Fighter Group's 99th Fighter Squadron, led the Red Tails when group commander Colonel Benjamin O. Davis was recalled to Washington to defend the group to Air Force commanders. (USAF Official)

Captain Andrew "Jug" Turner, commander of 100th Fighter Squadron of the 332nd Fighter Group. (USAF Official)

Tuskegee Airmen: Pilots of the 332nd Fighter Group attend pre-mission briefing. (USAF Official)

Pilots of the 332nd Fighter Group's 99th Fighter Squadron in April 1945. (USAF Official)

The close working relationship of a pilot and his crew chief, shown here, was crucial to success. (piemags/Alamy Stock Photo)

MAPS

Map 1: Bombing range of the Fifteenth Air Force   8

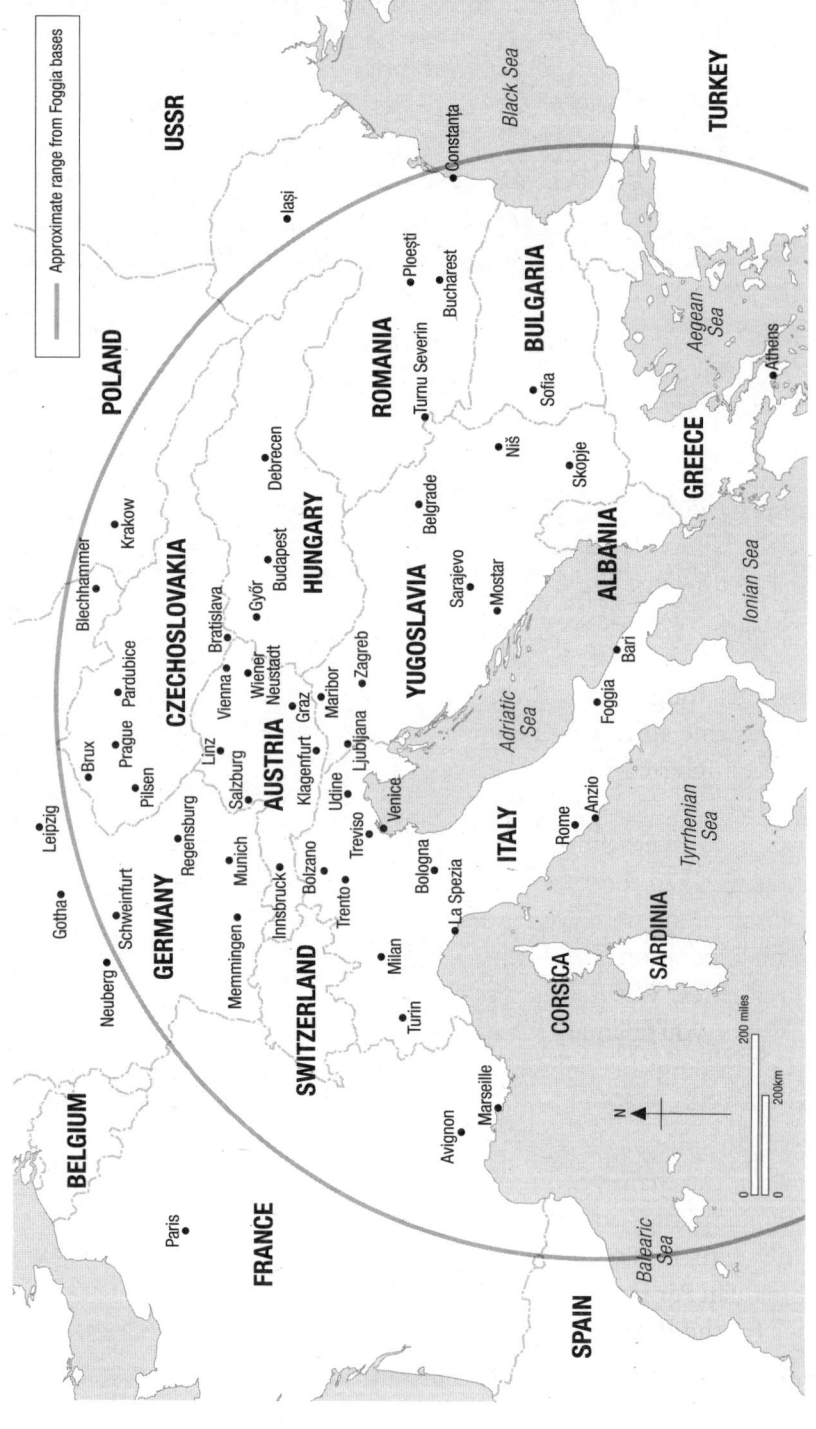

FOREWORD BY CAPTAIN USN (RET.) ROY CASH JR.

Come fly with Tom Cleaver and experience the challenges, the successes, and the failures leading to the ultimate victory achieved by the Fifteenth Air Force against the Axis forces during World War II.

Tom Cleaver's account of the Fifteenth Air Force in its effort to disrupt the Luftwaffe's access to oil supplies is an epic tale. The Fifteenth Air Force fought not only against the German Luftwaffe, but also the very capable air forces of Romania, Bulgaria, Hungary, and Italy.

Often referred to as "The Forgotten Fifteenth" due to less publicity compared to the Eighth Air Force, the Fifteenth, which operated from bases in southern Italy, faced logistical and operational challenges that far outweighed those of the Eighth Air Force operating out of England.

Come along with Tom as the B-24 Liberator pilots and aircrews man up for Operation *Tidal Wave* – the first US mission against the Ploeşti oil refineries. Was it a success or a failure?

Maybe you're an aficionado of World War II fighter aircraft like the P-51 Mustang – a "fighter freak" like me; the story of how the Red Tails of the 332nd Fighter Group defied the racial norms of the era has echoes today. In spite of the ignorant racial attitudes and claims at the highest levels of the chain of command, the Red Tails acquitted themselves well as fighter pilots – and proved their racist detractors very wrong.

Fly with P-38s caught in a disastrous low-level interception by the Romanian Air Force that was that force's greatest day – and "the blackest day" for the P-38 in World War II.

Or fly with P-38 pilots Dick Willsie and Dick Andrews on a mission to Russia that saw Andrews land in Romania to pick up Willsie, his flight leader – "piggyback in a P-38."

Escort the "shuttle raids" to the Soviet Union and experience what the American pilots of the 325th "Checkertail Clan" found when they got to Ukraine.

Whichever role you'd prefer or choose, you'll encounter plenty of action along the way to Wiener Neustadt or Salzburg, Austria, to the railyards in Milan, Italy, flying cover for the Checkertails over Steyr, Austria, or maybe as wingman for one of the Red Tails escorting B-24 Liberators to Friedrichshafen, Germany.

You could also help repulse an attack by 20 enemy fighters from "six o'clock low," and then be ready for the final Red Tails victory en route to Prague, racking up at least four enemy fighters as the final victory for the 332nd Fighter Group. And the final prize: you'll see how the Fifteenth Air Force's primary objective at Ploești fared in the end… emphasis on "the end."

In short, Tom Cleaver has brought to life the thrills, dangers, and, ultimately, a tsunami of action worthy of *Twelve O'Clock High*.

Roy Cash Jr.
Captain, USN, Ret.
Former commander of "Top Gun"

AUTHOR PREFACE

Starting with the first mission on November 2, 1943 – to the Messerschmitt assembly plant at Wiener Neustadt – and finishing with the attack on the Salzburg main marshaling yard on May 1, 1945, the Fifteenth Air Force bore the brunt of an especially difficult campaign. Major General Nathan F. Twining – the Fifteenth's primary commander through the conflict – said at the end of the war, "The cost to us, in both men and materiel, has not been small, but with that indomitable American spirit and know-how, we have surmounted all obstacles to accomplish our mission."

The Eighth fought one enemy: Germany, and its air force, the Luftwaffe. The Fifteenth fought not only the Luftwaffe – its main opponent – but also the air forces of Romania, Bulgaria, Hungary, and the Italian Social Republic founded out of the ruins of Mussolini's Italy. Toward the end of the war, these smaller air forces – particularly the Hungarians – fielded better, more able pilots than the average Luftwaffe *Nachwuchs* (late recruit) from mid-1944 onwards. The Romanian Air Force ended its fight with the country's surrender at the end of August 1944, and the Bulgarian Air Force ceased operation shortly thereafter when the country was overrun by the Soviet Red Army. But the Hungarians and Italians fought on to the final days of the war in 1945. American pilots frequently thought they were up against Germans when they were intercepted by Hungarian pilots, and their three squadrons of Bf-109s racked up a respectable score fighting the Mustangs and Lightnings of XV Fighter Command.

The 332nd Fighter Group – better known as the "Red Tails" – fought more than a foreign enemy in the skies. They fought and won a battle every day of their service for recognition of African Americans' skill and ability as pilots, against the racial prejudices of a mostly Southern higher command in the US Army Air Force (USAAF), with even its chief General Henry H. "Hap" Arnold resisting their initial formation and later doubting their combat competency. Their fight for recognition and opportunity is now recognized as one of the initial moves in the "Second Reconstruction" of the mid-20th-century civil rights movement that transformed the United States. Their story provides a firm reminder of the need for memory and for the study of events that make us uncomfortable – as good history must always aim to do. We need history not to confirm that how we feel now is right, but rather to teach us more about where we come from than we can know ourselves. I am proud to tell this story to a new audience.

The Fifteenth's primary mission was the destruction of the Luftwaffe, followed by the destruction of Axis oil refineries. Ploești, the most famous of the Reich's refineries, became a familiar target from high altitude. The Fifteenth's final accomplishment was the destruction of the German ball-bearing industry.

The most common name for the Fifteenth among the airmen who served in the force was "The Forgotten Fifteenth." This was in recognition of the outsized publicity campaign surrounding the much-larger Eighth Air Force in England. As an author, I dealt with the aftereffects of that situation, with the relative paucity of earlier works on the Fifteenth Air Force as compared with the massive library of multiple group histories and personal memoirs available for the Eighth. There is literally only one group history available for each of the fighter groups that made up XV Fighter Command. There are no group leader memoirs and few by individual participants.

Like the Twelfth Air Force and all the other American combat units in the Mediterranean Theater of Operations (MTO), the Fifteenth Air Force suffered from the prioritization of the war in northeastern Europe over the six-month lead-up to the Normandy landings and the 11 months following to VE Day. Replacement aircraft were hard to get; at times, the P-38-equipped units couldn't field 20 airplanes in total for a mission. The P-51B Mustangs that were largely replaced in the Eighth Air Force by the summer of 1944 soldiered on with XV Fighter Command through the end of the war. The Red Tails didn't receive their first P-51D until December 1944, six months after the

AUTHOR PREFACE

31st Fighter Group – followed rapidly by the 325th and 52nd Fighter Groups – had completely re-equipped with the most important version of the Mustang to see combat, and the P-51Bs they received in June and July 1944 were hand-me-downs from the 325th Group as they received P-51Ds.

Personnel replacement was also difficult. In December 1944, the 31st Fighter Group had 38 pilots for all three squadrons, with many experienced veterans having completed their tours in November. The story was the same across all the groups until replacements began flooding in during January and February 1945. Several of the group war diaries mention that it was a good thing the weather in the winter of 1944–45 was so bad, as it limited the number of missions flown and eased the personnel replacement problem.

Nevertheless, despite all of this, the Fifteenth Air Force accomplished what it had been created for. By mid-August 1944, just before the Romanian surrender, the Ploești oil fields and refineries had been reduced to ruins in a bombing campaign that had got going against the most important target in Europe really only in late April 1944. When combined with the attacks against the synthetic oil industry in Germany carried out by the Eighth Air Force, those four months saw the German fuel supply drop by 80 percent. As Air Force planners had predicted and German leaders had known, such destruction of the main resource necessary to fight a modern industrial-technological war led to a rapid decline on the part of the Luftwaffe. "Where is the Luftwaffe?" was a common question among Allied flyers in both the Eighth and Fifteenth Air Forces from September 1944 to the end of the war the following May.

I hope that this book will be a major contribution to ending "Forgotten Fifteenth" among those interested in aviation history and particularly the air war of World War II.

Thomas McKelvey Cleaver
Encino, California
2025

I

BLACK SUNDAY

Adolf Hitler's powerful Wehrmacht possessed an Achilles' heel: Germany had no large oil deposits in its territory, an essential requirement for maintaining and operating a first-rate 20th-century war machine. Hitler and his generals knew that Germany could not hope to wage the coming war without a reliable supply of crude oil; on the opening day of World War II, Germany itself produced just 0.02 percent of the world's crude oil.

Beginning in 1933 when he came to power, Hitler had supported the work of the chemical firm I.G. Farben, which had developed a process for creating high-quality gasoline from low-grade lignite coal, a fuel that was abundantly available in Germany. While more costly than refining crude oil, the process was economically viable when fully developed. The full-scale development of the synthetic fuel industry was well under way by 1936, with 13 such plants in operation on September 1, 1939, and more under construction. By 1940, the industry was producing 72,000 tons of oil products per day, half of the Wehrmacht's requirements.

To make up the other half, Hitler had turned during the years before the outbreak of war to developing a relationship with Romania and Hungary; while an alliance with Hungary was concluded in 1938, taking control of Romania – which had the most significant oil reserves inside Europe – was more involved.

Romania's oil industry was the most advanced in Europe, centered on the city of Ploeşti, 35 miles north of the capital of Bucharest.

The first oil refineries at Ploești were created in 1859, supported by strong foreign investment because Romania had neither the technical nor financial resources to create the industry on its own. During World War I, Romanian oil was so important that Ploești was taken by Imperial German forces in 1916, following Romania's decision to join the Allies in the war. When postwar reconstruction was completed in the late 1920s, the Romanian oil industry was completely owned by foreign companies. The Astra Română and Unirea refineries were both joint British–Dutch operations; Steaua Română was French–British–Romanian; Sirius Concordia was a joint Belgian–French–Romanian company; Standard Oil of New Jersey owned the Română Americana complex, the largest refinery; Romanians controlled Creditul Minier, the smallest refinery.

By the mid-1930s, the Ploești refinery complex was composed of 13 refineries that between them produced all the oil that Germany would require in the looming war. A formal alliance between Germany and Romania did not come about until 1940. Following the defeat of France that June, the Soviet Union – which was allied with Germany through the Hitler–Stalin Pact – demanded the return of Bessarabia and Bukovina provinces, which had been ceded to Romania in the Treaty of Brest-Litovsk of 1918. Hungary demanded the part of Bessarabia ceded in 1918, while Bulgaria demanded Dobruja. Hitler needed the continuing support of the USSR, while Hungary and Bulgaria were formal German allies. He convinced Romania's King Carol II to accept the demands and cede the territories, while offering a German guarantee for the remaining Romanian territory; German troops and aircraft arrived in July 1940.

In the face of popular outrage over the ceding of territory, King Carol appointed the Hitler-allied fascist leader General Ion Antonescu as prime minister, then abdicated in favor of his 19-year-old son, Mihai, on September 6, 1940. From then until the Romanian surrender in August 1944, Antonescu led a tight fascist dictatorship that suppressed any resistance to German domination of the country. Hitler had gained control of the oil resource he required without firing a shot, while his forces were invited to take control of Romania.

Interestingly, the foreign ownership of the Ploești refineries that the Germans took control of would prove valuable to the Allies when war came, particularly when the British, French, Belgian, and American engineers who had developed the industry and had left the country in the face of the German takeover were able to provide detailed targeting information for each refinery.

A measure of the importance of Ploești was demonstrated by a statement by German General Alfred Jodl, that the Russians could achieve no success on the Eastern Front that would equal the disaster if the Romanian oil fields were captured. Hitler agreed, stating that if the Ploești refineries were destroyed, the damage to the Wehrmacht would be irreparable.

Allied target planning was often hit-or-miss throughout the war, and the planners often found the operational air force commands opposed – ranging from moderately to intransigently – to taking the targeting suggestions and converting them into actual missions. This was not the case with Ploești. Its crucial importance to the German war machine was blindingly obvious to everyone from the outset. Churchill called Ploești "the taproot of German might." The problem was that in 1940–42 there were no airfields on which to base bombers that were within close enough range for the existing bombers to strike the refineries; it was not until 1942 that there would be a bomber available in the region with the range to get to the target and return.

The first airstrike against Ploești was mounted by the Red Air Force on July 13, 1941, following the German invasion of the USSR. The six Pe-8 bombers that bombed the Astra Română and Unirea Orion refineries caused significant damage, setting over 9,000 tons of oil on fire and destroying a large number of storage tanks and railroad tanker cars. Four of the six bombers were shot down by defending German fighters, which even the Soviets declared was too high a price, and there were no other significant raids on Ploești. The Black Sea port of Constanța was a site for petroleum storage and shipping, and was hit by over 50 small Soviet air raids until the German forces captured the airfields in Crimea where the bombers were based in late 1941.

That changed in the summer of 1942 with the arrival in Egypt of 23 B-24D Liberators of the HALPRO detachment.

Following the US entry into the war after Pearl Harbor, the USAAF planned to establish an air force in the China–Burma–India Theater of Operations. The Tenth Air Force, based in British India, would include a heavy bombing force charged with organizing attacks on the Japanese Home Islands from bases in China.

Colonel Harry A. Halverson was a member of Hap Arnold's "bomber mafia," going back to his work on the around the world flight of 1924 and his participation with Carl Spaatz, Ira Eaker, and Pete Quesada in the flight of the Fokker C.2 "Question Mark," which set a record of 150 continuous flying hours using air-to-air refueling in 1929. Halverson was given command of the 98th Bombardment Group (Heavy) located at Barksdale Army Air Forces (AAF) base in Louisiana, one of the first USAAF units to equip with the B-24 Liberator, in March 1942. His orders were to create a special, secret bombing group, using the best crews in the 98th, for a then-unspecified secret mission. The special unit was officially named Halverson Project 63, shortened to Halverson Project and finally to HALPRO. Halverson chose 23 of the 98th's 36 available crews for his project. They were moved to Page AAF outside Fort Myers, Florida, in March, where training began in long-range operations. Halverson gained the solid support of the young aircrews when he got all the second lieutenants promoted to first lieutenant.

The B-24Ds were the first model of the Liberator deemed fully combat-capable, with armor, self-sealing fuel tanks, and defensive gun turrets in the nose, dorsal, belly, and tail positions. These bombers were delivered straight from the factory on April 28, 1942, and were then flown to Wright Field in Ohio, where the unreliable belly turrets were removed and two 400-gallon auxiliary fuel tanks were installed in the forward bomb bay.

Originally, it was planned that HALPRO would fly from Florida to Brazil, then on across the South Atlantic to Africa, across sub-Saharan Africa and South Asia, and over the Himalayas to a base at Chekiang in eastern-central China that would put the bombers in range of Japan.

The force began departing Page AAF in small formations in mid-May. Halverson's training paid off when no one was lost flying to Accra, Gold Coast, despite having to contend with tropical weather that forced several crews to depend on dead-reckoning navigation.

By the time HALPRO was fully assembled in Khartoum, Sudan, in late May, its mission had been overtaken by events. A recently launched ground offensive by the Imperial Japanese Army in China had captured its planned base at Chekiang. On May 28, 1942, the Liberators flew to the Royal Air Force (RAF) base at Fayid, Egypt, where they became the first USAAF combat unit to arrive for operations in the Mediterranean Theater. The British could support HALPRO in Egypt, which would allow the bombers to attack targets in Greece and Sicily as well as the Western Desert battlefield in North Africa.

The USAAF Planning Division quickly realized that if the bombers flew from airfields in Palestine, they would just be in range to attack Ploești. Thus, Ploești became the first strategic European target for the USAAF, only six months after Pearl Harbor. When HALPRO arrived in Egypt, Field Marshal Erwin Rommel's Afrika Korps was in the process of kicking the British Eighth Army out of Libya, creating an emergency situation. Planners believed that if even the small HALPRO force could hit the refineries, the strike might be effective enough to cut some of the fuel Rommel depended on. Plans were quickly made. The full force could not be used, due to ten bombers still requiring major maintenance for problems that had developed during their flights from Florida to Egypt. Only 13 B-24s would take part in the attack on Ploești.

Although Romania as a German ally had declared war on the United States a week after the United States and Germany exchanged their declarations of war on December 11, 1941, the United States had not declared war in reply. Now, the United States finally declared war on Romania on June 5, 1942, to legitimize the pending attack against Romania's oil industry.

The 13 crews that would fly the mission first learned about it when their names were announced on June 10, the day before the mission was to be flown. Briefing for the attack was held on the morning of June 11. Given the size of the force, the decision was made that the attack part of the mission would be flown at night, to lessen the likelihood of enemy fighters intercepting the bombers. The crews would fly to the target and make their attack individually, since none of them were trained for night formation flying. The official briefing was held in the presence of British authorities, who had warned the Americans not to violate Turkish airspace; since the Turkish government was known to be considering closer cooperation with the Axis, the British feared that such a violation of Turkish neutrality would push the government to enter the war on the Axis side. The maps at the briefing showed the route the crews would take: departing from Egypt and flying around neutral Turkey, then across the Black Sea into Romania and on to Ploești. Such a mission was barely within range; if the crews were able to accurately navigate, they would arrive over Ploești at sunrise. Once they had hit the target, they were to cross the Black Sea, again fly around Turkey, and land at the RAF air base at Habbaniya, Iraq.

However, after the official briefing, when the British had left, Colonel Halverson told the crews to fly directly to Romania across Turkey and return to Iraq by the same route, since he did not trust the weather forecast or the crews' navigation capabilities to get to Ploești and return otherwise.

The first bomber took off at 2230 hours on June 11, 1942. All were airborne and on their way by 2300 hours. As they flew over Turkey, the Liberators were met with searchlights and some limited gunfire, but none of the bombers were hit. Over the Black Sea, they climbed to bombing altitudes between 28,000 and 30,000 feet. Arriving over Romania at dawn, the Liberators approached Ploești individually at around 14,000 feet, as they tried to find their targets while flying through heavy cloud cover that frustrated the navigators. Antiaircraft fire and a few enemy fighters were encountered as the crews dropped 24 tons of bombs. Since the crews didn't possess the training to bomb accurately in darkness, the raid inflicted no real damage. One crew bombed the Romanian harbor of Constanța. At Ploești, a string of six 500-pound bombs fell in the town, killing three civilians and injuring three others. Only the B-24 "Blue Goose," flown by First Lieutenant Ed Cave, hit one of the targeted buildings at Ploești. Overall, little damage was inflicted and there was no reduction in oil production.

During the raid, Adjutant Pilot Vasile Pascu of the Romanian Air Force's Escadrila 59 managed to take off in his IAR-80A fighter, against orders. He found one B-24 and fired all his ammunition at it, claiming he had set it afire. However, no wreckage was found and HALPRO recorded no bombers lost to enemy action, with only two receiving any hits from ground fire.

As the bombers departed Romania, several crews realized that they did not have the fuel to return successfully to Iraq, even flying directly across Turkey. Cave finally realized he would have to land in Turkey. When he approached the airfield outside Ankara, he saw that two other B-24s had already landed on the field. A total of four B-24s landed at Ankara and the crews were interned by the Turkish authorities. They were eventually released seven months later, after the war situation in the Mediterranean had changed to the Allies' advantage, leading the Turks to release the men as a gesture of goodwill while the country changed from pro-Axis neutrality to pro-Allied neutrality. In the meantime, Cave's co-pilot Eugene Zeisel and three other men managed to steal one of the B-24s and fly it to Cyprus. In November 1942, Cave and his navigator Harold Wicklund were allowed by local authorities to "escape" from their place of detention; they managed to get to the British consulate at Mersin, where the consulate's MI6 officer arranged for them to be smuggled aboard a Norwegian cargo ship that took them to Haifa, Palestine; there they were flown on to Egypt.

Four bombers led by Colonel Halverson managed to cross Turkey and land at Habbaniya, while another five landed at other fields in Iraq and Syria. Halverson was awarded the Silver Star for leading the mission.

Following the Ploești raid, the HALPRO Liberators and their crews were joined by B-17 Flying Fortresses from India that had participated in the fight for the Dutch East Indies in the spring of 1942. The combined force became the 1st Provisional Bombardment Group, in the newly formed Ninth Air Force; then later the 376th Heavy Bombardment Group, fighting through the North African campaign in 1942–43.

The commitment to destroy Ploești was formally made a part of Allied grand strategy at the Cairo Conference in February 1943. The case was made by Winston Churchill, who believed that targeting Romania's oil refineries and mounting a campaign to destroy them would deal the "knockout blow" to the German war effort.

Once the commitment to attack Ploești was made at Casablanca, planning for a decisive strike began almost immediately. Given that Ploești was supplying somewhere between 30 and 50 percent of Axis fuel requirements, it was believed that demolishing the refineries enough to take them out of the war for a significant period would have an immediate effect on German operations. Most particularly, it would provide the Western Allies with a way to significantly aid the Soviet Union in the aftermath of the German surrender at Stalingrad and go some distance to meeting Stalin's demand for a second front in Europe, which was not possible at that time.

The truth was, the United States was not in a position to mount a mission big enough to really accomplish this goal. Eighth Air Force in Britain was still struggling to get enough bombers to mount significant raids against Germany. Mounting even a more modest-sized mission would require diversion of bombers from Britain to provide a force large enough to have any real chance of inflicting the kind of damage that was demanded of such a mission.

General Hap Arnold ordered his staff to renew planning for a strike on Ploești in March 1943. The mission would be the responsibility of the Northwest Africa Allied Air Force, commanded by Arnold's longtime comrade in arms, General Carl A. "Tooey" Spaatz; the two had worked together going back to their service in the 1916 Pershing Expedition to capture Pancho Villa, through service in World War I and the 20-year interwar struggle to create an effective air force. Two plans were conceived: one was a medium-scale high-altitude attack launched from Syrian bases; the other was a large-scale low-altitude attack launched from Libya, conceived by Colonel Jacob E. Smart. Smart and his staff could only count on a maximum force of 200 bombers, which meant they had to maximize the chance that the force would get to the target without significant losses, and that the attack would be effective.

A low-level attack meant that the bombers would evade enemy radar until the last minute, making interception difficult, and the bombing itself could be conducted with greater accuracy. Flying at low level also meant that enemy fighters would be unable to attack the bombers from below, and that side attacks from the same altitude would be difficult.

But there were significant disadvantages to such a plan. It meant that bombers designed to operate at high altitude would be engaged in combat at an altitude of around 200 feet from approach through the attack and egress. Accurate navigation would be difficult. The view from low level meant that navigators would have little opportunity to compare their map position with landmarks outside. Navigating to the target would require near-perfect timing and piloting, along with excellent chart interpretation. Pilotage itself with the difficult-to-fly B-24 would result in pilot fatigue as the pilot wrestled his bomber through propwash from preceding aircraft while maneuvering in order not to strike the ground or hit trees or telephone poles, which would be difficult to see until the bomber was almost right on top of them. Additionally, attacking at low level meant the force would be vulnerable to all enemy antiaircraft weapons from 20mm cannon to 88mm artillery. Should the defenders somehow gain advance knowledge of the incoming force, the bombers would be easy targets.

Despite the reservations, this plan was accepted in June. Using HALPRO's experience, it was decided that the operation would be flown in daylight in a low-level attack during the last leg of the bombers' approach to the target to avoid being detected by German radar. The code-name for the mission was Operation *Statesman*, later changed to Operation *Soapsuds*, and finally to Operation *Tidal Wave*. The plan was approved by Arnold in late May.

By the time the *Tidal Wave* plan was accepted by both President Roosevelt and Prime Minister Churchill that June at the Trident Conference, the Allies had reversed their position in the Mediterranean from a year earlier. All of North Africa from Egypt to Morocco was now under Allied control. All five groups due to be involved had flown missions in support of Operation *Husky*, the Sicilian invasion, including several effective low-level missions that proved the concept for the Ploești attack.

Operation *Tidal Wave* was set to take place on August 1, 1943. General Lewis H. Brereton was given operational control, and the mission would be led by Brigadier General Uzal Girard Ent, commander of IX Bomber Command. In mid-July, the B-24s were taken off Sicilian operations and commenced intensive training for the Ploești mission. Crude scale replicas of the various refineries had been assembled in the desert south of Benghazi, Libya, which proved to be a valuable training aid, even though there was a constant battle with scavenging Bedouins to maintain the structures. A highly detailed scale model of the Ploești refinery complex had been built in Britain and was flown to Benghazi to be studied by the crews. Oblique drawings of the targets were also produced so the pilots and navigators would know how their target would look when they turned onto their final attack heading. Results of the runs made against the dummy targets showed remarkable accuracy as missions were repeated and the pilots gained confidence about low-level flying.

General Brereton, who was initially a skeptic about the mission, became so committed that he threatened to relieve any group commander who gave it less than full support. This put him at odds with General Ent, the mission commander. When Ent drew up a petition he wanted the five group commanders to sign, outlining the difficulties and dangers of the mission as planned, he was nearly replaced; realizing that his opposition would result in more harm than good, Ent finally threw his support behind the mission. Ent was not the only dissenter; the 98th's Colonel John R. Kane was convinced the plan was so dangerous it would result in the destruction of the

Pyramiders; he did not change his views. Many crews were upset that the mission involved a 2,400-mile flight to and from the target, the longest since the original HALPRO mission; unlike HALPRO, this mission would involve formation flying, which increased fuel usage; and flight engineers worried that the engines would suffer from oil starvation on such a long flight, since oil consumption was already high in the desert environment in which the bombers operated, with engine changes performed at 50–60 hours rather than at the 200 hours that was considered "standard." The biggest complaint among the crews was that the plan depended on the enemy being surprised, since even if the large formations weren't spotted over Albania and Yugoslavia and reported, there were plenty of spies in North Africa to pass on rumors regarding the low-level practice missions.

Regardless of all this, it was clear the mission would be flown as planned. Bomb bay fuel tanks were installed in the bombers, increasing fuel capacity to 3,100 US gallons. The high-altitude Norden bombsights were replaced with simple low-level bombsights. The bomb loads were 500-pound and 1,000-pound high-explosive bombs, supplemented by incendiaries. All bombs had delayed-action fuses that varied from 45 seconds to six hours.

The original plan envisioned a strike force of 154 bombers, but this was increased to 178 bombers with 1,751 aircrew: the largest commitment of heavy bombers and crewmen by the USAAF to that time. After taking off from airfields near Benghazi, the bombers would rendezvous over Benghazi and formate in the following order: lead group would be the 376th, with General Brereton flying in the right seat in group commander Colonel Keith Compton's plane; the 93rd would be the number two; then would come the 98th, with mission commander General Ent flying with Colonel Kane; the 44th; and the 389th. At the last minute, Brereton was ordered not to fly the mission since he would be too valuable to the enemy if shot down and captured; General Ent would fly with Compton in the B-24 "Teggie Ann."

The target assignments were as follows: White I – the Română Americana complex – was the lead 376th Group's target; Concordia Vega (White II) and the Standard Petrol Block and Unirea Speranta (White III) refineries would be hit from two directions by the 93rd, which would divide for the attack; White IV – the Astra Română and Unirea Orion refineries – was the 98th Group's target; White V – the

Columbia Aquila refinery – was the target for half of the 44th, while the other half of the group would separate at the initial point and go after the Creditul Minier refinery at Brazi (designated Target Blue); the 389th Group would also separate from the others and hit the Steaua Română refinery at Câmpina (Target Red).

Once in formation, the Liberators would cross the Mediterranean and Adriatic Seas, passing near the island of Corfu; after landfall was made, they would fly over the Pindus mountains in Albania, cross southern Yugoslavia, and enter southwestern Romania, where they would drop to low level and turn east toward Ploești. Using predetermined checkpoints, each group would approach their target from the north, with all targets struck simultaneously to overwhelm the defenses.

In an attempt to hide their intentions of attacking Ploești from the enemy, the USAAF had flown no photo-reconnaissance missions over the complex before the attack. Thus, they did not know that, following the HALPRO attack, the German and Romanian armed forces had placed strong antiaircraft defenses around Ploești, until a defecting Romanian pilot landed in Sicily with in-depth information about Ploești's defense. Most important was the fact that well-trained German crews manned the majority of the defenses. Luftwaffe General Alfred Gerstenberg's defensive plan had created one of the heaviest and best-integrated air defense networks in Europe. German and Romanian antiaircraft artillery included 21 88mm batteries operated by the German Flak-Division 5 and 15 88mm batteries operated by the Romanian Regimentul 7 Artilerie Antiaeriană for a total of 36 heavy flak batteries with four of the highly effective 88mm guns in each, 144 guns in all. Additionally, the Germans operated ten medium and light 37mm and 20mm batteries, with the Romanians operating six; these were concealed in haystacks, railroad cars, and fake buildings. Fifteen Würzburg radars provided fire control. Additionally, smoke generators and 23 barrage balloons were deployed. The Luftwaffe's contribution to the aerial defense of Ploești included 48 Bf-109G-6 fighters flown by JG 4 (Jagdgeschwader 4) and 12 Bf-110F night fighters operated by 11./NJG 6 (11.Staffel, Nachtjagdgeschwader 6). The Romanian Air Force had *escadrile* equipped with 61 IAR-80As, 62 IAR-80Bs, 45 IAR-80Cs, 53 Bf-109G-2 and G-4s, and 51 Bf-110Cs. Altogether, the ground and air defenses made the Ploești oil refineries the fourth-most heavily defended target in Europe, after Berlin, Vienna, and the Ruhr.

Although this information was received five days before the attack, no changes were made to the attack plan.

Additionally, in the days before the mission, rumors flew through the five groups that losses exceeding 50 percent were expected. Colonel Kane contributed to the atmosphere of dread when he told his crews that if they succeeded in destroying the targets, the mission would be considered successful even if there were no survivors. Many worried about their chances of survival despite being issued escape and evasion kits containing money, including a $20 gold coin, and counterfeit Romanian ration cards, in addition to a silk map of the country, while others took the kits as a sign that they would be the ones to make it back if shot down.

On August 1, those crewmen who had managed any sleep were awakened at 0400 hours and fed breakfast. The strike force began taking off from their home airfields around Benghazi shortly after dawn, with all airborne by 0730 hours. The takeoffs were made more difficult by the limited visibility caused by dust kicked up when the first aircraft took off. Engines strained to lift large bomb loads and additional fuel. One B-24, "Kickapoo," crashed during takeoff, with two men miraculously surviving the explosion and fire when the pilot hit a concrete pole while attempting to land. The remaining 177 aircraft departed safely.

The formation reached the Adriatic Sea without further incident, but then the 376th Bomb Group's "Wongo Wongo," piloted by Lieutenant Brian Flavelle, experienced an unexplained malfunction and began flying erratically before plunging into the sea below. Flavelle's friend, Lieutenant Guy Iovine, flying "Desert Lilly," dropped out of the formation and descended to look for survivors, in the process narrowly missing "Brewery Wagon'" flown by Lieutenant John Palm. No survivors were spotted, but due to the additional weight of fuel, Iovine was unable to rejoin the formation.

One of the myths of Operation *Tidal Wave* which has been believed ever since 1943 was that the lead navigator was in "Wongo Wongo" while the deputy lead navigator was in "Desert Lilly," and that their loss led to the later navigational difficulties that were experienced. In an interview that Robert Sternfels conducted in 2000 with Colonel Compton – pilot of the B-24 "Sandman" on the mission – Compton stated that the lead navigator was HALPRO veteran Captain Harold Wicklund, who was aboard "Teggie Ann."

The confusion was compounded by the inability of the lead formation to regain cohesion since it was under orders to maintain strict radio silence. As a result, ten other crews returned to friendly airfields. Keith Compton led the formation as it turned northeast after crossing Corfu and flew across Greece, Albania, and Yugoslavia into Bulgaria. As they flew over Yugoslavia and Bulgaria, the formations were detected by German radar in Sicily and other stations on the Adriatic Coast. In addition, a message from Ninth Air Force confirming the departure of a large bomber formation had been intercepted by the Germans and relayed to other Luftwaffe units, including Jagdfliegerführer Rumänien (Romanian Fighter Command). So the Ploeşti defenses were alerted to the probable attack. The American mission leaders were unaware that their presence was now known to the Germans, or that the defenses had been alerted and were ready for them. The presence of the bombers was confirmed by the pilots of two Bulgarian Air Force B-534 fighters that had been launched in an unsuccessful attempt at interception, who got close enough to spot the Liberators in the distance headed toward Romania.

The bombers now faced a daunting 9,000-foot climb over the cloud-shrouded Pindus mountains. During the climb to around 11,000 feet, the 376th and 93rd Groups, which were using high power settings, pulled ahead of the other formations, disrupting the synchronization of the separate attacks. Orders allowed them to break radio silence in such a situation to rebuild their formations, but the strike proceeded without correction. Colonel Kane, now leading the three rear groups, did not agree with Compton's decision to utilize higher power settings, and his stubborn refusal to increase power meant that the other two groups could not change their settings to catch up; the trailing groups fell even further behind as the bombers flew on toward the target.

Once over the mountains, the bombers descended to 2,300 feet as they crossed the Danube River. Compton slowed and made small turns to provide an opportunity for the three groups to his rear to catch up; unfortunately Kane had fallen too far behind to make this up. Although the formation was now split between the two leading groups and the three trailing groups, all five made the navigational checkpoint 65 miles from Ploeşti. At that point, the 389th Bomb Group turned for its separate, synchronized approach to the target. Unfortunately,

Compton's speed changes and maneuvering had thrown off lead navigator Wicklund's navigational calculations.

As they flew on to Ploeşti at 500 feet altitude and 190mph – which made identifying checkpoints difficult – Colonel Compton and General Ent were using their own charts to navigate while co-pilot Captain Ralph Thompson handled the controls. Navigator Captain Wicklund had given Compton an estimated time of arrival for Floreşti, where he was supposed to make his turn, before Compton had thrown things off with his speed and direction changes. As they came up on the time Wicklund had given for arriving at Floreşti, Compton looked out and saw a town ahead that he took to be the right one. He took the controls and turned prematurely toward Ploeşti at what was actually Târgoviste – halfway to Floreşti – following the wrong railroad line for his approach to Ploeşti. Neither Wicklund nor Ent, who were also navigating, caught the error. The 376th and 93rd Groups were now headed straight at Bucharest. Facing disaster, several crews broke radio silence to draw attention to the navigational error, but Compton was not monitoring the group radio circuit and didn't hear the warnings. Both groups now had to face the extensive air defenses around Bucharest in addition to those waiting at Ploeşti.

Compton recognized his error as Bucharest became visible in the distance. With no way to maneuver the formation back to the correct heading, Compton asked General Ent for permission to order the two groups to hit targets of opportunity, to which the general assented. Compton came up on the group circuit and gave the order, then turned "Teggie Ann" north toward Ploeşti.

Behind him, the 93rd's commander, Lieutenant Colonel Addison Baker in B-24 "Hell's Wench," had already led his group in a turn to the north and was now committed to a separate attack on what turned out to be the Columbia Aquila refinery, which was assigned to half of the 44th Group. In minutes, the bombers were over the outskirts of Ploeşti, where they came under fire from the massed defenses, with the sky now filled with 20mm and 37mm tracers in a curtain of fire, coupled with the orange explosions of 88mm shells.

Romanian and German fighters, which had been scrambled earlier, were at first directed to climb to 16,000 feet, since the bombers were expected to attack at high altitude. The error was quickly corrected and the fighters were vectored to attack the low-flying enemy. The IAR-80s of Grupul 6 Vânătoare spotted the oncoming formations at 1150 hours near Săbăreni.

JG 4's Hauptmann Wilhelm Steinmann spotted the B-24 "Brewery Wagon," which had broken off from the 376th Group's formation after pilot Lieutenant John Puck noticed Compton's navigation error and attempted to bomb the refineries alone. The B-24 had been badly hit by defending flak and had jettisoned its bombs on an empty factory while trying to escape. Steinmann closed on the damaged bomber and opened fire, setting two engines on fire. "Brewery Wagon" crash-landed in a field near Tătărani, the first B-24 shot down. Palm and the other seven surviving crewmen were taken prisoner.

Baker's co-pilot was Major John Jerstad, who had volunteered for the mission despite having completed his tour. The two manned the heavy controls of the Liberator, but were unable to miss hitting a balloon cable that threw them off course. At the same time, an 898mm shell exploded in the nose section; "Hell's Wench" caught fire and flames from its burning fuselage stretched back toward the bomber behind them. In minutes, every plane in the 93rd's formation had taken hits, with several catching fire. Crewmen threw themselves out of the burning bombers despite the fact they were now too low for their parachutes to deploy before they hit the ground. Several Liberators flew into the ground as they took what evasive action they could, exploding on impact and adding their smoke to that the enemy were putting up with their smoke generators, obscuring the target ahead. Those gunners aboard the bombers who were still able to manned their .50-caliber guns and exchanged fire with the defenders on the ground.

Baker and Jerstad knew "Hell's Wench" was a goner, but they maintained their speed and stayed in the air as fire ate at the bomber. Unable to stay in the air with his bomb load, Baker jettisoned his bombs and maneuvered through, below, and among the refinery structures as the 93rd's surviving Liberators followed. Afterwards, surviving crewmen of the mission related that it seemed to take forever to get through the refinery, despite the fact that the attack lasted mere minutes. Their bombs turned the refinery into an inferno of flame and smoke.

"Hell's Wench" was now a mass of flames but it continued to take fire from the ground. Baker attempted to gain altitude so that his crewmen had a chance to bail out. None made it out alive before the B-24 fell off on its right wing and dived into the ground, killing all aboard in the explosion. Addison Baker and John Jerstad were posthumously awarded the Medal of Honor for their action "above and beyond the call of duty."

"Jose Carioca" was immediately behind "Hell's Wench." The Liberator was shot down by an IAR-80 whose pilot half rolled and flew under the bomber upside down, raking its belly. The B-24's wings sheared off and the fuselage careened down a street to crash into the Ploești Women's Prison. Of the 101 civilians killed and 238 injured in the attack, half died when the three-story building exploded in flames. While 40 women survived, there were no survivors from "Jose Carioca's" crew.

Major Ramsay D. Potts, flying "The Duchess," and Major George S. Brown, piloting "Queenie," encountered heavy smoke over Columbia Aquila that obscured the target. They led the rest of the 93rd to successfully bomb the Astra Română and Unirea Orion refineries that were the targets for the 98th Group. The 93rd lost 11 B-24s over Ploești of the 36 that made the attack; only 15 of the bombers returned to Libya.

Following Compton's order to attack "targets of opportunity," the majority of the 376th's B-24s bombed the Steaua Română refinery at Câmpina, while five headed directly into the conflagration at the Concordia Vega refinery. The five, led by Lieutenant Norman Appold, bombed a distillation plant of the refinery and hit it so hard that 40 percent of the refinery was destroyed in the resulting fire. At Steaua Română, gunners in the hills of Câmpina, overlooking the refinery, fired down at the formation.

As the 93rd and 376th Groups attacked, Colonel John R. Kane's 98th Bomb Group and Colonel Leon W. Johnson's 44th Bomb Group made the prescribed turn at Florești and headed toward their respective targets, the Astra Română and Columbia Aquila refineries. The three trailing groups arrived at Ploești as the first two were attempting to re-form for the trip back to Libya. The defenses were on full alert; the bombers faced raging oil fires, heavy smoke, secondary explosions, and delayed-fuse bombs dropped earlier by the 93rd Group.

The Liberators of both groups flew parallel to the Florești–Ploești railroad, with the 98th to the left and the 44th on the right; in so doing they became targets for Gerstenberg's *Die Raupe* ("The Caterpillar"), a disguised flak train armed with heavy and light antiaircraft weapons, which opened fire on bombers flying past at treetop level. The train was already running as the big bombers came up on either side, hard to miss so close and so large. Gunners from both the 98th and 44th responded to the threat; their massed fire blew the locomotive's boiler, killing many gun crews.

Kane realized that his target had already been hit, but it was impossible to shift to any other target in the time left before they would be over the refineries. He and Johnson pressed on toward their targets, with both formations taking heavy losses while their gunners continued engaging the gun crews in their positions directly below on the ground.

Behind Kane, First Lieutenant Robert Sternfels in the B-24 "Sandman" battled to keep the bomber under control in the violent propwash of the preceding aircraft; he and co-pilot First Lieutenant Barney Jackson had to move their control yokes from stop to stop as they fought to stay in the air and upright. Too close for any evasive maneuvering, Sternfels saw a barrage balloon cable just ahead. He managed to swing the nose just enough to avoid it being sliced by the cable, which was caught and severed by the propeller on his number three engine; portions of the cable rapped around the prop hub while a long strand broke loose, slicing through the fuselage without injury to anyone inside. Approaching the refinery, he saw bodies fly through the air when a preceding Liberator exploded. The fires sent flames hundreds of feet above the low-flying bombers.

Seconds later, "Sandman" penetrated the wall of smoke and flame. The big bomber rocked with the delayed explosions below them from bombs dropped by the 93rd's B-24s. The bomber leaped skyward when bombardier First Lieutenant David Palaschek dropped their bombs. An instant later, "Sandman" popped into clear air just in time to be caught by the automatic camera aboard First Lieutenant Donald Johnson's "Sneezy," to become the iconic image of Operation *Tidal Wave*, in which the B-24 races away with the burning Astra Română refinery to its rear.

Leon Johnson's 44th Group caught hell as they raced into the wall of fire put up by the Columbia Aquila Refinery's defenders. "Sad Sack II," piloted by First Lieutenant Henry Lasco and co-pilot First Lieutenant Joseph Kill, flew toward the refinery 50 feet above the ground. They entered the black cloud, bouncing from the propwash of those ahead and nearly hitting the ground. Just as he released their bombs, the navigator was hit by a 37mm shell that tore away his chest. The number two engine took a direct hit and was immediately feathered. Bursting out of the fire, Lasco and Kill maneuvered toward six other bombers. Intense ground fire struck the fuselage, exploding the top turret and killing the flight engineer, while taking out the radio operator in his position behind the pilots. As the pilots tried to move into the formation for protection, the B-24 was hit in the rear fuselage by two attacking Romanian-flown Bf-109s. One waist gunner had his legs amputated by a burst of fire. "Sad Sack II" was a flying wreck, increasingly difficult to control with ammunition cooking off in the rear fuselage and the crew other than the two pilots wounded or dead.

One Bf-109 circled and attacked from ahead, hitting Lasco who fell over on his controls. Kill managed to pull the pilot off the controls and fly the bomber into a crash in a cornfield, where it crumpled and caught fire as it touched down. Kill's legs were both broken in the crash. The wounded crewmen managed to pull themselves out of the burning wreck, only to be attacked, beaten, and robbed by Romanian peasants before soldiers arrived and rescued them.

Nine of the 16 B-24s that Colonel Johnson led into the attack were lost. Colonels Kane and Johnson were both awarded the Medal of Honor for their leadership.

The defending fighters that finally entered the battle with the arrival of the three trailing groups had been on alert on their airfields for several hours as enemy radar tracked the oncoming attackers and local observers reported seeing them overhead. Radar contact had been lost when the bombers came out of the mountains and dropped to low level for their final approach. At this point, the fighters were ordered to take off, but they were vectored high in the expectation that the attackers would use standard tactics. The reports from ground observers failed to get through to the fighter controllers in time to correct the mistake, which allowed the first two groups to hit their targets without aerial opposition.

Romanian pilots in IAR-80s were the first to drop down; they spotted Colonel Baker's formation from the 93rd as it turned north to make its attack but were too far away to attack the bombers before they were over the target. The Romanians did manage to make runs on the first two groups as they came off their targets. They were quickly followed by the 50 Luftwaffe-flown Bf-109s that had finally got the new information about where the enemy could be found.

Two Bf-109s were shot down by B-24 gunners in their first attack, but then the other German pilots found the American formations as they began to break up due to ground fire. The Germans broke into two- and four-plane flights and went hunting damaged Liberators straggling behind the others. The fight became a muddled free-for-all when the Romanians joined their allies, swarming the bomber formations.

The most successful American attack was by Lieutenant Colonel James T. Posey, who took 21 of the 44th's B-24s for a separate attack on Blue Target, the Creditul Minier refinery just south of Ploești. Although the bombers ran across the same air defense batteries that had engaged the 93rd, Posey maintained such a low-level approach that some of his bombers actually flew through tall grass and were damaged by hitting ground obstructions. Since this refinery had not been previously hit, visibility was good over the target. The Liberators lined up as they had trained to do over Libya and pilots were able to hit their assigned targets. Amazingly, the 21 bombers – all carrying heavier 1,000-pound bombs – managed to hit their targets without loss, though two were later shot down as they headed toward Bulgaria. Posey's bombers had managed to show what might have been, but for the two major mistakes of the force becoming split and Compton's premature turn for the target.

The 389th Group, led by Colonel Jack Wood, bombed the Steaua Română refinery – Red Target – that had been previously hit by the 376th Group. Cloud cover made it difficult to spot the Dealu Monastery that was their initial point. Wood also became confused on reaching Târgoviste and the group took a wrong turn heading toward Bucharest; no one in the following planes came on the radio circuit to warn of the incorrect change, but fortunately it was quickly corrected by Wood's navigator; the bombers went even lower as they took up the correct heading. Like Posey's force, they were hitting a target that had not been accidentally attacked earlier, and were approaching as they had trained to do. This attack was more complicated than the others, requiring the group to split into three detachments to hit several targets, which proceeded as they had rehearsed at Benghazi.

The 389th lost four aircraft in the attack, including "Ole Kickapoo," flown by Second Lieutenant Lloyd Herbert Hughes; previously dropped bombs detonated as the bomber flew only 30 feet above the target and ignited leaking fuel, which set the B-24 on fire. Despite this, Hughes held his course for bombardier Second Lieutenant John A. McLoughlin. As it came off the target, "Ole Kickapoo" nosed down and cartwheeled into a riverbed, killing six crew members, while two gunners and the bombardier survived to become prisoners. Hughes was awarded the Medal of Honor for his sacrifice. The attack was the most successful of all; the Steaua Română refinery did not become fully operational again until after the war.

Returning by way of Bulgaria, B-24s from different groups banded together for protection. All were damaged to varying degrees. The big question for many of the crews was whether they had the fuel to get home to Benghazi, since they had used more fuel than planned in the attack, and fuel tanks on many had been holed by enemy fire. The bombers that had lost engines were in even more desperate situations as the surviving engines were burning more oil and fuel, making them likely to fail as they faced the long climb back over the mountains. The Bulgarian Air Force launched over 50 of its obsolete Avia B-534 fighters from three groups over Karlovo. Pilots Podporuchik Peter Bochev, Kapitan Tschudomir Toplodolsk, Poruchik Stoyan Stoyanov, and Podporuchik Hristo Krastev of the third group launched each shot down an already-damaged B-24, the first victories of the war for the Bulgarian Air Force. They were awarded the Order of Bravery, personally presented by Tsar Boris III. Each was also awarded the Iron Cross First Class a month later by the German embassy. The losses were not one-sided; several Avias were shot down by defending gunners in the B-24s.

Over Yugoslavia, two B-24s collided with each other, while five were shot down over the Ionian Sea by ten Bf-109Gs of JG 27 that intercepted them after taking off from Kalamaki airfield in Greece. Two of the attacking fighters were shot down by defenders in their initial head-on pass. After a second pass brought down two B-24s, the eight remaining Messerschmitts attacked the bombers in flights of two. The defenders shot down another Bf-109G, but three more Liberators went down before the enemy fighters were forced to break off.

Of the 167 bombers that attacked Ploești, only 88 made it back to Libya, with 55 suffering varying amounts of battle damage. Forty-four were lost directly over the targets to flak and fighters, with an additional 44 lost to air defenses over the Balkans and to ditching in the Mediterranean, while eight were interned after landing in neutral Turkey. One B-24 that landed in Libya 14 hours after departing had 365 bullet holes in it; its survival was due to the light armament of four 7.92mm machine guns in the Bulgarian Avia B-534s that had peppered it.

Personnel losses included 310 killed or missing; 108 were captured, 78 interned in Turkey, and four rescued by partisans in Yugoslavia. Three of the five Medals of Honor awarded – the largest number for any single American air action ever – were posthumous. These medals were on top of 56 Distinguished Service Crosses (DSC) and 41 Silver Stars awarded for valor. Every man who went on the mission was awarded the Distinguished Flying Cross (DFC). Over 100 Purple Hearts were awarded. Operation *Tidal Wave* was the costliest USAAF mission in the European Theater of Operations (ETO), and proportionally the costliest Allied air raid of the war. August 1, 1943 was later referred to by surviving crewmen as "Black Sunday." The estimated 40 percent loss in refining capacity at Ploești refineries was not borne out in fact. This was proven optimistic when it was subsequently discovered by reconnaissance flights on August 3 and 19 by 60 Squadron South African Air Force (SAAF) Mosquitos that the Română Americana and Unirea refineries had not been hit. Additionally, the Romanians and Germans had worked energetically on repairs and bringing previously idle equipment back into operation, while production was vastly increased at the undamaged refineries.

By September 1943, when the Enemy Oil Committee issued their appraisal of Ploești bomb damage from *Tidal Wave*, which stated there was "no curtailment of overall product output," the Ploești refineries were producing more oil than they had before the attack. Of the bombed refineries, Creditul Minier and Columbia Aquila restarted production in late 1943, while Steaua Română partially restarted production in January 1944. Overall production for the rest of 1943 was higher than it had been before the raid.

The Royal Romanian Air Force claimed 20 confirmed air victories for the loss of one IAR-80B and one Bf-110; 15 more were claimed by

Romanian antiaircraft guns. Luftwaffe claims were 25 bombers shot down by fighters and German flak, with losses of five aircraft. Another 11 fighters – two Romanian and nine German – were damaged.

Ninth Air Force's General Brereton officially criticized Ent for the command mistakes made – particularly Compton's too-early turn at Târgoviste and Kane's failure to keep up with the two lead groups that split the attack – but there were no official reprimands. Brereton's report stated, "The decision of the commander to execute an attack from the south after his formation had been lost and missed its IP was unsound. It resulted in wrong targets being bombed, destroyed coordination, and sacrificed the benefits of thorough briefing and training of the crews." He then softened the rebuke, stating, "Although tactical errors and erroneous decisions are pointed out above, no blame is attached to any commander or leader participating in the mission for decisions which were made on the spot under the stress of combat. On the other hand, IX Bomber Command is deserving of the highest praise for its excellent staff procedure and leadership displayed in the planning, training and execution of this most difficult mission."

The Ninth Air Force never launched another major heavy bomber mission before it was transferred to Britain that fall to become the USAAF tactical air force for the invasion of northern Europe. On August 2, the command could not have fielded 50 serviceable B-24s. The 44th, 93rd, and 389th Bomb Groups were quickly returned to the Eighth Air Force. The surviving bombers of the Ninth's 98th and 376th Bomb Groups flew their last mission against targets in Italy on September 20, 1943; the two groups were then transferred to the newly created Fifteenth Air Force.

Despite the enormous losses, *Tidal Wave* was played out in both the British and American press as a heroic success. King George VI later wrote President Roosevelt that "The gallantry with which the crews pressed home their attacks at a very low level was beyond praise, and their devotion to duty in spite of heavy losses has stirred the hearts of all who fight with us in the cause of freedom."

Both the Germans and Romanians were stunned by the bravery of the Americans who flew the mission. The Romanians were particularly impressed that there were so few civilian casualties.

While later studies would demonstrate that *Tidal Wave* inflicted more damage to Ploești than any subsequent mission flown during the campaign against the refineries in the spring and summer of 1944, it was clear on August 2, 1943 that Ploești would not be knocked out by a single raid. General Spaatz submitted a report to General Arnold in late August, in which his main point was that knocking out Ploești would take a sustained campaign flown by a full air force.

Fortunately, when Spaatz wrote his report, the decision had already been made to create that air force. The mission of the Fifteenth Air Force would be to destroy Ploești.

2

THE FIFTEENTH AIR FORCE TAKES SHAPE

The Fifteenth Air Force was brought into being as a result of two factors: geography and climate. Geography was crucial. The importance of Romanian oil in fueling the Axis war machine had been recognized by Allied strategists since the war's beginning. Romania lay a daunting 1,300 miles from Britain, putting the Balkan oil fields beyond the reach of Eighth Air Force bombers. On the other hand, the oil fields were less than 600 miles distant from the air base complex at Foggia, Italy, which the Allies took control of in November 1943 following the invasion of Italy that September.

Weather was equally important. Britain and northern Europe were notorious for overcast and soggy weather. In sharp contrast, Italy was thought of as being mostly sunny and clear. To Allied planners, the Foggia airfields could support a strategic air campaign against the Third Reich with missions being flown when the weather hobbled operations from Britain. Thus, when the Fifteenth stood up in November 1943, top airmen reckoned that they would be flying in a more permissive environment. The predictions were wrong. During the first two months of operations in the winter of 1943–44, the Fifteenth's heavy bombers managed to conduct operations on just 30 days. Throughout 1944, the Eighth actually operated 20 percent more often than did the Fifteenth, and conditions worsened in the winter of 1944–45, the coldest in Europe in more than a century.

THE FIFTEENTH AIR FORCE TAKES SHAPE

Starting with the creation of IX Air Force Bomber Command in the summer of 1942, the USAAF's small heavy bomber force in the Mediterranean attacked enemy ports, airfields, and ships in support of Allied ground forces in North Africa and to prepare for the invasion of Sicily. IX Bomber Command was joined in November 1942 by XII Air Force Bomber Command following the US invasion of French North Africa. These two forces were united in the spring of 1943 as the North African Strategic Air Forces. Following the successful invasion of Sicily that summer, USAAF Headquarters decided to unite the Mediterranean heavy bomber forces in the separate Fifteenth Air Force. The stated purpose was to mount major strategic raids in southern and eastern Europe. This decision also allowed the Ninth Air Force to be transferred to Britain where it became the USAAF tactical air force for support of the invasion of northwest Europe and subsequent US ground operations in France, the Low Countries, and Germany.

Lieutenant General James H. "Jimmy" Doolittle – America's most famous aviator – was notified in mid-October 1943 that the Northwest Allied Strategic Air Force that he now commanded after bringing the Twelfth Air Force to North Africa a year earlier would become the Fifteenth Air Force on November 1, 1943 with his headquarters in Tunis, Tunisia becoming headquarters for the new air force. Things moved quickly after the command was established and a month later the headquarters was moved to Bari, Italy on December 1, 1943, where it would remain throughout the rest of the war. Doolittle's fledgling air force comprised three B-17 groups previously part of Twelfth Air Force and the two B-24 bomb groups that had formed IX Air Force Bomber Command. The long-range P-38s of the 1st, 14th, and 82nd Fighter Groups from Twelfth Air Force were assigned to the Fifteenth from the outset, joined a month later by the 325th Fighter Group, known as the "Checkertail Clan" for the distinctive yellow-and-black checkers on the vertical and horizontal tail surfaces of their fighters. The Checkertails were newly equipped with the first P-47 Thunderbolts assigned to the MTO. The two Twelfth Air Force B-26 Marauder-equipped medium bomber groups were also temporarily attached, but returned to the Twelfth Air Force in the spring of 1944. At its strongest, Fifteenth Air Force would grow to an authorized strength of 21 heavy bomb groups and seven fighter groups, half the size of the Eighth Air Force. Both the Eighth and Fifteenth Air Forces were joined in the US Strategic Air

Forces (USSTAF), commanded by Carl Spaatz, who was now based in England, where he would be in close contact with General Dwight Eisenhower when he was transferred from the Mediterranean in late December to take command of the Allied Expeditionary Forces set to participate in the coming invasion of Europe, Operation *Overlord*.

Two months after taking command of the Fifteenth, General Doolittle was transferred by order of USAAF commander General Hap Arnold to replace General Ira Eaker as commander of the Eighth Air Force. In part, this change was due to Arnold's loss of faith in Eaker, his long-time friend and ally in the creation of the USAAF, who had not fulfilled Arnold's hopes in the first year of operations by the Eighth from Britain. An additional reason was that Doolittle had experience working with Eisenhower, who trusted the airman from the year they had spent together in North Africa; this personal connection would be important when it came time for Eisenhower as Supreme Commander to control air and ground forces for the invasion. Doolittle was succeeded in command of the Fifteenth by Major General Nathan F. Twining, who came to Italy from the South Pacific, where he had commanded the Thirteenth Air Force in the Solomons and Rabaul campaigns.

Twining was another of the "founding fathers" of the Air Force. He came from a military family: his older brother Merrill B. Twining attained the rank of general in the Marine Corps; his younger brother Robert B. Twining was a captain in the US Navy; and his uncle Nathan Crook Twining was a Navy rear admiral. After graduation from West Point in 1919, Twining transferred from the infantry to the Air Service in 1922, where he became involved in pursuit aviation, flying fighters until 1937. On graduation from the Air Corps Tactical School at Maxwell Field and the Command and General Staff College at Fort Leavenworth – and having caught the eye of General Arnold for his operational leadership as he had risen in command – Twining was assigned to Air Corps Headquarters in Washington as a member of Arnold's staff. Following the outbreak of war, he was a senior planner on the Air Staff, then went to the South Pacific in the summer of 1942 as chief of staff to the Eleventh Air Force. He was promoted to command the Thirteenth Air Force in January 1943 and led the USAAF contingent in the Allied air forces through the end of the Solomons campaign.

With the Eighth Air Force receiving priority for equipment with the B-17, it was decided that the B-24 Liberator would be the primary offensive weapon of the Fifteenth Air Force. The B-17 was flown by the three bomb groups in the 5th Bombardment Wing that had originally been assigned to the Twelfth Air Force, while the B-24 was flown by the 12 bomb groups assigned to the 47th, 49th, 55th, and 304th Bomb Wings.

The B-24 originated in a 1938 request by the US Army Air Corps (USAAC) to the Consolidated Aircraft Corporation that the company produce the B-17 under license. In response, company President Reuben Fleet and a group of Consolidated executives visited the Boeing factory in Seattle, where they studied the B-17 and listened to Boeing's presentation of proposed developments. Fleet and his team were unimpressed and on their return to San Diego he told Hap Arnold that he had decided Consolidated would submit a more modern design of its own.

After studying Consolidated's initial proposal, in January 1939 the USAAC formally invited the company to submit a design study for a bomber which would have longer range, higher speed, and a greater ceiling than the B-17, with the specification being written in such a way that the Model 32 would be the winning design. Following submission of the design study, the Air Corps awarded the company a contract for the prototype XB-24 in March 1939; the contract required that the prototype should be completed and ready for test flying before the end of the year. In April 1939, contract #12464 increased the USAAC's order to seven additional YB-24s. In the event, the prototype was finished and Consolidated had it ready for the first flight on December 29, 1939. While the design was simple in concept, it was also technically advanced for its time.

What Consolidated proposed was in many ways the antithesis of the B-17. While the Flying Fortress in all its manifestations was an elegant, visually pleasing design, what Consolidated designated the Model 32 was close to aerodynamically ugly with a deep slab-sided fuselage, a shoulder-mounted wing and twin vertical stabilizers, and rudders adapted from the Consolidated Model 31 flying boat that would become known as the PB2Y Coronado. The deep fuselage was designed around two bomb bays, each the size of the B-17's single bomb bay and capable of carrying 4,000 pounds of bombs, double the Flying Fortress's 4,000-pound maximum load. The fuselage design earned the Model 32 the nickname "Flying Boxcar." An unusual four-panel set of all-metal, "roller-type" bomb bay doors operated like the enclosure of a rolltop desk, retracted up the fuselage sides; this created minimum aerodynamic drag, allowing the bomber to maintain a high speed over the target. Since the airplane had a low fuselage ground clearance, the fact that the roller-type bomb bay doors could be opened and raised on the ground gave crews and ground support personnel easier access than would have been the case with normal bomb bay doors.

The item that really made the Model 32 different was designer David R. Davis' wing, a high-efficiency airfoil design that allowed both a relatively high airspeed and long range. The wingspan was six feet more than that of the B-17, but with overall less wing area, resulting in a 35 percent higher wing loading compared with the B-17. The thick wing resulted in increased tankage while providing increased lift and speed, but also had unpleasant flight characteristics at higher weights operating at high altitude in bad weather – the exact operating conditions that would be experienced over the Alps on operations with the Fifteenth Air Force. Additionally, the wing was also more prone to take on ice in those operating conditions than the B-17's. The result was a loss of lift that gave unpleasant experiences. On operations out of Italy, this condition led to a widespread saying among crews that "The Davis wing won't hold enough ice to chill your drink." Finally, the wing was more easily damaged than the B-17's wing; there are many photos of B-24s hit by flak with a wing blown off or with one or both wings folding up as the main spar failed. This was of particular importance to crews, since such situations meant that escape from the airplane was virtually impossible.

One other new thing the Model 32's design incorporated was use of a tricycle landing gear, the first such installation in a heavy bomber design. Unfortunately, the surrounding nose structure was light enough that the nose and the forward fuselage and nose gear were prone to collapse on landing if damaged by flak, which led to many numerous fatal crash-landings. The tricycle gear used differential braking and differential engine thrust for ground steering, which also made taxiing problematic.

Flight testing began in January 1940. While the XB-24 did have both longer range and higher speed than the B-17, it had a lower operational ceiling. This would never be resolved; one former B-24 bombardier recalled, "We were always down in the flak field, jealously watching the

THE FIFTEENTH AIR FORCE TAKES SHAPE

B-17s fly 3,000 feet higher, above the flak." The initial tests revealed that the XB-24 was deficient in several areas. It failed to meet the contractually specified speed requirements: maximum speed was only 273mph instead of the specified 311mph. Consolidated's fix was to replace the mechanically supercharged Pratt & Whitney R-1830-33s with turbosupercharged R-1830s. Directional stability was also faulted, with the result that tail span was increased two feet. The XB-24 was re-designated XB-24B.

Despite formal US neutrality in the war that began in September 1939, official US military procurement policy was that American military requirements could be deferred to allow delivery of equipment to Britain and France. The military was satisfied with this due to the added advantage that the new US types could be assessed in the European combat conditions. On November 9, 1940, the first six YB-24s were released for direct purchase by Britain under contract #F-677. The YB-24s were redesignated LB-30A. Since the Liberator had the range to fly direct from the United States to Britain, one of these first airplanes was modified by the RAF as a transport and became "Commando," the official transport that Prime Minister Winston Churchill would use through the rest of the war.

The Liberator carried a ten-man crew. The pilot and co-pilot were together in the cockpit, just ahead of the wing. The navigator and bombardier were in the nose, fronted with a framed "greenhouse" plexiglass nose for the B-24D; they were also provided with two .30-caliber Browning M1919 machine guns for forward defense. The radio operator sat behind the pilots, facing sideways, while the flight engineer's position was adjacent to the radio operator behind the pilots. Four gunners were located in the rear fuselage aft of the bomb bays, where they operated the waist guns, a lower gun, and a tail gun position. The B-24D – which was the first combat-capable sub-type – had an upper turret with two .50-caliber machine guns, operated by the flight engineer, a retractable "ball turret" with similar armament in the belly, and a power-operated two-gun turret in the tail. A power-operated nose turret with two .50-caliber weapons would replace the "greenhouse" nose beginning in late 1943 as the result of combat experience.

When flying the Liberator, it was necessary to get "on step." This meant climbing to about 500 feet above cruise altitude, leveling off, attaining a cruising speed of 165–170mph, then descending to the assigned altitude.

Failing to do this resulted in the bomber flying slightly nose high, using more fuel. The B-24 was sensitive to weight distribution due to the narrow-chord Davis wing. A heavily loaded B-24 created difficulties flying at speeds under 160mph. The controls were heavy, especially if the control rigging was not properly tensioned; in combat the co-pilot had to assist the pilot in operating the controls to get the response time high enough to allow successful flight in formation. Because B-24s leaked fuel, they were flown with the bomb bay doors cranked slightly open in order to dissipate potentially explosive fumes. Eighth Air Force B-24s took lower casualties than B-17s due to the fact they were given shorter, safer missions. This was not the case in the Fifteenth Air Force, where the bomber's long-range capability was what allowed the Fifteenth to strike as widely across southern and eastern Europe as it did.

A total of 18,482 B-24s were built by September 1945. The USAAF operated 12,000, with a peak inventory in September 1944 of 6,043. The US Navy received 977 PB4Y-1s – Liberators originally ordered by the USAAF. The RAF received 2,100 B-24s of various sub-types that were used as bombers – primarily in the Far East – and for long-range maritime patrol in the battle against U-boats in the Atlantic; the Royal Canadian Air Force (RCAF) flew 1,200 B-24Js; and the Royal Australian Air Force (RAAF) operated 287 B-24Js in the Pacific. The Liberator holds the record as the most-produced bomber, heavy bomber, multi-engine aircraft, and American military aircraft. The only other airplanes produced in greater numbers are the German Bf-109 series, the British Spitfire series, the Soviet Yak1-9 series, and the Soviet Il-2 Shturmovik. Production of the B-24 in the United States was the largest production effort for one product in the war. According to the *Willow Run Reference Book* published February 1, 1945, the Ford Motor Company broke ground on Willow Run on April 18, 1941, and the first B-24 came off the line on September 10, 1942. The Willow Run plant had the largest assembly line in the world with 3,500,000 square feet of production space. At its peak in the summer of 1944, one B-24 was finished per hour and 650 B-24s were produced per month. Such were the production numbers that more aluminum, aircrew, and effort went into the B-24 than any other aircraft in history.

Overall production of B-24s increased throughout 1942 and 1943. Consolidated Aircraft increased the size of its San Diego factory by 300 percent and built a large new plant outside Fort Worth, Texas, where knock-down kits of the B-24H shipped from Willow Run were assembled. Douglas Aircraft assembled B-24s from Ford parts at a new government plant built in Tulsa, Oklahoma with Reconstruction Finance Corporation funds, producing a total 962 D, E, H, and J models. Bell Aircraft produced B-24s at a factory near Marietta, Georgia, northwest of Atlanta, and North American Plant B in Grand Prairie, Texas started production of the B-24G in 1943. In mid-1944, production was consolidated at the Consolidated Aircraft Company in San Diego and the Ford Willow Run factory. By 1945, Ford was producing 70 percent of all B-24s in two nine-hour shifts and overall produced half of the total 18,500 Liberators.

The "definitive" B-24 was the B-24H, introduced in 1943. It formed the majority of the Liberators assigned to the Fifteenth. The B-24H was ten inches longer than the glass-nosed B-24D, with the new electrically powered Emerson A-15 nose turret above the bombardier's position to reduce vulnerability to head-on attack. The tail turret had larger windows for better visibility, while the Martin A-3 dorsal turret received an enlarged "high hat" dome. The waist gunner positions were enclosed with Plexiglass windows, laterally offset to reduce interference between the waist gunners. It was fitted with an improved bomb sight, autopilot, and fuel transfer system. Willow Run produced 3,100 B-24H Liberators. The B-24J was similar to the B-24H, but used a modified, hydraulically powered Consolidated A-6 turret due to shortages of the Emerson turret. The B-24J featured an improved type C-1 autopilot and an M-1 series bombsight. Consolidated, Douglas, and Ford all manufactured the B-24H, while North American made the slightly different B-24G. All five plants switched over to the almost identical B-24J in August 1943.

The conditions in which men flew and fought in the B-24 are truly remarkable. One crewman described them thus:

> Bone chilling cold was the constant companion of every Liberator crew member. Air ingress was everywhere, especially at the bomb-bay doors, which had nothing even remotely resembling seals. Missions were flown with the waist windows open and, of course, the bomb-bay doors were open during the bomb runs, which typically lasted 10–15 minutes. Temperatures at 25,000 feet varied from zero to as much as 70 degrees below zero Fahrenheit. Only the flight deck was equipped with heaters, and their operation was erratic.

Crew members wore electrically-heated suits, including gloves and slippers – the forerunners of electric blankets. These failed frequently, so it was always advisable to wear heavy, or at least medium-weight, flying suits and boots over the electrically-heated suit – severe discomfort and frostbite could be the result of not doing so.

Besides the cold, there was the noise. The aeroplane's fuselage was uninsulated, so engines, propellers and slipstream combined to set up an ear-splitting din despite the earphones and helmet ear flaps that were worn. This, perhaps, was a blessing in disguise, for the steady drone of four good engines was truly a security blanket. Best of all, the noise created by the aircraft made it impossible to hear anything but the most proximate of flak detonations. Watching flak blossom in silence was unnerving enough – had the sound effects that accompanied the bursting of the shells been audible to the crews, bomb runs would have been all the more frightening.

On the other hand, the high noise levels tended to isolate crew members, especially those in turrets. A crew member could suffer anoxia without his buddies knowing. More than one B-24 returned to base with a dead gunner in his turret, the victim of a faulty oxygen system or an incorrect oxygen hook-up. To combat this, crews in my group – the 459th Bomb Group – conducted regular oxygen checks. These were usually initiated by the bombardier when flying at altitudes above 10,000 feet.

In keeping with their total disregard for crew comfort, Consolidated's engineers gave little thought to the need for urination, despite B-24 mission lengths frequently exceeding eight hours. Most aeroplanes had relief tubes at the pilot's and co-pilot's stations – some also had them in the ball turret and in the waist. There were no such provisions in the nose of the Liberator, so most navigators, bombardiers and nose gunners just held it. Any use of the pilots' relief tubes at altitude during a mission was likely to bring on tirades of vulgarity from the ball and tail turret gunners, because urine discharged from the tubes would swirl in the slipstream and freeze on the turrets, obstructing the gunners' views. Crew members seldom used the relief tubes anyway because their layered clothing and other items such as parachute harnesses made it very awkward.

THE FIFTEENTH AIR FORCE TAKES SHAPE

The main base for Fifteenth Air force bombers was the Foggia airfield complex on the plains of Italy that form the "spur on the boot" of the peninsula. There were multiple malarial swamps through the area, which had a major effect on operations for those units unfortunate enough to be based near one. Repairing the existing airfields built by the Italians and laying out new ones in what would become the Foggia air complex was a difficult job; USAAF aviation engineers struggled against rain, mud, and shortages of heavy equipment that winter to bring Foggia up to fighting trim. By the end of March 1944, there were 20 operational airfields in the Foggia aviation complex, which allowed the heavy bombers to finally move from their North African airfields as new bomber units originally scheduled to join the Eighth Air Force arrived weekly from the continental United States beginning in February 1944, with the last unit arriving in April. Based at Foggia, all of Occupied Europe was now within range of American heavy bombers.

The cold, wet weather that had predominated in October gave way in November to better weather that allowed an increase in missions just as the Fifteenth Air Force came into existence on November 1, 1943. The Fifteenth launched its first mission on the day the air force was formed; the target for the B-17s was La Spezia naval base in northern Italy. The Fifteenth's first "strategic" mission, a long-range attack on the Messerschmitt factory at Wiener Neustadt near Vienna was flown on November 2. Because the Foggia airfield complex was still under repair after its recent capture, the B-24s flew from bases in Tunisia.

Liberator pilot Captain Ben Konsynski of the 376th Bomb Group's 513th Bomb Squadron recalled the mission:

> We flew the 2 November 1943 attack from Enfidaville, in Africa, in aeroplane #42, which was the B-24 we had brought over from the states. On the way to the target we lost three superchargers and couldn't stay with the formation, but continued to the target and dropped our bombs. Since we were not in formation, and were being continually attacked by ME 109s, every crew member was busy

either shooting or reporting what was happening in our vicinity. We saw several B-17s picked off when they were out of formation and expected the same to happen to us… By running the engines at full throttle and descending from the target we picked up speed, still under attack. We caught our formation and were going so fast we flew right through it and out in front, so we had to cut the throttles all the way back to get back into the formation. The '109s continued to attack the whole formation. We made an emergency landing in Bari, Italy on a 4000 ft runway with one application of brakes. We had to cut back one, two and three engines and baby number four in order to make the turn at the end of the runway. Our left rudder was completely shredded, we had flak fragments in our right tire and the British mechanics who worked on our plane reported we had 181 holes in it mostly from '109s. Not one of our crew was hit.

The force of 74 B-17s and 38 B-24s reached Wiener Neustadt and dropped 327 tons of bombs; the results were deemed impressive, the bombs having destroyed a large aircraft assembly shop and damaged another, wiped out two hangars and cratered runways and taxiways.

The 14th and 82nd Fighter Groups provided escort for the mission, which was recorded in the war diary of the 14th Group as "a long dull escort." During the return flight, the 14th's pilots, now flying new P-38J Lightnings, went down on the deck in search of targets of opportunity. They returned to base claiming nine locomotives and a train, with 25 tanker cars destroyed. The 48th Squadron's First Lieutenant John Hurley flew so low in his attack that he lost three feet of his right wing when he knocked down a tree that fortunately wasn't big enough to bring him down in the collision. He recalled that, after losing more than half of his right aileron, the flight home to Lecce airfield in southern Italy was "hairy" when it came to making turns. First Lieutenant James Eddins took a 37mm flak hit that knocked out his right engine and set off the ammunition in the nose gun bay; the explosion ripped off the gondola's outer skin from the nose to the windscreen, with a piece hitting his left propeller but not damaging it. He managed to make the 500-mile return flight successfully despite this damage. Second Lieutenant Ray Trombley was shot down during the attack on the tanker cars but turned up a prisoner of war in Hungary after first being presumed dead.

The 82nd Fighter Group's Lightnings found no enemy aerial opposition over the target and the P-38s remained at high altitude, returning to base without incident.

In his memoir, *I Could Never Be So Lucky Again*, Doolittle described the mission: "Our B-17s and B-24s hit the Messerschmitt factory at Wiener Neustadt, a 1,600-mile (round trip) mission that netted excellent results. That facility was turning out about 250 fighters a month. We estimated we put it out of action for at least two months." Doolittle recalled that some 150 German fighters attacked the Allied bombers before, during, and after their bombing runs, even flying though their own flak. He lost six B-17s and five B-24s that day. Though Bf-109 production at Wiener Neustadt was cut roughly 75 percent, the Germans proved exceedingly resilient, and soon the rate began rising again.

The 1st Fighter Group, which had remained based Tunis, Tunisia throughout the Sicilian campaign and the invasion of Italy, finally received orders to leave Tunisia in late October when they were transferred to the Fifteenth Air Force. Advance groups in the ground echelon had been sent on by sea in the last week of October, docking at Cagliari in Sardinia – where the group would be initially based – on October 31.

On November 6, the group's air echelon moved to Djedeida, 60 miles from Tunis. The base was occupied by an RAF Wellington bomber squadron, and the fighters had to be taxied half a mile on muddy roads and taxi strips to get to the runway. They had originally been told their stay at Djedeida would be "about a week," but that week turned into a miserable month as the winter rains arrived in North Africa; pilots had sent their warm clothing on to Sardinia and were caught short by the weather. The group's war diary said of the stay that, if Djedeida was not the most miserable place they stayed during the war, it was among the top contenders. Food was limited to C-rations, and the near-constant cold rains made everyone miserable.

The 1st Group flew one of the longest missions of the Mediterranean air war on November 10, escorting B-24s to Athens. The mission required the Lightnings to fly to Sicily for a fuel stop before the rendezvous with the bombers, with a fuel stop at the 82nd's base at Lecce on the return; in total, the mission lasted nine hours. Leading White Flight, Captain Bob "Smokey" Vrilakas spotted a Bf-109 that was approaching the rear of Blue Flight. When his repeated calls to break right resulted in no response from Blue Flight, he led White Flight in a break toward the enemy fighter, which broke off its attack run and dived away.

Between November 2 and 13, the 82nd flew 11 uneventful missions to targets in northern Italy, Albania, and Greece. November 14 saw the 82nd Group fly its first productive Fifteenth Air Force mission: 48 P-38s escorting 48 B-25 Mitchells from the 321st and 340th Bomb Groups to Sofia, Bulgaria. This was the first USAAF mission against a Bulgarian target and 15–20 defending fighters rose to contest the Americans; the results for the Lightnings were claims of five destroyed, one probable, and three damaged; First Lieutenant Jack Walker – one of two original officer pilots still flying with the group – claimed the probable. Over the rest of the month, the group escorted bombing missions to Athens, which were hampered by bad weather.

The most memorable of these missions was flown to Kalamaki airdrome on November 15. Again, 48 Lightnings escorted a similar number of Mitchells from 321st and 340th Groups. The Luftwaffe scrambled Bf-109s from JG 27, a group of which attempted an interception tactic that the 97th Squadron's Second Lieutenant Don Foley had never seen before. He later recalled that he watched some ten Bf-109s out of range to the right climb until they were some 2,000 feet above the P-38s:

> They rolled over and started straight down in formation. Something was going wrong. I think the leader had in mind to dive through us, attack the bombers and then go home. But they were picking up too much speed and one of them shed a wing. The leader had no alternative but to break off the attack. When they pulled out, they went in all directions but didn't hit anybody. They were now at our level or slightly below and we had the advantage.

Foley turned into one enemy fighter, but a second appeared alongside. "We were each standing on a wing and were canopy-to-canopy at less than 50 feet for about ten seconds; our heads were bent back and we were each looking directly at the other. Why we didn't touch is beyond me, it was that close."

At that moment, Foley's left engine quit cold. He called for help but none arrived, and his fight with the two Bf-109s continued.

"They appeared to be very inexperienced and still learning their aircraft, which saved me." Given an opening, Foley nosed over and dived straight at the ground. "They pulled out of their dives shortly after they came after me. I believe it was because they had seen their comrade lose his wing in such a dive." Foley pulled out low over the Gulf of Corinth and stayed low as he flew across the body of water. As he approached the Ionian Islands he spotted two P-38s and joined with them for protection. "We stayed low until we were out of range of the guns on Corfu." Foley was one of the 14 P-38s claimed that day by the pilots of IV./JG 27 (IV.Gruppe, JG 27) though no 82nd Group Lightnings were lost that day.

When the 82nd escorted B-24s to Sofia on November 24, they were again intercepted by Royal Bulgarian Air Force Bf-109s. In the ensuing fight, the 96th Squadron's Major William Litton was later given credit for a Bf-109 destroyed, as was the 97th's First Lieutenant Jack Walker, while First Lieutenant Charles Hicks scored a probable. Jack Walker's victory made him an ace.

As would be the case with P-38s in England, these long-distance high-altitude missions were difficult for the pilots since the heating system in the P-38F G and H models was notorious for its lack of heat. Flying in cold cockpits for several hours was extremely uncomfortable and reduced pilot effectiveness. The missions also put a strain on the older model P-38s, which had been in use since the North African campaign.

At the beginning of December, all three P-38 groups were operating at half strength after the Sicilian and Italian campaigns. The problem was that the replacement aircraft that were expected that fall were in high demand and had been diverted for delivery to VIII Fighter Command, which had demonstrated in the Schweinfurt mission of October 14 that VIII Bomber Command could not cope with the losses that came on missions flown beyond escort fighter range. The 55th Fighter Group, which became operational in England shortly after "Black Thursday," as the Schweinfurt mission came to be known, and the 20th Fighter Group were both short of Lightnings and their full equipment was given top priority over the units in the MTO.

The P-38 was the only US fighter that was produced at just one factory throughout the war – Lockheed in Burbank, California. Delays in changing over from the P-38G to P-38J production models had created a supply bottleneck over the summer and early fall of 1943, which would not be fully resolved for the Lightning groups in the Fifteenth until early 1944. As the 14th Fighter Group had prepared to transfer to the Fifteenth Air Force at the end of October, P-38Js had begun arriving to replace the war-weary P-38G and H Lightnings they had used since North Africa. The group considered themselves lucky, since the 82nd and 1st Groups would not receive any replacements until early 1944.

The 95th Squadron's historian wrote for the record at this time about the missions the 82nd Group had flown in November:

> There were many instances of mechanical failure on missions, due to the aging condition of our aircraft, lack of repair parts, and poor weather conditions for maintenance work. Replacements of airplanes promised during the month did not arrive and many of our P-38s are becoming flying wrecks. Replacement pilots, having been trained on the latest type of P-38s in the States, are puzzled by the sign of our old Fs and Gs still being used in combat.

On December 6, the 82nd Group escorted Liberators to bomb Eleusis airfield in Greece. The bombers were intercepted by enemy fighters and the group claimed four destroyed, two probables, and two damaged. Two of the Bf-109s shot down were credited to the 96th Squadron's First Lieutenant Leslie "Andy" Andersen. Second Lieutenant Gene H. Chatfield, who had never flown a P-38 before joining the 97th Squadron two weeks earlier, received credit for an Fw-190 destroyed.

Meanwhile, on November 29, the 1st Fighter Group's Lightnings were finally able to leave Africa behind when they flew to a new base at Monserrato, Sardinia; only two missions were flown – on December 4 and 8, escorting B-26s to Italian targets – before the group made a further move to the Italian mainland, setting up at Gioia del Colle airfield, known as Foggia No. 3 airfield in the newly completed Foggia complex. The P-38s flew to the new base on December 9 with an advance ground party flown over in C-47s. The remainder of the ground echelon left Sardinia on December 20 and docked in Naples two days later.

The Gioia airfield had little to recommend it in terms of any creature comforts for the men, and poor facilities for operations. The group's war diarist noted that the runway was a grass strip with many low spots, which led to the field getting very muddy when it rained. The winter rains did nothing to improve matters regarding life on the field. There was no housing on the airfield beyond tents, which were difficult to maintain on the stony ground. Within a matter of days everyone had moved into some wooden structures nearby that were rumored to have been Italian chicken coops.

With the introduction of H2X radar, which allowed the bombers to hit a target despite cloud cover, the 14th Group managed to fly 52 missions over the winter and early spring of 1944, with 49 being bomber escorts to targets in southern Germany, Austria, and northern Italy. On December 6, one lagging Bf-109 of 15 that attacked the bombers over Czechoslovakia before diving into the cloud cover was shot down by the 49th's First Lieutenant Oliver Bryant. Another mission to Munich on December 9 resulted in an Me-262 appearing 3,000 feet above the 49th's Lightnings; it dived through their formation and disappeared into the clouds below. Two other Me-262s were spotted as the Lightnings turned for home, but they also dived away when a flight of four P-38s turned toward them.

On December 10 the 82nd's Lightnings escorted Liberators to Sofia again and claimed nine Bulgarian-flown Bf-109s destroyed, one probable, and four damaged, losing one P-38. Andy Andersen became the group's 18th ace when he shot down a Bf-109 for his fifth kill. Squadron mate Second Lieutenant Hiram Pitts was credited with two Bf-109s downed and a probable. The 97th Squadron's Captain Charles Spencer, First Lieutenant Charles Hicks, and Second Lieutenant Paul Jorgensen each claimed a Bf-109 destroyed and First Lieutenant Walker claimed an Fw-190.

Another mission was flown to Sofia on December 20. Twenty-four enemy fighters came up. Their pilots were described as "first class" in the mission report. Three P-38s were lost against claims for three Bf-109s shot down and four damaged. The 97th Squadron's First Lieutenant Hicks and Second Lieutenant Donald T. Foley claimed two of the three shot down.

On December 21, group commander Lieutenant Colonel George MacNicol – who had been advising Eighth Air Force on operation of their newly-arrived P-38s – was returning to Italy from England in a B-24 when it crashed on takeoff, killing all onboard. MacNicol was replaced by deputy group commander Major William Litton, who received promotion to lieutenant colonel in February 1944.

On Christmas Day, the group escorted B-24s to bomb the marshaling yards at Udine in northern Italy. In a 40-minute fight, intercepting German fighters led by *Experte* (ace) Oberleutnant Otto Schultz, *Staffelkapitän* of 6./JG 51 (6.Staffel, JG 51), used hit-and-run tactics against the defending P-38s, shooting down six Lightnings and damaging two others so badly that they were scrapped after returning to base. Schultz was credited with shooting down Major Hugh Muse, commander of the 95th Squadron, and the 96th Squadron's Second Lieutenant Hiram Pitts. The 96th's Major Litton claimed the sole Bf-109 destroyed. Oberleutnant Schultz had fought against the 82nd in North Africa, claiming nine Lightnings destroyed; he survived the war with 73 victories. The Germans reported losing three Bf-109s, two of which must have been victims of 82nd pilots who were killed that day. Bomber crewmen witnessed three Bf-109s being shot down by P-38s.

The 14th Group had only run across enemy fighters twice since they became part of the new air force: two Bf-109s were shot down during a mission to Torino on December 1, followed by two Fw-190s during a mission to Marseilles the next day. They finally had a major engagement on December 20 while escorting B-17s to bomb Eleusis airfield outside Athens. Lieutenant Colonel Oliver Taylor flew group lead with the 49th Squadron. When enemy fighters were spotted, he quickly gave engagement orders, then led his flight of four to attack a flight of Bf-109s:

> At the proper moment, I lined one of them up in my sight, pressed the trigger button, and nothing happened! In an instant, I realized the pilot whose ship I had borrowed for the day had the various buttons on the steering column rewired to suit his own personal predilection, a not uncommon practice among our seasoned pilots. My frustration led to a lapse in judgement as I stayed with the Germans until I could discover which button fired the guns. During my frenzied search for the right gun control combination, I did damage one and probably destroyed another.

Once Taylor had figured out the mystery of the gun controls:

> I found myself practically on top of another Me 109, a bit above and to his right rear, but unaware that he was in a nearly vertical

dive, I caught him with a long burst from machine guns and cannon full in the cockpit. He seemed to be disintegrating in slow motion. A moment later, I realized I was heading straight down.

Taylor was now in the most dangerous part of the P-38's flight regime: diving with a rapid buildup in speed:

> There was no response to the controls and an increasingly violent vibration of the entire ship with extreme bucking of the steering column. The airspeed indicator showed a blurred 550 mph and the altimeter read less than 10,000 feet. Just before I blacked out I recall deciding to try retarding my throttles and getting awfully close to the ground.

Taylor blacked out and came to moments later to find the P-38 climbing straight up and about ready to stall out at 20,000 feet. As he recovered from the stall, Taylor looked up and found the 49th Squadron above:

> Getting a firm grip on myself, I very calmly, in well-modulated tones, told them where I was and to make a 360-degree turn and form on me. They acknowledged my call and proceeded to try. The next thing I knew, P-38s were whizzing by me, followed by a call: "Colonel, if you would raise your flaps, it would be easier for us to form on you." I not only had my flaps extended, but also was just barely making flying speed. With a very red face, I cleaned up the ship, was joined by the others, and headed for home.

The 14th ended 1943 with a mission to Verona on December 30. Many enemy aircraft were spotted in the distance, but only a few attempted to engage the Lightnings. The 48th Squadron's First Lieutenant Harrison Hannah was seen to destroy two, but was in turn shot down by a third, ending up a prisoner of war.

During the same period, the 1st Group flew two missions to Greece, one on December 14 and one on December 20. They met no opposition on the first mission, which experienced poor weather over Greece and kept the enemy on the ground. The weather was again poor for the second mission, and four pilots crashed on return due to bad weather and the lack of a homing device at Gioia, which led to the pilots letting down in the poor visibility to discover they were in the nearby mountains.

The 1st Group had received no replacement aircraft since the summer of 1943. By the end of the year, the squadrons were hard pressed to put up eight to ten P-38s for a mission: it was only possible by dint of scavenging and cannibalization of other aircraft by the mechanics. When the Fifteenth was founded, the command reported that none of the three P-38 groups assigned was at more than half strength.

On Christmas Day, the 1st Group escorted B-17s to bomb Udine. There was a continuous overcast over northern Italy; this resulted in the 94th and 71st Squadrons picking up the wrong B-17 formation and escorting them to Bolzano, while the 27th Squadron provided the sole escort to the B-17s that went to Udine. 27th Squadron leader Robert Kipper experienced oxygen failure and had to abort, leaving Captain Bob Vrilakas to take the lead. Before they got to the target, the squadron was bounced by four Fw-190s that popped out of the clouds unexpectedly, forcing the P-38s to drop their belly tanks earlier than planned. In the inconclusive fight that followed, the P-38s became separated from the rest of the formation. Vrilakas led them back toward home, but the fighters soon faced a fuel shortage. Vrilakas later wrote in his diary about what happened:

"We got homing to the closest airfield, which was 30 miles behind the front lines at Tremili." Vrilakas found a hole in the clouds near the field and led the squadron through it to land. The 79th Fighter Group was based there, which was fortunate for the Lightning pilots. Once on the ground, the weather got worse. The pilots were put up for the night by the 79th. "They fed us a Christmas dinner which really hit the spot since we'd had nothing since before takeoff." The next day, rain prevented any flying. Each of the 79th's squadrons had their own club, and Vrilakas and his pilots heard the newly released "Pistol-Packin' Mama" and "Paper Doll" while visiting. When they went to bed at 2330 hours, it was still raining. By the next morning, the weather had improved enough to allow the P-38s to take off by 1030 hours. "We gave the 79th a buzz job and headed home." Shortly after they landed back at Gioia at 1130 hours, the light rain turned to hail.

The three P-38 groups were joined in Fifteenth Air Force by the 325th Fighter Group, the Checkertail Clan. An increase in production of the Republic P-47 Thunderbolt following the commencement of operations at Republic's second factory in Evansville, Illinois, in the spring of 1943 allowed several fighter groups in the Mediterranean equipped with the P-40 to re-equip with the Thunderbolt. The first to do so was the 325th, which left southern Italy and returned to Tunisia, basing at Mateur airfield, for the transition to the P-47, on September 22, 1943. While the groups that followed the 325th would be fighter-bomber groups attached to the Twelfth Air Force, the Checkertails would take on the bomber escort role with their Thunderbolts when they transferred to the Fifteenth Air Force in November.

The first Thunderbolt appeared at Mateur on October 11, 1943, when group commander Lieutenant Colonel Bob Baseler landed the P-47 he had picked up at the aircraft assembly base at Bizerte. The North African rainy season soon arrived, and the 325th moved to the all-weather Soliman airfield on November 4, where it resumed training using the paved runways. When President Roosevelt's airplane arrived in North Africa on the way to the Tehran Conference, the Checkertails were chosen to escort the presidential Douglas C-54 – unofficially known as "The Sacred Cow" – when the president flew on to Cairo.

To expedite training, VIII Fighter Command sent Majors Lewis W. "Bill" Chick, Bill Madole, and Archie Hill to Soliman on December 3, to fly as unit leaders on the 325th's initial missions. Bill Chick, a veteran of the 4th Fighter Group who had flown Spitfire Vs and Thunderbolts in Britain, was the most experienced of the three. A man of action who had joined the RCAF before the US became involved in the war, Chick was dissatisfied with the passive escort tactics that were used by the Eighth Air Force, in which the fighters were to stick with the bombers at all times as close escort. He was extremely happy to learn on arrival in Tunisia that General Doolittle supported implementing new fighter tactics in the Fifteenth, in which the fighters would stay with the bombers until enemy fighters were sighted, at which point the escorts were to go after them. As Chick later recalled, "He wanted us to destroy the enemy fighters whenever we saw them so that we wouldn't have to engage them again tomorrow." Following completion of training, Chick wangled a transfer from Eighth to Fifteenth Air Force and then to the 325th, where he took command of the 317th Fighter Squadron.

The group's ground crew began moving back to Italy, where the Checkertails would operate from Foggia Main airfield, between December 1 and 3. The pilots flew the P-47s over to the new base on December 9; weather interfered with the transfer and the last Thunderbolts didn't arrive until December 11, when the air echelon flew over in C-47s. While the group was still short of maintenance personnel, P-47 operations began from Italy on December 14, with an escort mission to Kalamaki, Greece that turned out to be a "milk run," as were the next five flown between then and the end of the year. The Checkertails did get to fire their guns in anger on the fourth mission to Innsbruck, Austria: Captain "Spot" Collins destroyed a Ju-52/3m sitting on the Ancona airfield that he spotted during the return flight, while Major Chick strafed a ship moored in the port of Rozzeto di Abrizi, flying through a hail of defending flak without damage.

By late December, Foggia Main was so overcrowded that the 325th was transferred to Celone airfield, known as Foggia No. 1, on December 30; rains had turned the airfield into a "real mudhole," but it later became a good field when it dried out and the grass came in, as Captain Herschel "Herky" Green recalled. The group still managed to fly a mission that day, providing target withdrawal support for B-17s that bombed Verona. The mission turned into the group's baptism to aerial combat in the Thunderbolt when they came across several Bf-109s preparing to attack the bomber formation and shot down three. The 319th Squadron came out on top when Flight Officer Richard Catlin claimed two and the third was credited to Second Lieutenant Clarence Greve.

While a major reason for creating the Fifteenth Air Force had been the expectation of better flying weather, the Italian weather in late 1943 was so bad that only six Combined Bomber Offensive (CBO) missions could be flown in the final seven weeks of the year. The storm fronts brought low clouds, poor visibility, rain, and occasional snow. Captain Green later recalled, "This required us to do considerable instrument flying, climbing through multiple layers of clouds to our escort altitude and descending through them on our return."

3

THE FIFTEENTH IS BLOODED

New Year's Day 1944 saw a heavy rainstorm with high winds blow over many of the 325th's tents at Foggia No. 1, scattering their contents across the field. The mess tent was also blown down and the turkeys for the group's new year celebration were scattered, though they were recovered and – after thorough cleaning – were served to the men the next day in a delayed celebration. Captain Green recalled locals saying the storm was the worst seen in southern Italy in many years.

The new year of 1944 saw the Fifteenth Air Force begin to extend its reach, with missions flown into Austria and Hungary while preparation was made to join the Eighth Air Force in the Combined Bomber Offensive over Germany.

The 14th Group's P-38s ran into the Aeronautica Nazionale Repubblicana (ANR) – the reconstituted Italian Fascist air force – during an escort mission to Villa Perosa in northern Italy on January 3, 1944. Several Macchi C.205 "Veltro" (Greyhound) fighters attacked the 49th Squadron's Lightnings and dived away before the Americans could react. The Italians scored in their attack: Second Lieutenant David Fritz failed to join up after the brief encounter. The 48th's Lieutenant L.D. Wells was also missing when the group landed back at their Foggia base.

On January 4, the 82nd's Lightnings escorted B-17s to Sofia, where they found very little opposition, with the only claim being a Bf-109 damaged. On the way back to Italy, pilots from the 97th Squadron came across an He-111 bomber towing a Gotha Go-242 troop transport glider; both were shot down. Official credit was given to the squadron as a whole since seven pilots hit the Heinkel (the glider received no separate credit). January also saw the group move from their base at Lecce to Foggia No. 11, also known as Vincenzo airfield, which would be their home for the rest of the war; the move was completed on January 11.

The 14th and 1st Groups provided escort on January 7 for a mission to bomb the Messerschmitt aircraft factory at Wiener Neustadt in Austria. The lack of P-38 replacements in the 1st Group was so bad that the group could put up only 20 Lightnings of an official 48 assigned. The 16 P-38s of the 94th and 71st Squadrons ran into two waves of enemy fighters totaling 50–60 Bf-109s and Fw-190s. The 94th's Lieutenants Meredith and Griffith were shot down in flames over the target, while Lieutenant Devenney's fighter was so badly damaged he was forced to bail out over northern Yugoslavia, where he was able to contact partisan forces which returned him to Italy in March.

The 71st's squadron leader, Major Horace Hanes, was hit in his right engine; he too successfully bailed out over Yugoslavia, and was rescued by partisans who were able to return him to Italy in late February. Lieutenants Owens and Corbett were missing in combat, while Flight Officer Lee Rowe's Lightning was seen to get hit in the cockpit, after which it fell away out of control.

While the 1st Group experienced the majority of combat on the mission, First Lieutenant Max Wright of the 14th's 48th Squadron claimed a Bf-110 destroyed. Overall, the Wiener Neustadt mission boded ill for the Fifteenth's escorts; the 1st Group had only 32 P-38s left after the mission. Re-equipment was desperately needed if the unit was to remain operationally effective. There was a need for longer-range escorts if the new air force was to effectively participate in the Combined Bomber Offensive.

Once in their new home at Foggia, the 82nd Group escorted B-24s on a mission to Sofia on January 10, during which the Lightnings engaged in combat with 25–30 Bulgarian Air Force defenders as the force approached the target. The P-38 pilots demonstrated clear superiority over their Bulgarian opponents, with group commander Lieutenant Colonel Oliver Taylor, First Lieutenant Robert Margison, and Second Lieutenants Paul Wilkins and Cleveland Tatum of the 37th Squadron; Second Lieutenants Robert Cowie and Ralph Sebring from the 48th; First Lieutenant Harold Simpson and Second Lieutenants John Grant,

Robert Hoke, and Roy Liles of the 49th Squadron each claiming one Bf-109 destroyed.

Life at the new Foggia bases was far from easy for the Lightning pilots. The weather in January and February was bitterly cold while the winter rains turned the airfields into muddy swamps with mud so deep that boards had to be laid for foot traffic. Taxiing a P-38 on a pierced-steel planking (PSP) taxiway covered in icy mud was like ice skating: if a pilot applied too much power to break free of the gunk, there was a real danger of sliding into the airplane ahead in the takeoff line, with disastrous results. The tents were heated using improvised stoves made from a 55-gallon fuel drum cut in half and upended over rocks, with 100-octane fuel dripping from an upended drop tank outside through copper tubing; a petcock controlled the amount of fuel, which was ideally enough to keep a low fire going on the rocks inside the drum. Lighting off such a Rube Goldberg contraption could be literally explosive. Several 1st Group pilots lost all their belongings and were lucky to escape with their lives when their tents went up in flames from such an explosion. Later versions used a bed of sand which the vaporized fuel saturated, which was comparatively safer. The 1st Group's base at Salsola in the northern tier of airfields in the Foggia complex turned out to have a mosquito breeding ground in a swamp just north of the field when spring finally arrived. Food was basic. Groups supplemented the official diets with hunting parties sent into the mountains to obtain whatever was available, along with negotiations with local Italian farmers for supplies of fresh vegetables and such. When aircrews went on leave to Cairo or Algiers, they left with considerable sums of cash and long lists of food items to obtain for their return.

The fact that the living conditions in the Fifteenth were what they were, rather than the far more comfortable Eighth Air Force bases in England near cities such as London, meant there were far fewer visits by war correspondents, which contributed to the lack of public awareness of the Fifteenth as compared with the Eighth.

The 1st and 14th Groups escorted B-24s to Piraeus, Greece on January 11. The 16 1st Group P-38s were left alone over the target when the second wing of bombers aborted just short of the target, taking the 14th Group's Lightnings with them. A force of 25–30 JG 27 Bf-109s made an appearance over the target but the P-38s fended off their attack, claiming two destroyed; all the Lightnings returned to Salsola safely.

The 14th escorted bombers to hit the airfields around Rome on January 13. Enemy fighters had been scarce during previous missions to the Italian capital, but both German and Italian fighters rose to contest the Americans this time. Individual battles swirled from 25,000 feet to right on the deck. Seven pilots from all three squadrons claimed one enemy fighter each destroyed, while Lieutenant Ralph Sebring collided head-on with a Bf-109; the enemy fighter disintegrated, while Sebring's P-38 lost ten feet of the right wing. He was last seen struggling to keep the fighter upright to bail out, but was never heard from after.

Two days later, the 14th Group returned to Austria, escorting bombers to Klagenfurt. Lieutenant Enoch Lemon later wrote his impressions of the battle over the target in his diary: "Just as we neared the target, someone broke radio silence, calling 'Ten bogies are making passes at the rear bombers!'" The 37th Squadron made a 180-degree turn and headed back over the bomber stream. "Next thing I knew, there were Me-109s all around us. Blue and Green flights turned into some 109s that were coming up on us from behind." Lemon then saw Lieutenant Tom "Dub" Smith get midaired by a Bf-109 that hit the Lightning between its tail booms and took out the right engine.

Smith later recalled the incident in which he should have gone down. "I could see enemy fighters all around and realized I would be very easy pickings, so I decided to jump out before any of them had a chance to make a pass at me. I told my flight I was bailing out, and would see them after the war." Smith released his canopy, unfastened his harness, rolled down the side window, and pulled off his helmet and oxygen mask. "Realizing a map might be handy, I pulled them out and discarded until I found one of the area I was in."

Smith's airspeed indicator read 110mph as the airplane lost 25–30 feet of altitude a minute. "I discovered that by turning into the dead engine I could gain altitude at a rate of about 200 feet every full rotation. I continued this maneuver all the way back." Smith had to stand on the right rudder with both feet to make his turns. With the cockpit open and having removed his gloves, "It was so cold that my feet and hands were nearly frozen." The left engine was overheating; when it started detonating, Smith pulled the throttle back to cool it, losing altitude in the process. "I had little hope that I would ever get back, and was looking for a likely place to belly land."

Smith flew over the coast at Fiume, where the enemy opened up with antiaircraft fire. "Having no canopy, I could hear the 88mm rounds go past me and heard it when it burst. The air became so turbulent it almost turned my ship over." Smith dived for a cloudbank. Once in it, his elevator started vibrating so badly he thought it would come off. Banging on his radio brought it back to life and he was able to receive a heading for home. "I decided it was worth taking a chance to get back to base."

Turning back toward the coast:

> My good engine quit due to overheating. I called in my position and started to let down. At about 6,000 feet, the engine caught again, apparently having cooled off. I arrived over our base at 4,000 feet, still undecided if I would bail out or belly land. When I tried taking my feet off the rudder, the ship spiraled to the right, which would put me into the path of the elevator if I decided to jump. I made a practice landing in the air and saw that it might be possible to hold the nose up sufficiently to land if I didn't bring it in too fast.

On the ground, Flight Surgeon Dr Wiliam Curtis watched Smith's landing. "He went back out over the town of Foggia and made a perfect belly landing on the grass. By the time I got to the plane, he was standing to the side and trying to light a cigarette. Gas was everywhere. I yelled at him to stop, then loaded him into the ambulance and let him have a cigarette."

On January 24, the 82nd flew a second mission to Sofia, escorting B-24s. This time the formation ran into aerial opposition well before they arrived over the target when a mixed formation of 12 Bf-109s and Fw-190s attacked the bombers head on north of Skopje, Yugoslavia. The Lightnings quickly went after the enemy and a dogfight ensued. The enemy pilots were good; the 82nd pilots claimed two destroyed, a probable, and three damaged in exchange for two P-38s shot down. Captain Clayton M. "Ike" Isaacson – who had been with the 96th Squadron since September after completing a tour in B-25s with the 321st Bomb Group – was credited with a probable Fw-190, later upgraded to destroyed.

The Checkertails flew five unopposed escort missions to Italian, Austrian, and Bulgarian targets between January 4 and 10, during which their only loss was the 317th Squadron's Lieutenant Miller, who failed to return from the mission on January 10 due to unknown causes. The 319th's Captain Green recalled that, for the P-38 pilots, aircraft identification was easy – all single-engine aircraft were the enemy. Once the 325th was flying missions as part of the escort force, "This caused us to expend considerable effort avoiding attacks by P-38s." Some Checkertails were willing to entertain the thought that Miller had been the victim of their alleged friends in the three P-38 groups.

January 13 saw the Checkertails engage 25 Bf-109s during a bombing raid against airfields in the vicinity of Rome, claiming three shot down. Newly promoted Captain Spot Collins claimed one as his seventh victory, while Major James Toner and Lieutenant John M. Forrest each claimed one. The group's next five missions were again "milk runs," but on January 19, during a mission escorting B-17s to bomb Contocello airfield near Rome, Major Chick and Flight Officer Edsel Paulk each claimed a Bf-109 destroyed when the group caught a formation of the enemy fighters attempting to attack the Fortresses from the rear.

Major Chick reported, "I initially attacked the leader, diving on him. I missed and pulled up from my dive and fired at the wingman from about 50 yards. He burst into flames and started down. I followed him down from about 8,000 feet to 4,000 feet and watched him crash." Paulk reported, "There were four of us and two of them, so it was a question as to who would get to them first. We all shot at them. After Major Chick got the first one, the second one tried to get away, but I was able to make a quick turn and keep on his tail until I saw him smoking and the pilot bailed out."

Two days later, on January 21, during a fighter sweep over the Florence area, the Clan engaged a formation of Fw-190s and claimed four destroyed. They were credited to Captain Raymond Hartley Jr. and Lieutenants Harry Carroll, William Elliott, and Fielder Smith.

Captain Hartley wrote a long and detailed report of how he scored his first victory:

> We were at 15,000 feet, about six minutes south of Florence when, at 1225 hours, Lieutenant Elliott called out bogies at 11 o'clock. Major Tirk, who was leading the squadron, instructed Lieutenant Elliott

to go after them – I led my flight down with Elliott's. The bogies were Fw 190s; there were five or six flying south in a line abreast formation at about 10,000 feet, and we peeled off after them when they were almost directly beneath us.

Elliott led his flight after the three to the left, while Hartley led his flight after the two to the right. "Elliott's flight, being ahead of us, opened fire, and the Fw-190s started split-essing. I saw one roll over and up trailing smoke and fire, and moments later a 'chute opened."

Hartley then opened fire on the leader of the two he was chasing. "My Fw did a split-s and then a half roll, and I was able to follow him through despite the fact I was still carrying my wing tanks. I finally released my wing tanks as we pulled out of a dive at 2,000 feet." Hartley forgot to switch to his main tank and momentarily lost speed when the engine cut briefly due to fuel starvation. As a result, another P-47 flew past him in pursuit of the Fw-190 he had attacked:

We chased the enemy fighter down to the deck and quite a way south. The leading P-47 fired several bursts and I thought I observed several explosions along the wing of the Fw, although I was well behind and it was hazy. Then that P-47 broke off the chase, banking away to the left despite me calling him to keep going. I continued the chase. Although the pilot was weaving as if to look behind him, I apparently took him by surprise when I fired from close range.

Hartley's fire scored hits on the left wing and fuselage bottom. The Fw-190 initiated a long climbing turn to the right. "I adjusted my lead and observed hits on top of the fuselage. The FW then rolled slowly onto its back and a large sheet of flame came out of its belly at the wing root. The pilot then split-essed into the ground from about 100 feet. This was between 1230 and 1235 hours." Just before the enemy fighter crashed, Hartley had to pull back on his throttle so that he didn't overrun his opponent.

With the Anzio invasion on, the 325th flew fighter sweeps over the enemy airfields in the vicinity of Rome to limit Luftwaffe attacks on the invasion. The sweep flown on January 22 saw the Checkertails dodge ground fire throughout the mission. South of Rome, the Thunderbolts ran across 12–15 Bf-109s. Captain Collins flamed two for victories seven and eight, while future ace Second Lieutenant Robert Barkey claimed his first victory. The remaining two Bf-109s were credited one each to Major Chick and Lieutenant Elliott. Two Checkertail pilots were reported missing.

Barkey reported afterwards, "Two of us were over Guidonia airdrome, near Rome, when we spotted about 12 Me 109s below us, so we dove on them. We were less than 30 feet from the ground and traveling at about 400 mph. When I was about 50 feet behind a Me 109 I got a good burst into his tail. I could see pieces fly off, he rolled over and crashed."

The ten missions flown between January 23 and 29 were uneventful, but January 30, 1944 would see the Checkertails score their first "big day" as part of the Fifteenth Air Force.

Over January, USAAF intelligence had discovered from monitoring Luftwaffe radio traffic that German fighters were scrambled about 15 minutes before the heavy bombers arrived over their targets. Armed with this knowledge, Lieutenant Colonel Baseler and the group operations staff came up with a plan that they submitted to Fifteenth Air Force mission planners to launch the 325th on a fighter sweep covering five enemy airfields in the Villaorba and Udine areas. To gain surprise, the Checkertail Thunderbolts departed at 0945 hours and flew 300 miles north over the middle of the Adriatic Sea – out of sight of land and at an altitude of 50 feet to avoid detection by German radar. Over the Gulf of Venice, the P-47s climbed to higher altitude. When they arriving over Villaorba airfield at 1145 hours, with the three squadrons stacked from 15,000 feet to 19,000 feet, 60 German fighters were spotted taking off, in addition to a number of transports and bombers fleeing the airfields.

The 317th Squadron's Captain Herky Green had the most successful day of any USAAF pilot in the Mediterranean Theater during the war. He later recalled:

> I had been sick and hadn't flown for about a week, but there was no way I was going to miss this mission. I was leading the 317th and was considered one of the "old timers." We had never trained for this type of mission, but our pilots were up to the challenge. We were so low that the undersides of our airplanes were streaming water from the

spray kicked up by our props. The mission was even more hazardous because the sea was unusually calm and a heavy haze hung low across the horizon completely obscuring the horizon.

Like the others, Green was drenched with sweat from flying under such conditions by the time they got to Venice. "There were no visual references. Maintaining altitude under such close tolerances required unbelievable concentration. The maximum 20–30 feet clearance we maintained could be lost in the blink of an eye. All the leaders could do was fly on instruments while others hung on hoping their leaders were doing a good job."

Once over the airfield complex, Green spotted several large aircraft flying at very low altitude in a loose gaggle approaching one of the airfields. He nosed over, followed by his wingman, Flight Officer Cecil Dean, his element leader, First Lieutenant George Novotny, and his wingman, Flight Officer Edsel Paulk. Diving vertically, Green had to throttle back in the dive and the Thunderbolts still pulled out with too much speed for accurate shooting. "We were still very fast when we hit them." The enemy aircraft turned out to be 11 Ju-52 trimotor transports, strung out in intervals for landing. Green started firing at the last in line and worked his way forward. Having shot down four, he pulled up to go around for a second pass, but by the time he came around, the rest of them had been shot down by the other members of the flight.

Element leader Novotny recalled, "I picked out a couple that turned to the left and destroyed them both. After turning to rejoin my flight, I saw a little Hs-126 right in front of me, so I gave him the works. One burst and he disappeared. Only a few pieces were left and they fluttered harmlessly to the ground."

Green led the others in a climb to 10,000 feet; when a Bf-109 dived past, the flight turned to chase the enemy fighter. As he recalled, "We never did get back to altitude the rest of the fight." Flight Officer Paulk came close to shooting at Green when both pursued a Bf-109 up a dry riverbed, but Green dropped back out of the way while Paulk scored the Bf-109. When the enemy fighter crashed, Paulk pulled up and flew right through high voltage power lines that crossed the river he hadn't spotted. Balls of blue fire flashed from the severed wires, but the P-47 climbed away safely.

When Green turned away from that fight, he ran across a Macchi C.202 "Folgore" that passed him flying the opposite direction:

> Turning as quickly as I could, I dropped behind him and closed the gap to a reasonable range. He was flying flat on the deck, pulling up over trees, fences and houses. I was trying my best to catch him. He made a tight 360-degree turn and then straightened out. I gained a couple hundred feet of altitude and dived on him. He made another 360 and I followed him. When he started a third 360, I was in range and let him have it. The pilot must have been hit, for the airplane executed a perfect snap roll at that low altitude, coming back almost level before the right wing hit the ground and he cartwheeled away in a ball of flame.

Green was now alone, but still wasn't done. "As I climbed through 15,000 feet, heading home, I saw a twin-engine plane 5,000 feet below and behind me. I made a turn and descended in a right turn to come down on his tail. As I approached, I recognized it as a Do-217." Green opened fire, hitting the left engine, which caught fire. The next burst was all tracers, the reminder that Green had run out of ammo. "I pulled to the side and watched him crash land and explode." Green turned again for home. "I spotted another, but decided discretion was the better part of valor and didn't try to score number seven. It was tempting."

On arrival back at base, Green discovered that the regular pilot of the plane he had flown did not subscribe to the group's idea of carrying only 400 rounds per gun to save weight, but opted for the full 800 rounds per gun that the P-47 could carry. "His armorer just attached two of the 400-round belts, each of which had the five tracer rounds just before the end of the belt. I actually had another 400 rounds per gun than I thought I had!"

The Checkertails had achieved an amazing success in the mission. Green's A Flight was credited with 15 – six for Green, while Dean had shot down three Ju-52s, Paulk had shot down two Ju-52s and the Bf-109, and Novotny had shot down two Ju-52s as well as the Hs-126. Colonel Baseler claimed a Ju-88 for his last victory, and Captain Collins and Lieutenants Carroll, Brewer, Dorety, Emmonds, Edwards, Jones, Kerns, Suehle, Ketcher, Whiteside, and Hogg each claimed a Bf-109 for a total of 28 kills, with seven more claimed probable.

Major Chick's flight ran into six Bf-109s which attacked the four P-47s head on. Chick scored two victories shooting the enemy fighters off a P-47 they were attacking. He later described the fight: "It was a real hassle, and Hollywood would have given a million to have gotten the overall picture of the action on film. It still scares me to think of all the near misses and mid-air collisions I almost had."

The cost was two P-47s missing. Green's six victories tied him with Spot Collins as the Checkertails' leading aces with nine victories each.

The 82nd Group also saw heavy action that day while escorting B-24s to bomb targets in Udine. The formation was attacked by Bf-109s as it approached the target. In the fight that erupted, the 97th Squadron's commanding officer (CO), Major Charles Spencer – who had only taken over command eight days earlier – was shot down when he and Second Lieutenant Claude Skinner engaged ten Bf-109s that attacked the rear of the bomber formation. Skinner saw Spencer shoot down one enemy fighter and engage two others that were forced to break away smoking. At that point, Skinner was forced to dive away to escape a Bf-109 on his tail. As he broke free of the pursuing German fighter, Skinner looked up and saw a P-38 he identified as Spencer's "going down in a slow spiral as if it was out of control." Spencer received a posthumous Silver Star for his leadership on this mission.

The 95th Squadron's First Lieutenant Lee Thompson led his two flights into a fight with the Germans attacking the bombers' rear. After closing on a Bf-109 that dived away, Thompson and his wingman Second Lieutenant John Batie found themselves momentarily alone. Thompson spotted a twin-engine airplane below and dived on it. Identifying it as an "Me-210," he closed on the fighter but was forced to pull up when the rear gunner opened fire. He got below the enemy plane and opened fire, hitting the right engine which caught fire. Batie was able to confirm that the quarry went in and exploded when it hit the ground. Thompson recalled, "I decided we were far enough north we might run into enemy reinforcements, so we turned back south." He then spotted an Fw-190 attacking a B-24. "We were closing on him pretty fast. Hoping to prevent him getting away, I started firing at greater than optimum range; he split-essed right through my fire. I continued on toward the bombers."

Thompson saw Batie dive after the Fw-190. He later recalled, "When he landed back at Foggia, his plane was a mess. Most of the plexiglass was missing from the canopy and his right boom was bent. He'd gotten into compressibility chasing the '190, saw the Fw-190 go straight in, and had to use rim tab to get out of the dive."

First Lieutenant Dick Willsie came to prominence in the group during the mission. He had arrived in December, transferred from the 414th Night Fighter Squadron in which he had flown "Reverse" Lend-Lease Bristol Beaufighters. As the bombers turned away from the target, Willsie found himself alone. He spotted a P-38 with three Bf-109s on its tail and turned into the enemy fighters, breaking up their attack. Suddenly, he found himself surrounded by a formation of 30 Bf-109s. Willsie shot at one and then another of them while he maneuvered desperately to get away. Just as he ran out of ammunition, he was able to break free and turn toward Foggia. When he landed 20 minutes behind the rest of the group, he found he'd already been listed as "missing in action." His fight got Dick Willsie the first of three DFCs that he would be awarded during his tour with the 82nd.

On January 30, the 14th Group flew an escort mission to northern Italy, where 25–30 enemy fighters were spotted. However, the Germans were in no mood for a fight and turned away, diving to escape before the Lightnings could close. The next day, the group was so short of airplanes they could only send 26 P-38s on another mission to Klagenfurt. Fortunately, the enemy didn't make an appearance and the Lightnings returned with no losses.

On February 1, good news arrived for the 14th and 1st Groups that they would finally receive replacement aircraft. Pilots from both groups were flown in B-17s to England, where they collected brand-new P-38H Lightnings and returned via Gibraltar and Algiers on February 12. The two groups were close to full strength for the first time since before the Sicilian invasion in the previous summer.

The reinforcement was just in time for what came in February. Weather closed down flying in Italy during the first nine days of the month; as it cleared, the Fifteenth Air Force prepared to become a full partner with the Eighth Air Force over Germany.

At the beginning of February, General Arnold wrote to General Spaatz – newly installed as commander of the US Strategic Air Forces in Europe – regarding the concerns of Air Force high command for the way the Combined Bomber Offensive was being handled. Arnold was frankly worried that RAF Bomber Command might overshadow the USAAF's effort, concluding, "Already, the spectacular effectiveness of their devastation of cities has placed their contribution in the popular mind at so high a plane that I am having the greatest difficulty in keeping your achievement in its proper role, not only in publications, but unfortunately in military and naval circles, and in fact, with the President himself."

In the year since VIII Bomber Command had received approval of Operation *Pointblank* at the Casablanca Conference and for the goals agreed to at the recent Cairo Conference, it was clear none of those goals had come close to being achieved. The leaders of the Western Allies were confronted with loud Soviet calls for opening the long-delayed "Second Front." Jimmy Doolittle recalled Spaatz saying to him when Doolittle was informed he would be going to Britain to take command of Eighth Air Force, that it was "time to fish or cut bait." On taking the new command, General Doolittle sent a public message to those he now led: "During the next few months it is mandatory that we secure complete air superiority over the German Air Force in this Theater... we must adopt every expedient to improve the effectiveness of the Air Force."

First developed in November 1943, the goal of Operation *Argument* was the destruction of the German aviation industry, which was to be accomplished by a series of closely spaced attacks against aircraft factories. Planners believed such a blow, delivered over a short period, would keep the enemy from being able to repair factories one at a time, leading to the repair capacity collapsing as it was stretched beyond its limits. The continuing bad weather over the winter of 1943–44 had kept the plan from being implemented, but new long-range forecasts gave a possibility of a break in the storms during February that would allow a window in which to mount such attacks. This was to be the first time that Eighth and Fifteenth Air Forces would work in conjunction with each other. Operation *Argument*'s goal was achieving air superiority by hitting targets that the *Jagdwaffe* would have to defend.

While the Eighth Air Force waited for the promised good bombing weather to arrive, the Fifteenth Air Force took part in one of the most controversial missions of the war in Italy. The Allied armies were engaged in the Second Battle of Cassino as they tried to break through the Gustav Line of German defenses and move north to Rome.

Acting more out of frustration than military necessity, General Clark approved a mission in which the Fifteenth's B-17s and B-24s bombed the Benedictine Abbey of Monte Cassino. Intelligence suggested the ninth-century abbey was being used as an observation post to observe the whole region. The mission was scheduled for February 15. Unfortunately, imprecise bombing resulted in only 10 percent of bombs dropped hitting the target; Clark's command compound at Presenzano, 17 miles away, was hit by 16 500-pound bombs which blew up a few yards from the general's trailer. The resulting ruins became a perfect defensive position for the German paratroopers who moved in; they held the position against until May.

In England and central Europe, three frustrating months of bad weather ended on February 19. USSTAF's weather section identified two extensive high-pressure areas, one in the Baltic, which – if it moved across Europe as anticipated – would leave clear skies or, at worst, scattered clouds over the Continent, and one just west of Ireland, which would give good weather over the Eighth's bases in Britain. The resulting battles became known as "Big Week."

Eighth Air Force mounted its largest mission to date on February 20 when 1,003 B-17s and B-24s bombed aircraft production factories in the Brunswick–Leipzig region, which was only 80 miles south of Berlin. Losses were 21 bombers and four escorting fighters, while the results were more than had been expected in their wildest dreams; four assembly plants in Leipzig had been hit hard. The Luftwaffe admitted losing 53 Bf-109s and Fw-190s, and 25 Bf-110s. VIII Bomber Command had been prepared to lose 200 bombers.

On February 21 the targets were aircraft factories in Brunswick and Braunschweig. The weather over Germany was not as good as the day before and bombing results at Brunswick were not what was hoped for. The city was hit by area bombing as 762 bombers followed H2X-equipped pathfinders. Again, the 16 losses were lower than expected.

The forecast was favorable for visual bombing on February 22, with the high-pressure ridge moving south and opening up Regensburg and Schweinfurt. Weather over Italy was also good. Fifteenth Air Force would enter the battle with a strike against Regensburg while Eighth Air Force bombed Schweinfurt, Gotha, Bernburg, Oschersleben, Aschersleben, and Halberstadt.

Bad weather over Britain forced 3rd Air Division commander General Curtis LeMay to cancel the Schweinfurt mission, while the 2nd Division B-24s ran into poor weather crossing the Channel; unable to re-organize, they were recalled. Only 1st Air Division's B-17s flew into Germany, where the weather forced them to seek targets of opportunity; only 99 of 466 bombers hit their primary targets. This time 41 bombers were lost while fighters claimed 60 enemy fighters shot down.

Better weather over Bavaria and Austria allowed 183 Fifteenth Air Force B-17s and B-24s to strike Regensburg, while 118 B-24s bombed the Messerschmitt factory at Obertraubling. Losses were 14 bombers shot down over Regensburg. The target was at the edge of P-38 coverage; the bombers were forced to shoot their way in and out, unescorted over the target.

Sergeant Loyd Lewis, a B-24 flight engineer in the 449th Bomb Group who flew the February 22 mission in the Liberator piloted by First Lieutenant Carl Browning, recalled, "Everything seemed to be going OK, when all of a sudden I spotted fighter planes very far out at three o'clock. They were diving down into the clouds and out of sight. I remember getting on the intercom and announcing the enemy planes. This was the last I remembered. I was hit and knocked unconscious." Lewis regained consciousness a few days later in an Austrian hospital and was told his bomber had been attacked by Bf-109s and Fw-190s. Browning, the bomber's pilot, had been stunned by a shell burst, and the B-24 went into a dive. The co-pilot had managed to right the bomber and help the crew bail out.

The weather forced a break on February 23, but both air forces struck targets on February 23 and 24. Eighth Air Force's 1st Air Division's five wings bombed Schweinfurt, while 2nd Division's B-24s hit Gotha. LeMay's 3rd Division bombed aircraft component factories and assembly plants in northeastern Germany and Poland. The Fifteenth sent 87 bombers to Steyr, Austria.

The 1st and 2nd Air Divisions had almost continuous fighter cover; they suffered persistent, concentrated attacks over Gotha and Schweinfurt. The B-24s that bombed Gotha lost 33 of 239. As at

Schweinfurt, losses were considerably less, with only 11 shot down while the escorts claimed 37 against a loss of ten.

The 87 Fifteenth Air Force B-17s that bombed Steyr experienced attacks by single-engine fighters while Bf-110s fired rockets at long range. The rear formation was hit hard; all ten Flying Fortresses from the 2nd Bomb Group were shot down, while the rest of the formation lost another seven. The 82nd Group's P-38s had just moved into position behind the last group of bombers as they approached the target, when they found a swarm of German single- and twin-engine fighters attacking the formation. The Lightnings intervened and in the running battle over the target, the P-38 pilots claimed eight enemy fighters shot down and destroyed. Lieutenant Gene Chatfield recalled:

> We were right on schedule to take up target support when we heard the bombers calling for help. We increased speed and got there as fast as possible. We got there just as the bombers were starting their bomb run. I could see formations of '109s and Me-410s above and behind the B-17s. They would break out of their gaggle and attack the rearmost bomber, shooting it down in flames. We only had 28 P-38s of the original 42 that took off.

The P-38s spread out wingtip to wingtip so they looked at first glance like a much larger force than they were, and headed toward the enemy gaggles. "We plowed into the enemy and forced them to break off their attacks on the bombers." The final claims were five Bf-109s, one Me-410, and two Bf-110s. Despite the enemy's determined attacks, the aircraft components factory that was the target was heavily damaged.

On February 25, the Fifteenth's bombers returned to Regensburg. Unfortunately, the older model P-38s flown by three Lightning groups did not have the range to accompany the bombers to the target. As a result, the undefended formations lost 29 B-17s and B-24s, with the 301st Bomb Group losing 11 B-17s.

That night, snow fell on both the East Anglia airfields and Germany. Almost all air operations in northern Europe came to a halt for the next six days. "Big Week" was over.

Despite the losses on the final missions, the Fifteenth Air Force units had performed well. The results at the Messerschmitt factories in Regensburg – the heart of Bf-109 production – were particularly good. When these were coupled with the heavy damage inflicted on the Obertraubling factory on February 22 and 25, in which many buildings were destroyed and scarcely any escaped damage, overall Bf-109 production was reduced from 435 planes per month in January 1944 to 135 per month in March. Regensburg did not recover scheduled production levels until June 1944.

Regardless of the comparatively small size of the forces that flew the two "Big Week" missions, the overall contribution by the Fifteenth Air Force to the goals of Operation *Argument* was immense. The Fifteenth was now blooded and had the experience to take on the mission for which it had been created: the destruction of Ploești.

4

THE FIFTEENTH AIR FORCE COMES OF AGE

The "Big Week" missions had clearly demonstrated that the Fifteenth Air Force would not be able to take part fully in the Combined Bomber Offensive until there were fighter escort units equipped with an airplane that had sufficient range to escort the bombers all the way to the target and back. Such was beyond the ability of the P-38 groups based at Foggia. The P-51B Mustang had appeared in Britain in the fall of 1943. The Air Force bureaucracy had initially assigned the fighter to units in the tactical Ninth Air Force – primarily because the RAF had put the earlier Allison-powered Mustangs to use in fighter-reconnaissance units due to that fighter's inability to fly and fight at the higher altitudes required in Europe. However, Eighth Air Force had been able to have the Ninth's 354th "Pioneer Mustang" group assigned to operational control of VIII Fighter Command until needed for the invasion of Europe. The second Ninth Air Force unit equipped with the P-51B – the 353rd Fighter Group – was also seconded to VIII Fighter Command. The Eighth was able to convince General Eisenhower that the 357th Fighter Group, also initially assigned to the Ninth, should be directly assigned to VIII Fighter Command in exchange for a P-47 group, and that future deliveries of the P-51B to Britain should be made available for re-equipping existing VIII Fighter Command units using the P-47. By April 1944, there were five units assigned to VIII Fighter Command flying the Mustang, and the air war over Germany had been transformed.

THE FIFTEENTH AIR FORCE COMES OF AGE

By February 1944, production of the long-range Merlin-powered Mustang had risen to the point that General Twining was able to argue successfully for XV Air Force Fighter Command to be assigned additional fighter groups that would be equipped with the new fighter, and for the Checkertail Clan's P-47s to be replaced with P-51Bs. The Twelfth Air Force's 31st Fighter Group, which had flown Spitfires since the unit first entered combat in England in the summer of 1942, would be the first group to re-equip with the Mustang and be reassigned to the Fifteenth Air Force.

Shortly after the 31st Group learned that they would be re-equipping and joining the Fifteenth Air Force, the 52nd Fighter Group discovered that they too would be trading in their Spitfires for the new Mustangs, and would soon be flying long-range escort for the heavy bombers rather than the tactical missions they were flying in support of the forces at Anzio. The 52nd was based at Borgo Poreta airfield, outside the town of Aghione on the island of Corsica off the central Italian mainland, which placed them closer to targets in Austria and southern Germany than the escort groups based at the Foggia complex. They handed over their Spitfires to the Free French Air Force unit with which they shared Borgo Poreta in early March 1944 and began transition training led by another Pioneer Mustang pilot. The 52nd had been primarily equipped with the older Spitfire V, and the pilots found that the Mustang's Merlin-60 series engine and two-speed supercharger made flying the new fighter "exhilarating as hell," in the words of one.

The Fifteenth's 325th Fighter Group continued to fly missions with the P-47 Thunderbolt. Following their first "big day" on January 30, the group found little combat on the few missions flown during the bad weather in February. In the meantime, the Checkertails discovered that their new base at Lake Lesina in the Foggia complex was "one of the most malaria-ridden places in Italy," as Herky Green later recalled. Green first experienced the initial signs of the disease on the mission he flew on February 1. "The harbinger of my severe case of malaria first appeared symptomatically while I was flying a fighter sweep in the Orvieto-Viterbo area." Green found himself feeling semi-dazed and half-asleep, unable to concentrate on flying. By the time he landed three hours later, he was running a temperature. Flight Surgeon Captain Theodore Marquardt diagnosed malaria and confined Green to his tent in the squadron where he could be observed constantly. Green's temperature finally broke on reaching 105 degrees, but recovery took the remainder of February. Several other pilots and ground crewmen were also infected by the mosquitos. A major effort to drain the swampy ground near the field finally solved the problem.

While Green was ill, the Checkertails escorted a mission to bomb the marshaling yards in Verona on February 14, during which they were engaged by 25 Bf-109s and five Macchi C.202s, claiming six Bf-109s and a C.202 destroyed. On March 3, a mission to Rome was hit by 18 Bf-109s and Fw-190s that went after the bombers. Five pilots claimed four Bf-109s and two Fw-190s.

While ill, Green was promoted to major in late February. He later wrote that the promotion caused him to look back on the year of combat he had experienced. One of the few combat pilots ever to admit that initially he was so scared of being killed in combat that it had adversely affected his performance for his first missions, Green thought about the six times he had returned from a close-fought battle which could easily have gone the other way:

> I suddenly had the realization that I wasn't going to be killed in the war! The irrationality of that revelation had no bearing. As long as I believed it was true, for me, it was true. From the time of that realization, I became uninhibited in combat. I wasn't reckless and didn't take unnecessary risks, it was just that I no longer was concerned about personal safety. That meant that what talent and skill I had as a fighter pilot could be exercised one hundred percent. I know that sounds crazy; maybe it was.

Green's newfound sense of fearlessness manifested itself on the escort mission he flew on March 11, when the Clan took B-17s to attack the Padua marshaling yards. As the formation neared the target, it was intercepted by 65 enemy fighters in two formations. Green and his wingman attacked what he recalled were "30–40 enemy fighters." He reported, "There were so many it was difficult to choose which to shoot first. I got on the tail of the closest '109 but I couldn't hit him because I was dead astern and in severe prop-wash." When the enemy fighter rolled over and dived away, Green followed. "Now that I could get my sight on him, I started getting hits around the cockpit. Immediately there were explosions and he caught fire and went out of

THE FIFTEENTH AIR FORCE COMES OF AGE

control." Green and others reported that the enemy pilots they engaged in this battle seemed "more aggressive than usual." Three P-47s, flown by Lieutenant Colonel Tick, First Lieutenant J.H. Jones, and Flight Officer Knox, were shot down. Green and Lieutenants Butler, Jones, Clark, Kerns, and Chesney were credited with one Bf-109 each, while Lieutenant Carswell was credited with a C.202 destroyed and Captain Rynne received credit for two Bf-109s.

The 318th Squadron's First Lieutenant Bob Barkey reported that he and squadron commander Lieutenant Colonel Tick were surrounded by Bf-109s that attacked the squadron, and that he saw Tick's Thunderbolt catch fire. "I saw Tony bail out, but his 'chute was on fire. I was stunned that it all could have happened so quickly." The enemy pilot who shot down Tick managed to slow roll his fighter in front of Barkey moments later. "I opened fire and was rewarded with hits all over his fuselage just before he blew up."

Green's new confidence was rewarded on March 18 when the Clan ran into 30 enemy fighters attempting to attack the bombers they were covering.

> I spotted a '109 on my left making a pass on another P-47. I broke into him and at the same time he broke toward me and nosed down. They always wanted to head for the ground when things got tough. I broke down too, and almost blacked out from pulling so many Gs. I came out right on his tail in a vertical dive. I opened fire and when I pulled out of the dive at 15,000 feet, he was on fire and continued out of control to crash.

Overall, the Checkertails were credited with seven Bf-109s and two Macchi C.205s destroyed in the fight.

The evening of March 18 was clear and cold over southern Italy. During the night, the massive Vesuvius volcano began a major eruption. By the next day, Fifteenth Air Force personnel at the Foggia airfield complex could see the 50,000-foot-tall smoke pyre rising from the mountain, and ash from the eruption was falling on the airfields nearly 60 miles from Vesuvius. The eruption, which continued belching rocks and ash for the next week, disrupted Allied air operations over Italy more completely than anything the Germans had accomplished in all the combat since the North African invasion. There was fear that there could be additional eruptions and more destruction. Fortunately, the bomber bases were not as disrupted as was feared.

Herky Green was promoted to command the 317th Squadron on March 25 when Major Chick, the previous CO, completed his tour. A few days later, the group moved to a new airfield at Lesina, 45 miles north of the Foggia complex, which put them out of the increasing aerial congestion.

On March 17, the three P-38 groups attempted to recreate the success the Checkertails had found on January 30 with their surprise attack on enemy airfields in northern Italy. The 1st, 14th, and 82nd Groups managed to put up 90 Lightnings between them. The target was the Maniago–Udine airfield complex in northeastern Italy. Even though the P-38s flew 350 miles to the target at 30 feet above the Adriatic to avoid radar, a mixed force of ANR and Luftwaffe fighters was waiting for them as they swept in over the airfields. The air battle lasted for over half an hour. Though the enemy fighters were aggressive, they weren't very successful. The top score among the Lightnings was achieved by the 1st Group, which claimed three Ju-88s, three Ju-52s, three Do-24s, and an He-111 destroyed on the ground by strafing, though only one aerial victory. The 14th Group was tops for aerial claims – four Bf-109s and two C.205s shot down – while the 82nd Group claimed three in the air. Claims were submitted for a total of 20 enemy aircraft destroyed by all three groups in strafing attacks.

Fortune began to change for the P-38 groups on March 20, when 97th Squadron CO Major John Litchfield ferried a brand-new silver P-38J to the 82nd Group's base at Vincenzo from Foggia Main. The 95th Squadron won the right to receive the new airplane in a coin flip after Litchfield landed and everyone had a chance to look at the shiny new fighter. The new airplanes continued to trickle in over the remainder of the month; some of the older F and G model Lightnings were destined to fly with the group until finally replaced in May. The 14th and 1st Groups were also re-equipped with the new Lightning.

Production of the P-38J, which had commenced in August 1943, had ground to a halt that fall when the sub-contractors producing the new radiator cores experienced delays in deliveries due to bottlenecks in supplying parts. This resulted in "stopgap" production of the P-38H, which used the earlier radiators and cooling system of the P-38F and G, along with the newer Allison engine that powered the P-38J; the resulting airplane was not a success, since the cooling problems and engine failures associated with the earlier versions were exacerbated with the newer, more powerful engines.

Finally, the delivery delays of the P-38J radiator cores were solved in January and production resumed; the backlog of fighters coming off the production line and forced to sit idle on Empire Boulevard at the south end of Burbank Airport (where the Lockheed factory was located) while awaiting their radiators was quickly resolved, with a burst in numbers of available new-production P-38s. The Fifteenth's P-38 groups – which had been forced to wait for replacements over the fall of 1943 while the British-based groups were re-equipped – were the beneficiaries of the sudden largesse; VIII Fighter Command's three P-38 groups soldiered on with the defective P-38H until they received P-38Js in May, a situation that contributed to General Doolittle's decision to re-equip these groups with P-51s during the summer of 1944.

The biggest improvement associated with the P-38J was increased range. This resulted from the fact that the cooling system no longer used the outer leading edge of the wings. These spaces were therefore converted to 110-gallon fuel tanks, which increased the total internal fuel capacity from the 300 gallons of the earlier P-38s to just over 700 gallons; with two 150-gallon drop tanks, the total fuel was 1,000 gallons. The result was an increase in range from the 1,700 miles of the previous Lightnings to a maximum range for the P-38J, and later P-38L, of 2,300 miles.

While the new fighters were an improvement on the earlier P-38s, difficulty with controlling engine heat at high altitude over Europe continued. The 14th Fighter Group, which had received P-38Js in late February, discovered that the new radiators created cooling problems for the carburetor intercoolers which were now mounted below the engines, near the radiator cores; this initially created problems for the new Lightnings on winter flights over the Alps. Captain Jim Stitt, engineering officer in the 37th Fighter Squadron, recalled:

> The big new radiators had so much capacity that they could drop the carburetor air intake temperature down to the point that we were not getting good fuel vaporization. We modified our planes by installing doors in front of the intercooler to close off the passing air to control the temperature. Control cables were run through the radiator and

worked off the flap motor. They worked just fine and eventually we educated our pilots on the proper operation.

We also had a problem of freezing oil in the oil coolers. When the oil started to freeze the engine oil temperature gauge would go up, and the natural reaction of the pilots was to open the oil cooler door a little more. If you did that, the additional air through the oil coolers would freeze the oil solid, and there would be no oil circulating and you could lose an engine very quickly. The pilots picked up on this and eventually we operated our P-38s at high altitude without trouble.

This information was passed on to the 1st and 82nd Groups and considerably eased their transition to the new fighters when they were delivered. The information was also provided to VIII Technical Command for use with their P-38s in Britain. In addition, the fixes that the 14th's engineers came up with were passed on to Lockheed and began appearing on the production line with the P-38J-25-LO subtype.

The failure of the Anzio invasion force to break out of the beachhead before the surprised Germans could surround the area, and the failure of Fifth Army to break through the Gustav Line despite repeated attempts, led to the development of Operation *Strangle*. This involved both the tactical Twelfth Air Force and the Fifteenth Air Force in a campaign throughout the Italian peninsula to destroy road and rail transportation, bridges, rail marshaling yards, storage facilities, and anything else that resupplied the forces that were so relentlessly blocking the Allies in southern and central Italy. *Strangle*'s objective was to deny the enemy resources to aid the next major Allied ground offensive, which was already in planning to occur after the winter rains ended.

Mediterranean Allied Tactical Air Forces developed the Operation *Strangle* plan in late February and issued orders for its commencement on March 19, 1944. The Fifteenth Air Force was assigned the destruction of marshaling yards and railroad repair facilities in the major northern Italian cities. The series of Fifteenth Air Force attacks on Axis air force bases in northern Italy prior to the outset of *Strangle* assured there would not be effective enemy air opposition to the missions.

March 22 saw the 82nd Fighter Group fly its first Operation *Strangle* escort mission, escorting B-24s to bomb the marshaling yards in

THE FIFTEENTH AIR FORCE COMES OF AGE

Verona. The only opposition came from the antiaircraft gun defenses surrounding the city, and no losses were suffered by either the bombers or the fighters.

On March 26, the 82nd Group's Lightnings escorted B-17s to Steyr, Austria, which was a major waypoint on the enemy's resupply route from Munich to Bologna. As the Flying Fortresses crossed into northern Yugoslavia, they rendezvoused with the P-38s; 15 minutes later an enemy force of some 15 Bf-109s and at least one Bf-110 attempted to attack the rear of the bomber formation. Two four-plane flights from the 97th Squadron led by Captain Litchfield, reinforced by the three-Lightning "spare" flight from the 95th Squadron led by First Lieutenant Orson Osborne, turned back and with an altitude advantage for once, the Lightnings dived into the enemy formation. After a quick fight during which their opponents displayed a noted lack of aggressiveness, they claimed five destroyed, a probable, and three damaged.

Lieutenant Darrel Skinner, leading Litchfield's second flight, put a long burst into a Bf-110; the left engine caught fire and it shed parts, one of which hit Skinner's left engine, knocking it out. When Skinner broke away, wingman Second Lieutenant John Aiken finished it off. The 95th's Lieutenant Osborne shot down one Bf-109 and put a long burst into a second, which caught fire and was then finished off by his wingman, Second Lieutenant Gene Chatfield. Back at base, the mandatory coin flips when two pilots claimed the same airplane shot down – since there were no half-scores in the 82nd – resulted in Aiken receiving credit for the Bf-110 and Chatfield for the second Bf-109 that Osborne had hit. Additionally, Chatfield received a DFC for the victory.

On March 27, the 306th Fighter Wing was created by order of General Twining. Up to now, the Fifteenth's fighter groups had been assigned to one or the other of the air force's bomb wings; now all the fighter groups were assigned to the 306th Wing, which would from that point on function in the Fifteenth Air Force as the equivalent of VIII Fighter Command in the Eighth Air Force from its headquarters at Torremaggiore, 60 miles north of the 82nd's Vincenzo airfield. Brigadier General Dean C. "Doc" Strother took command of the new wing. An inspirational leader known for a "hands-on" leadership style, Strother flew operational missions on several occasions with the P-51 groups during the Ploești campaign in the summer of 1944; he commanded the Fifteenth's fighters through the war's end.

The B-24s that the 82nd's 96th and 97th Squadrons were scheduled to meet up with on a mission to Verona on March 28 were late, so the group joined a formation of B-17s. When the bombers were 20 miles northwest of Ferrara, pilots spotted a formation of 24 enemy fighters turning in to attack the formation. Checkertail P-47s flying high cover engaged a second formation of Bf-109s at 28,000 feet, above the first group spotted by the Lightning pilots. In the 15-minute fight, Lieutenant Colonel Chester L. Sluder, who had arrived ten days earlier replacing Lieutenant Colonel Baseler as 325th Group CO, scored his first victory. Lieutenants Jones and Folkes were also credited with a Bf-109 each.

The star of the fight was Second Lieutenant John R. Booth, who was credited with four Bf-109s shot down in an epic fight, though he initially claimed only one. Booth later recalled, "As we reached the target and about 40 Bf-109s and Macchi 202s engaged us, I found myself alone in a fight with six '109s. One made a head-on pass at me. As we passed, our planes collided wing to wing." The Bf-109's right wing was ripped off at the root by the impact. The enemy fighter fell away to the right and collided with a second Bf-109; both exploded as they hit. Booth lost four and a half feet of his Thunderbolt's right wing, but he was still able to outrun two additional Bf-109s, though he could not maneuver his fighter. "I had to belly in back at base because my plane had a tendency to fly sideways."

Booth claimed the first Bf-109 he fired at and was credited with not only that victory but the second fighter his victim crashed into. His gun camera film was later developed and showed that he had kept firing his guns after the collision, and that he had shot down the two Bf-109s that attacked him as they flew into his bullets and caught fire. Booth's quadruple was one of the strangest multi-victories claimed by any American fighter pilot during the war.

While the Checkertails fought it out above, the 82nd's pilots engaged the Bf-109s they had first spotted, as well as others that dived on them from the dogfight overhead. Captain Litchfield went after a Bf-109 that dived away from the Thunderbolts. The Lightning accelerated in its dive and was soon locked in a compressibility dive as Litchfield found his controls frozen. He was preparing to attempt a high-speed bailout when the controls revived as he passed through 3,000 feet, having used every bit of his strength pulling the yoke back to keep the P-38 from tucking its nose into a terminal velocity dive from which there was no escape. As he pulled out, the aggressive Litchfield spotted two Bf-109s in formation and went after them. He out-turned one and got in a good burst that resulted in the pilot bailing out; his parachute only opened just before he hit the ground, the fight was at such a low level.

The 96th Squadron's Lieutenant Art Larkin also ended up down on the deck when he went after a Macchi C.205 flown by Tenente Giovanni Pittini of the ANR's 1° Gruppo Caccia (1st Fighter Group) that dived through his flight after Larkin had dropped to 9,000 feet when his wingman experienced oxygen failure. A solid burst in the enemy fighter's fuselage behind the cockpit forced Pittini to bail out.

March 29 saw the first operation mission for the 96th Squadron's new P-38Js when they escorted B-24s to bomb the rail yard in Milan. Beyond marking a "first" for the record book, the mission was otherwise uneventful since enemy fighters failed to make an appearance. No bombers or fighters were lost on what was listed on "one of our few milkruns" by the squadron war diarist.

The 95th Squadron took their new P-38s to Sofia the next day when they escorted B-17s to the Bulgarian capital. With the arrival of the new replacements, the 82nd had sufficient Lightnings available for all three squadrons to fly the mission. When enemy fighters attacked the rear of the bomber formation, the 95th's Captain Lee Thompson led two flights to break up the attack. He later recalled, "Visibility was not too good in the target area. There was a very high overcast blotting out the sun and a gray haze. The radio was busy as unprotected bombers called for help. Our fighters couldn't cover all the boxes. Eventually we spotted a lone Fw-190 sitting back out of the bombers' range. We were still out of range when he spotted us." Thompson pulled up his nose and fired at the '190, despite being far out of range 4,000 yards to the enemy fighter's rear. "A second or two later I saw a small flash on his right wing. A one-in-a-million lucky shot! It apparently damaged his landing gear as they dropped down, making him a sitting duck." Thompson closed to a position 200 yards behind his opponent. "I fired a long burst and pieces flew off in all directions. As the pilot bailed out, I had a glimpse of four more Fw-190s as they appeared from around a small mountain to my left." Thompson turned into the new enemies and opened fire. "They broke to the left without returning fire and kept going in the direction of Sofia."

Lieutenant Colonel Sluder assumed command of the Checkertails on April 1, 1944. His route to a fighter cockpit had been roundabout. Joining the Air Corps in 1935, he was assigned after flight school graduation to the 9th Bomb Group, flying Martin B-10s. In April 1937, he wangled a transfer to the 8th Pursuit Group, just as they re-equipped with the new Curtiss P-36 Hawk. That June, he was ordered back to Randolph Field, Texas as an instructor in the Pursuit Squadron. By the time he got out of instructor duty, his students included Bob Baseler, whom he replaced in the Checkertails; "Buzz" Wagner, the first official Air Corps ace of World War II; Dave Schilling, who would become a legend as a leader of the 56th Fighter Group; and Charles M. McCorkle, who commanded the 31st Fighter Group at the same time that Sluder led the Checkertails through the Ploești campaign.

April finally saw the coming of spring with improving weather. On April 2, the Fifteenth flew a major mission to bomb Steyr, Austria. The 1st Fighter Group engaged in their first combat in the new P-38J Lightnings escorting the bomber formation to the target. A large gaggle of enemy fighters attempted to attack the B-24s as the bombers neared the target. The enemy's main tactic was to dive through the bomber formation and then climb away in pairs that looked for any bombers damaged in the first attack. The 94th Squadron's Captain Ralph Thiessen led his flight in a dive into the middle of the enemy formation; that began a 25-minute fight between the shiny new silver Lightnings and the enemy Bf-109s. Thiessen shot down three in quick succession, catching them as they climbed away from their attacks. Four other Bf-109s were claimed by other pilots in the group, but the enemy managed to shoot down three Liberators.

The 82nd Group provided cover for the bombers over the target. Flak from the defending guns below was intense and accurate, so that enemy fighters broke off most attacks while they waited for the bombers to come out of the flak field. Nevertheless, the 82nd's Lightnings were hard pressed to defend themselves against the enemy fighters that attacked the escorts. First Lieutenant Charlie Pinson recalled:

> Six '109s came down out of the sun on the P-38s. With my first burst, I hit the lead '109, which was closing on a P-38, and it exploded

in a ball of red flame and black smoke. The other '109 pilots were startled by that and pulled back up, then turned back and dived on us again. I was hard pressed from that point on, turning into each attacking '109 in a head-on pass, then reversing to go head to head with another. The '109s didn't get any good shots, but I made no more hits either. After about 20 passes, the '109s broke off and climbed away into the sun.

The 14th Fighter Group provided withdrawal support for the bombers. First Lieutenant Enoch Lemon, who led the 37th Squadron on the mission, recalled that by the time they arrived over the bombers, he only had ten Lightnings left after several had aborted and returned home, escorted by their wingman. "The 48th Squadron called out bogies below the bombers and went after them." Lemon was about to order his P-38s to drop their underwing tanks and follow the 48th when "someone called 'Look at the 110s coming in!' They were coming in level to the bombers and closing fast. I knew I didn't have time to come around behind them, or they would get the bombers, so I dove head-on at them."

Lemon came upon a formation of 16–20 twin-engine fighters, but they broke and dived away before he could attack. He came on a second formation of 25, which the Lightnings were able to attack before they could get away. Lemon went after a flight of four that split up into two pairs. When he went after the closer pair, their rear gunners opened up on him. He closed on the rear Bf-110 and concentrated his fire on the cockpit; the gunner was hit and quit firing. "I closed and let him have it. Pieces peeled off the left engine, and it began pouring black smoke. Then I saw his left wing start to come apart and disintegrate from the tip inward." As that one fell away on fire, Lemon caught the leader and opened fire. "There was a large flash under his left wing that looked like one of his rockets had exploded and the engine caught fire." As that '110 fell off into its death spiral, Lemon broke off to deal with a Bf-109 that came at him. By this point, all three 14th Group squadrons were engaged. Lemon fired at two more '110s with effect, then began gathering the rest of his P-38s for the flight home.

Despite the 1st Group providing cover during the approach, the 82nd providing cover over the target, the 14th providing withdrawal support, and the 325th's P-47s providing high cover over the target,

20 bombers were lost in total to the intense, accurate flak and defending enemy fighters. The four fighter groups claimed a total of 36 enemy fighters destroyed. The 14th claimed 22 of that total, an indication of how hard the enemy went after the bombers following their attack. The 14th Fighter Group was awarded the Distinguished Unit Citation for this performance.

The Steyr mission was Colonel Sluder's first as the Checkertails' group commander. It was also one of Herky Green's first missions since his recovery from malaria. Green later recalled that the Checkertails were "about 50 miles east of Klagenfurt" when they spotted a mixed formation of approximately 20 Bf-109s and Fw-190s maneuvering to intercept the bombers. "The fight lasted ten minutes, during which three Bf-109s were destroyed."

The Checkertails had another "big day" on April 6 during an escort mission to Zagreb, Yugoslavia that was intercepted by 40 enemy fighters 60 miles southwest of the target. In the ensuing 30-minute battle, ten pilots in the group each claimed a Bf-109 destroyed. The next day, Green scored his first victory since February, when he spotted a Bf-110 below his formation and dived on it. "I closed to very close range. After I fired a few bursts, his left engine exploded and the plane began to spin. The fuselage was burning, but the pilot managed to pull out of the spin. Evidently he was attempting a belly landing. I gave him another short burst and a moment later he hit the ground and cartwheeled in a ball of fire."

April saw the first of the fighter groups that were re-equipped with the P-51 Mustang join the Fifteenth Air Force when the 31st Fighter Group was officially transferred from Twelfth Air Force on April 1. The transfer was made more palatable to everyone in the group with the news that they would leave their current muddy base at Castel Volturno on the west coast of Italy and transfer to San Severo airfield, a prewar Italian air force base on the Foggia plain 20 miles north of the city of Foggia near the Italian east coast on the Adriatic Sea. Not only did the new base possess a 5,000-foot hard-surfaced runway, but there were permanent buildings for aircraft maintenance and quarters; for the first time since their arrival in North Africa in November 1942, pilots and ground crews would be able to live indoors. Previous doubts about the transfer to the Fifteenth died off and the move was completed by April 5.

The group's veteran Spitfire pilots did not originally see the loss of their Spitfire VIII and IX fighters and their replacement with the Mustang as a positive development. The pilots were now firmly attached to their Spitfires after using them for 18 months in combat over North Africa, Pantelleria, Sicily, and Italy. In fact, over the last three weeks of March, the group's three squadrons had seen considerable combat with Luftwaffe fighter units over the Anzio beachhead. The Spitfires came out on top in nearly all these combats in terms of claimed victories versus losses. The final Spitfire missions were flown over the beachhead on March 30, 1944.

It took until mid-April before two P-51Bs and a pilot from the 354th "Pioneer Mustang" group in England arrived to initiate conversion training. The statement that the new fighter was superior to their beloved Spitfires, with much longer range, was initially received with disbelief by the pilots. However, group opinion began to change as the pilots got the chance to fly the P-51s, which turned out to be far easier to fly than the Spitfire – particularly for landing and takeoff, with the Mustang's wider-spaced landing gear – and almost as maneuverable as their previous mounts.

Switching from Spitfires to Mustangs involved more than learning to fly a different airplane. The flying itself was different. With Spitfires, the group operated by individual squadrons, putting up two or three flights – 8–12 aircraft – for a patrol that lasted a maximum of almost two hours, flown at medium altitudes of 18,000–25,000 feet. P-51 missions were a minimum of four to five hours, and all three squadrons flew together in group formation, at 28,000–30,000 feet. The first training missions flown involved flights up and down nearly the entire length of the Italian peninsula. Once 108-gallon metal drop tanks were added to the repertoire, missions could push seven hours in duration. "Oh my achin' ass!" became a common complaint among the pilots.

Perhaps the most important thing the former Spitfire pilots learned was that the P-51 really was superior to the Spitfire. The P-51B's armament of four .50-caliber machine guns was superior to the Spitfire's two 20mm cannon and four .303-caliber machine guns for overall hitting power, though initially ammo feed jamming caused trouble until the VIII Fighter Command solution of using electric motors to power the ammo feed was adopted in early June. Maneuverability of the

Mustang was on the same level with the Merlin-60 powered Spitfires, with light and easy control forces like the British fighter. Gradually, the pilots began to accept that they really had "moved up in the world," as group commander Colonel Charles M. McCorkle reported.

Major Paul Gillem, commander of the 307th Squadron, recalled ferrying the new fighters from Algiers to San Severo:

> Our instruction was limited to how to start the engine and what power settings we would need. Our takeoff was spectacular! And almost tragic. Our instructor had neglected to warn us of the terrific torque that big four-bladed propeller generated. About the time we got airborne, we also veered off the runway, aimed at a large RAF Avro York transport that was just taxiing in. It was the private plane of Prime Minister Winston Churchill! We barely missed taking it and him out of the war! We just did clear, by wartime standards. Most of us also failed to notice that the canopy ejection lever in a P-51 is located where the gear retraction lever is in a Spitfire. The net result? All those canopies popping off, almost in unison, all over the sky, with these hot rock pilots from Italy at the controls. We had to return and have them replaced before flying to Italy. All in all, quite a trip!

The 31st Group flew their first operational mission on April 16, 1944, a 450-mile flight to Turnu Severin, near the Romania–Yugoslavia border, escorting B-17s and B-24s to attack the marshaling yards. No enemy aircraft were encountered on this initial operation. The only problem that arose was when a B-24 gunner opened up on a flight of P-51s that approached the bombers, mistaking their silhouette for Bf-109s – a common occurrence with the P-51B and C-model Mustangs. Unfortunately, the errant gunner managed to hit the 309th Squadron's Lieutenant Howard Baetjer's fighter, which lost most of its coolant, forcing him to bail out 150 miles inland in Yugoslavia.

The next day, the group escorted B-17s to bomb the marshaling yards in Sofia, Bulgaria. After the bombers made their run, a force of 35 Bf-109s made several slashing passes against the formation. Colonel McCorkle was leading the 309th Squadron, and they went after the enemy fighters. McCorkle claimed two while Captain Charles Brown claimed one.

THE FIFTEENTH AIR FORCE COMES OF AGE

Several missions were flown by the P-38 groups in the last half of April into Romania, with Bucharest the target of three attacks over April 15–17. The first mission on April 15 drew a large response as both the Luftwaffe and the Romanian Air Force put up a strong defense. The 82nd Group's 37th Squadron saw most of the fighting, with five pilots putting in claims for the six enemy aircraft the group claimed destroyed in the battle. The missions flown on the next two days saw no enemy response. Lieutenant Lemon wrote in his diary that "We looked all over for something to shoot at but couldn't find a thing."

On April 18, all three P-38 groups flew a mission to strafe enemy airfields in the Udine area of northern Italy. The 31st Group was assigned as high cover, flying at 28,000 feet, while the Checkertails gave intermediate cover at 20,000 feet. The target was covered by solid overcast that extended down to only 500 feet above the ground in some places, with haze below, when the Mustangs arrived. The P-38 attack stirred up major enemy opposition, with some 50 Bf-109s and Macchi C.205s rising to meet the American fighters. The 309th Squadron was below the overcast layer, but it was difficult to spot the enemy in the haze, and only one claim for a probable was submitted on return.

Above the overcast, the 307th Squadron ran into 35 Bf-109s and Fw-190s, but again only claimed two probables. The 308th Squadron engaged 30 Bf-109s, claiming two shot down and three probables. Overall, the weather was so bad that the 308th lost two pilots who collided in the murk.

On April 20, the mission to escort B-24s to bomb the marshaling yards at Monfalcone in northern Italy was also hampered by poor weather that affected the bombers' accuracy since they could only bomb through the few holes found in the overcast. The weather was bad enough to ground the Luftwaffe, and no enemy fighters were encountered.

By mid-April, more P-38Js had arrived in the Mediterranean and the three Lightning groups said good-bye to their older P-38 F, G, and H models by the end of the month.

With the good weather, the 1st Group managed to fly 18 escort missions to northern Italy, southern France, and Austria over the month, and even to Braşov, Romania on April 16, which was the group's 1,000th mission since their arrival in the Mediterranean Theater. April saw the group's pilots claim 37 enemy aircraft destroyed, ten probables, and 35 damaged, against a loss of four pilots.

The Fifteenth Air Force reached its full complement of units by the end of April. Fifteen bomb groups operated B-24s while six flew B-17s. The three P-38 fighter groups were joined by the 31st and 52nd Fighter Groups with their new P-51Cs, while the 325th continued flying their Thunderbolts, though they were scheduled to switch over to P-51s in May. The end of May saw the arrival of the last fighter group to join the Fifteenth when the 332nd Fighter Group was transferred from Twelfth Air Force following its re-equipment with P-47 Thunderbolts. Problems with the supply of replacement aircraft were eventually worked out as the P-51 Mustang reached full-scale production at North American's second factory in Dallas, Texas and Lockheed straightened out their sub-contractors, finally ensuring a steady supply of P-38s.

5

TARGET PLOEȘTI

The Ploești campaign in the spring and summer of 1944 was intimately tied to the plans for the cross-Channel invasion of France. When General Dwight Eisenhower arrived in Britain in January 1944 to become Supreme Commander, Allied Expeditionary Force, it was recognized that fairly soon he would have to take supreme command of the Allied air forces to insure that all efforts went to achieving the necessary conditions to support the invasion.

General Carl Spaatz, commander of the US Strategic Air Forces, understood that when this operational control shift happened, all air force operations other than those specifically directed at preparation for the invasion and support of it once it became reality would take a lower priority. Thus, in January and February 1944 he pushed hard for the Eighth and Fifteenth Air Forces to achieve the goal of Operation *Pointblank*: the destruction of the Luftwaffe as a force capable of opposing the invasion and the creation of Allied air superiority over northwestern Europe.

Spaatz fully agreed with his planning staff that destruction of the German oil industry, which would deny the Luftwaffe the fuel it needed to fight the Allied air forces, was a top priority for the success of *Pointblank*.

Professor Solly Zuckerman was a personal friend of both Air Marshal Sir Arthur Tedder – second in command to Eisenhower at Supreme Headquarters Allied Expeditionary Force (SHAEF) and the man who would control the Allied air forces for the invasion – and Spaatz.

Zuckerman became the chief architect of the Allied Expeditionary Air Force's plan. In January 1944, he returned to London from the Mediterranean, after completing a study of the bombing campaigns in Pantelleria and Sicily.

The Allied planning staff responsible for creating the invasion plans concentrated on what was known as the Transportation Plan, which aimed to deny the enemy the ability to move troops and supplies from Germany into France, Belgium, and the Netherlands. This called for the Eighth Air Force and Bomber Command to concentrate their main efforts on destroying the German railroad system, while the US Ninth Air Force and RAF Second Tactical Air Force concentrated on the destruction of the French railroad system and the roads in northern France leading to Normandy. With its carefully stated measurements of success and statement of goals, it appealed to Zuckerman's scientific mind, and he became a convert.

Spaatz agreed that the Eighth could knock out the railroad system in Germany by bombing marshaling yards, railroad stations, and railroad bridges, with the Eighth's fighters going after trains by strafing. He was adamantly opposed to the part of the plan calling for employment of the strategic air forces in bombing the French railroads, pointing out the limitations and capabilities of strategic bombing, which did not have the accuracy to be used against an Allied country, where such bombing was bound to result in the certain killing and injuring of French civilians in large numbers. Thus, he advocated that the oil campaign, in addition to being seen as an integral part of *Pointblank* by denying fuel to the Luftwaffe, should be viewed as a playing a key role in the pre-invasion destruction of German resources, since it would adversely affect road transport and the Wehrmacht's ability to employ mechanized forces against the invasion.

USSTAF planners estimated that German gasoline production could be reduced by 50 percent with 15 raids against Ploeşti by the Fifteenth Air Force and with Eighth Air Force flying ten strikes against the German synthetic oil industry. These were the Wehrmacht's only two sources of fuel for maintaining the capability of fighting a modern mechanized war. During a February 15 meeting, Spaatz argued to Eisenhower that destroying the panzers' gasoline supply would be a far greater blow against the enemy than destroying easily repaired railroad marshaling yards, and would be of equal importance in grounding the

Luftwaffe. Knowing he could not get the SHAEF planning staff's focus away from the Transportation Plan, Spaatz pointed out that an aerial offensive against oil would only need half of Eighth Air Force's bombers, and that Fifteenth Air Force was not directly involved in air operations to support the invasion. He was saddled in making his argument by the Air Force's history of over-promising decisive results by striking "strategic" targets, the failure of the ball-bearing campaign the previous fall being the prime example bought up by the invasion planners in opposing the oil campaign. Spaatz was unsuccessful, even with General Arnold's unstinting support in Washington with the Joint Chiefs.

In a letter to Arnold dated March 6, 1944, Spaatz laid out his argument in favor of the oil plan: "A concentrated effort against oil, which would represent the most far-reaching use of strategic air power that has been attempted in this war, promises, I believe, more than any other system, a fighting chance of ending German resistance in a shorter period than we have hitherto thought possible."

In a meeting at SHAEF Headquarters on March 25, 1944, Eisenhower pressed VIII Bomber Command's General Frederick Anderson about the likelihood of success for a campaign against oil. Anderson was forced to confess that the Air Force "could not guarantee that the attacks of oil targets would have an appreciable effect during the initial stages of Overlord." He did say that a campaign against the synthetic oil industry "would have a decisive effect within a period of about six months." Eisenhower, who was focused on the immediate problems of putting an army into France and keeping it there, came down against Spaatz's proposal. Prime Minister Churchill expressed dismay during a British War Cabinet meeting on April 3, when he was told that Bomber Command estimated that the Transportation Plan would create 80,000–160,000 French civilian casualties as the result of strategic bomber attacks on key marshaling yards. As a result, Churchill favored the proposed oil campaign, due to his concern that the deaths of French and Belgian civilians would create political problems for the Allies. In the end, RAF Chief of Staff Air Marshal Sir Charles Portal pushed a compromise proposal that both Eighth Air Force and Bomber Command could mount a campaign against oil once the Allied armies were in Normandy and any German counterattack had been blunted. Also, it was decided that the heavy bombers would not be used on French transportation targets, which would be assigned to the medium bombers and fighter-bombers of the US Ninth Air Force and RAF Second Tactical Air Force.

After repeated refusals by Air Chief Marshal Charles Portal to permit renewed attacks on Ploești following this decision, Spaatz turned to bureaucratic subterfuge. Shortly after SHAEF had taken control of the strategic air forces on April 1, Spaatz asked Tedder to allow the Fifteenth Air Force to mount a mission against Ploești, convincing him with the argument that since the main target was not the oil fields but the Ploești railroad marshaling yards, with the goal of crippling the main railhead for shipping petroleum products to Germany, the mission was part of the Transportation Plan. Spaatz defined the mission this way since Tedder was not convinced of the need to start the oil campaign before the invasion. Tedder granted Spaatz's request. The mission Spaatz ordered on April 5 was actually part of the oil campaign, since it was expected that the 95 B-17s and 135 B-24s that went to Ploești would end up dropping many of their bombs on the refineries; in fact, there was considerable refinery destruction. This result demonstrated that the oil refineries were very vulnerable to high-altitude bombing attack. This attack and the three that followed in April and early May were later justified by an Army Air Forces Evaluation Board report which noted, "The direction of flight... plus the compactness of the target area made bomb spillage in the refinery well-nigh inevitable."

The 82nd Fighter Group provided target cover for the mission. Enemy fighters made no serious attempt to attack the bombers. One "Fw-190" (most likely an IAR-80 flown by the Romanians) attempted an attack on the 95th Squadron, but was chased away. The 14th Fighter Group, which provided withdrawal support, reported that its pilots spotted a total of 12 enemy fighters, which kept their distance and made no attempt to engage. The bombers reported good coverage of both the marshaling yard and the nearby Română Americana refinery.

Following these missions, Spaatz again met with Eisenhower to press for approval of the oil campaign since he had demonstrated that the strategic air force could hit the refineries and inflict significant damage. Eisenhower again refused; the meeting grew so heated that Spaatz threatened to resign if the Supreme Commander did not change his mind. A compromise was found that allowed Spaatz to attack oil targets in Germany on days when the weather prevented attacks on transportation targets. On April 20, Tedder agreed to further attacks on the Ploești refineries by Fifteenth Air Force on days when they could not attack transportation targets in southern France and Austria.

While the bureaucratic battle over attacking Ploești raged among the air force leaders, on April 18 P-38s from the 1st, 14th, and 82nd Groups flew a strafing mission to hit the Aiello landing ground near Udine in northern Italy. They received cover from the 325th's Thunderbolts and the 31st's Mustangs. The weather was "lousy," with visibility so reduced that the pilots had difficulty spotting the target, which turned out to be virtually empty of enemy aircraft.

The Mustang pilots approached the target from the Adriatic. As they approached Udine, they experienced some very accurate enemy flak, with the result that 309th Squadron CO Major "Jug" Jared was shot down when he took a flak hit in his engine. He entered the cloud deck below, but never made it out of his airplane. While the P-38s found little action, the 31st ran into some 50 Bf-109s that had taken off on the approach of the American force. Due to the bad weather, only the 309th's Captain George G. Loving Jr. was able to claim one destroyed. The 307th Squadron, flying high cover, ran across 25 enemy fighters above the cloud cover, but again the poor visibility resulted in only two claims for "damaged." The most successful of the 31st's three squadrons was the 308th, which was flying top cover above the poor-visibility layers. In the fight that followed, First Lieutenant Frederick O. Trafton shot down one Bf-109 and damaged a second, while First Lieutenant Thomas Byrnes also destroyed one Bf-109.

Spaatz took advantage of Tedder's agreement and ordered the first strike directly against the refineries to take place on April 21, 1944, though the mission was billed to Air Marshal Tedder as another "transportation strike" against the Ploești railroad.

The mission was unsuccessful due to the weather. Halfway to the target, the force was recalled due to the adverse weather that had been encountered en route since shortly after the force crossed the Yugoslavian coast. However, most of the bombers failed to receive the recall and proceeded on. The 31st Fighter Group, which was flying its first major escort mission, also failed to receive the recall. The Mustangs continued on with the bombers. The weather worsened by the minute. Despite this, mission leader Major James D. Thorsen hit the crossing point of the Danube River on time, with the correct heading, altitude, and airspeed. A moment before arrival over the checkpoint, a hole opened in the thick overcast that allowed them to visually confirm they were crossing the Danube at the proper point.

Minutes later, German fighters appeared out of the clouds, vectored to the Mustangs by radar. The 307th Squadron chased off a mixed formation of 18 Bf-109s and what was reported as "Fw-190s" which were undoubtedly Romanian-flown IAR-80s, since there were no Fw-190-equipped units in Romania. The 307th's Second Lieutenant Reginald C. Gilbert shot down two Bf-109s and damaged a third before the enemy fighters broke off and dived away through the clouds. First Lieutenant Frederick L. Bohl shot down what he claimed as an Fw-190.

When the Mustangs arrived directly over Ploești, the bombers were nowhere to be seen, since they had been delayed due to navigational errors in the bad weather; they would not arrive for another 35 minutes. The 36 Mustangs were attacked by a force of 60 enemy fighters that appeared out of the clouds. Major Thorsen called the break, and the 308th Squadron was the first to engage, claiming four shot down, four probably shot down, and two damaged for no loss. Captain Leland Molland claimed two of the four shot down while First Lieutenant Trafton claimed one of the other two, with the fourth enemy fighter claimed by Second Lieutenant George D. Hughes.

The 309th Squadron encountered the biggest enemy formation; in a hard-fought encounter, squadron pilots claimed seven shot down. Again, the pilots were unfamiliar with the IAR-80s they encountered and came up with some strange aircraft identifications. Major John W. Meador claimed an Fw-190 destroyed; Major Samuel Brown claimed two "Fiat G-50s" destroyed; First Lieutenant John M. Ainsley claimed a Bf-109 and a "G-50" destroyed, along with another "G-50" and an Fw-190 damaged; First Lieutenant Raymond F. Harmeyer claimed a "G-50" destroyed and another damaged; Flight Officer John A. Felton claimed a Bf-109 destroyed; and First Lieutenant John R. Busley claimed a "Reggiane Re.2001!" The claims for Italian fighters that were no longer operational were undoubtedly Romanian IAR-80s with which the Americans were unfamiliar.

The 14th Group's P-38s claimed an additional ten destroyed, in a series of fights that began when 35–40 enemy fighters identified as Bf-109s, Fw-190s, and G.50s (again, IAR-80s were misidentified as Fw-190s and the obsolete G.50) were spotted going after the bombers. Group commander Colonel Oliver Taylor claimed two, while the

48th Squadron's Second Lieutenant William Church claimed a "G.50" destroyed. The 37th Squadron had the greatest success, with squadron CO Major Kenneth Gaskin credited with three, First Lieutenant Frank Phillips credited with two, and First Lieutenants Marvin R. Elston and Porter McClain credited with one each. The 1st Fighter Group's P-38s covered the bombers during their withdrawal and reported no enemy contacts.

Bomber gunners claimed ten. The total 35 enemy fighters claimed destroyed in a mission that had been recalled was one of the best achievements in any Fifteenth Air Force mission so far. The 31st received a special commendation from General Twining for their performance. After this battle, the former Spitfire pilots of the 31st were finally convinced they were flying the best fighter in the Army Air Forces.

The rest of April saw the 31st go from success to success, with a few operations called off for rain.

On April 23, after a day of rain following the first Ploeşti mission, the target was the Messerschmitt factory at Wiener Neustadt. At briefing, the pilots were told they could expect air opposition to number 50–200 at any time, with enemy fighters coming at them from the Po Valley on to the target.

Colonel McCorkle again led the group. They arrived at the rendezvous point on time; there were no bombers to be seen. The group circled for 40 minutes; at one point a German fighter formation flew overhead, but the Mustangs made no move to go after them as they concentrated on using as little fuel as possible. Soon after, Flying Fortress formations appeared.

Opposition was strong: 50 miles short of the target, a large formation of Bf-109s made a "company front" ("twelve o'clock high") attack that failed to bring down any of the bombers, while the enemy fighters broke away before the Mustangs could intervene. Colonel McCorkle, who was flying with the 309th Squadron, engaged a formation of Bf-110s with his flight, shooting down two of the rocket-carrying fighters in his initial pass. First Lieutenant John Ainsley, McCorkle's element leader, and his wingman First Lieutenant Richard L. Grose each claimed a Bf-110. They were then engaged by a formation of Fw-190s coming to the aid of the twin-engine fighters; McCorkle shot down one Fw-190 while Ainsley damaged two. With three claims, Colonel McCorkle became a double ace with a score of ten.

The 4th Fighter Group's Major James A. Goodson and his fellow Eagle, wingman First Lieutenant Bob Wehrman, who had flown from England to provide final operational training to the 31st's new Mustang pilots, were flying the mission with the 307th Fighter Squadron. Twenty Bf-109s tried to jump the Mustangs shortly before the bombers arrived over Wiener Neustadt. In the fight that followed, Goodson claimed two destroyed. First Lieutenant Carroll A. Pryblo and his wingman Second Lieutenant John T. Nelson each claimed a Bf-109 destroyed.

The 308th Squadron had the worst record of the day, with three pilots lost for two Bf-109 claimed destroyed. Lieutenants Trafton and Johnson were each shot down by their opponent's wingman after scoring the two victories.

The next day, the group escorted bombers back to Ploești for a third Transportation Plan attack on the rail yard adjoining the refineries. This time, the few enemy fighters that were vectored to the bombers stayed well away and refused combat. Over Niš, Yugoslavia, pilots of the 307th and 309th Squadrons spotted enemy twin-engine fighters well below their altitude. The 307th's Second Lieutenant Gilbert hit a Ju-88, knocking off one wing with concentrated fire in the wing root.

The 307th also managed to scare up six enemy fighters when they got to Ploești. Lieutenant Gilbert got into a fight with an obvious veteran in an IAR-80 that he managed to misidentify as an Fw-190, claiming only a "damaged" as the enemy pilot outflew him in the engagement. Lieutenant Linton flew into the cone of fire from another P-51 attacking a Bf-109 and exploded when he was hit in his engine. Lieutenant Bohl shot down a Bf-109 for the only score.

A separate bomber formation hit the marshaling yards in Bucharest with excellent results. Combined with the destruction of the Ploești marshaling yard, enemy transport operations were reduced by more than half.

Rain over the next four days resulted in canceled missions, other than a short trip to Piombino on the Italian west coast. When the Mustangs arrived at the rendezvous point, they found that the bombers had arrived early and flown on. They caught up with their charges 20 miles inland and the bombing was carried out successfully. On the way back to San Severo, the 307th Squadron ran into nine Bf-109s and claimed five shot down for the loss of one Mustang.

At the end of April pilots and ground crews from the Checkertail Clan showed up at San Severo to learn about the P-51, since the Checkertails had been notified that they would re-equip with Mustangs over the month of May so they could join in the full-on Ploești campaign that Air Marshal Tedder had finally signed on to after the good results obtained in the April missions.

The 52nd Fighter Group, which had turned in its Spitfires in mid-April and commenced conversion to the Mustang, was declared ready for operations in early May. Morale in the group was now considerably better than it had been when its pilots were flying Spitfires, since they had been assigned to Coastal Command at the conclusion of the North African campaign, in which they flew cover missions for Allied convoys that were not attacked by Axis forces. Over the first half of May, the group flew escort missions to southern France and northern Italy to gain experience in the bomber escort role.

While the 52nd Group prepared to re-enter air combat, another Transportation Plan mission was flown to Ploești on May 5, in which the 31st Group provided target cover for the bombers. The mission was led by Major Thorsen, flying with the 307th Squadron's Mustangs, which ran into over 100 enemy fighters – Germans in Bf-109s and Romanians in IAR-80s, which were accurately identified this time. The enemy made aggressive attacks against both the bombers and the escorts. First Lieutenants George D. McElroy and Ernest Shipman each claimed a Bf-109 destroyed – the first of their victories. Major Alvan C. Gillem scored his second Bf-109 and First Lieutenant John A. Frazier claimed a Bf-109 destroyed and another damaged. The 309th Squadron, which provided withdrawal support, tangled with the enemy fighters and held them off the bombers. First Lieutenant John M. Ainsley claimed a Bf-109 shot down and a second damaged, while Lieutenants Murray D. McLaughlin, David C. Wilhelm, and Raymond F. Harmeyer each claimed a Bf-109 destroyed. The 308th's First Lieutenant Leonard H. Emery made the group's ninth claim of the mission for a Bf-109 shot down.

The P-38s of the 82nd Fighter Group also provided withdrawal support for the bombers. The 96th Squadron was covering some straggling B-24s when they were attacked by 25–30 enemy fighters identified as Bf-109s and "Fw-190s" (undoubtedly IAR-80s) over Kraljevo, Yugoslavia. "Tail-end Charlie," Second Lieutenant Bob Klos, was hit in the first pass and his P-38 caught fire. He successfully bailed out, but partisans later reported finding his body. Klos' flight leader, First Lieutenant Neil Kloutz, was able to damage one of the attacking fighters. Pilots later reported that these enemy fliers were "obviously experienced," maintaining top cover as two-plane sections dived on the Lightnings.

Lieutenant Roland "Tuffy" Leeman led his flight of four 95th Squadron P-38s to reinforce the 96th; Leeman made a pass and claimed one aircraft damaged, but then his Lightning was hit in the right engine and he had to break off. When the rest of the 96th and 97th Squadrons appeared, the enemy broke off their attacks and headed back toward Romania. In the brief battle before the enemy turned away, Lieutenants Hal Johnson and Bob Miller of the 95th, and the 96th's Lieutenants Andy Blakely, Joe Cardimona, and Terry Coleman each claimed a Bf-109 destroyed.

The 14th Fighter Group's Lightnings also provided target cover. While they did not run across any of the defenders over the target, they did run into some heavy, accurate flak. The 49th Squadron's First Lieutenant Norm Jackman – flying the last mission of his tour – recalled, "My plane suddenly jumped and rang like a bell. The air was suddenly full of flak bursts and I later discovered several shrapnel holes in my P-38. The AA [antiaircraft] over Ploeşti was the heaviest I had ever seen. Several bombers exploded or went down in flames."

The group was then hit by enemy fighters as it came off the target and turned for home. In the 15-minute fight, the 48th Squadron's First Lieutenants Michael Wagner and Walter White each claimed a Bf-109 destroyed, while other pilots put in claims for seven enemy fighters damaged.

The 325th spent most of May writing *finis* to their six months flying the P-47 Thunderbolt.

Herky Green recalled that, following a week in which very little of the enemy was seen, May 5 saw the action pick up on an escort mission covering B-24s attacking the marshaling yards in Turnu Severin, Romania. Twenty-five enemy fighters intercepted the Checkertails 40 miles east of the point at which they were to rendezvous with the bombers. The enemy pilots – who appeared to be more experienced and aggressive than those the group had met in April – dived on the Thunderbolts in twos and fours, zooming back up after a pass.

An additional ten Bf-109s got into the fight over the target area. The 325th claimed four Bf-109s shot down in the fight.

No action took place during the mission to Belgrade two days later, which found the 42 P-47s circling the rendezvous point for over 30 minutes as they waited for bombers that never showed up. After three days of poor weather, the Checkertails again took the bombers to Wiener Neustadt, which was attacked successfully, though the fighter pilots were disappointed not to run across any opposition.

Two days later, a mission to Bologna in "iffy" weather saw the group lose five pilots to weather. Green recalled that when they departed their base, the sky was clear but as they flew on to the target, clouds appeared and grew in intensity until the sky was completely overcast with some cloud tops as high as 28,000 feet. Arriving at the target, which they spotted through a hole in the clouds, the Checkertails circled for an hour but the bombers never appeared, having been recalled due to the poor weather. The missing pilots – who most likely succumbed to vertigo after entering the clouds – were First Lieutenants John L. Brower and Joseph P. Folkes, and Second Lieutenants Edward V. Nuniveller, John M. Forrest, and Richard C. Scott.

A fighter sweep the next day over Ferrara, Verona, and Lake Garda gave the 317th Squadron a chance for combat when they spotted 20–25 enemy fighters that initiated a 25-minute dogfight. First Lieutenants Frank J. Butler and Eugene H. Emmons each claimed a Bf-109 destroyed, while First Lieutenant Arne E. Aho and Second Lieutenant Cecil Dean claimed a Bf-109 damaged each.

On May 10, the 31st Group's Mustangs provided target cover for the B-24s on a mission to Wiener Neustadt. Penetration cover was provided by 52 14th Group P-38s, while P-38s of the 14th and 82nd Groups covered the withdrawal. The mission was met over northern Italy and Austria by more than 120 defending enemy fighters. With poor weather at San Severo, the Mustang pilots were forced to climb through more than 15,000 feet of clouds before breaking out around 20,000 feet into clear air.

The 14th Group's Lieutenant Colonel Oliver Taylor was leading the 37th Squadron's 16 P-38s when he spotted contrails from what he identified as 16 enemy fighters – type unknown – approaching from the northwest, 3,000–4,000 feet above the P-38s. Taylor led his Lightnings in a climbing turn to meet the approaching enemy. In the midst of the climb, Oliver suddenly realized as the enemy got closer that he was up against some 30–35 Bf-109s. The enemy fighters dived on the Lightnings, which were forced into a Lufbery circle to defend themselves. First Lieutenant Enoch Lemon recalled that they were in the Lufbery for 30–40 minutes, with the enemy attacking them from the sides. "I realized Colonel Taylor was not going to break out, and several pilots were announcing they were low on gas so I screamed for all P-38s to follow me. We managed to break out and down." When Lemon called for the break, Colonel Taylor called for help to "brush off" the enemy fighters. The 48th Squadron's fighters responded, followed by two flights from the 49th Squadron; as they came into sight, the enemy fighters broke away. Lemon, who was flying his last mission of his tour, considered the 37th Squadron lucky that "we got out of that unscathed."

Lemon scored one Bf-109 destroyed and two damaged, while Second Lieutenant Wesley Hancock also destroyed one. The 48th Squadron's First Lieutenant Walter White and Second Lieutenant Paul Winston scored one each. The 49th Squadron's Captain William Palmer and Second Lieutenants Warren Jones and John Penning were also credited with one Bf-109 each. Despite being outnumbered in their fight, the 14th's Lightnings all returned to base safely.

Over the target, the Mustangs engaged enemy fighters and the 309th Squadron made claims for two, with First Lieutenant Raymond Harmeyer scoring his fifth victory. There were so many enemy fighters over the target that the Mustang pilots concentrated on breaking up attacking formations without sticking around for a dogfight. The flak over the target was intense and accurate, firing heavy field barrages and tracking barrages. One B-24 exploded over the target due to a direct hit before it dropped its bombs, while another spun in after taking hits in both engines on one side.

The 1st Fighter Group's P-38s provided withdrawal cover; the 94th Squadron picked up the last B-24 group coming off the target and escorted them without incident. Over Graz, Yugoslavia, a straggling B-24 was attacked by a dozen enemy fighters. P-38s engaged them and initiated a running fight that broke up 50 miles south of Graz. Three Bf-109s were claimed destroyed in the fight, which saw Lieutenant Frank Lathrope forced to bail out shortly after he shot down a second Bf-109 when he was attacked by the wingman; partisans picked him up, and Lathrope returned to the squadron by the end of the month. The other squadrons did not run across any enemy fighters as they concentrated on shepherding cripples out of Yugoslavia.

As these battles happened, the 52nd Fighter Group completed its move from Corsica to its new base at Madna, on the Italian mainland. The advance party was flown to the new base between May 13 and 16, to meet the pilots who flew over on May 17, with the main party traveling from Corsica to Naples by LSTs on May 19–20, then transported by truck to Madna. The move was completed by the 20th. By then, the 52nd had already flown their first escort mission.

On May 18, Fifteenth Air Force flew the first mission planned to directly attack the Ploești refineries. Poor weather reduced the planned attack force from an original 700 bombers to only 206 B-17s and B-24s. In addition to the poor weather, the smoke dischargers at Ploești effectively obscured the targets. Only eight bombs hit the Română Americana refinery. The escorting fighter groups, however, did come across enemy defenders.

The 31st Group were now on their fourth escort mission to Ploești, putting the performance of their Mustangs to maximum advantage providing target cover. Only 12 enemy defenders opposed the formation over the target. First Lieutenants William J. Dillard and James L. Brooks of the 307th Squadron were each credited with the destruction of a Bf-109. The 308th could only claim a probable and a damaged Bf-109s, and the 309th Squadron claimed two damaged IAR-80s.

The 82nd Group was briefed to provide withdrawal support, but the bombers they expected to rendezvous with never appeared. After a 20-minute wait, the P-38s turned for home. Spotting enemy aircraft on the ground at Niš, Yugoslavia, six pilots from the 95th Squadron made a strafing attack, claiming a Ju-52 destroyed and an unidentified twin damaged. Three Bf-109s were spotted approaching the field, but they were able to escape because the Lightnings were running low on fuel. After crossing the Adriatic, enemy aircraft were spotted on the airfield at Scutari and a strafing run netted an He-111 claimed destroyed and a radial-engined fighter damaged.

The 14th Group's P-38s also found only a few enemy fighters in their sector. First Lieutenant Tom Yarwood of the 48th Squadron put in the only claim for the group, for a single Bf-109 destroyed.

While the other groups found slim pickings over Ploeşti, the 1st Fighter Group picked up a wing of B-17s coming off the target that were being swarmed by a mixed group of Bf-109s and IAR-80s. All three squadrons dived into the attackers, and in the 25-minute fight that ensued, the P-38s accounted for seven "Fw-190s" (again misidentifying IAR-80s), three Bf-109s, and a Macchi C.205 destroyed.

Lieutenant Frank Williams recalled, "Just after we rendezvoused with the bombers, I called in two enemy fighters making a head-on pass at them. As I went under Sprengel's flight, I saw two more coming down from three o'clock; as I continued to turn left, I spotted two more at nine o'clock climbing to attack. I broke into them and opened fire, getting hits on the second one and seeing hits from my wingman on the first." Williams and his wingman then came under "friendly fire" from another flight of four P-38s that damaged his fuel lines; after taking what seemed like "a long time" to figure out how to control his fuel feed to stop gas coming in the cockpit, Williams got things squared away. "There was a lone bomber whose wing was on fire, that was covered by a flight of P-38s." Williams and his flight stayed with the other fighters covering the bomber until they were out of the target area:

> I was on two engines because my wing tanks hadn't been hit, but when I ran them out and switched to the other tanks, I had to turn off my right engine because all the fuel had drained from the right side tanks. My hydraulic system was also out and my nose gear door was hanging open. I could just hold my position at 16,000 feet. We then left the bombers and took a direct course toward home. My left supercharger regulator was out, which meant I had a hard time staying above 16,000 feet. We were at mid-point over the Adriatic at 5,000 feet when I finally ran out of gas. I had a hard time getting out of the cockpit but made it on the third try.

Williams made it into his raft, then waited for rescue. After an hour, a passing PBY attempted a landing, but the waves were too strong and it turned away. Thirty minutes later a C-47 spotted him, and was able to call for a launch, which arrived 20 minutes later. "A shot of whisky, a cup of coffee, and plenty of cigarettes had me back to normal in a few minutes."

Four of the 11 enemy fighters were shot down by the four pilots from the 94th Squadron led by First Lieutenant Cecil Quesseth, who went to the aid of a straggling B-17 that had attracted eight to ten of the defenders. Quesseth claimed two, while his wingman and the element leader each claimed one – all as "Fw-190s." The B-17s – which were all from the 463rd Bomb Group – had lost six of their number before the Lightnings arrived on the scene and drove the enemy off the bombers. The report made by the bombers on their return to Foggia resulted in the 1st Fighter Group receiving its third Presidential Unit Citation for the mission.

The newcomers of the 52nd, assigned to withdrawal cover, did not meet any opposition. The war diary for the 2nd Squadron lamented that the group had not had the luck of the other groups. It was noted that the mission lasted five-and-a-half hours from takeoff to touchdown, which was nearly five times the length of any mission they had flown in Spitfires. Like the 31st, they had difficulty in maintaining a 36-plane group formation, since the 52nd had previously not flown any single mission at more than squadron strength. In all, the pilots returned with more confidence in their new mounts and their ability to operate them effectively.

The Checkertails flew their last five missions in the P-47 between May 18 and 25. The final mission on May 25, in which the 325th flew penetration escort for an attack on the airfield at Wöllersdorf, Austria, was the only one on which enemy aircraft were encountered. Just after they rendezvoused with the bombers, 15 enemy aircraft bounced the bombers northwest of Zagreb. The Checkertails then bounced the enemy fighters, shooting down six Bf-109s. First Lieutenant Don Kerns was credited with two destroyed for his second and third victories; his performance on the mission resulted in his being awarded a DFC for leadership and aggressiveness. The citation provides a good description of the fight: "He broke up the enemy formation and drove them from the area. During the aerial battle he successfully destroyed two enemy fighters, and saved a fellow pilot from two aggressive enemy fighters. Under his protective cover the bombers were thus enabled to complete a highly successful bombing mission unmolested."

First Lieutenant Robert Barkey destroyed a Bf-109 for his fifth kill as he became the 325th's newest ace. Lieutenants Hiawatha Mohawk (the only Native American fighter pilot in the USAAF), Robert Rausch, and

Robert Bass also scored one Bf-109 each. All the Thunderbolts returned safely to base.

During their six-month association with the P-47, the Clan had experienced some tough air combat, which provided pilots with experience that would be put to good use once they began flying the P-51 Mustang. Over these six months the Checkertails had flown 97 combat missions, during which they claimed 153 victories at a cost of 38 losses, only seven of which were air combat losses; five P-47s were shot down by flak. The rest of the losses were the result of the winter weather and mechanical problems. Six pilots became aces in the Thunderbolt: Major Herky Green scored ten victories, plus three in the P-40; First Lieutenant Eugene Emmons scored nine; Major Lewis W. "Bill" Chick was credited with six victories; First Lieutenant George Novotny gained five victories in addition to three in the P-40; Captain William A. Rynne and First Lieutenant Edsel Paulk both scored five, all in the P-47, while five other pilots scored four victories each in the Thunderbolt. A further 66 Checkertail pilots scored one to three victories in the fighter.

While flying their final operations in P-47s, the Checkertails had also been checking out in the new P-51s that were delivered over the first half of May. By May 25, they were declared ready for operations with the Mustang. The P-47s were handed over to the 51° Stormo of the Italian Co-Belligerent Air Force, which would use the fighters to the end of the war.

There was one detail about the P-51 that nearly had fatal results for several pilots. Herky Green was the first Checkertail to confront the phenomenon, on his first flight. Having flown the earlier Allison-engined P-51 at Wright Field, Green believed he knew more about the new fighter than anyone else in the group. He climbed to 5,000 feet and initiated a maneuver he had flown many times in the P-40 – a loop from cruising without advancing power. "The Mustang reached vertical with its airspeed dropping rapidly, and everything came unglued." Green's controls were suddenly non-responsive. "No matter what I tried, I could not regain control of the airplane." He finally realized that the fighter was in an outside spin; then he saw the horizon, which meant he was in an inverted flat spin. "I knew I must be getting close to the ground. There was no time for recovery. Bailing out was the only choice I had." He reached futilely for the canopy release, then realized he was looking where it would be in a P-47.

He then grabbed the canopy release but couldn't get anything to move, having failed to release the safety. Finally, with everything lined up, he managed to open the canopy and fell out of the cockpit. "The chute snapped open, and I heard just a split-second of whine, then boom! I looked down past my feet and there was the plane in a small hole in the ground."

Green hitched a ride back to base with a passing jeep driver. There he found out what had caused his near-fatal mishap: the P-51B was equipped with an 85-gallon fuel tank in the rear of the cockpit that the Allison model had lacked. With more than 30 gallons in the tank, the P-51B had a center of gravity dangerously close to the rear limit. It was placarded for no maneuvers with more than 30 gallons aboard, because stability would be non-existent. "My stupidity and ego caused me to take the plane without a proper briefing and nearly got me killed." Once on operations, other Checkertail pilots would report getting into a turning fight and suddenly having to push forward on the stick to keep the airplane from turning tighter and a high-speed stall. "It did not take us long for everyone to become very aware of this critical problem and heed the placard warning."

On May 24, the 52nd Group finally caught the enemy and scored the group's first victories in the Mustang on a mission to Vienna, where an aircraft factory was bombed; these were the first aerial victories claimed by the group since their early days in North Africa. The Mustangs were assigned as close support for four groups of B-17s from the 5th Bomb Wing, flying penetration, target, and withdrawal cover. The mission leader was First Lieutenant Bob Curtis, CO of the 2nd Squadron. Shortly after rendezvousing with the bombers over Bleiberg, enemy fighters were encountered over the target. Curtis led his flight to bounce a flight of Fw-190s spotted below them. Curtis went after one of the enemy fighters but lost it in the haze created by the bombing. First Lieutenant Jack Schneider followed Curtis with his flight; in the melee, he and wingman Second Lieutenant Dan Zoerb shot down an Fw-190 that exploded in midair under their combined fire. Lieutenants "Dixie" Alexander – a former 133 Eagle Squadron pilot – and Dick Lampe chased two Fw-190s to the deck, where Alexander sent his into a flaming crash on the edge of Vienna, while Lampe claimed a probable after losing his heavily smoking target in the haze and smoke. With this, Alexander's score sat at four destroyed.

Lieutenants "Junior" Adams and James Hoffman became separated from their flight and joined up with Curtis and Lieutenant Barry Lawler just before Curtis spotted a formation of ten Bf-190s headed north at 15,000 feet. The four Mustangs dived into the enemy formation and in the ensuing fight, Curtis and Lawler were each credited with a Bf-109 destroyed and a second damaged; Hoffman and Adams combined forces to destroy one Bf-109, with Hoffman also destroying two others while Adams shot down an additional Bf-109. Dixie Alexander, Bob Curtis, and Barry Lawler were each awarded a DFC for their actions in the mission.

On May 29, the 52nd returned to Austria on a mission to hit the Messerschmitt factory at Wiener Neustadt, led by Captain James O. "Tim" Tyler, 4th Squadron CO. Approaching the target, the 4th Squadron was ahead of the other two and became engaged in a big fight with several single- and twin-engine enemy fighters. Captain Tyler and Lieutenants Norman Cross and William Hanes each scored two Bf-100s, claiming two others as probables. Lieutenants Richard N. Evans, James D. McCauley, and Bradley Smith were each credited with a Bf-109 destroyed.

The 5th Squadron, led by squadron CO Captain Edwin W. Fuller, encountered an enemy fighter formation at 26,000 feet over Altenmarkt. First Lieutenant Walter Zelinski shot down a Bf-109 that was going after Fuller, who then shot down another Bf-109 he spotted as he turned to evade the Bf-109 that Zelinski had shot down. Lieutenants James H. Johnson and Jim Empey also destroyed a Bf-109 each. This was the group's best day in the war so far, with 14 confirmed victories and three probables for a loss of two P-51s.

The next day the group returned to Austria, escorting bombers to Wels. The 2nd Squadron, which had missed out in the previous day's fighting, ran into 20 Bf-109s near Vordenberg. A flight of four 2nd Squadron Mustangs led by First Lieutenant Sully Varnell dived on two Bf-109s that spotted the Americans and attempted to break away, chasing them to the deck, where Varnell shot one down. He then spotted a Ju-88 and pursued it, putting a burst into the right engine, then the fuselage; the Ju-88 exploded and crashed 20 miles northeast of Linz.

The 5th Squadron's First Lieutenant Stan Rollag spotted three Bf-109s at 23,000 feet, climbing to attack the Mustangs. Rollag chased one down to 6,000 feet, where he put a burst into the engine and the fighter caught fire, going straight in to crash just north of the Danube.

As Rollag scored his victory, Dixie Alexander was lost just after shooting down the Bf-109 that was his fifth victory, making him an ace. He later recalled after the war that just after he hit the enemy fighter and started to pull up, his engine sputtered and stopped, leaving him no alternative but to make a crash-landing in a small clearing. Climbing out of his fighter, he saw a line of bullet strikes across his cowling and realized he'd been shot down by his victim's wingman. Before he could escape into the woods, he was captured by German troops attracted by the crash.

The most successful of the May Ploești missions took place on May 31, when the Fifteenth Air Force hit four refineries with 481 bombers. The Concordia Vega refinery was struck by 156 bombs, destroying the boiler house and putting the plant out of operation for more than two weeks. Română Americana was hit by 37 bombs, damaging the boiler house and crippling operations for a month. For the escorting fighters, the mission was memorable because the enemy chose to make a maximum effort to inflict serious losses on the Americans.

For the 52nd Group, the May 31 mission turned into what the group war diarist called "a red letter day." The group encountered some 34 enemy aircraft in the target area, claiming 15 in the fight that followed.

The 2nd Squadron led the way with nine claims for enemy fighters destroyed. First Lieutenant Bruce Kellam was first to spot the initial enemy presence time, which he identified as "four Fw-190s" (IAR-80s) and two Bf-109s at 16,000 feet. Closing behind one of the "Fw-190s," Kellam missed when he opened fire at too great a distance. He closed from 150 to 50 yards and opened fire a second time, putting strikes over the enemy fighter's fuselage. His wingman, Lieutenant Riley, witnessed the subsequent crash north of Bucharest.

As Kellam scored his victory, Lieutenants Carl Bellis and Barry Lawler went after one of the two Bf-109s. Both opened fire and their target rolled right and headed for the deck. Bellis then lost sight of Lawler and the Bf-109; Lawler followed the enemy's dive, finally coming within range at an altitude of 1,000 feet. When he hit the engine, the enemy pilot quickly bailed out. Lawler climbed back to find Bellis, discovering his wingman just as he shot down another of the "Fw-190s."

First Lieutenant Arthur Jonson led his flight onto a formation of "Fw-190s" and shot down a leader and wingman in quick succession. Element leader First Lieutenant Fred Ohr – the only Korean-American pilot in the USAAF – caught a nearby Bf-109 and flamed it after chasing it from 4,000 feet down to just over the trees and hitting it with a long burst at a range of 200 yards. Ohr's victory was the 52nd's 200th since entering combat in North Africa in November 1942. Not to be outdone, Sully Varnell shot down a Bf-109 and an "Fw-190."

The 5th Squadron's final victory was scored by First Lieutenant Dan Zoerb, who spotted a Bf-109 with its gear down in the landing pattern of an airfield five miles north of Bucharest. His first burst scored hits and the enemy pilot retracted his landing gear and tried to turn away at low altitude. Zoerb pursued him, then saw the enemy fighter's prop stop turning a moment before it nosed down and crashed in a field below.

The 5th Squadron scored six victories. Captain Edwin Fuller claimed two "Fw-190s," while Lieutenants John Karle, Stanley Rollag, Charles Denham, and John Schumacher each claimed. Denham made his score by colliding with his target, then bailing out to be captured. Lieutenant Karle suffered damage to his Mustang that forced him to bail out over Yugoslavia when his engine failed.

The 4th Squadron, which flew high cover, didn't come across any opposition; First Lieutenant Frederick "Ted" Bullock recalled that from his altitude with the rest of the squadron, the day was exceptionally clear, with smoke from the oil fires over the target rising to over 20,000 feet.

The 31st Group sent the 307th and 308th Squadrons to Ploești, while the 309th escorted B-17s that bombed the marshaling yards at Oradea, Romania. Over Ploești, smoke from the generators in the refineries obscured the air overhead; the group saw only 11 enemy fighters, and before they could maneuver for an attack, a squadron of P-38s dived through their formation and took those fighters on. When the bombers they were responsible for withdrew from the target area, the Mustangs turned back to San Severo, where all landed safely.

Over three days before the Ploești mission on May 31, the 82nd Group flew three strafing missions against airfields in Yugoslavia, with good results. Unfortunately, on the final mission of two on May 29, First Lieutenant Tuffy Leeman was among six P-38 pilots whose Lightnings were damaged by flak over the airfield they attacked. Leeman was pilot of "Sad Sack," one of the original P-38Fs that had been flown from England to North Africa in the fall of 1942, to cover Operation *Torch*. This mission was the fighter's 183rd, and marked only the second time it had been hit by enemy fire. On touchdown, the nose gear collapsed from what was later found to be damage from the enemy fire that had hit "Sad Sack's" nose. Both engines had been turning when the nose dropped, and both props were driven into the ground, seriously damaging the engines and their mounts. With this heavy damage, "Sad Sack" ended its career, the last P-38F flying operations in the MTO. Though they flew the Ploeşti mission, their assignment was withdrawal support, by which time the skies over the target were so smoky they were unable to spot any enemy fighters and returned scoreless.

The 14th Fighter Group's P-38s turned out to be the Lightnings that had dived through the 31st's formation to attack enemy fighters. Unfortunately, the smoky, hazy conditions allowed the enemy fighters to break off and get away in the poor visibility.

On the last day of May, the 1st Fighter Group flew its fourth escort mission to Ploeşti; enemy fighters shot down two P-38s in the poor visibility caused by the smokepots in the refineries, which created a cloud that rose to 20,000 feet. May had been a grueling month; the group had flown a mission every day, with several days seeing double missions. By the end of the month, the 27th Fighter Squadron reported that it had only 21 pilots available; with a mission flown each day over the last ten days of May, they had flown every day without a break.

By the end of May, XV Air Force's Fighter Command had three experienced P-38 groups, two newly experienced P-51 groups – the 31st and 52nd – and a third, the 325th, which had flown its first mission, an escort to southern France, on May 29. All the bomber groups assigned to the Fifteenth had arrived by mid-April and seen action in the May missions.

The battle for Ploeşti was about to take a very different turn.

6

SHUTTLE TO RUSSIA

The 325th Fighter Group began operations with its new P-51s on May 27, 28, and 29, 1944, flying missions to cover bombers striking marshaling yards at La Blanchard in southern France on the 27th and Turin on the 28th, with a strike on the Wöllersdorf airfield in Austria on the 29th. Herky Green recalled that enemy opposition was non-existent at all three targets, which allowed the Checkertails to become more familiar with their new mounts.

All that changed on the morning of June 2, 1944. For days, rumors had run through the group that they would be involved in a big operation of some kind, though Green recalled, "Our speculations were never close to reality." At the morning briefing on June 2, the pilots learned they would escort four groups of B-17s to bomb the marshaling yards at Debrecen, Hungary, then fly on to the Soviet Union, landing at Piryatin airfield, south of Kiev in Ukraine.

Operation *Frantic*, seven shuttle bombing operations flown by US aircraft based in Great Britain and Italy during the summer and early fall of 1944, resulted from a long-term USAAF decision to use Soviet bases, allowing bombers to hit targets beyond the range of their British and Italian bases and thus opening new German-held areas of Europe to the strategic bombing campaign.

Frantic was dismissed by the Germans as American propaganda to impress the Soviets, who had been demanding that the Western Allies take steps to take German pressure off the USSR since the German invasion in June 1941. The *Frantic* missions also revealed significant tensions between the Western Allies and the Soviet Union, exacerbated by such events as the Luftwaffe attack on Piryatin during the first mission flown by the Eighth Air Force at the end of June 1944.

The USAAF made its first informal request for basing privileges at Vladivostok in the spring of 1942, during planning for the Doolittle Raid. However, following the German invasion the Soviets decided they would take no action in the Far East that might give the Japanese an excuse to break the Non-Aggression Pact signed in 1940 after the Nomonhan Incident in Manchuria. The Doolittle raiders were forced to fly to China, where all crashed, save for one that went to Vladivostok safely – proving the value of Siberian bases.

The first formal request for joint basing came at the Moscow Conference of Allied foreign ministers in October 1943; the American delegation raised this with Foreign Commissar Vyacheslav Molotov, with no immediate result. A month later at the Tehran Conference, President Roosevelt proposed using Soviet airfields as bases for bombers and reconnaissance aircraft. Surprisingly, Stalin agreed to the plan "in principle." Operation *Baseball* envisioned basing three heavy bomber groups in Soviet territory. Stalin agreed to this in a meeting with Ambassador W. Averell Harriman on February 2, 1944. Harriman cabled Roosevelt "Stalin approves project limited to 200 bombers and six airfields." Only three bases were established. By this point in the war, Soviet victory was assured.

After the Soviet approval, USAAF Eastern Command was established at Poltava in Ukraine, led by General Alfred Kessler, in late April. Poltava was designated USAAF Station 559 (AAF-559). Poltava and Mirgorod (AAF-561) were for the heavy bombers, while Piryatin (AAF-560) was for fighter escorts. Heavy construction equipment and bulky supplies arrived in Murmansk and Archangelsk, where they were transported by train to Ukraine. Delicate negotiations allowed 42 round-trip ATC missions to bring further supplies and key personnel from Iran. Nearly everything had to come from the United States, including high-octane aviation fuel and steel-plank runways. The bases were further from the front than the USAAF wanted; despite the best efforts of US engineering personnel, they were barely adequate for heavy bombers.

In May 1944, General Frederick Anderson, Deputy Chief of Staff for Operations, USSTAF and his staff visited Moscow and the three bases. They found conditions allowed approval of operations. Operation

Baseball became Operation *Frantic* when it was realized in late May 1944 that calling the first mission "Operation *Frantic Joe*" could be taken as an unflattering reference to Stalin. It was shortened to *Frantic*, becoming the operation's code name.

Bombing German targets was not the primary American reason for pushing to create Operation *Frantic*. US leaders wanted to establish a numbered air force in Siberia for B-29 operations after the USSR entered the Pacific War following the defeat of Germany. It was hoped that these operations would provide a model for trust and cooperation between the two emerging superpowers, which was considered essential for establishing postwar relations.

For their part, the Soviets viewed the American presence, and the exposure of Soviet people to American ways, with trepidation. Stalin considered that the need to obtain information about superior American technology outweighed the security threat, though he ordered that contact between Americans and Russians be strictly limited. Red Air Force officers assigned to the project were ordered to learn as much as possible about US equipment and operational concepts.

The catastrophic Luftwaffe attack on the Ukrainian bases at Poltava and Mirgorod in June in which 43 B-17s – one-third of those that had flown from Britain – were destroyed, poisoned the well for cooperation. Soviet refusal to allow night fighters and radar-directed antiaircraft guns for defense against subsequent German attacks was followed in August by Soviet non-cooperation as the Red Army entered Romania. In September, the Soviets refused to allow use of the bases to support the Warsaw Uprising or for repatriation of American prisoners of war; this was seen by the Americans as the final straw. By September most targets remaining as the Wehrmacht retreated into eastern Europe were in reach of US bombers flying round-trip missions from Italy.

When the 325th Fighter Group was chosen to fly the first shuttle mission, Group CO Lieutenant Colonel Chester Sluder informed only four staff officers, so they could assist with preparations. Sluder recalled the preparations:

> This first shuttle mission was classified Top Secret, but we were able to make our preparations without compromising the program. This included equipping selected airmen and ground officers with new

uniforms, then transporting them to the various bomb groups on 1 June. They boarded the B-17s the next morning for the trip to Russia. On 2 June we held our briefing at 0300 hours. Brigadier General Strother, commander of Fifteenth Fighter Command, instructed us about proper behavior in Russia.

The Mustangs took off at 0700 hours and rendezvoused with the bombers off the coast of Yugoslavia an hour later. The 48 Checkertails were the sole escort. Sluder recalled "We got to Debrecen without incident, then proceeded on to Russia." No defending fighters were encountered. A Checkertail ground crewman was aboard the only bomber hit by flak; he parachuted safely with the others.

When the formation crossed the Dnieper River in central Ukraine, the fighters turned for Piryatin while the bombers headed to Poltava and Mirgorod. Sluder was navigating using three unrelated charts, each to a different scale. He was unable to raise the direction-finding station at Piryatin. Sluder recalled, "That part of Russia is pretty featureless, and I was navigating using time and distance. It became apparent we had overshot Piryatin and so I reversed course, planning to return to the Dnieper and follow it to Kiev." It didn't help that they were flying over a solid undercast.

Once past the Dnieper, the undercast changed to broken clouds, allowing glimpses of the ground below. Herky Green remembered, "The country was flat like a pool table, and the area was colored a springtime shade of unbroken green. Someone called out that P-39s were parked beneath us." The 64 Mustangs in the Checkertail formation were 2,000 feet overhead. Having discovered an airfield to land at, "Each of us took the shortest landing approach. We came from all points on the compass, landing upwind, downwind and crosswind."

The P-39 Airacobras were supposed to provide top cover when the Americans arrived. Spotting the Americans overhead, the Russians took off. "It was only by the grace of God no one was killed that day! When I landed, I had 15 gallons of fuel remaining. I was anxious to get on the ground!" The Americans discovered they were at Piryatin, where they were supposed to be.

The Checkertails remained at Piryatin for several days. By the second day, some pilots had convinced a Russian woman named Nadia, who worked in the mess hall as a food server – and spoke no English – to answer questions by the others about what was for breakfast with "The same old fucking thing!"

Due to bad weather, no missions were flown from Piryatin until June 6, which saw the Americans escorting the B-17s to bomb Galati airdrome in Romania, where they encountered 16 enemy aircraft. Sluder, who shot down an IAR-80 that he claimed as an "Fw-190," elaborated, "Shortly before reaching the target I spotted a pair of Fw-190s climbing toward the bombers. I let down behind them and deliberately overflew the first, thinking my second flight would take care of him. I clobbered the leader; the wingman got away. I should have been greedy and shot him down first!" Suddenly Sluder found himself evading six other enemy fighters. "Captain Roy Hogg nearly got himself killed shoving them off of my tail!" Hogg claimed two "Fw-190s," his fifth and sixth victories, making him an ace.

Just before Sluder scored, First Lieutenant Cullen J. Hoffman came across a Ju-88 that he shot down for his fifth victory, becoming the first American pilot to score while flying from a Soviet base. First Lieutenant Robert Barkey claimed a Bf-109 for his fifth, making three new aces from one mission. His wingman, future ace First Lieutenant Wayne Lowry, claimed his first, a Bf-109.

Herky Green got into a turning fight with a Bf-109. "He was blazing away at me, but he obviously didn't have enough lead to finish me. We kept turning, with me slowly but surely out-turning him. Seeing the futility of remaining in the fight, he split-essed and lived to fight another day."

First Lieutenant Barrie Davis recalled how he, Wayne Lowry, and Bob Bass got separated from the others. "While mixing it up with Me-109s trying to attack the bombers, we became separated from the rest of the Checkertails." When Bass disappeared, Davis and Lowry flew to Piryatin together. Lowry saw an approaching airplane; thinking it was Bass, he let it get close enough to open fire on Davis. Lowry broke into the Bf-109, following it in a 20,000-foot dive before he managed to explode the enemy fighter. Davis remembered, "The first rounds evidently hit my cockpit, because I remember only a big bang, then I seemed to awake from sleep to find myself in a self-flying airplane." His canopy was gone and his right wingtip had taken hits. He managed to get back to Piryatin, where he experienced difficulty getting his tail down for landing. After landing, "We found the 109 had done more than chew up my right wingtip. He had shot nearly all my tail off, hit all four blades of the prop, and made a mess of 'Mayfair 24.'" There was also an unexploded cannon shell in the cockpit fuel tank, which still held some 15 gallons of fuel. The Checkertails lost two P-51s in the fight.

The weather closed in over Ukraine after this mission, and didn't break until June 11, when the Americans returned to Italy. The takeoff saw one Mustang crash, while eight others had to abort and return to Piryatin. Their target on the way was the Focşani airfield in Romania. Over the target, 12 enemy fighters attacked a straggling B-17 and were engaged by Green's flight. "After the enemy's initial attack, I saw two Fw-190s about 3,000 feet below the bomber formation. I went after one, attacking from the five o'clock position. My wingman took the other. I opened fire and got hits on the right side of the fuselage and the right wing, but I had to pull off because another Fw-190 was on my tail." Lieutenants Ferdinand E. Suehle, Richard S. Deakins, and Benjamin H. Emmert were each credited with a Bf-109 destroyed. The straggling B-17 was shot down; it was carrying all the photos that had been taken in Russia.

Green tried to get flight pay for the 317th Squadron's ground crewmen who had flown the mission. "There seemed to be rules against that, so I put them in for Air Medals, which came through."

The consensus was that the operation had been highly successful. The shuttle missions were not abandoned, but they were suspended until the issue of airfield defense could be resolved. The Soviets refused to allow the United States to provide defenses and the Red Air Force lacked the capability to provide protection. Plans to permanently station three heavy bomber groups on Soviet airfields were abandoned.

Just before the 325th Group flew the mission, 12 new pilots reported in. Several had been stateside instructors in P-47s. One, First Lieutenant Art Fiedler, would eventually become a Checkertail legend. To give them more time in the Mustang, Fiedler and four others were sent to Casablanca to pick up new Mustangs and fly them back to Lesina. By the time the Checkertails returned from Russia, they were completely checked out in the P-51s. Fiedler was assigned to the 317th Squadron and flew his first missions as Herky Green's wingman.

While the Checkertails flew to Russia, the 31st Fighter Group escorted B-17s to Ploeşti on June 6, flying target cover for the 55th

Bomb Wing's B-24s. The bombing was unsuccessful due to the smoke screen covering the target. Enemy fighters showed up, attacking from several different directions. Three Bf-109s attacked the 308th Squadron. Lieutenants James A. Jacobs and John A. McKean shot down one of the three – the squadron's 100th victory – but the other two went after Jacobs, who managed to outrun them. Six others attempted to attack the formation from the 307th's side. Captain Samuel J. Brown and Second Lieutenant James Smith each got one. The others shot down two B-17s. Fifteen enemy Bf-109s were spotted by the 309th Squadron when they attacked the bombers. Major Victor E. Warford and Second Lieutenant Albert J. Carey destroyed a Bf-109 each.

Once the decision had been made to give complete priority to Operation *Overlord* in northwestern Europe over the Mediterranean Theater, personnel replacement became spotty; many times, tour-expired pilots had to remain past the end of their tour until replacements had arrived. In June 1944, the 31st received replacement pilots who were graduates of Advanced Training, but had no specialized training in fighters. The group was forced to create its own fighter training school to give these pilots the opportunity to gain battle readiness. Originally it was planned to obtain some "war weary" P-40s for this training; however, the first one obtained was in such sorry shape it would have been dangerous to use. Thus, the newcomers were forced to step up to the P-51B and train in them now that brand new P-51Ds were arriving in the group. Fortunately, there were no training casualties, and the pilots who completed the six week "cram course" became successful operational pilots.

The month of June began slowly for the 52nd Fighter Group, which flew only four missions between June 1 and 8; high winds forced cancellation of missions planned for June 7 and 8. With a change in weather on June 9, the group flew an escort mission to Munich to provide penetration, target, and withdrawal support. However, as they approached Udine in northern Italy, they came across enemy fighters attacking a formation of B-24s. Sixteen Mustangs went after the attackers, leaving only 29 of a planned 55 to provide escort to Munich.

First Lieutenant Jack Schneider led a flight from the 2nd Squadron to attack a mixed formation of Bf-109s and Fw-190s attacking five B-24s. Schneider overran his target, which was shot down by wingman Second Lieutenant Frank Grey. Second Lieutenant Barry Lawler went after a Bf-109 attacking a Liberator and hit it solidly; the enemy pilot rolled inverted at 5,000 feet and bailed out.

4th Squadron CO Captain Tim Tyler saw four Bf-109s attacking a B-24, and another enemy fighter formation maneuvering to attack the bombers. He ordered First Lieutenant Robert L. Burnett III to take eight Mustangs and head off the enemy. When the enemy pilots spotted the incoming P-51s, they broke off their attack and dived for the deck, followed by four of the P-51s. Dogfights broke out in which five of the enemy fighters were shot down. First Lieutenant Ted Bullock, who shot down his first enemy fighter in the fight, later noted in his diary, "I'm no longer a virgin! Got into a fight over Udine and destroyed a Me-109. I took three short bursts on the 109, hit its glycol tank, and he went in. Burnett got two and Shorty spun one in. Group score was 14 and 1 probable. No losses. Not bad. Really a thrill and good luck."

5th Squadron's Blue Flight leader, Lieutenant Joe Blackburn, spotted a B-24 under attack by six Bf-109s. The four Blue Flight Mustangs, followed by two from Green Flight, went after them. The Bf-109s headed for the deck, pursued by the Mustangs. At 300 feet, one leveled out and was hit with two bursts fired by Second Lieutenant Bob Karr; it rolled over and exploded when it crashed. A moment later, First Lieutenant Jim Carnie hit another at 2,000 feet, which also exploded when it went in. Green Flight leader First Lieutenant James Holloman spotted two Bf-109s approaching to land at Casara airfield and shot down one. Lieutenant Blackburn caught two Bf-109s as they took off and downed one after a five-mile chase over the Tagliamento River.

The 29 Mustangs that stayed with the bombers ran into a formation of 20 Bf-110 and Me-410 twin-engine fighters with a top cover of ten Bf-109s and Fw-190s, near their rendezvous point with the bomber formation. First Lieutenant Kellam, who had assumed leadership of the 2nd Squadron, turned into the enemy formation and scattered the Bf-110s. Lieutenant Sully Varnell got a Bf-110. Failing to get any hits with his first burst of fire, he closed on the target. "On my second and third bursts, I observed strikes on the left engine, wing and fuselage. Pieces came off and the left engine stopped. Streaming black smoke, the Me-110 attempted to level off to crash land, but went over on its back at 2,000 feet and broke up on impact." Second Lieutenant Arthur G. Johnson closed on a Bf-109; after his third burst the canopy came off and the pilot came out, pulling his ripcord as soon as he was clear of his burning mount. The victories were each number five for Varnell and Johnson, now the group's newest aces.

As the Liberators approached their target, James Hoffman shot down a Bf-109 as it pulled up from an attack. Lieutenant Kellam spotted six Bf-109s and broke up their formation, then shot down one. Overall, June 9 was a major victory for the 52nd, with 14 enemy fighters claimed destroyed and no losses to the group or the bombers they were escorting. In recognition of this achievement, they were awarded the Distinguished Unit Citation.

By late May 1944, it had been found that the biggest problem the Ploești campaign faced was the fact that large formations of heavy bombers flying at 25,000 feet could be picked up by German radar when they were far enough out that there was time to deploy the smoke generators in the refineries, so that by the time the bombers arrived, the target was so obscured that accurate bombing was difficult and often impossible.

In the face of this, planners organized another low-level attack that would prevent the enemy having the necessary warning time to obscure the target. This time, the attackers would be P-38s, which could hit the Românǎ Americana refinery, primary producer of high-grade aviation gasoline for the Luftwaffe. The 82nd Fighter Group would dive-bomb the refinery, protected by the Lightnings of the 1st Fighter Group.

At dawn on June 10, 1944, 46 82nd Fighter Group Lightnings from the 95th, 96th, and 97th Fighter Squadrons, each carrying a 1,000-pound bomb on the right wing shackle and a 310-gallon ferry tank on the left, took off under the leadership of 96th Squadron CO Lieutenant Colonel William Litton. They had practiced dive bombing an island off the Italian coast for a week and felt they had a good chance at success. At the same time, 48 P-38s of the 1st Fighter Group's 27th, 71st, and 94th Squadrons led by mission leader First Lieutenant Armour Miller took off from their base at Salsola. The Lightning formations joined up over Manfredonia, Italy at 1,500 feet.

The fighters remained at 1,500 feet – low enough to evade enemy radar – as they crossed the Adriatic. Over Yugoslavia, 12 82nd Group P-38s and nine from the 1st Group aborted for mechanical failures, leaving 36 "bombers" and 39 escorts. The pilots stayed as low as possible when they crossed the mountains into Romania. Dick Willsie, now the squadron operations officer, with more than 40 missions under his belt making him the most experienced pilot in the squadron, recalled, "Once we got past the mountains, we would go into Romania on the deck – and I mean we were to remain at 50 to 100 feet altitude when we came out of the mountains."

Low-level formation flying is difficult under the best circumstances, let alone when two formations are flying on the deck under radio silence for two-and-a-half hours. It turned out that the low-level flying did not achieve the expected result, since German air-defense radar spotted the fighters over Yugoslavia before they entered Romanian airspace, losing the element of surprise. To cap things off, shortly after they came out of the mountains, the two groups got separated. Approaching Ploești, both groups accelerated as they punched off their drop tanks over the open fields.

With Soviet armies attacking from the northeast, the Romanians had sent the experienced pilots of the Bf-109-equipped Grupul 7 Vânătoare to meet the threat. Thus, Ploești's primary air defense was the responsibility of the IAR-80 equipped Grupul 6 Vânătoare, with occasional reinforcement from Grupul 1's Bf-109s. In total, the defenders had no more than 30 Bf-109s and 70 IAR-80s. However, with the early radar reports now definite about the US attack, Oberst Edu Neumann – who headed the German defenses – and his assistant controller, Capitan Comandor Aviator Gheorghe Miclescu of the Romanian Air Force, scrambled all their defenders as the P-38s spread out over the Romanian plain. Having identified the attackers as *Jabos* – fighter-bombers – Neumann expected an attack on airfields. There was sufficient time to recall the Bf-109Gs of Grupul 7, which flew back from the Russian Front and were able to refuel at Popesti-Leordeni airfield in time to meet the attack.

As the American force got closer, all operational IAR-80s of Grupul 6 – led by 15-victory top ace Capitan Aviator Dan Vizante – took off and clawed for altitude. The Bf-109s of the Luftwaffe's I./JG 53 and III./JG 77 took off from Pipera airbase near Bucharest. Among the scrambling *Experten* were I./JG 53's *Gruppenkommandeur*, Knight's Cross holder Major Jürgen Harder, Leutnant Rupert Weninger, Leutnant Erich Gehring, and Unteroffizier Willi Dreyer, each of whom would raise his score in the coming battle. Within minutes, Capitan Vizante and Grupul 6 were in position.

As the 1st Group formation passed Popesti-Leordeni airfield, pilots in the 27th Squadron spotted four Do-217 bombers attempting to land. Three flights of the 71st Squadron broke off from the group formation and went after the bombers, downing all four. However, they were now separated from the rest just as 20 Romanian Air Force IAR-80s that they misidentified as Fw-190s dived on them. Four P-38s went down in the first pass as the others tried to turn with the enemy. All the advantages the heavy P-38 had over the lighter IAR-80 at high altitude were canceled out in dogfights waged at altitudes between 100 and 300 feet.

The battle was fought in a shallow valley filled with more than 40 aircraft. Airplanes of both sides fought erratically, attacking while trying to avoid one another and the ground. Two P-38s went down when they snagged the ground with their wingtips, an indication of how hot the battle was, while two IAR-80s collided and several others were hit by their own defensive ground fire.

In the four-minute battle, the 23 intercepting Romanian pilots claimed 23 P-38s for a loss of two of their own. The 71st Squadron lost nine of its 16 P-38s. Second Lieutenant Herbert "Stub" Hatch Jr. – element lead for Cragmore Green Flight – managed to shoot down five IAR-80s. His success made Hatch one of the few P-38 "aces in a day." He later recalled the battle: "At the end of the little shoot-down over the enemy airfield, as we pulled up slightly off the airfield to turn back north again, somebody hollered, 'Cragmore, break left for Chrissake.' I instinctively looked off to my left and there was a whole flock of what appeared to be Fw-190s headed in from 2 o'clock high to my position. (I later learned they were Romanian IAR-80s.)"

The entire 27th Squadron broke to the left. As Hatch continued around, an IAR-80 flashed past and pulled right across in front of him. "He was so close – fifty to seventy-five yards away – that all I could see in my ring sight was the belly of his fuselage and the wing roots. I opened fire with all four of my .50-caliber machine guns and the 20mm cannon, and I damn near blew him in half. I blew a two-foot hole in his fuselage directly beneath the cockpit."

As he rolled out, Hatch glanced to his right and saw the other IAR-80s at his two o'clock. "There were four IAR-80s in the lead. I did the only thing I could do. I turned sharply to my right, pulled up, and opened fire again. The leader was 150 to 250 yards away, nearly head-on and slightly to my left. I set the lead IAR-80 on fire with a burst that went through the engine, the left side of the cockpit, and the left wing root."

The enemy fighter rolled to his right and passed Hatch on his left. "I didn't see him crash, but my gun-camera film showed the fire, and my wingman, 2d Lieutenant Joe Morrison, confirmed that he crashed." The other three IAR-80s continued on to attack the Green Flight leader and his wingman, who were both shot down.

"As I continued to turn to my right, my wingman stayed with me. I saw another IAR-80 right up behind one of my tentmates, 2d Lieutenant Joe Jackson, who was Cragmore White-4. I closed in on him from about his 5 o'clock and tried to shoot his canopy off from less than 100 yards." The enemy pilot had already set Jackson's P-38 on fire. "The P-38 rolled over and went in, and Joe was killed. I did get my burst into the IAR-80's cockpit area, however, and he followed Joe right into the ground."

Hatch cranked down his combat flaps to continue turning at low speed. "I then saw one of our 38s coming head-on at me with an IAR-80 on his tail." Hatch was still at around 300 feet and the Romanian fighter passed over, missing him by 50 feet:

> I pulled my nose up and opened fire on him head-on from a distance of 150 to 200 yards. He kept coming at me head-on and I thought to myself, I can hold as long as you can, you son of a bitch. And then I shot the bottom half of his engine off. He nosed down, still shooting at me, and I had to dump the yoke hard to miss him. He was burning when he went over me – not more than three feet – and part of his right wing caught my airplane and knocked about three inches off the top of the left rudder.

Three more IAR-80s made a pass from Hatch's left and he turned so fast that he lost wingman Morrison. He missed his shot but a moment later he saw two others diving on another P-38:

> I snap-shot at the leader from about a 100-degree deflection. I hit his left wing and shredded the aileron, and he fell off and went in. He was so low there was no chance for him to recover. I kept on going around to my left and shot at the second one, which was going away from me on my left. I hit him, but I'm not sure if he went in. I know I knocked a bunch of pieces off his cowling and fuselage, but I did not have time to see what happened to him.

Hatch looked up to see another IAR-80 diving from his two o'clock, firing at him. "I just shut my eyes and involuntarily hunched down in the cockpit. I thought I had bought the farm right there. But he missed me. God knows how! I was a sitting duck for sure." As Hatch continued to turn, he saw another IAR-80 and closed on him. His guns fired only ten rounds and quit; he was out of ammunition.

> I cannot adequately emphasize what a melee it was. There were at least 24 P-38s in that little area, all of them at low altitudes. Somewhere between 25–30 IAR-80s were also in there. None of us, Romanians or Americans, was at more than 200–300 feet, and some of us were quite a bit lower. The topography was a kind of little hollow with some hills on each side of it. It was by far the wildest melee I saw in the sixty-odd combat missions I flew. It was a wild, wild few minutes.

In fact, the whole fight lasted three to six minutes according to the squadron report.

Out of ammunition, 600 miles into enemy territory, and all alone, Hatch went looking for some company. He quickly ran across First Lieutenant Carl Hoenshell, another 27th Squadron pilot, and they joined up. Minutes later, Hatch heard wingman Joe Morrison calling for some help:

> Hoenshell and I turned back to look for Joe. We finally picked him up down at about 200 feet. After we got him headed in our direction, we started to climb out of there to the west. Joe's airplane looked like a lace doily. The two IAR-80s that had gone right over the top of me had then gone right down on Joe's tail. His P-38 was flying, but just barely. And Hoenshell and I were both out of ammunition.

The three were soon joined by the 94th Squadron's Second Lieutenant John Allen. "We were happy to see him and hoped that he had some ammunition. When we called to ask, we found that his radio was out and we couldn't talk to him."

They continued on to the west, and moments later ran into a flak nest. Morrison got separated from the others and they had to turn around a second time and go back to get him. "Finally we got out of Romania into Yugoslavia and climbed to about 12,000 feet." Hatch and Hoenshell were S-turning above Morrison when Hatch spotted six Bf-109s at his eight o'clock. "I hollered to Hoenshell, 'Bogies! High at eight o'clock.' He saw them, too, and called 'Joe, hit the deck.'" Morrison stuck his nose down and dived for the deck:

> Carl, Allen, and I held the turn as best we could, and when the 109s broke formation and came at us from six o'clock, we turned up into them, hoping to scare them off by looking like we were ready for a fight. Well, they didn't scare worth a damn. When Hoenshell, who was leading, hollered on the radio, 'Hit the deck, Hatch!' I didn't waste any time. I rolled my airplane over on its back and split-essed out of there.

One Bf-109 chased Hatch while two of the others went after Hoenshell. "There was an undercast beneath us and I didn't have the faintest idea where the hell the mountains were – Yugoslavia is full of mountains – but there was no choice at that point." With the Bf-109 gaining, Hatch dived through the undercast. "I was hitting close to 600 miles per hour when I came through the bottom into a valley between two high ridges. The Lord was sure with me that day!"

Hoenshell was shot down by the Bf-109 that pursued him as far as Bulgaria, where he crashed. Wounded in the fight, he died in hospital the next day.

When he felt certain he had lost the pursuing Bf-109, Hatch climbed back above the cloud deck and tried to find the others:

> I heard Joe hollering for help, but my fuel level was getting down to the point where I couldn't afford to turn around and go back. I continued on toward Foggia. As I flew across the Adriatic, I was one wrung-out boy. I was wet with sweat. I was tired. I had gone past the point of being scared. I was just all shook up. The business of enjoying that kind of combat might be true for some people, but for this boy – well, I was just damn glad to be out of there and headed for home.

Hatch was the first 71st Squadron pilot to return. "It was noon, and my elapsed time on the mission was six hours and fifty-five minutes.

I don't think I had enough gas to make it around the circuit if I hadn't been able to land on the first approach." Hatch's "ace in a day" score of five destroyed – along with two probables and another damaged – and Hoenshell's three were among the claims for 18 destroyed made by 1st Group pilots in the battle. Both Hatch and Hoenshell were awarded the DSC for the mission. The heaviest losses were suffered by the 71st Squadron, which was caught at low altitude at cruising speed by enemy fighters. Unable to get up to speed while trying to evade at low altitude, the squadron lost ten Lightnings shot down.

Hatch was very happy later that night when his wingman, Joe Morrison, walked into the officer's club. Morrison had managed to fly his damaged P-38 across the Adriatic, but the good engine finally failed as he got to the coast of Italy, and he was forced to crash-land on the beach near Bari. He had managed to hitch a ride on a passing Army truck that dropped him at the base gate. "To say I was glad to see him was a definite understatement."

Moments after the 71st Squadron was engaged by the enemy, the 94th Squadron ran across several low-flying aircraft. Two Do-215s and one IAR-80 were shot down as the Lightnings flew through them. First Lieutenant Merrill Adelson claimed an Me-210 and an He-111 that he hit while they were trying to lift off from the Pipera airbase; he also claimed the destruction of the IAR-80.

In the fight with the 71st Squadron, Capitan Aviator Dan Vizante shot down two P-38s, solidifying his position as top IAR-80 ace. The Romanians claimed 23 P-38s of which the 1st Fighter Group lost a total 24, with many others crippled. The group's P-38s were thoroughly routed and played no further part in the mission. The battle over Popesti-Leordeni airfield was the high point of Romanian Air Force resistance to the USAAF.

Willsie and the rest of the 82nd Group – not knowing of the 1st Group's battle and still right on the deck as they approached Ploești – overflew Pipera airbase looking for their missing escorts. Once past the field, they began their climb to 10,000 feet to make the attack. At that moment, 40 Bf-109Gs of Grupul 7, I./JG 53 and III./JG 77 made their interception. Willsie recalled, "It was as though the roof fell in on us. There were Messerschmitts and heavy flak bursts everywhere." Of the 34 Lightnings that attempted to make the attack, only 24 were able to bomb the target; nine were lost to flak and fighters, while another ten were badly damaged. During this fight, the Bf-109 flown by Gefreiter Helmut Köditz was shot down and he was killed when his "Weisse Drei" crashed near Broşteni. He was claimed by the 96th's First Lieutenant John Sognia. A second Bf-109 made a successful belly landing at Horsesti, with minor battle damage.

The P-38s were able to initiate their dive bombing before the smoke generators had the chance to fully cover the refinery. Willsie described the result. "Unfortunately, despite the fact that we hit the cracking plant, a storage tank and three refinery units, the bombing was not effective because of our evasive maneuvers; everyone was flying to get away from the interceptors, and the refinery was not seriously damaged."

Willsie took a flak hit in his right engine. "I feathered it, stayed on the deck and got out of there." Climbing slowly over the mountains back toward Yugoslavia, he ran into three Bf-109s searching for stragglers. As they came after him, he turned and flew through their formation, causing them to scatter. "I split-essed for the deck and executed that classic maneuver known as getting the hell out of there."

Climbing to get over the mountains, Willsie came across another P-38 with an engine out. "He looked pretty badly shot up and had several large holes. I could tell from his markings he was from the First, but when I tried to contact him, his radio was out. I pulled ahead of him and motioned for him to follow me. He gave me a thumbs-up, and I led us back to Foggia. The trip seemed longer than it really was, as I was waiting for either of us to lose our good engine."

When they arrived over the 1st Group's Salsola base, the other pilot indicated that his instruments were out and he couldn't land. Willsie moved in close and flew them both into the pattern, staying with the other through the final approach. "When he touched down, I pulled up and flew on over to our base and landed."

Recalling the reputation of the P-38 being a bad single-engine aircraft, Willsie explained, "You have to understand. I'd had a lot of experience on the P-38 before joining the 82nd, and I had experienced my share of engine failures. So I was completely comfortable with the airplane. I wouldn't recommend flying around on one engine to a low-time pilot, but I felt fine with it in that condition."

The surviving 27th Squadron P-38s strafed an airfield that they came across on their return. Coming off the run, they were engaged by 30–40 Bf-109s, of which they claimed four shot down.

June 10, 1944 was recorded as the "blackest day" in the combat history of the P-38. The 1st Group and the 82nd's 30 total loss was the worst suffered during a single mission by any American fighters in World War II. The Romanian claim of 51 shot down was nearly twice the actual loss, but 23 P-38s failed to return from the mission. American claims of 33 shot down were also more than double the actual Romanian loss of 14 – only ten of which were fighters. The inflated claims from both sides demonstrate the intensity of the battle over Ploești.

Most important, despite all the sacrifice, the Română Americana refinery had survived without serious damage. As Willsie put it, "We pretty much felt like we'd gotten kicked pretty hard that day. It took a lot of hard work by the ground crews for us to be ready for the mission we flew on the next day."

Despite the battering of June 10, the next day the 82nd escorted a B-24 mission to Constanța, Romania that saw the target destroyed. This mission was also flown by the 52nd Group. The bombers' targets were the oil storage facilities. Constanța was 680 miles from the 52nd's base at Magna, so distant that the field order for the mission read, "provide escort on penetration to the prudent limit of endurance for four groups of the 47th Bomb Wing."

Enemy fighters and flak were encountered over Yugoslavia, and the bombers were late to the rendezvous. Contact with enemy fighters happened at 0845 hours over Yugoslavia, when the group came across a mixed formation of German and Bulgarian fighters. The 2nd Squadron's Lieutenant Bob Curtis shot down two enemy fighters in this first encounter, and a third half an hour later during the squadron's return flight to Italy. Curtis' three victories raised his score to six. The 5th Squadron's First Lieutenant James Empey shot down two Bf-109s and Second Lieutenant Calvin Allen also shot down a Bf-109. The combined score of 13 was offset by the loss of the 2nd Squadron's Second Lieutenant Joseph Riley, who was shot down and killed. First Lieutenant James Hoffman's Mustang was badly shot up, but he was able to fly back to the group's base at Madna and land successfully. 5./JG 301 bore half the enemy casualties, losing Feldwebel Gunter Ifert and Unteroffizier Hans Gerling killed, while Feldwebel Paul Becker and Unteroffizier Herman Erchen managed to bail out after being wounded. The 52nd's war diary stated, "There was no disposition on the part of the enemy to avoid combat. In view of the evident ability of the enemy pilots, there was some surprise expressed at the evidence of poor marksmanship on their part."

By the time they neared the target, the 2nd and 5th Squadrons had been forced to turn back after the fight left them with insufficient fuel to continue, leaving only the 4th Squadron to provide 15 minutes' cover over the target before it was forced to turn back.

June 13 saw the 31st Group return to the German airfields that had been targeted unsuccessfully on June 9. This time the air was clear and the enemy came up to contest the mission. Thirty enemy aircraft, including both single-engine Bf-109s and Fw-190s and also twin-engine Bf-110s and Me-410s, were encountered. The Bf-109s and Fw-190s attempted to pull the escorts away from the 5th Bomb Wing so the rocket-carrying twin-engine fighters could make their attacks. The 309th's Captain Muray D. McLaughlin scored two Bf-109s destroyed; the first of these was the group's 300th victory since entering combat in North Africa in 1942.

That same day, the 52nd again escorted bombers to Munich. Defending Luftwaffe formations were up in force. The 52nd confronted over 90 enemy fighters, engaging in a series of running battles. On the way to the target, Luftwaffe fighter formations tried twice to entice the Mustangs away from the bombers. Finally, as the force approached Landshut in Bavaria, five Fw-190s were spotted closing in on the bombers. Seven P-51s of the 5th Squadron dived on them. The enemy spotted the intercepting Mustangs and broke for the deck. The original seven Mustangs were joined by four more 5th Squadron P-51s and dogfights broke out when ten more Fw-190s joined in, along with three Me-410s and a Ju-88. Lieutenants John Heller, Calvin Allen, and Victor Trevsik were each credited with destroying two Fw-190s, while Lieutenants Matthew Broder and Robert Anderson claimed a shared seventh Fw-190. Jim Empey shot down an Me-410 and recalled, "East of Munich at 26,000 feet, my flight leader called a flight of Fw-190s. We started down on them. At lower altitude, I spotted an Me-410 and made three passes on it, trying to lower my speed. On the fourth pass, I got dead astern and shot up both engines and the cockpit. The enemy aircraft crashed and burned."

The remaining three victories went to the 2nd Squadron's Lieutenant Barry Lawler, who claimed an Me-410 destroyed, while the 4th Squadron's

Junior Adams claimed an Fw-190, and the 4th Squadron's Lieutenant Robert Burnett claimed a Bf-109.

Despite the large enemy response over Munich, the 82nd's Lightnings got no reaction, while the 1st Group's P-38s ran into Bf-109s as the bombers they were escorting neared the target. Lieutenant Warren "Beans" Campbell remembered:

> Nearing the target, we ran into 15–20 Bf-109s that were above us. The squadron leader started a slow climb to meet them. Blue-Two started to experience engine trouble and dropped further and further behind. I throttled back to stay with him. Suddenly, he managed to correct his engine problem. His older G model was lighter than my J model and as a result he accelerated and pulled back into formation; I was all by myself with enemy aircraft bearing down on us. I looked back and saw an Me-109 diving on me from eight o'clock with all guns blazing. The tracers were falling behind me but they seemed to be getting closer. I ducked and put my head between my legs. After what seemed like an eternity – probably three seconds – I looked up and to my surprise and horror all I could see for a fraction of a second was the wing and part of the underbelly and tail surface of the 109, less than 100 feet in front of me. At first all I could think of was that if I had my guns firing, I would have blasted him out of the sky. As we flew back home, I began to think about how close we had come to a mid-air collision. It was several hours after we landed before the cold chills stopped running down my spine.

The Checkertails also flew the Munich mission. This was Art Fiedler's first mission as an official Checkertail. He recalled how he learned on the afternoon of June 12 that he and the other three newcomers assigned to the 317th Squadron would be on the next day's mission. At the briefing, Fiedler found himself taken aback when the pilots were informed they might meet as many as 450 enemy aircraft over the target.

With the briefing over, the pilots headed for their aircraft. Fiedler's was one of the new P-51Cs he had helped ferry from Casablanca:

> While I awaited engine-start time, the second hand on the cockpit clock seemed to stagger from second to second so slowly that I asked

the ground crew four times to check their wristwatches. They had gone through this many times before with new pilots and were great as they joked with me to help pass the time and take my mind off the obvious – would I pass muster? Finally it was time and soon the air was filled with the sound of Merlins coughing to life and then in a few seconds all were turning over.

The fighters taxied to the runway, where they lined up two abreast for takeoff at 15-second intervals. "The takeoff was a new experience – one that made the heart beat faster. As my aircraft hurtled down the runway, I jockeyed the throttle to stay in position beside my leader. I could see four aircraft still accelerating on the runway ahead of me, and knew there were two more 15 seconds behind me." Lift-off came at 110mph, followed by a gentle left turn. "By the time we were flying past the runway in the opposite direction, all sixteen aircraft in the squadron had joined up. As I looked around the sky, I could see one squadron ahead of us, and the last one completing its takeoff below."

Two P-51s crashed at the end of the runway when they failed to achieve flying speed. Fiedler's tent mate, First Lieutenant Kidder, made a late takeoff after experiencing difficulty starting his engine; when he joined up from the low position, he went too high and too wide, and the prop of another Mustang cut his tail off. "It was probably just as well that I learned about this on returning from the mission, rather than as it happened."

As the formation reached 17,000 feet over the Adriatic, Fiedler's engine suddenly surged with an increase in power and he jumped ahead of his flight. Quickly retarding the throttle, he returned to position. "No one told me the supercharger cut in at that altitude, and since I had never been over 10,000 feet in a P-51, I had never experienced this totally unexpected phenomenon. It was a big change from the P-47." As they crossed the Po Valley, Fiedler put his 20/10 vision to work, looking for the 450 enemy fighters. "I saw dots ahead, and called 'Bogies! Two o'clock high!' After a long moment, a sarcastic voice came back, 'That's flak.' How was I to know, since I had never seen flak before?"

The Mustangs crossed into Austria over the Alps, heading north-northeast to cross into Bavaria. A reminder that the P-51B still had many "bugs" to work out was shown in the 11 mechanical aborts that left only 34 Mustangs escorting the bombers over the target. "To the north, I spotted two contrails and immediately called them out. This time no one said a word as they crossed our path 500 feet above us and I identified them as Fw-190s. Nothing happened; no one went after them." A moment later, he spotted another airplane approaching at high speed, followed by several Mustangs whose wings flashed fire at what he identified as a Bf-109. "It was being chopped to pieces as they flashed past only 100 yards away. It was a fantastic experience, to be at ringside and see an aircraft literally torn apart on my first mission."

The 317th Squadron didn't run into any opposition. After they returned to base, Fiedler proudly reported the three aircraft he had seen. "I was flabbergasted when the old hands reported the 40–50 enemy aircraft they had seen in the area. That was when I realized there was more to this game of combat than knowing how to fly an airplane. One also had to develop an intangible thing called combat sense if he expected to do the job we were there for and survive."

Herky Green, Fiedler's flight leader on the mission, had a very different experience. He became separated from the squadron and returned to base alone.

> In the Udine area, I saw six Macchi 205s at 32,000 feet headed toward Venice. I started climbing to their level from behind. After about four minutes I caught them 20 miles south of Venice. As I closed in from six o'clock, three of them spotted me and split-essed. The other three continued straight and level. When I fired on the last plane, hoping to work my way up and get all three, the other two promptly rolled over and headed for the ground. Immediately, the one I opened fire on exploded and started to burn. It was my fourteenth victory and my first in the P-51.

While Fiedler saw only three aircraft, Green shot down a C.205; Lieutenants Paul P. Tatman and Wayne Lowry each shot down a Bf-109 and Lieutenants Cullen Hoffman and Eugene Emmons each damaged an Fw-190. Lowry later described his victory:

> I was so sure of my newfound power in the P-51 that I actually trapped a Me 109 at 30,000 ft while I was at 20,000 ft. He kept trying to get away and I kept cutting him off. I must have stalled out 50 times trying to get to his altitude. The Mustang was really screaming over

such treatment, as I relaxed full power only momentarily to boot her out of the notion of flipping. I suppose there were moments when I could have been clobbered, but somewhere around 28,000 ft the German pilot lost his nerve and attempted to dive by me. That was his mistake, and it led to a one way trip to Valhalla for him.

On June 14, an "all-out" mission was flown to Budapest; all fighter groups were involved. Bombers attacked the Szony oil refinery. The 52nd Group and the Checkertails found their parts of the escort were "milk runs"; Herky Green noted "the weather was about perfect, though, so it was a nice day for sightseeing."

The 14th Fighter Group's P-38s also participated. Whereas the Checkertails found no opposition, the 14th encountered almost too much; the 49th Squadron saw all the action while B-24s hit the Petfurdo refinery. The 49th's Captain Don Luttrell recalled:

> We were well back in the bomber stream. By the time the B-24s arrived, the other groups had hammered the refinery, which was burning furiously. There was a cloud of black smoke rising from the target to around 25,000 feet that was miles across. The other two squadrons went around the smoke column to the east while we went to the west alone. We were perhaps watching the bombs falling more closely than we should have when suddenly someone called out "51s at nine o'clock!" A moment later, Clyde Jones called "51s hell, those are 109s!" Suddenly we had what seemed like the entire Luftwaffe to ourselves. I have never seen so many black crosses on so many planes.

The pilots punched off their tanks and followed mission leader First Lieutenant Lou Benne as he climbed toward the enemy. Benne shot down one Bf-109, then called for the squadron to form a Lufbery while he called out for help. A moment after Benne destroyed a second Bf-109, his P-38 was hit by several enemy fighters. The right engine was damaged, the left engine caught fire, and a 20mm round shot out the instrument panel. He was so low when he bailed out that his parachute had barely opened when he struck the ground so hard it knocked the wind out of him. Before he could recover, he was captured.

Luttrell later commented, "I will never forget the melee that evolved. I'd been scared many times. I went into the fight chewing gum under my mask, and came out of it with the gum strung back and forth between my teeth. I was freezing in the cockpit when I dived into the fight, and when I came out I was burning up." There were P-38s and enemy fighters everywhere. Luttrell followed Clyde Jones in a right turn. "As Clyde rolled and turned back left, a 109 swooped through us, firing at him. In an instant he was a ball of fire; you could not even see the outline of the plane in the fire. The 109 pulled up, putting himself right in front of me, and I gave him the same treatment he'd just given Clyde. Clyde was gone, the German was gone, and I was all alone looking for company."

As it turned out, Clyde Jones was not killed. After the war when he returned from prison camp, he recalled the fight:

> I looked back over my shoulder and there was a 109, with fire flashing from his guns. Everything in my airplane disappeared. The instrument panel was gone. And then his fire must have hit the fuel lines that ran through the cockpit and also hit the oxygen tank; all of a sudden there was an explosion! I twisted the wheel, kicked the rudder, and went into a vertical dive. Fire was everywhere in the cockpit. My gloves were so burned I couldn't get a grip on the canopy release, but using both hands I managed to pull it and the canopy went. I was still in my harness, and I got sucked out of the cockpit into a 500 mile an hour wind as far as the seat belt allowed. I managed to hit the harness release and I was sucked out of the cockpit. I got hit by the right boom on my head behind my ear and was knocked unconscious. When I came to, I was quite low. I managed to pull the ripcord and only swung twice before I hit the ground. I barely missed going into the fire of my airplane that hit the ground below me. I pulled up my legs and landed flat on my butt and injured my spine so I couldn't walk.

Jones was found by farmers and threatened with a lynch mob until a Hungarian Army officer arrived on the scene and rescued him.

Above, Luttrell was still in the fight. "There must have been 75 109s swarming around." The surviving P-38 pilots broke out of the Lufbery and managed to evade the enemy. The 49th lost five pilots – Louis

Benne, Clyde Jones, Bill Williams, John McLaughlin, and Wesley Jule, who was killed. The others were taken prisoner; McLaughlin died in captivity. Nearly all of the ten Lightnings that returned had some kind of damage from the fight. Amazingly, Luttrell's P-38 didn't have a scratch on it. Despite being badly outnumbered, First Lieutenants Louis Benne and Tom Purdy were credited with two each, while First Lieutenant Houston Musgrove was credited with one destroyed. Second Lieutenants Swanson Short and Jack Lenox destroyed three each. Second Lieutenants Moses Long, Don Luttrell, John Thomas, and George Johnson were credited with one each, for a total of 15 shot down in the 15-minute battle.

The 31st Group escorted the 5th Bomb Wing's B-17s to hit synthetic oil refineries. They found no enemy action over the target, but while heading home the 308th Squadron ran across 12 Hungarian Air Force Me-210s over the Drava River that stayed to fight it out. Squadron CO Lieutenant Colonel William A. Daniel, Captain Samuel J. Brown, and First Lieutenant Edmund Antonini were each credited with the destruction of one Me-210.

The 82nd Group's First Lieutenant Gene Chatfield led the 97th Squadron on the mission. He later recalled, "Our intelligence discovered that the Germans were ferrying aviation fuel from Ploești to Germany, flying at night and stopping over for the day at the airfield at Kecskemet, Hungary. Our mission on the 14th was to destroy the planes and facilities there." On arriving over the target, the 82nd split into squadron formations, with the 96th and 97th Squadrons circling just out of range from flak while the 95th Squadron came strafing across the field before the defending gunners were aware of them. "As the gunners concentrated on the departing strafers, the rest of us safely made our bomb run." The huge six-engine Me-323 "Gigant" transports were right where they had been on the reconnaissance photos. "These wood and fabric ships loaded with aviation fuel made a fire that could be seen for miles, and our bombs took care of the hangars and machine shops. All in all, it was quite a day!"

The 95th Squadron claimed eight destroyed. Mission leader Major Phillips and Lieutenants Carlyle Abbott, Barry Butler, Jack Joley, and Roy Harman were credited with one Me-323 each, while Lieutenant Jim Holloway was credited with an Me-323 and an Fi-156 "Storch" destroyed. Lieutenant Charles Eberty was credited with a Bf-109.

They strafed ten oil tank cars on a railroad siding next to the airfield, turning them into blazing wrecks. The 97th Squadron was credited with the destruction of both hangars with their bombs.

A major strafing mission to southern France involving all six of the Fifteenth's fighter groups was planned for June 15. The 31st Group drew the airfield at La Jasse airdrome. While the 308th and 309th Squadrons flew cover, the 307th dropped down and strafed the airfield, which proved to be "sparsely populated" as the war diary noted. Lieutenant Colonel Daniel and Captain Brown were credited with one Ju-88 each. An Me-410 escaped unscathed. As the 307th's Mustangs pulled off their runs, 15 enemy fighters arrived overhead and attacked the 308th Squadron. In the fight that followed, First Lieutenant Walter J. Goehausen came away credited with three Bf-109s destroyed. Defending flak was described as "murderous," and was responsible for the loss of Second Lieutenant Derrick Boyd, whose Mustang crashed and exploded after passing over the field.

The Checkertails went to the Pujuat and Château Blanc airfields at Avignon. The fields had already been hit, so they strafed a locomotive with 30 boxcars and several oil tank cars. Four Bf-109s were engaged at low level just off the coast; First Lieutenant Hiawatha Mohawk destroyed one, and one other was damaged by Captain R.E. Hartley. Five P-51s were lost and two were missing. Herky Green recorded in his diary that "The meager results in no way justified these losses."

The 82nd Group aborted their mission when they encountered heavy fog west of Corsica. The 1st Fighter Group managed to evade the fog; their low-level approach surprised Orange Plan de Dieu airdrome, where the 71st Squadron flew high cover at 10,000 feet while the 94th and 27th Squadrons strafed the airfield. The 71st's Lieutenant Robert Spitler shot down an Fw-190 he spotted stalking the attacking squadrons. The 94th Squadron's Lieutenant Don Greenley damaged a Bf-109 that attacked the strafing Lightnings. Two Bf-109s, an Fw-190, and four Ju-88s were destroyed by strafing. The 94th's Lieutenants Dugglesby and Crandall were shot down in flames by the defending flak. The squadrons attacked two trains, destroying both locomotives.

The 14th Group's Lightnings were assigned to the Orange/Caritat airfield complex near Avignon. The 37th Squadron flew high cover while Lieutenant John Schill led the other squadrons on their strafing run, which saw the destruction of nine enemy aircraft on the field.

Afterwards, two locomotives on the Marseilles line were strafed. The 37th's Lieutenant Robert Powers and the 49th's Lieutenant Warren Semple were lost to flak. The 37th's Lieutenant Bill McClain, who experienced mechanical failure on both engines during the approach to the airfield and was forced to crash-land, was fortunately immediately rescued by resistance personnel and hidden from the Germans; he became a member of the Maquis and fought with them until Operation *Dragoon*, when he was liberated by an American armored unit and returned to the group at the end of August.

The "all-out" mission on June 16 was assigned to hit several synthetic fuel refineries around Vienna. The mission was particularly costly to the 1st Fighter Group, whose target was the Labau oil blending plant near Vienna. During the run-in to the target, the 94th Squadron ran across 30 enemy fighters and engaged them in a 20-minute running battle. Lieutenant Philip Smith destroyed one Bf-109, while Lieutenants Bob Van Sice, Charles Dollarhide, and Chester Heien claimed one Bf-109 destroyed and one probable each. Over Lake Balaton in Hungary, the squadron lost Lieutenants George Loughmiller, Thomas Vitale, and Samuel Barnes, killed.

Lieutenant Jim Fairhurst saw all three go down: "Just after our first break, I looked off my left wing in time to see three P-38s get it. One burst into flame all over and around the cockpit (Loughmiller), the second went into a slow spin to the right trailing coolant (Barnes) and the third stopped flying and went by me like some giant hand had hurled it across the sky. I saw the third guy (Vitale) hit the silk."

The 82nd Group sent the 95th Squadron, led by Lieutenant Chatfield, who also led the group for the mission, and the 97th Squadron, led by Lieutenant Leeman. Forty miles from Lake Balaton, two Bf-109s dived on the trailing 95th Squadron flight; the whole squadron went after them as they continued their dive, and were followed by two Fw-190s. The running fight ended up over Veszprém airfield, where another 12 enemy aircraft were encountered in the landing pattern. Lieutenant Paul Mass recalled that his flight was just crossing over the bombers at 26,000 feet when the two Bf-109s came through them. "Lieutenant Holloway jettisoned his tanks and rolled over to go after them and I did too. We caught up with them and I fired a long burst at the second one in a perfect overhead pass. As I went past the bomber formation, I heard someone call 'Look at those little friends go.'" In a moment, Mass was in a compressibility dive, which was almost always fatal in a P-38:

> My airspeed was reading well above 500 indicated and was rising rapidly. I pulled back on the control yoke but the only response was heavy buffeting. I cranked in a little 'up' elevator and decided I would bail out when the horizon started to come up. It soon felt like the aircraft was starting to pull out. I blacked out completely and when I came to, the aircraft was climbing in a shallow angle at around 5,000 feet. The bombers reported that one of the 109s went down, but no victory claim was made. I never attempted that screaming dive again.

Lieutenant James Holloway was credited with a Bf-109 in the fight over the airfield; Lieutenant Jack Joley destroyed two Bf-109s, while Lieutenants Barry Butler, Gerard Cavanaugh, and Tuffy Leeman got one each. Leeman was firing on a second enemy fighter when his guns jammed, denying his fifth victory.

Lieutenant Bob Carpenter shot down an Me-210 but then disappeared in a fight with a Bf-109. His wingman, Lieutenant Cavanaugh, reported that the fight got down to the deck and progressed south toward the lake. "I saw Lieutenant Carpenter chase a 109 and fly through a cloud. When I rejoined a P-38 I thought was his, it was another pilot. I didn't see him hit or hear him on the radio."

The 95th claimed eight destroyed for the loss of three. Their opponents were most certainly the new 101 "Puma" Group of the Royal Hungarian Air Force, which were flying their first combat and claimed six P-38s shot down.

The Checkertails escorted B-24s to bomb the Nova oil refinery at nearby Schwechat, Austria. North of Lake Balaton the Mustangs ran into 11 Bf-109s and claimed four shot down.

The 52nd Group escorted B-24s from the 47th Bomb Wing to bomb refineries at Bratislava, Czechoslovakia. Arriving at Lake Balaton for rendezvous with the bombers eight minutes early, the Mustangs were then forced to circle for 42 minutes before the Liberators appeared. Five minutes later, a pilot in the 2nd Squadron spotted 12 Bf-109s at 28,000 feet preparing to attack the bombers. The squadron prepared to bounce them, but the 1st Group's 95th Squadron got there first (in the fight described above). Ten minutes later a formation of 25 Me-210s was spotted and the squadron went after them, with one flight of four breaking up the formation, though some persisted in their attack on the bombers. They were met by another 2nd Squadron flight that forced them to turn away. Simultaneously, 30 Bf-109s hit the last squadron of bombers and the remaining 2nd Squadron P-51s engaged them. When the dogfights – that ranged from 26,000 feet to the deck – were over, the squadron claimed five Bf-109s and five Me-210s destroyed. Sully Varnell scored two Me-210s, while Dan Zoerb destroyed a Bf-109 and shared a Me-210 with Lieutenant John Clarke. Captain Fred Ohr destroyed a third Me-210, while Lieutenants Richard Lampe, Willard Pretzer, and Jack Schneider destroyed one Bf-109 each; Barry Lawler destroyed the fourth Me-210. The fifth Me-210 was shared by Lieutenants Art Johnson and Dennis Riddle. The group lost 4th Squadron's Lieutenant F.R. Crawford, who was attacked by four P-38s.

The 31st Group escorted B-17s of the 5th Bomb Wing to Vienna, where they found the opposition light. The 309th's First Lieutenant Richard L. Gross got one Bf-109 while Major Victor E. Warford went after two Bf-109s and shot down one. Over the target, seven Bf-109s attacked the 308th's Mustangs, diving from up-sun through the fighters; Thomas W. Byrnes destroyed one. Following the mission of June 16, heavy rain prevented more missions until June 22.

The mission of June 22 saw the 31st Fighter Group equipped with brand new P-51D Mustangs when they escorted B-24s to Trieste to attack oil refineries. The weather was still marginal, forcing the bombers to go to their alternative, Pola. The weather there was also marginal, with total cloud cover, and the results were unobserved. The mission marked five stand-downs in a row for weather and a sixth that should have been a stand-down. Better results were obtained on the 23rd, when the group flew their seventh mission to Ploești. As the Mustangs approached the target, eight Fw-190s and Bf-109s dived through the 307th Squadron's formation. First Lieutenant Robert E. Riddle dived after them, shooting down two Fw-190s and damaging two others. First Lieutenant James L. Brooks destroyed a Bf-109 and damaged a second, and First Lieutenant Maurice D. Surratt got his first victory, a Bf-109.

The 308th Squadron found good results over Ploești. Captain Thomas W. Byrnes claimed an Fw-190 destroyed while future MTO top ace First Lieutenant John J. Voll scored the first of an eventual 21, an Fw-190. Captain Robert J. Goebel also scored a Bf-109, his fifth victory.

The 309th, flying roving top cover over the target, saw only two enemy aircraft in their vicinity; they dived away when several Mustangs turned to go after them.

The 52nd Group also suffered through the six rainy days of rain; the group's war diarist noted that the canceled missions would make it difficult to achieve the group's goal for June of shooting down 100 enemy planes. On June 21, an uneventful mission was flown to Turin. Everyone hoped for better luck on the mission scheduled for June 23.

On the June 23 Ploești mission, the group flew approach and target cover for the B-24s of the 47th Bomb Wing. Arriving at the rendezvous point, mission leader Captain Tim Tyler found B-17s but no B-24s; determining the bombers had gone on ahead, he led the Mustangs toward Ploești. Approaching the target at 0940 hours, pilots of the 2nd Squadron spotted 20 Bf-109s and ten of the 14 P-51s dived after them; the four left behind as high cover then spotted another gaggle at 29,000 feet and climbed to intercept them. The ten P-51s diving on the larger formation watched the Messerschmitts break and head for the deck. The Mustangs went after them, joined moments later by four more P-51s from the 4th Squadron. Two minutes later, another formation of 15 IAR-80 fighters mistakenly identified as Fw-190s dived on the American fighters. Dogfights broke out all over the sky.

Over the next 20 minutes, 12 enemy fighters were destroyed, with five claimed by 2nd Squadron's pilots and seven by the 4th's. Dan Zoerb's victory made him the newest ace in the 2nd Squadron. Captain Bob Curtis and Lieutenants Dennis Riddle and Dick Lampe claimed one Bf-109 each; Lieutenants Jack Schneider and Willard Pretzer shared the last Bf-109.

Mission leader Tim Tyler and Lieutenant Frank Tribbett led the 4th's claims with two Bf-109s each; Lieutenants George Goettelman, Bob McCampbell, and Ted Bullock destroyed one IAR-80 each, claimed as "Fw-190s."

The 4th's Lieutenant Ted Bullock wrote about the mission:

Boy! What a day this was. Had a mission to Ploești. As we neared the target, we encountered more E/A than I've ever seen before. All types

– 109s, 190s, MA 205s and MA 200s. Really a sight. Dogfights all over hell, parachutes, flares, and what-not. I was in McCampbell's flight. We got into a hell of a scrap with some MA 205s. Mac got one, spun him in. I took a couple of 90 degrees deflection shots. I didn't see anything, but Mac confirmed one for me when we got back. Said he blew all to hell. Tribbett got two, Tyler two, George one also. We lost Burwell somewhere in the deal. The 2nd got five, the 5th none, lost one each.

The mission was Bob Curtis' introduction to the P-51D; he wrote about it after the war: "This was my first mission in a P-51D with a bubble canopy that provided such wonderful visibility, but somehow fouled up the air flow in a high speed dive and produced a porpoising effect that helped the diving 109s and 190s to get away. As C.O. I got the first D model on 18 June, but was never smart enough to give it up after learning of its limitations." Curtis was flying the early P-51D-5, which lacked the later dorsal fin extension that largely solved the directional stability problem.

With the 12 victories scored in this mission, the 52nd Group set a new Fifteenth Air Force record for victories in a month – 102. The record came at the cost of losing Lieutenants F.B. Fisher from the 5th Squadron, D.C. Robinette from the 2nd Squadron, and G.N. Burwell from the 4th Squadron, all over Romania.

The Checkertails also flew the Ploeşti mission. Herky Green recalled, "We always expected a fight from the Germans when we went to Ploeşti and we were not disappointed." As they approached the target, they ran into 35 enemy fighters turning to attack the bombers. "I saw three Me 109s heading toward the bombers. I pushed my nose down and started after them. I came down on the last plane and fired a long burst into it. I could see hits all along the fuselage and engine. The 109 burst into flames and started spinning toward the ground, out of control." The victory was number 15 for Green. Four enemy aircraft were claimed. Lieutenants Edward L. Mueller, Peter C. Osterhus, and David C. Hanson were all seen to parachute successfully after they were shot down.

With the improving weather, the 31st flew a fighter sweep to Bucharest on June 24, but only one enemy fighter was spotted; it was quickly claimed by the 307th's Second Lieutenant Dave Mann.

The Air Sea Rescue patrols that day – which were normally "quiet duty" – found the most action of all. The 309th's Lieutenants Frederick L. Bohl and William H. Schanning were attacked by 30-plus Bf-109s over the Adriatic off Ancona. They turned and ran for home, outrunning the enemy fighters. A short time later, group flying exec Lieutenant Colonel Yancy E. Tarrant and the 307th's Lieutenants Don H. Pensinger and Lance J. Kerwin were chased by the same group of enemy fighters, which they also successfully outran.

The Checkertails ran across 36 enemy fighters north of Bucharest; five Bf-109s and IAR-80s were shot down, with First Lieutenant Wayne Lowry claiming a Bf-109 and an Fw-190 (a misidentified IAR-80). Art Fiedler latched on to his first enemy fighter – a Bf-109 – and managed a "probable."

The 52nd also came up dry on the June 24 mission; several pilots ran so low on fuel that they had to land at other airfields in Italy to refuel. Their June 25 mission to France was also recorded as a "milk run."

On June 25, Group CO Colonel McCorkle led the 31st on a mission covering the B-24s of the 49th Bomb Wing as they hit bridges and marshaling yards near Avignon. Approaching Avignon, the Mustangs ran across a formation of nine enemy fighters that stayed to fight. McCorkle scored his 11th victory, a Bf-109, while First Lieutenant Robert E. Riddle scored victory number five – another Bf-109 – and First Lieutenant Carl H. Brown shot down his first. Neither of the other two squadrons saw any action.

June 26 proved to be an unlucky day for the Luftwaffe when defending fighters rose to meet the 31st and the B-24s of the 55th Bomb Wing they were escorting to bomb the marshaling yards in Vienna. Thirty Me-410s with an escort of 20 Bf-109s were spotted when the Mustangs arrived at the rendezvous point. Major Samuel J. Brown, who was leading the 307th Squadron, dived into the Me-410s with wingman Flight Officer Edward Jay, breaking up their formation. Brown scored two destroyed while Jay destroyed one before the enemy knew what had hit them. Clawing his way up to the Bf-109 escorts, Brown hit one that immediately fell off and traced a smoky trail to the ground below. The rest of the Bf-109s broke and dived for the deck while Brown and Jay turned back to go after the confused formation of twin-engine fighters; Brown destroyed a third Me-410, his fourth victory of the mission, as Jay knocked down the wingman for his second victory.

The Bf-109s that broke for the deck did not get away; the rest of the 307th fell on them, chasing the enemy fighters over the treetops. Lieutenant Dave Mann got one before he was attacked in turn by another, which shot him down as his element leader, First Lieutenant William E. Schanning, went after another Bf-109.

The 308th Squadron had mixed results. John Voll shot down victories two and three for his scoreboard. Squadron operations officer Captain Thomas W. Byrnes destroyed one Bf-109 and then was shot down while going after a second; he went in on fire from 2,000 feet and the Mustang exploded when it hit the ground.

The 309th Squadron claimed three, with Flight Officer Charles W. Bratton and First Lieutenant George G. Loving Jr. credited with a Bf-109 each, while Lieutenants John W. Shropshire and George Warren shared credit for a third Bf-109.

Of the 16 claims, credit for nine put the 307th Squadron in the group lead with 122 victories to date. Major Brown now had 13.5 victories, putting him second behind the Checkertails' Herky Green, the current MTO top ace with 15.

The 52nd Group's action started with an attack on B-24s of the 304th Bomb Wing by three Bf-109s over Lake Balaton. They were spotted by Ted Bullock, who was leading a flight of the 4th Squadron for the first time; he broke up the attack before they got to the bombers – shooting down one – and later wrote in his diary:

> Had a mission to Vienna today. I led my first flight and got a 109. Chased three of them right through the bombers and really shot him up. Glycol and smoke streaming from him and he went straight in. After I'd shot him, I pulled up and a P-51 made head-on pass at me and shot a bunch of holes in my right wing. Got back without too much trouble. Tyler got 2, and Frye 1. The 2nd got 4, 5th got 7. No losses.

The Bf-109 was Bullock's second of an eventual 15. The running battle with the enemy interceptors lasted 35 minutes. The wild nature of the fight is shown in the claims for Bf-109s, Bf-110s, Me-410s, and Ju-88s.

On June 26 the Checkertails met the Eighth Air Force bombers that had flown their first Russia shuttle mission when they bombed the marshaling yards at Debrecen, Hungary and provided escort to Italy. Green recalled, "It was a quiet mission with no incidents." The Checkertails welcomed the arrival of Major Deacon Hively's 334th Squadron of the Eighth Air Force's 4th Fighter Group, which stayed for several days.

The 82nd Group experienced their best single day's score to date on the Vienna mission, despite the fact that by the time they encountered their first enemy aircraft over Lake Balaton, the force was down to only 26 Lightnings due to four mechanical aborts and the failure of six pilots from the 97th Squadron to join back up after losing the formation in a turn en route. The enemy fighters that the group came across over Lake Balaton made passes to try to get the Lightnings to drop their underwing tanks, which the Americans refused to do. The main formation of 50 Bf-110s, Me-210s, and Me-410s showed up 20 minutes later, coming in from the northwest for a diving attack on the bombers. Two Me-410s that made a pass on the 96th Squadron were met head-on, with one going down destroyed and one breaking off damaged. The main force then dived on the Americans in groups of four to six in trail. The 95th and 97th Squadrons intercepted them before they got to the bombers. The enemy tried to evade the P-38s by diving for the deck but the Lightnings easily caught up with them. In a 12-minute battle over the treetops, 12 were shot down and five damaged. The total score for the 82nd was 14 destroyed, with the 95th Squadron leading the score with nine; Lieutenant Holloway shot down two Me-410s and a Bf-110 to make ace with five victories. Paul Mass recalled when shooting down his Bf-109, "The pilot jettisoned his canopy, then pushed himself up and out, threw his left leg over the side and rolled out head first. He did a half somersault, coming right toward me and I thought 'He's going into my left prop!' He went past my cockpit, between the left engine and the nacelle, a foot away from the prop. I'm sure he also thought he was going to hit me." The 95th Squadron mission leader, First Lieutenant Ray Allen, and his wingman, Second Lieutenant Allen Wisner, were shot down in the fight.

June 27 saw the weather continuing to be good over Italy when the 31st escorted bombers to Budapest, where it turned out the weather was so poor that 30 enemy fighters lurking in the 9/10ths clouds were able to bounce the 308th Squadron as the Mustangs neared the target. In the wild fight that followed, First Lieutenant Joseph B. Sheehan destroyed an Me-410 and probably shot down a Bf-110 that he was forced to break away from when he came under attack from another enemy fighter. John Voll shot down a Bf-109, while Lieutenants Goebel and Goehausen shared a Bf-110. In the confusion, Major Charles Lamont was heard to call he was bailing out, never to be seen again, while Lieutenant William J. Baetjer, recently returned from a bailout over Yugoslavia, was seen to bail out over the target, this time being taken prisoner.

The 309th's Captain Murray McLaughlin destroyed a Ju-88 while Lieutenant Maurice Cloutier destroyed an Me-410. The 307th Squadron became separated from the group in the clouds and missed the fight.

The 52nd Group also flew the Budapest mission. The 2nd Squadron found success in the cloudy sky when they came across a formation of Bf-110s forming up to attack the bombers and claimed ten destroyed. The height of the success was Sully Varnell's claim for three Bf-110s, raising his score to 12. James Hoffman and Frank Grey claimed two 110s each.

The mission of June 28, in which the group escorted B-24s of the 55th Bomb Wing to hit the Bucharest marshaling yards again, was frustrating for the Mustang pilots. Thirty enemy aircraft were spotted over the target by pilots in the 307th, but when the P-51s turned toward them, they dived away. The 308th's pilots spotted six to seven Bf-109s that stayed out of range. The 309th made up for the other squadrons' frustrations when Major Vic Warford shot down one of two Bf-109s that dived through the squadron formation to go after the bombers, while his wingman, Lieutenant Stanley J. Vashina, probably destroyed the other, which disappeared in haze.

The 52nd also managed to find a few enemy fighters in the hazy sky and claimed two destroyed. Bob Curtis wrote about the fight in his diary that night:

> I was Red Leader on bomber escort when, near Bucharest at 28,000 feet about 1100 hours, we saw six E/A at 3 o'clock attacking the bombers. I called a turn and dropped tanks and we started toward the bombers. As we approached them, 12 Me 109s passed us at 12 o'clock, slightly below. Blue Flight attacked the E/A while my flight provided top cover. (There was no dogfight as these 109s quickly fled the scene when they saw Blue Flight pursuing them.) Shortly after a Me 109 passed in front of me from 2 o'clock to 12 o'clock. I chased

it and closed slowly in a dive. I fired a burst at 300 yards, slowing it down. I fired another burst at 200 yards and then overran the E/A. He turned into me and opened fire but stalled out and crashed in a field.

First Lieutenant Frank Empey scored his fifth victory and wrote about it later: "I was Number 4 in Yellow flight. We were at 28,000 feet SW of Bucharest headed north when two Me 109s passed under us from 9 o'clock to 3 o'clock. We turned and dived on them. I fired a couple of bursts at one Me 109. It was way out of range, but I saw four strikes on the tail and wings. The Me 109 leveled out slightly at 18,000 feet, then to my surprise the pilot bailed out."

On return from this mission, the 31st found themselves playing host to the Mustangs of the Eighth Air Force's 4th Fighter Group, who were returning to England via Italy after flying the second Operation *Frantic* mission. Entertainment for both groups was provided that night with a screening of gun camera film from the Budapest mission while the 309th's pilots enjoyed their beer ration day: four bottles of cold American beer each. Fortunately for hangovers, weather canceled the next day's mission.

The Checkertails also flew this mission and ran into all the action the others had missed. North of Bucharest they encountered a large formation of Bf-109s and IAR-80s of the Romanian Air Force. In a wide-ranging fight, the group claimed 17 destroyed; Flight Officer Robert H. Brown was the top scorer with three Bf-109s, followed by Art Fiedler who claimed two Bf-109s destroyed, along with Second Lieutenant J.J. Stacy who also scored two Bf-109s. First Lieutenants Wayne Lowry, Paul Jensen, and George Sweeney, along with Second Lieutenant Barrie Davis and Flight Officer Phillip Sangermano, claimed an IAR-80 destroyed each. Second Lieutenants William Murphy, P.J. Kastner, and John M. Simmons each claimed a Bf-109 destroyed.

The 31st's last mission of the month on June 30 would have set a record for distance, escorting B-24s 650 miles one way to Blechhammer in occupied Poland. However, by the time the Mustangs arrived at the rendezvous point over Lake Balaton in Hungary, the weather had deteriorated to the point that the bombers they were assigned to cover abandoned the original mission and bombed what the fighter pilots described as "some obscure little town in Austria." The only enemy aircraft encountered were two Bf-109s that dived through the formation and disappeared into the clouds without a shot being fired.

The 52nd Group also flew the Blechhammer mission. Their bombers stayed the course and bombed the synthetic oil plants; there was no enemy aerial opposition. The 5th Squadron became separated from the rest of the group on the return and ran into a mixed formation of Bf-109s and Fw-190s, claiming two of each destroyed. These brought the group's score for the six weeks they had been flying Mustangs to 133 destroyed.

The Checkertails provided withdrawal support for the bombers and found the enemy in their part of the formation also unwilling to contest their flight home.

In retrospect, June 1944 could be seen as the decisive month, the time when Things Changed. Within a month of the "blackest day" on June 10, the Romanian Air Force had suffered decisive losses to its leading fighter units, with 56 of its top pilots killed or wounded. Fifteenth Air Force had received all the promised bomb groups, and the P-51 Mustang force had grown, allowing the Ploești campaign to grow and expand, making full use of these resources. It was overshadowed by the world-changing news from Normandy, but the result of the battles in eastern Europe that happened simultaneously to the invasion were crucial for the success of Operation *Overlord*.

7

RED TAILS

Lieutenant Colonel William Momyer, commander of the 33rd Fighter Group, had not wanted the African American-manned 99th Squadron in his unit and had done everything he could to belittle them and set them up for failure while they were part of it. Following the successful conclusion of the Sicilian campaign, Momyer wrote a memorandum to General Hap Arnold, Chief of the USAAF, regarding what he claimed was the poor performance of the 99th, which he specifically stated to be the result of the squadron being manned by African Americans who were unable to fulfill the role of pilots as well as could white men. He cited the poor record in air-to-air combat, difficulties with maintaining the squadron operationally, and command deficiencies on the part of the squadron commander and senior flight leaders. He further claimed that the squadron did not fight as a team, broke formation when attacked, chose to attack undefended targets instead of the briefed defended targets, avoided bad weather and, in general, performed poorly. He closed by stating: "It is my opinion that they are not of the fighting calibre of any squadron in this group. They have failed to display the aggressiveness and daring for combat that are necessary for a first-class fighting organisation. It may be expected that we will get less work and less operational time out of the 99th FS [Fighter Squadron] than any squadron in this group."

Momyer then carefully sent the memo up the chain of command in an effort to obtain as much written agreement by senior air force commanders as possible by the time it reached Arnold's desk. Momyer's immediate superior, Brigadier General Edwin House, Commander of XII Air Support Command, agreed and took responsibility for the memo, which became known from that point as the "House Memorandum"; the report was sent up to and endorsed by Major General John Cannon, deputy commander of the Northwest African Tactical Air Force. Cannon sent it on to Lieutenant General Carl Spaatz, deputy commander of the Mediterranean Allied Air Forces, who added his opinion that the 99th should be reassigned to coastal patrol duty in a location such as the Panama Canal Zone.

When the memo was leaked in Washington, "all hell broke loose" in the memory of Gladwin Hill, at the time the Associated Press' "Man with the Eighth" who was home on leave. Major Benjamin O. Davis, commander of the 99th Squadron, was called to testify before a Congressional committee evaluating the 99th's performance and the viability of the Tuskegee Program, which trained the first non-white pilots and ground crew of the USAAF.

Like all congressional committees in the Democratic-majority Congress at that time, this committee was chaired by a white Democrat from the South and included several others as senior members. Their power in Congress came from seniority created by the one-party "Solid South", based on "Jim Crow" white supremacy and the exclusion of African Americans from political and social involvement, in what was later called "American Apartheid," which was cited by the Nazis when they came to power as the model for excluding Jews and other groups in Germany. It was also significant that the majority of the senior officer corps of the American military at this time were from the South and equally committed to the policy of "Jim Crow." The press supported that view without question. After the memorandum was leaked in Washington, a *Time* magazine cover story was titled "Experiment Proved?" Its thesis was that the 99th might be disbanded on the strength of the House Memorandum.

Davis departed Pantelleria to return to Washington on September 2, 1943. He later explained, "I was absolutely enraged. I was sure that all the aces were held by the Army Air Force, especially with the correspondence going up through channels the way it did, and the statement by General House that a Negro didn't possess the physical qualifications that would make him a good fighter pilot."

When Davis left, George "Spanky" Roberts assumed command of the 99th while Lemuel Custis became operations officer. The same day that Davis left for the United States, advance elements of the 99th moved from Licata to the Italian mainland following the Allied landings at Salerno. They were assigned as a fourth squadron to the 79th Fighter Group, a white unit that still flew P-40s, commanded by Colonel Earl Bates, who held different beliefs from Momyer and who dealt with the men of the 99th no differently than he did with the other, white, squadrons. The 99th's combat experience changed considerably. The 79th's war diaries never mention the skin color of the 99th's pilots. Colonel Bates made sure that the squadron routinely flew missions with the others; he assigned the 99th's pilots to lead mixed formations of aircraft from all four squadrons.

In Washington, Davis testified before Congress in early January 1944. Accustomed to remaining publicly composed in the face of overt racism, he reacted strongly to the biased questions of the congressional interrogators, and stated with some passion that the pilots and crewmen of the 99th Squadron were "no different from any other Americans at war in other USAAF squadrons," and that their performance was the equal of other units manned by white personnel. He later said, "I recall saying something to the effect that overseas, the reception given to black people on the ground was much more pleasant and more favorable than the reception given to black people on the ground here in the United States. I also stressed the determination of the members of the 99th to demonstrate their abilities and set the stage for the oncoming combat units that were still training in the states."

He further explained that the 99th had received only 26 pilots since being formed, as compared to 30–35 pilots assigned to the other fighter squadrons in the same period, pointing out that this shortage meant his pilots flew up to six sorties per day, more than the sortie rate for white pilots, and contributing to operational exhaustion of his fliers. He detailed the fact that the ground-attack missions assigned to the 99th Squadron meant the pilots were less likely to encounter enemy aircraft, accounting for the low air-to-air score.

After hearing Davis' testimony, General Arnold stated publicly that he would take no action until an official study was completed comparing the performance of the 99th Fighter Squadron with that of other P-40 units in the Twelfth Air Force, to establish whether the criticism in the House Memorandum was accurate. Arnold himself was still not convinced that black aviators could perform well in combat, and privately advocated their relocation to a rear defense area as suggested by his long-time friend and comrade Spaatz.

Fortunately, editing the subsequent report became the duty of Colonel Emmett M. "Rosie" O'Donnell, chief of Arnold's Advisory Council and even then a "legend" in the USAAF. Most importantly, O'Donnell was not a Southerner. Born in Brooklyn, New York in 1906, he had joined the Air Corps in 1930 following graduation from West Point in 1928. In 1941, he had pioneered the dangerous flights through Japanese-controlled airspace in the Central Pacific to bring the B-17s of the 14th Bomb Squadron from Hawaii to the Philippines before Pearl Harbor. He had established an outstanding combat record in the battles to defend the Philippines and the Dutch East Indies following the outbreak of war on December 7, 1941, serving as operations officer of the Far East Air Force, and had earned the DFC on December 10, 1941 for attacking a Japanese heavy cruiser and its escorting destroyer in one of the surviving B-17s.

Bucking the opinions of superior officers, when O'Donnell finished editing the report, he included a cover memo, in which he "urgently recommended that this entire subject be reconsidered," pointing out the absurdity of racial discrimination in wartime, and observing that one to four squadrons were "but a drop in the overall war effort." He concluded, "I feel that submitting such a proposal (to disband the 99th) to the President at this time would definitely not be appreciated by him. He would probably interpret it as indicating a serious lack of understanding of the broad problems facing the country."

The edited report was released on March 30, 1944. It concluded that the 99th Fighter Squadron had performed as well as the white P-40 squadrons with which it flew in combat. President Franklin Roosevelt never saw the report. Davis said of the events, "If that G-3 evaluation had not been made, God knows what would have happened." The 99th was allowed to stay in combat.

According to Davis, the report had a secondary effect. "It eventually sent us to the Fifteenth Air Force, and took us out of the nasty, dirty close air support business, and put us into a sort of glamour business – escorting bombers. Sometimes things turn out for the best, and that's exactly what happened." Following his successful defense of the

99th Squadron's combat record, Davis was promoted to lieutenant colonel and assigned as CO of the newly formed 332nd Group, composed of the 100th, 301st, and 302nd Fighter Squadrons, manned by graduates of the Tuskegee Program.

On January 2, 1944, 332nd Group personnel loaded aboard a transport, headed for Italy, arriving in Taranto on February 3. The three squadrons were initially assigned to Montecorvino airfield, where they found themselves flying war-weary P-39 Airacobras on coastal patrols from Palermo to the Ponziane Islands, the mission that General Spaatz had privately suggested as the best utilization of pilots he refused to consider "qualified for combat." On February 15, 1944, two P-39s from the 100th Squadron were vectored to intercept a Ju-88 over Naples. Unfortunately, the enemy bomber easily outclimbed the clapped-out Airacobras and accelerated into the distance, disappearing in the clouds. Davis renewed his efforts to obtain a "clean" combat assignment for the group.

On February 21, the 100th Squadron was transferred to Capodichino airfield, where the 99th Squadron was operating successfully as part of the 79th Group. The 100th continued flying coastal patrols, made even harder for the pilots as they watched pilots of the 99th Squadron fly combat missions over the Anzio beachhead. They were joined by the 301st and 302nd Squadrons on April 15. On April 25, the first P-47s – castoffs from the 325th Checkertails who were now re-equipping with the P-51B Mustang – arrived. Their yellow-and-black Checkertail Clan markings were quickly painted red overall, the new group identification marking for the 332nd; due to this marking, they were destined to become known as the "Red Tails." On April 30, ten more Checkertail Clan P-47s arrived and the 332nd began full-on conversion training.

By late May, they were considered qualified on the Thunderbolts. Their first operational assignments were strafing missions flown in support of the troops of VI Corps as they finally broke out of the Anzio beachhead. On May 27, the group transferred to Ramitelli airfield, one of the outlying airfields of the Foggia complex, where they were finally transferred to the Fifteenth Air Force.

Over the course of June, the 332nd flew escort missions for Fifteenth Air Force bombers to northern Italy and Yugoslavia. Their first escort mission was flown on June 8 escorting bombers to the city of Pola; no enemy opposition was encountered. That was not the case the next day,

June 9. Thirty-nine P-47s of the 301st and 302nd Squadrons departed Ramitelli at 0700 hours and rendezvoused with the 5th, 49th, 55th, 57th, and 304th Bomb Wings, for targets in Munich, Germany.

Four Bf-109s dived on a group of Liberators as the formation approached Udine, resulting in a major dogfight. Completing their firing pass, the Bf-109s turned left, allowing Second Lieutenant Wendell Pruitt to latch onto one. He later described the fight: "As the Jerries passed under me, I rolled over, shoved everything forward, dove and closed on one at 475 mph. I gave him a short burst of machine gun fire, and discovering that I was giving him too much lead, I waited as he shallowed out of a turn. Then I gave two long two-second bursts. His left wing erupted in flames." Pruitt's wingman witnessed the German pilot bail out; the Bf-109 exploded when it hit the ground.

Captain Ray E. "Red" Jackson spotted five or six Bf-109s "eleven o'clock high," and closed on them, losing the rest of the flight. He opened fire on one and it fell into a spin. Another Messerschmitt made a head-on pass. The P-47 stalled when pulled up and the Bf-109 was quickly on his tail. As Jackson maneuvered to escape the enemy fire, First Lieutenant Charles Bussey – leading eight P-47s – caught up with the four remaining Bf-109s. Second Lieutenant William Green fired at Jackson's pursuer, followed an instant later by Bussey, whose fire blew the tail off the enemy fighter. Back at base, Bussey's wingman reported he saw the pilot bail out and the fighter explode, resulting in Bussey and Green sharing the victory.

Unaware he'd been saved, Jackson pushed his throttle "through the gate," activating the P-47's water injection system, and accelerated into some low clouds in a last desperate attempt to evade his pursuer. Emerging from the clouds, Jackson spotted another Bf-109 and turned into it. When he opened fire, hitting the enemy fighter's belly, he recalled, "Metal flew off his left side, then the Nazi pilot bailed out over a German airfield." Dropping to treetop level, Jackson headed for home.

Meanwhile, Lieutenant Frederick Funderberg spotted two Bf-109s 500 feet below at "nine o'clock." Followed by his wingman, Funderberg dived on them, firing a quick burst that caused pieces to fly off his target. As the flight passed under the enemy fighters, he and his wingman found themselves face to face with a second pair of Bf-109s. Funderberg fired a quick burst and the P-47's eight machine guns tore one of the German fighters apart.

Simultaneously, Second Lieutenant Robert Wiggins spotted a Bf-109 to his left at the same altitude; he turned into it and fired a full deflection burst. Pieces came off the enemy fighter, but the pilot made a quick shallow dive to gain speed, then zoomed up and climbed away.

The five victories came against the death of Second Lieutenant Cornelius Rogers, while the P-47s of Captain Floyd Rayford and Second Lieutenant William Hunter were damaged by flak that also superficially wounded Rayford.

The Thunderbolts began arriving back at Ramitelli, where Republic tech reps and two senior officers from Fifteenth Air Force Headquarters had been lecturing pilots about the P-47's peculiarities. A major was telling the pilots – whom he called "boys" – that they should avoid a slow roll in a P-47 below 1,000 feet due to its weight. As he said that, Wendell Pruitt and wingman Lee Archer – known as "the Gruesome Twosome" – screamed across the field wingtip to wingtip on the deck; they pulled up over the assembly, throwing the Thunderbolts into slow victory rolls. As they recovered and entered the landing pattern, the indignant major screamed at them, "You can't do that!" Looking at the smiling crowd of pilots, he climbed down from the truck he was standing on and stalked off.

On June 11, the 301st and 302nd Squadrons sent 30 P-47s to cover the 5th and 55th Bomb Wings' raid on Smedervo, Yugoslavia. Bombing results were good, though there was no enemy air opposition. Two days later, on June 13, the two squadrons flew a 32-plane mission, escorting the 5th and 49th Bomb Wings to Munich. Again, the Luftwaffe appeared over Udine, but only four of the 11 enemy fighters made any attempt to attack the formation. One P-47 was damaged, but the bombers were successfully protected with no losses.

The June 14 mission to Budapest found the Luftwaffe's response even less enthusiastic. Twenty-nine P-47s from the 301st and 302nd Squadrons escorted the 5th, 49th, 55th, and 304th Bomb Wings. While 15 Bf-109s and seven Me-210 twin-engine fighters were spotted, they made no attempt to attack either the bombers or their escorts.

Another long-range mission was flown on June 16 when 40 P-47s from all three squadrons of the 332nd covered a maximum effort against targets in the Bratislava area. The Red Tails were responsible for escorting the bombers from Banja Luka to the target. After a break caused by rainy weather in mid-month, the group flew escort for another maximum-strength mission to Bucharest–Giurgiu in Romania. Both missions passed without incident, to the frustration of the group's pilots.

June 23 saw the uneventful long-distance trips north come to an end. The operational order that day sent 41 P-47s from the 100th, 301st, and 302nd Squadrons on a low-level strafing attack to northwestern Italy against the Airasca-Pinerolo landing ground, which was strategically located a mile west of Airasca in the Piedmont region, led by 100th Squadron commander Captain Robert Tresville. The mission was beset by problems from the start, when Gwynne Peirson's P-47 crashed on takeoff, though he survived. As they flew north, four other P-47s aborted, leaving only 36 Thunderbolts in formation when they flew across the Tyrrhenian Sea at an altitude of less than 100 feet in hopes of taking the target by surprise.

The air was hazy over the water, with a cloud base less than 1,000 feet, through which very bright glare from the sun created glittering reflections on the water. As they approached Cape Corse, pilots found it exceedingly difficult to see the horizon through the haze and sun glare on the water below. Suddenly, Second Lieutenant Sam Jefferson dropped his Thunderbolt too low; the fighter caught a prop tip on the water that flipped it into the water, where it exploded on impact.

Moments later, Lieutenant Earl Sherrard's P-47 pancaked into the sea below; fortunately, he was able to scramble out before his fighter sank and was later picked up by Air Sea Rescue. Second Lieutenant Charles B. Johnson circled Sherrard's sinking fighter trying to see if he was still alive, and flew into the shimmering water. Sadly, the Thunderbolt sank almost immediately, taking Johnson down with it.

A few minutes later, mission leader Tresville, leading Lieutenants Dempsey Morgan and Spurgeon Ellington as the second section, looked out and saw his wingman, Second Lieutenant Willard L. Woods, dropping so close to the water that his wing tanks were beginning to kick up rooster-tails of spray. Tresville frantically gestured at Woods to pull up. Woods looked over in time to see Tresville's P-47 hit the water, stripping off his drop tanks and ripping the ailerons off while the propeller bent back over the cowling. The fighter bounced off the water back into the air momentarily, then it plunged back into the water, leaving only the tail out of the water. Woods reported that Tresville appeared to be looking at a map when it happened. Radio silence kept the deputy formation leader from learning of Tresville's loss, which prevented his assuming navigational responsibilities. The pilots never found the target and turned back.

Tresville was the only black West Pointer in the group other than Colonel Davis and was well liked. His loss was keenly felt by all. Samuel Curtis remembered him, "Tresville was a fantastic guy. He was smart, he was bright, he was strong, he was well coordinated. He would have gone far." Captain Andrew "Jug" Turner assumed command of the 100th Squadron following Tresville's death.

The mission to Sofia on June 23 met no opposition. Two days later, the three 322nd Group squadrons sent 20 P-47s in five flights on a long-range strafing mission to attack troops in Yugoslavia. When Freddie Hutchins' left drop tank failed to release, he and wingman Larry Wilkins were forced to return early to Ramitelli. Lieutenants Wendell Pruitt and Gwynne Peirson continued on; however, strong winds forced them off course and they missed the troop concentration despite searching for some 15 minutes. They turned back for Ramitelli.

Near the port of Trieste, they spotted what they identified as a "German destroyer" steaming from the port. In reality, this was the former Italian World War I destroyer *Giuseppe Missori*, which the Kriegsmarine had taken over and converted to a large torpedo boat, designated *TA-22*. The two made a strafing run on the ship, which set it smoking from a small fire. Lieutenants Joseph Elsberry, Joseph Lewis, and Charles Dunne, who were also returning to Ramitelli, spotted the smoke and turned to investigate. They joined up with Pruitt and Peirson, who were circling to make a second attack, and the six Thunderbolts strafed the ship, setting fires. At that point, Elsberry, Lewis, and Dunne flew toward Trieste while Pruitt and Peirson decided to make one more pass since the ship was now on fire. The two then joined up with the others over Trieste, where the Thunderbolts strafed installations around the harbor, and shot up several trucks and the wharf at nearby Muggio. A sailboat that fired on them off Isola was strafed and sunk.

On return to Ramitelli, Pruitt and Peirson reported that the ship was left "sinking." In fact, while it was heavily damaged, *TA-22* did not sink, though it also never fought again. It was towed back to port, where it was decommissioned in November 1944. In April 1945, with Allied armies approaching, *TA-22* was scuttled.

The next day, June 26, 36 Thunderbolts from the 301st and 302nd Squadrons escorted a maximum effort mission to the Lake Balaton area of Hungary. Two flight leaders were forced to abandon their war-weary thunderbolts fighters due to mechanical problems. First Lieutenant Andrew Maples bailed out near Termoli, on the outbound leg, and was rescued; unfortunately, First Lieutenant Maurice V. Esters, who bailed out near Vetacandrija, was never seen again.

The mission on June 27 saw 37 Thunderbolts from the same two squadrons escort the 5th and 47th Bomb Wings to Budapest; although no enemy aircraft were encountered, the P-47s flown by Lieutenants Larry Wilkins and Washington Ross were damaged in a collision after landing back at Ramitelli. On June 28, a similar mission escorted the 304th Bomb Wing to the Ferdinand area in northern Italy. Again, there were problems with the increasingly weary Thunderbolts. During takeoff, Lieutenant Edward Laird's P-47 left the runway and crashed, killing him. First Lieutenant Mac Ross survived an emergency landing at Lecce airfield when his engine failed. First Lieutenant Floyd Thompson was forced to bail out near Forli when his engine failed; he was immediately taken prisoner on landing by nearby German troops. First Lieutenant Alfonso Davis suffered a blown tire on takeoff but was able to lift off successfully and fly the mission; returning home, he successfully force-landed in an open field near Otranto.

The last day of June saw the full group escort five bomb wings attacking targets in Vienna. Of the 45 P-47s that took off, there were only two aborts, a vast improvement over the mechanical woes two days earlier. Again, the mission proceeded without any encounters with defending enemy fighters.

While the 332nd had started receiving unpainted "bubbletop" P-47D-30s to replace the older "Razorbacks," this mission became their final one flying Thunderbolts. Cast-off P-51B and C model Mustangs from the Checkertails had started arriving over the last ten days of June, supplemented by others from the 31st Fighter Group as the two veteran Mustang groups received new P-51Ds. Checkertail leading ace Herky Green recalled later, after delivering Mustangs to the group, that, "I thought it was a crying shame. These guys were being given our clapped-out fighters again and were expected to fly them in combat. And they were happy to get them."

Over the month of June, the 332nd's pilots had fulfilled everything Benjamin O. Davis had said about them in his Washington testimony, and had done so flying aircraft that were not in top condition. In 20 missions over 30 days, pilots of the 332nd had been credited with five enemy fighters destroyed in air combat, and successfully protected the bombers they were escorting with only four losses. The pilots were now experienced fighter escorts. The experience gained would pay dividends over the next two months as the campaign against Ploești reached its climax.

On July 3, the 99th Squadron was assigned to the 332nd. The assignment was bitterly resisted by the pilots and crews of the 99th, who had flown as part of regular air force groups they had integrated by joining, where they had proven themselves by their combat record. They saw being transferred to a segregated unit as a demotion. For their part, the pilots of the 332nd feared that the group's leadership positions would go to the more experienced 99th Squadron pilots; however, this did not happen. While the 332nd became the only four-squadron group in XV Fighter Command, a situation that put more pressure on group commander Benjamin O. Davis, a bigger problem was that the Tuskegee Program would prove unable to produce enough pilots for all four squadrons and the 477th Medium Bombardment Group then forming. The result was that combat tours in the 332nd would be much longer than in the other groups in the command.

By early July 1944, the 332nd's Thunderbolts had all been replaced with P-51B/C Mustangs, which were much better suited to the long-range escort missions that the group was assigned by XV Fighter Command. Several early accidents during the transition were traced to pilots attempting aerobatic maneuvers with the fuselage tank filled to the point that it affected the center of gravity, which moved beyond the rear limit, leading to loss of control. The same thing had happened to the other three Mustang groups in the Fifteenth when they initially converted. The problem disappeared soon after pilots received instruction regarding safe conditions for initiating aerobatics. Like all other Mustang groups in the ETO and MTO, the 332nd adopted the operating policy of switching to the fuselage tank after takeoff and using that fuel before switching to drop tanks and wing tanks.

The Mustang's arrival coincided with Colonel Davis' difficult decision to relieve Major Charles DeBow from command of the 301st Squadron,

B-24 Liberators drop their bomb loads on the Concordia Vega refinery at Ploești during Operation *Tidal Wave*, August 1, 1943. (USAF Official)

P-38s of the 14th Fighter Group provided escort for the Ploești missions. (De Luan/Alamy Stock Photo)

B-24 "Sandman" flies away after a run on the Astra Română refinery in Ploești, as photographed by the automatic camera aboard "Sneezy," during Operation *Tidal Wave*. (USAF Official)

A B-24 Liberator flies over the Otopeni airfield in Romania during an attack on the airfield on August 26, 1944. (USAF Official)

Left Chetnik commander Draža Mihailović organized the rescue of American air crews shot down over Serbia in Yugoslavia and their return to Italy in 1944.
(USAF Official)

Below In August 1944, Romanian Air Force leading ace Prince Constantin "Bâzu" Cantacuzino flew Lieutenant Colonel James Gunn, the senior American prisoner of war, to Foggia in Italy in his Bf-109G to arrange the evacuation of US and Allied prisoners of war as Romania prepared to surrender to the Soviets.
(USAF Official)

The Bf-109G flown by Prince Constantin Cantacuzino of the Romanian Air Force to take Lieutenant Colonel James Gunn to Italy. (USAF Official)

Ground crews of the 1st Fighter Group work on a P-38J Lightning. (piemags/Alamy Stock Photo)

A P-38J of the 1st Fighter Group flying over Italy. (piemags/Alamy Stock Photo)

31st Fighter Group commander Colonel Charles M. McCorkle (center) briefs group pilots. His P-51B "Betty Jane" – named for his wife – sports 11 of his final total of 12 victories. (USAF Official)

The 31st Fighter Group's Captain John J. Voll was the top-ranked USAAF fighter ace in the Fifteenth Air Force with 21 victories. His last Mustang was P-51D "American Beauty." (USAF Official)

A formation of P-51D Mustangs of the 31st Fighter Group's 508th Fighter Squadron fly formation for the photographer in October 1944. (USAF Official)

A P-51B Mustang of the 5th Fighter Squadron shows the distinctive yellow tail section adopted in October 1944 as identification of the 52nd Fighter Group. (USAF Official)

P-38J Lightnings of the 82nd Fighter Group fly formation for the photographer. The 82nd Group was the top-scoring P-38 group in the MTO. (ART Collection/Alamy Stock Photo)

Colonel Benjamin O. Davis, commander of the 332nd Fighter Group. He fought both the enemy and USAAF commander General Henry H. "Hap" Arnold to keep the 332nd on operations when those opposed to an African American unit in the Air Force accused the pilots of "not measuring up" in the spring of 1944. (USAF Official)

Major George "Spanky" Roberts, commander of the 332nd Fighter Group's 99th Fighter Squadron, led the Red Tails when group commander Colonel Benjamin O. Davis was recalled to Washington to defend the group to Air Force commanders. (USAF Official)

Captain Andrew "Jug" Turner, commander of 100th Fighter Squadron of the 332nd Fighter Group. (USAF Official)

Tuskegee Airmen: Pilots of the 332nd Fighter Group attend pre-mission briefing. (USAF Official)

Pilots of the 332nd Fighter Group's 99th Fighter Squadron in April 1945. (USAF Official)

The close working relationship of a pilot and his crew chief, shown here, was crucial to success. (piemags/Alamy Stock Photo)

replacing him with the 99th's Captain Lee Rayford, a combat veteran who had returned for a second tour. Davis' reason for this was that DeBow had failed to meet his expectations for "leadership in the air"; Davis also relieved Mac Ross – a fellow member of the first class of pilots to graduate from the Tuskegee Program – as the 301st's operations officer. A week after he was relieved, while engaged in a familiarization training flight, Ross' P-51 entered a shallow dive, then slammed into a hill; Ross died in the crash. Rumors flew through the group that the crash was a suicide; however, the accident's nature was suggestive of the plane's oxygen system having failed.

The 332nd flew its first Mustang mission on July 4, 1944. Colonel Davis led 40 P-51s from the three original squadrons, escorting the 5th and 47th Bomb Wings on a mission to southern France. Davis was forced to turn over flight lead to First Lieutenant Claude Govan when his radio failed. The next day the group put up 52 P-51s for another escort mission to southern France. Only two Bf-109s put in an appearance, failing to lure the Mustangs away from the bombers, and all aircraft returned safely; fuel shortage saw four Mustangs land on Corsica. On July 6, 37 P-51s took the 47th Bomb Wing to Latisana and Tagliamento–Casarsa in northern Italy. A fourth mission was flown on July 7, with 47 Mustangs covering the bombers on a mission to Vienna. Although the enemy failed to appear on these missions, the missions enabled the pilots to gain familiarity with the Mustang on longer flights, while the fact that large formations were put up on consecutive days spoke to the standard of maintenance the group demonstrated; this was a far cry from the early days of only two months previous, when the other three Mustang groups were lucky to keep half the original formation over the target following multiple aborts for mechanical difficulties. While the rest of the group flew these missions, the 99th Squadron received its first Mustangs.

The 332nd finally engaged in combat with the Luftwaffe during their fifth consecutive mission, flown on July 8. The three squadrons put up 46 Mustangs to escort the 304th Bomb Wing's attack on Münchendorf airfield. Twenty enemy fighters rose to oppose this. First intercepted by P-38s from the 82nd Group, one Bf-109 got through the Lightnings' formation and managed to attack First Lieutenant Earl S. Sherrard over the target, engaging him in a twisting fight that saw neither combatant attain a commanding edge. Sherrard wrung out his P-51 thoroughly before he was able to shake the Bf-109. Almost immediately, he was attacked by P-38s as the Bf-109 flew off. Eluding the Lightnings, Sherrard landed at the first Allied airfield he came across, his fuel and himself exhausted.

The weather held and the missions continued. On July 9, the group put up 32 P-51s from all three squadrons to finally go to Ploești, escorting the B-17s of the 47th Bomb Wing to hit the Concordia Vega Refinery. Although two Bf-109s and two "Fw-190s" (IAR-80s) were spotted, the 31st Group's Mustangs got there first and engaged the enemy fighters.

July 10 saw the 332nd begin a series of missions to soften up southern France for the coming invasion. The group's three squadrons put up 33 P-51s escorting 47th Bomb Wing B-17s attacking the Toulon submarine pens. Poor weather grounded the July 11 mission but on July 12 they escorted the 49th Bomb Wing's B-24s to bomb railroad marshaling yards in southern France and were jumped by 25 enemy fighters as the group crossed over the French coast.

In the battle, flight leader Joseph Elsberry engaged Fw-190s and shot down three. He spotted the first opponent as it made a pass on the bombers and started turning away. Elsberry turned toward the enemy fighter and hit it with a 30-degree deflection shot; the Fw-190 streamed heavy black smoke and fell off to the left. He then spotted a second Focke-Wulf as it turned in front and below him and dived toward the bomber formation. Elsberry put his Mustang into a 30-degree dive and rapidly closed on the fighter. As he moved into range, he opened fire and hit the enemy fighter's left wing, damaging the aileron and causing the Focke-Wulf to start a slow roll to the left. He closed on it as he continued to fire short bursts at it until it slammed into the ground attempting a split-ess to escape. Elsberry added power and climbed to re-enter the fight; a moment later he saw a third Fw-190 as it turned away from him to evade the Mustang. He drew a bead on it and fired a two-second burst that arced into his target at close to maximum range. The fighter fell off into a dive that the pilot made no attempt to pull out of, perhaps indicating he had been killed. It crashed and exploded, witnessed by Lieutenants Dunne and Friend.

Banking away, another Fw-190 shot past him in a steep dive. Elsberry flung his fighter to the right and followed. Opening fire, he found that only the guns in his left wing were operating, a common problem with the P-51B; pulling Gs in a fight could jam the ammo feeds. He booted right rudder to keep the Mustang aiming at the fleeing enemy fighter, and scored hits across the Focke-Wulf's left wing root. It started spiraling down, then straightened into a dive that the pilot never pulled out of and it exploded when it hit the ground.

While Elsberry was experiencing what he later recalled as his best day of the war, Lieutenant Harold Sawyer scored a confirmed kill, destroying an Fw-190 over Nîmes after it attacked the bomber stream. Six enemy fighters dived through the Liberator formation, then split-essed left, quickly followed by split-essing right to evade pursuers. Sawyer – who had dived after them – got into range and fired a burst at the last Focke-Wulf. He saw hits and the enemy fighter never pulled out of its second split-ess, slamming into the ground and exploding. An instant later, he spotted a second Fw-190 at ten o'clock, lining up to attack the bombers. Banking tight toward it, he gunned down this enemy fighter as well. In the midst of all this, Second Lieutenant George Rhodes was shot down; he bailed out near Viterbo, where he made contact with the resistance and returned to the group in August.

The next mission on July 13 saw the Red Tails return to Italian targets, with the three squadrons sending 37 Mustangs to escort two groups of B-24s of the 5th Bomb Wing, which bombed the Pinzano railroad bridge and the Vinzone viaduct.

On July 15, the 99th Squadron flew with the group for the first time on a mission to bomb the refineries at Ploești. The 61 P-51s escorted the 55th Bomb Wing. Their close escort of the bombers earned praise from the crews when they chased off eight Bf-109s harassing three straggling bombers near Kruševac. Colonel Davis had announced at the outset of bomber escort missions that the 332nd's primary mission was to "stay with the bombers, even if it meant protecting them with your life." This differed from the tactics pursued by the other Mustang groups, which had adopted the "free ranging" defense in which the pilots were free to attack enemy fighter formations spotted forming up before their attack, and to chase the attacking enemy as far as it took to shoot them down. While Davis' policy grated with some of the pilots, no one dared disobey him.

The next mission on July 17 saw the group return to southern France, flying escort for the Liberators of the 306th Bomb Wing to hit the

Avignon railroad marshaling yard and railroad bridge again. As on the previous mission, the Mustang pilots found the hunting good when 19 Bf-109s rose to challenge the Americans. Only three attacked the bombers, however, diving in at the B-24s in a line-astern formation from the bombers' "eight o'clock" position. The fighters split-essed when they spotted the P-51s descending on them, then made a series of left turns in an attempt to evade the pursuers. Lieutenants Luther "Quibbling" Smith, Robert "Dissipatin'" Smith and Larry Wilkins closed on the Bf-109s and shot them down, following them all the way to their final crashes.

Second Lieutenant Maceo Harris was in the thick of things and recalled:

> My flight leader and I went down on two bogies, and after they split-essed from me at about 18,000 ft, I pulled up all alone in a tight chandelle to the left. I tried to join another ship, but lost him when I peeled off on two more bogies that were after some bombers. The bogies turned steeply to the left, and P-51s were in the vicinity, so I kept on with the bombers because they were hitting the target. Flak was intense over the target, and I kept an eye on the B-24s for enemy fighters that might come in when the bombers left the area.

As the bombers left the target, Harris joined another P-51 and tried to contact him by radio. "My attempt was unsuccessful, so I peeled off alone on three bogies who were approaching a straggling bomber from the rear. They looked like P-51s, and I rocked my wings coming in." He recognized them as Bf-109s as they swung left away from the bomber. Harris maintained his distance as he circled the Liberator since the top turret gunner was firing at him. "When he stopped firing I came in very close to survey the flak damage. The number two engine was feathered and the number one was smoking moderately." Harris could receive the bomber on radio but it could not receive him. On learning the bomber's compass was shot out, he used hand signals to tell them they would be over Corsica in 40 minutes, and led the way. Arriving over Corsica, Harris could not raise "Blacktop" (the control tower). He buzzed the field several times to clear the runway, allowing the B-24 to make a two-wheel landing, then landed himself. "The B-24 pilot was Lieutenant Loerb from San Francisco.

He and the co-pilot appreciated my friendly aid, and kissed me after the manner of the French."

First Lieutenant Walter Palmer also experienced an eventful flight. After taking off through cloud cover, he failed to spot the rest of his flight as he circled over Ramitelli, so decided to catch up with them on his own. Over southern France, Palmer spotted an aircraft heading toward him, rocking its wings. He rocked his wings in answer. Rather than joining up from the side, the unidentified aircraft tried to "join up" from the rear as Palmer kept his eyes on his new "wingman." When he saw flashes as it opened fire, he identified the other as a Bf-109 and threw his Mustang into a turn to escape. After a series of turns, the enemy pilot realized Palmer was almost in firing position and split-essed for the deck. Considering his escape lucky, Palmer headed for Corsica to refuel.

Although four enemy fighters were spotted on the mission of July 19 when 48 Mustangs from all four squadrons escorted B-24s from the 49th Bomb Wing's B-24s for an attack on Munich-Schleissheim airfield, they were too distant to be intercepted. On July 20, the Red Tails escorted Liberators from the 47th, 55th, and 304th Bomb Wings to Friedrichshafen, Germany. Over Udine, 20 enemy aircraft attacked the bombers from "six o'clock low." Several other enemy fighters in groups of four each acted as decoys, holding formation to either side of the bombers. Lieutenants Joseph Elsberry, Langdon Johnson, and Armour McDaniel and Captain Ed Toppins destroyed a Bf-109 each. Although the aerial interception was fruitless, three B-24s were destroyed by a ferocious flak barrage over the target. Near Udine, several Mustangs picked up two flak-damaged stragglers and escorted them home.

Weather prevented the group's rendezvous with the bombers they were ordered to escort on July 21 when the 332nd sent 60 aircraft for withdrawal cover of the 5th Bomb Wing after they bombed the Brux synthetic oil refinery. The next day, they escorted the B-24s of the 55th Bomb Wing to Ploeşti. With 60 P-51s shepherding the bombers, the 20 German aircraft that were spotted made no effort to attack and were ignored in return.

As they came off the target, Lieutenant Jimmy Walker's flight spotted a damaged B-24 and dropped down to escort it. They were rewarded with a barrage of very accurate flak resulting in all the Mustangs being damaged to varying degrees; Walker was forced to bail out of his crippled P-51C when the engine seized over eastern Serbia. After shucking his chute, he ran across anticommunist partisans who united him with nine other shot-down Americans. Walker rejoined the 332nd in September after they were eventually rescued at night by a C-47 having spent 39 days in occupied territory.

The pace picked up as July drew to a close. On July 24, 35 P-51s covered B-24s of the 47th Bomb Wing attacking Genoa harbor. The next day, 46 Mustangs covered the 55th Bomb Wing when they bombed the Herman Göring Tank Works at Linz, Austria. On that mission, the 60 P-51s flew in three groups to cover the leading, middle, and rear formations. Forty Bf-109s attacked the last two eight-Mustang groups, which resulted in their losing Lieutenants Starling Penn and Alfred Carroll, who both became prisoners of war. Captain Harold Sawyer shot down a Bf-109 for his second confirmed kill, damaging two others.

Mechanical issues began to plague the 332nd due to this operational tempo, compounded by the war-weariness of their Mustangs in general. Although 61 Mustangs took off on July 26, 21 returned to base due to mechanical difficulties. This was due in part to the relative lack of experience with the P-51s; however, while many mechanics in other – white – groups had previous experience as mechanics in civilian life, this experience was often not available to black enlisted men in civilian life before entering the Army.

The 40 Mustangs that did complete the July 26 mission escorting the 47th Bomb Wing to Markersdorf airfield in Austria found the sky filled with opposing fighters. En route to the target they sighted two groups of six Bf-109s and a group of Fw-190s, but all kept their distance until the B-24s turned on their bomb run, when 18 Bf-109s attacked the Mustangs while ten more remained above as top cover; they split into two-plane formations, diving on the bombers. When they tried to avoid pursuit by split-essing, the Red Tails made short work of them. Captain Ed Toppins scored his fourth kill while Lieutenants William Green, Freddie Hutchins, and Leonard Jackson destroyed a single Bf-109 confirmed each. Lieutenant Weldon Groves shared a kill with a P-51 from another group. They lost Lieutenant Charles Jackson, who evaded capture and returned to Ramitelli on 28 August.

Good hunting continued the next day; while escorting the 47th Bomb Wing's attack on the Weiss armament works near Budapest, the Red Tails were jumped by 25 Bf-109s and Fw-190s north of Lake Balaton. They sent one Mustang down, smoking, in their initial pass and several others were damaged, including Captain Ed Gleed's Mustang, which had two guns shot out. Gleed tenaciously stayed on the tail of a Bf-109 and hit one wing, blowing it off and sending the enemy fighter hurtling to earth. As Gleed's flight climbed back up to escort the Liberators coming off the target, the B-24s were attacked by 12 Fw-90s, which were in turn intercepted by other group Mustangs, forcing them to break off their attacks. As the enemy pilots tried to flee, the Mustangs gave chase. In the ensuing running battle, Gleed closed on an Fw-190 and chased it all the way to the deck, where he caught it with a fatal burst. In the process, he had become separated from his wingman and was out of ammunition. He was in turn was attacked by two Fw-190s that hit his damaged Mustang as he stayed at treetop level and hedge-hopped between hills trying to shake off his pursuers. He streaked across a riverbed and between church steeples in a town; when he spotted a valley heading in the general direction of Ramitelli, he firewalled his Merlin and left both Fw-190s in his wake. When he landed back at Ramitelli, the Merlin quit from fuel starvation.

The rest of the 332nd had also been busy. Lieutenant Alfred Gorham scored a double, while Lieutenants Claude Govan, Richard Hall, Leonard Jackson, and Felix Kirkpatrick claimed one each destroyed. This eight-kill haul had been accomplished without sacrificing any bombers to enemy fighters.

Yet another mission to Ploești on July 28, escorting the 55th Bomb Wing, saw 14 Mustangs aborted for mechanical problems out of the 54 aircraft that took off. The seven enemy aircraft spotted in the target area were out of interception range. One Bf-109 stalked two straggling P-51s, but the pilot ran for home when the Mustangs broke into him.

Weather canceled the mission on July 29 but the next day 43 Mustangs escorted the 5th Bomb Wing's Liberators when they bombed the Tokol armament works in Budapest. What was identified as an "Re-2001" but was either a C.205 or a G.55 of the Italian fascist ANR air force was spotted flying a parallel course to Second Lieutenant Carl Johnson's straggling Mustang. Warned by his squadron mates just before the enemy fighter turned and tried to hit him with a 90-degree deflection shot, Johnson turned, pulled inside it, and shot it down with a few well-aimed bursts.

Minutes later, another Red Tails flight spotted a single Bf-109 and gave chase. Before they could catch it, a Checkertail Mustang swooped in and shot down the enemy fighter.

The last day of the month saw 65 Mustangs from the 332nd provide escort to the 47th Bomb Wing which was sent to hit Ploești. The Red Tails arrived at the rendezvous point on time, but had to wait five minutes for the bombers. One Bf-109 was spotted over the target, but was too far away to catch.

June and July 1944 had seen the Red Tails prove themselves the equals of any other fighter group in XV Fighter Command, despite being equipped with war-weary hand-me-down Thunderbolts and Mustangs from other groups in the command. In June, they had demonstrated their mastery of escort flying, and July had seen their Mustangs face off successfully with the Luftwaffe on many missions, during which the pilots acquitted themselves well in combat, while protecting the bombers so effectively that they received compliments from those units. By the end of the month, bomber crews welcomed the sight of Mustangs with red tails.

8

JULY 1944 – HIGH POINT OF THE CAMPAIGN

While the Red Tails were proving themselves to their detractors with the combat missions they flew in July 1944, the other groups in XV Fighter Command continued wide-ranging missions to France, Austria, Hungary, Yugoslavia, and Romania as they continued their battles against the Luftwaffe. July, which had the best weather of the year 1944, saw more missions flown daily than any other month in the Fifteenth's history, punctuated by intermittent bad weather lasting two to three days. In retrospect, July 1944 would be seen as the high point of XV Fighter Command's battle against the *Jagdwaffe*'s Bf-109s and Fw-190s.

The good weather during the first week in July saw the 14th Fighter Group fly consecutive missions to targets in Hungary, Yugoslavia, Romania, France, northern Italy, and Germany. Although enemy fighters were seen on all these missions, only Major Frank Robinson was able to score, when he destroyed an Fw-190 over Yugoslavia. This was due to the fact the 14th saw their main responsibility being prevention of attacks on the bombers they were escorting. If an enemy fighter formation was broken up, it was unlikely that it could reassemble in time to mount a second attack before the bombers had dropped their loads and withdrawn from the target area. Since the American escorts were frequently outnumbered, they followed a strategy in which scattering an enemy formation was more important than scoring individual victories.

The Budapest mission of July 2 was one of the biggest air battles fought by XV Fighter Command during the fast-paced month.

The 82nd Group was also on the scene, escorting B-24s to bomb the Almasfuzito oil refinery; the group saw the brunt of the combat that happened. Minutes before the bombers arrived over the target, 30 Bf-110s, Me-210s, and Me-410s were seen coming from the direction of Vienna. When the bombers made their turn at the initial point to begin their run to the target, the 96th and 97th Squadrons dropped their tanks and turned into the enemy formation, diving on them through a break in the cloud cover. One Bf-110 was shot down, but the rest were able to break away in the haze at this lower level that made visibility very poor. Responding to calls for help from the bombers that had come under attack from other formations, the Lightnings climbed back to the bombers and met attacks by Bf-109s and Fw-190s that dived on the climbing P-38s. The ensuing air battle extended from ten miles north to 30 miles south of Lake Balaton. Pilots claimed six Bf-109s and Fw-190s and a Bf-110 without loss. The bombers withdrew from the target unscathed. Major Claude E. "Hank" Ford, the 97th's commander, claimed the Bf-110 and a Bf-109. The 97th's Lieutenant Bob Griffin destroyed two Bf-109s while Lieutenant Jack Darrow claimed a Bf-109 destroyed. Lieutenant Jim Holloway, the 95th Squadron's newest ace, added to his score with a Bf-109 destroyed and squadron CO Major Warner "Warnie" Gardner claimed an Fw-190.

Target cover for the mission was flown by the 31st Fighter Group, now completely re-equipped with the new P-51Ds. The 307th Squadron was the first to tangle with the enemy when Flight Officer Edward Jay shot down two of three attacking Bf-109s while First Lieutenant Ernest Shipman shot down one Bf-109 of another group of three that attempted to attack the bombers as they came off their bomb run. The 308th's John Voll "made ace" when he shot down a Bf-109. As the bombers turned at the initial point and headed for the target, the 309th Squadron's pilots spotted 20 Bf-109s several thousand feet overhead. While two flights remained with the Liberators, the other two flights clawed for altitude with their opponents at 35,000 feet, diving on them when the P-51s reached 38,000 feet; First Lieutenant Robert D. Thompson managed to damage two Bf-109s before the rest dived away.

The Checkertails, reinforced by Major Deacon Hively's 334th Squadron from the visiting 4th Fighter Group provided

JULY 1944 – HIGH POINT OF THE CAMPAIGN

penetration, target, and withdrawal support for B-24s bombing the Rakos locomotive depot in Budapest. A formation of 40 Bf-109s was spotted as the bombers turned on their target run, and Second Lieutenant Barrie Davis shot down two of the six that dived on his flight. Davis recalled:

> I'll never forget that day, as I remained behind to escort some cripples home. We were jumped, but somehow only a single 109 pressed the attack. I finally latched on behind him and – unable to shake me – he rolled over and headed straight for the deck. We started at 25,000 feet, and with everything bent past the firewall, I was indicating well past 550 mph passing through 20,000 feet. My guns were spraying the sky, but not a damn thing was happening to the 109. Finally, at around 15,000 feet, bits of his airplane started coming off. First a wingtip, then a piece of cowling. They streaked past, scaring the hell out of me. I couldn't lay a gun on him and was shooting from pure fright. Finally – it must have been below 10,000 feet – the pilot jettisoned his canopy, pushed outward twice and bailed out. His chute ripped to pieces as he sailed past me. I felt right sick about it, so I guess nobody gets hardened to death.

When Davis pulled back on his stick to recover, he blacked out from G-force, coming round to find the Mustang climbing through 18,000 feet:

> I saw a burst of flak, and wondered what 20mm flak was doing at 20,000 feet. I broke right or left – I don't remember – and there was a 109 behind me popping off out cannon shells! I finally tacked onto his tail, and this time my shooting was a bit improved. I knocked out his oil cooler and set him on fire. His oil dumped all over me and I flew blind back to Lesina. The most memorable part of that mission was landing without being able to see any way but out the sides of my canopy.

When Davis landed, his crew chief thought his Mustang was throwing oil, and was glad to find out it was German oil.

The 4th's 334th Squadron, whose pilots had acted like they thought the Checkertails were in the "bush leagues" when they arrived on July 1 from their Russian shuttle mission, scored seven enemy aircraft shot down but lost six of their own. Deacon Hively lost his canopy when it was shot off, cracking his head. Despite the blood flowing into his eyes, Hively had managed to shoot down two Bf-109s and then successfully return to Lesina; he was awarded the DFC for the mission. The 334th had lost six of 18 pilots. Among their opponents over Budapest was Erich Hartmann of JG 52, destined to become the highest-scoring ace in history with a total 352 victories by the end of the war, who shot down four of the six Mustangs in his first combat with American fighter pilots. First Lieutenant Ralph Hofer was also lost, who was later discovered to have been shot down when he attacked an airfield near Mostar, Yugoslavia while returning from the mission.

The 52nd Group's P-51s provided withdrawal support for B-24s that had bombed the Shell oil refinery in Budapest. The 2nd Squadron, which was covering the center of the bomber formation, encountered some 50 Bf-109s and 12 Fw-190s that went after the Liberators. The squadron turned into the approaching enemy formation and broke it up. In the swirling fight that ensured, eight enemy fighters were shot down: Lieutenant Barry Lawler shot down two Bf-109s, while squadron leader Major Ralph "Doc" Watson and Lieutenant William Cowan destroyed one each; Lieutenant Dick Lampe shot down one Bf-109 and shared a second with Lieutenant Dennis Riddle. Lampe's score made him an ace with five and a half victories. Lieutenant Bill Bryan shot down two Bf-109s; during his return flight, he took a flak hit in his Mustang's radiator and was forced to bail out over Yugoslavia, where he fortunately was rescued by partisans and returned to the group a month later.

The 5th Squadron, flying at the head of the bomber formation, heard calls for help and spotted a formation of Bf-109s preparing to attack. They dived into the enemy and broke up the formation without scoring victories but leaving the enemy unable to execute their attack. Moments later they came across a second formation of enemy fighters that stuck around to fight. Lieutenants Dwaine Franklin and John McCarthy each destroyed a Bf-109, while Lieutenants Bob Carnie and Walter Zelinski were each credited with an Fw-190 destroyed.

The Lightnings of the 1st Fighter Group, like those of the 14th Group, covered the bombers during the approach over Yugoslavia and southern Hungary, completing their assignment and turning back before the enemy was encountered.

JULY 1944 – HIGH POINT OF THE CAMPAIGN

The Americans were opposed by the Bf-109s of the Hungarian Air Force's "Puma" Group, along with Bf-109s from all three *Gruppen* of JG 27 and II./JG 52. The Bf-110s were from ZG 1 (Zerstörergeschwader 1) and the Me-410s from I./ZG 76. The enemy force totaled over 170 fighters. While the Americans claimed 30 victories, they also lost 15 Lightnings and Mustangs in the massive fight.

The Checkertails escorted B-24s to bomb oil storage facilities at Giurgiu, Romania on July 3. Over the target, they encountered a force of 50 enemy fighters and engaged in a fast-paced battle that saw the group claim six destroyed, with Major J.E. Perry claiming a Bf-109 destroyed and Second Lieutenant Jack Houghton downing an Fw-190, while Lieutenants Bruce Cobb, S.E. Myers, Leland J. Stacy, and R.S. Bass each claimed a Bf-109 destroyed. Although the next day's mission to hit marshaling yards at Pitești, Romania saw no action for the Clan, the mission following, flown to Verona, Italy on July 6 saw the Clan adopt a new strategy, keeping 12 Mustangs over the target while the rest escorted the bombers on home; this resulted in an engagement with the ANR in which Jack Houghton destroyed a Bf-109 and Leland Stacy damaged a Macchi C.205 "Veltro."

The 82nd Group flew a fighter sweep over Romania on July 4. The only enemy planes spotted in the air were three Ju-52s with mine detonating rings, spotted northwest of Craiova. The 96th Squadron's Captain Dick Gangel and Lieutenants Art Kidder and Walt Carroll were credited with one each when they pounced on the lumbering transports. However, the "Tante Jus" didn't go down as quickly as expected, and a flight of the 97th Squadron also attacked one of them. Lieutenant Lee Lette, flying as "Tail-end Charlie," recalled: "we throttled back and even put down our flaps to take him individually. I made the eighth pass; his nose and left engine were afire and he blew up just as I squeezed the trigger. Coin flips determined the victory would go to one of the 96th's pilots."

Herky Green saw action on the next day's mission when the group escorted B-17s to hit the oil refinery at Blechhammer, Germany. Although he managed to get in shots at two different Bf-109s, Green was forced to pull away from each to keep the bombers covered after the Clan had broken up different enemy formations preparing to attack the formation. The Bf-109s had attempted to draw him away from the battle by diving for the ground. First Lieutenant Bruce C. Cobb and Second Lieutenant Jack H. Bond each destroyed a Bf-109.

After two "milk runs" on succeeding days, the 82nd ran across more action on July 7, escorting B-24s returning from a mission against a target in eastern Germany. Reaching the assigned rendezvous point north of Győr, Hungary, the Lightnings found no bombers, and circled for 20 minutes waiting for them. When they failed to show, the formation turned south. A few minutes later they overtook another B-24 formation 70 miles north of Lake Balaton. Just as the Lightnings joined up with the P-51s escorting this formation, four Bf-109s were spotted at low level and a flight of four from the 96th Squadron dived on them. The Lightnings were in turn jumped by another formation of six Bf-109s. A second flight from the 96th joined the fight; when the enemy broke away, they were two less, with Lieutenants Adelson and Carroll each destroying one of the enemy fighters. The 95th Squadron, which had maintained their station, spotted two of the Bf-109s evading the first fight and the squadron's second flight went after them. They were in turn bounced by six more Bf-109s. The 95th's Captain Joe Belton, who was leading the day's mission, shot down a Bf-109, as did Lieutenants Jack Joley and Jim Hardin. Belton's victory was credited as the 82nd's 500th victory since entering combat in North Africa nearly two years earlier.

The 82nd's opponents that day were the Bf-109s of the Hungarian 101 "Puma" Group's 1st Squadron. The Americans claimed five Bf-109s destroyed, but the Hungarians only lost one, flown by 12-victory ace Lieutenant Lajos Toth.

Green recalled that there were 11 Bf-109s waiting for the Checkertails when the B-17s they were escorting attacked the airfield at Zwölfaxing, Austria on July 8. "Their courage failed as soon as we went after them." The Bf-109s disappeared into the hazy sky, but not before First Lieutenant Wayne Lowry managed to destroy one and damage another that he lost in the haze.

The fighter sweep that the 14th Group flew to Vienna the same day, independent of the bomber formations, saw the 48th Squadron engage the enemy when the Lightnings were intercepted by Bf-109s from JG 27. Lieutenants Don Wimmer and Michael Brezas each destroyed a Bf-109, and claimed another damaged. Unfortunately, a JG 27 Messerschmitt claimed Second Lieutenant Henry Mitchell, while Flight Officer Bernard Martin went down when his fighter took a direct flak hit. Both were killed.

JULY 1944 – HIGH POINT OF THE CAMPAIGN

As all that action was happening, the 52nd Fighter Group found its share of combat escorting B-24s to Brașov and back. Missing their rendezvous with the 5th Bomb Wing's B-17s, the group took up defense of a B-24 formation. Two gaggles of about 15 Bf-109s total were spotted at 1015 hours, drawing Mustangs from the 2nd and 5th Squadrons to confront the enemy fighters. Over a fast five-minute engagement, the 4th Squadron's Lieutenants Ralph Peterson and Arnold Smith destroyed a Bf-109 each, while the newly arrived 2nd Squadron's Second Lieutenant Edmund Gubler took out a third Bf-109 for his first victory. Ten minutes later, more Bf-109s were spotted and the 5th Squadron joined the fight, scoring five quick victories. Lieutenants Calvin Allen and Bob Carnie dived on five Bf-109s spotted beneath the Liberators. While Allen went after one Bf-109, Carnie chased another enemy fighter to the deck; his speed got so high during the long dive that he was not able to pull out in time and he hit a tree that took off a wing, sending him crashing to his death. Allen, who had followed Carnie, avenged his flying mate by closing in on the Bf-109 and shooting it down.

As the bombers came off the target and headed home, the 4th Squadron's Major Franklin Robinson and wingman Second Lieutenant Richard Evans sighted two Fw-190s below them. They dived on the unsuspecting enemy and shot both down in the first pass.

After a "milk run" to Toulon on July 5, the yellow-tail Mustangs ran across some enemy pilots willing to engage in combat over Bergamo, Italy on July 6. First Lieutenant Charles Botvidson, scoreless after more than 100 missions with the group, shot down two of the Be-109s, while Captain Bob Curtis destroyed one for his ninth victory. He later reported, "Near Lake Garda at 28,000 feet, we saw eight Me-109s at 26,000 feet. We dropped tanks and dived on them. I closed on one and opened fire from about 500 yards. It rolled over and dived and I followed it to the deck, firing short bursts but seeing no strikes. I finally saw two hits on the fuselage and the pilot immediately jettisoned the canopy and bailed out at about 200 feet. The enemy aircraft crashed and burned." The group's final kill was shared between Lieutenants Frank Grey and William Cowan. Grey later reported, "This was by far my single longest encounter with an enemy fighter, and the pilot was the best of all I encountered. The engagement seemed to last forever, maybe as long as 15 minutes, with Cowan and I trading roles with him as hunter and hunted. Because of the difficulty of the victory, Cowan and I didn't want to flip for it, so we shared."

The next day, July 7, the 52nd escorted B-17s to Blechhammer and again found the enemy willing to fight. The 5th Squadron's First Lieutenant Bob Karr destroyed two of the Bf-109s and damaged a third while First Lieutenant Stan Bricker destroyed another. The victories came at the cost of Second Lieutenant Floyd who was seen to fall victim to a Bf-109 and killed.

The mission that the 82nd's Lightnings flew on July 8 was their best-scoring day since they had caught a formation of German transports over the Strait of Messina back in April 1943. The group's assignment to a fighter sweep ahead of the bombers on a mission to Vienna was a lucky break, since such sweeps were usually the province of the P-51s, while the P-38s were given the assignment of sticking with the bombers. The sweep's purpose was to flush out enemy fighter formations that were preparing to attack the bombers and break them up. The 96th Squadron's Lieutenant Charlie Pinson led 36 P-38s on what turned out to be one of the group's best-scoring days of the war.

The Lightnings were at 25,000 feet, 20 miles northwest of Vienna in a cloudless sky, when a formation of 16 Me-410s was spotted at 10,000 feet below them, climbing to position themselves for an attack on the bomber formations. Both the 95th and 96th Squadrons attacked while the 97th Squadron maintained high cover. The Me-410s were surprised and broke their formation, pursued by the P-38s. The two squadrons claimed 16 Me-410s shot down in the fight, without loss. Top scorers were Lieutenant Walt Carroll of the 96th and the 95th's Chuck Adams, who claimed three destroyed each, adding to each pilot's score and making both six-victory aces. The 97th's Bob Griffith scored his fifth when he shot down a Bf-109 that attempted to intervene in the larger fight. The 95th's Major Warner Gardner and Lieutenants Bob Haller and Jack Joley got one Me-410 each, while the 96th's Captain Dick Gangel and Lieutenants Merrill Adelson, Pelton Ellis, Andy McPhie, Charlie Pinson, and John Sognier were credited with one Me-410 destroyed each, and Lee Lette shot down an Fw-190.

Mission leader Charlie Pinson recalled:

> We had just entered the target area when 16 Me-410s were spotted 5,000 feet below and crossing our course. I ordered the 97th Squadron

JULY 1944 – HIGH POINT OF THE CAMPAIGN

to stay as high cover, and instructed the 95th to attack the left side. I took the 96th in a dive straight ahead, and as the enemy aircraft passed under us we turned and attacked from the right in a pincer. The maneuver was timed perfectly and the enemy was hit simultaneously from both sides. All the P-38s were coming in on the tails of the me-410s. At about 300 yards, we all opened fire and the Me-410s split up with eight going left and eight going right in an attempt to set up two defensive circles. However, the P-38s were able to shoot at them from directly astern. Each one had two or more P-38s on its tail and they were forced to try and escape individually.

I sighted in on the engine of the trailing Me-410 in the group that turned right and opened fire at 300 yards with a 15-degree deflection shot, down to zero degrees at 200 yards. I gave him a two-second burst and saw my cannon shells exploding and my .50-caliber strikes on the engine nacelle, wing root and fuselage. The right engine faltered and emitted black smoke and then flame streamed from it. He took a 90-degree right turn and then dived away in a right turn. I followed, firing short bursts at the left wing and engine and it streamed smoke. I saw an Me-410 pursued by two P-38s to my right, and I turned toward him; he flashed by and I continued a 360 back onto the first one. I followed him down into a valley where he leveled off and crash landed in a cultivated field. He didn't catch fire. I pulled up and joined the first flight of P-38s to pass by.

Lieutenant Larry Noel was credited with a Bf-109 downed without firing a shot. Over Vienna, he spotted a Bf-109 below and – contrary to standard procedure – peeled off and dived on it without notifying anyone. Suddenly there were other Bf-109s on his tail and he shouted into the radio, "Come on down and help me, I've got the whole goddamn Luftwaffe on my tail!" Lieutenant Tommy Vaughan replied, "Where y'all at Larry?" Noel replied, "I'm over the golf course, I'm over the golf course, hurry!" To which Vaughan replied, "What hole, Larry?"

Noel now had nine Bf-109s chasing him and shooting at him. "I pushed the throttles to the firewalls and tried every trick in the manual. I went through one village upside-down and saw a church steeple above me. I hauled around sharply and when one of the 109s tried to follow, it struck a tree with its wingtip and cartwheeled into the river." The others gave up the chase at that point and Noel returned to Vincenzo with five gallons of fuel remaining when he landed.

Total claims, including three Bf-109s and two Fw-190s that got involved, were 21 shot down and destroyed. The 82nd's score was almost triple the total of eight claimed by the other participating groups on the day's mission.

The 52nd Group's Captain Bob Curtis of the 2nd Fighter Squadron had the best day of his tour on July 8 during an escort mission to bomb the Florisdorf oil refinery in Vienna. He later reported:

> At 1200 hours, I was ESE of the target area leading the squadron formation when we saw 15-plus Me-109s attacking the lead bombers as they came off the target. I followed Blue flight as they dived on the enemy aircraft, and attacked one of four 109s that were attacking the bombers from six o'clock. The enemy aircraft took violent evasive action and I followed it down to about 5,000 feet, firing and seeing strikes. Then my windshield and canopy clouded over and I lost sight of him. My wingman Frank Grey saw the pilot bail out but his parachute caught fire.
>
> After my canopy and windshield cleared I closed on what I thought was the enemy aircraft I had followed down, but Grey later said it was a different airplane. I fired several bursts, saw strikes on the wings and fuselage, and as I turned away I saw the Me-109 crash and explode. Grey later said he saw me destroy two enemy aircraft in about one minute.
>
> Grey and I then climbed back toward the bombers. When we reached abut 14,000 feet, we saw eight Me-109s attacking a bomber at about 17,000 feet and two o'clock to us. We attacked them but they were very aggressive and skillful. A dogfight ensued and we eventually were forced to hit the deck. A Me-109 followed me down, firing at me, with Grey following and firing at it. After I leveled out on the deck, and after about three minutes of aggressive, skillful flying by the Me-109 pilot, I was able to get in position to fire a few bursts and get enough strikes to force the pilot to bail out.

Curtis was awarded the DSC for his actions on this mission. As that was going on, Major Ralph "Doc" Watson shot down a Bf-109. The remaining victories were scored by pilots of the 5th Squadron,

JULY 1944 – HIGH POINT OF THE CAMPAIGN

with First Lieutenant John Schumacher destroying one Bf-109 while Major Edwin Fuller damaged three and Second Lieutenant Lindsay Lundegaard damaged another. The cost was Second Lieutenant Glenn Crewe missing in action, and Second Lieutenant Charles Botvidson of the 2nd Squadron forced to bail out, though he was rescued and returned a week later.

Herky Green scored again on July 9. The Checkertails had been turned loose for a fighter sweep to Ploești and Bucharest, during which they spotted 12 enemy fighters in the distance, which fled before the Mustangs could reach them. Green recalled what then happened:

> We heard bombers west of Ploești calling for help. I led the 317th Squadron to see what we could do, and immediately saw the bombers being harassed by 109s. I dived from 28,000 feet to 20,000 feet and latched onto the tail of one. I closed to about 200 yards and was getting good hits when I saw another 109 attacking a P-51. I dragged my P-51 through a turn that made its rivets creak. I strained to ensure no one was behind me, then I broke sharply to the left and closed on the 109 from astern, firing several short bursts. It swelled in my gunsight, and then it blew apart, its wing spinning away in two chunks. Large pieces flew off and the pilot bailed out.

As it turned out, Green was the only Checkertail to claim a victory on the mission.

While Green was scoring his victory, Art Fiedler experienced a near-disaster. As he later recalled:

> I was flying Herk's wing when he took the entire squadron down in a vertical dive on those jokers. I could see Herk lining up on one of the Me-109s, and I was trying to get my gunsight on another when suddenly I found myself staring at a sheet of white! Almost immediately, I realized my windshield had iced over. Since we were closing on the Jerries rapidly, I also realized that since I couldn't see the 109 I was behind, I would either run into him or pass him by and he would blow me out of the sky. Instantly, I jerked the stick back in my lap and got out of there.
>
> Leveling off, I turned on the de-icer and using my fingernails and my knife frantically started clearing the windshield. Simultaneously,

I was trying to cover 360 degrees of sky to be sure some Jerry didn't sneak up on me. Finally, with the windshield almost clear, I looked around for some friendlies. The sky was empty. Suddenly at ten o'clock low something reflected the sun which I presumed had come from an unpainted American aircraft. As I visually searched that area, several orange-red bees passed directly over my canopy from behind. Tracers! Although I had concentrated on the area of the flash for 10–15 seconds, that was all the time it took for someone to latch onto my tail.

Without thinking, I racked into a vertical bank to the right. A quick glance over my shoulder showed four or five 109s right on my tail. The plane was violently bucking and pitching; whether from a high-speed stall or my tail surfaces being shot away, I couldn't determine. High G-forces squashed me down in the seat and prevented me from looking behind me. If I released pressure on the stick to get out of a high speed stall, but found instead it was someone on my tail, I would probably be dead. Letting up on the turn would allow anyone on my tail to get a lead on me and next his bullets would bind my cockpit or engine.

Finally, after making at least a 360-degree turn, I realized no 109 could outturn me this long, so I popped the stick and took a look behind me. The 109s were gone and again the sky was completely empty. But this experience wasn't wasted; never again did I forget to turn on and check my windshield defroster!!!

The 52nd Group also participated in the Ploești mission, with Sully Varnell copying Curtis' fight the day before and emerging from the fight with three Bf-109s destroyed, giving him a total of 15 and status as XV Fighter Command's second leading ace after the Checkertails' Herky Green. Fred Ohr, John Clark, and Jim Hoffman also destroyed a Bf-109 each; Ohr's victory was his fifth, and he became the only Korean-American ace in the air force. The group also came close to a "blue on blue" mistake when four Checkertail Mustangs closed on the 52nd's fighters. Before anyone could shoot, enemy aircraft were spotted diving on the bombers. Eleven P-51s broke off and went after them. In a five-minute battle, six of the eight were destroyed. Fred Ohr later reported on his ace-making victory:

I saw nine enemy aircraft at eight o'clock. We made a climbing turn into them and I closed on four, firing two short bursts at each. Three

JULY 1944 – HIGH POINT OF THE CAMPAIGN

turned left and one broke for the deck. I followed it and on the way down fired a long burst from astern and saw several strikes on the fuselage and wing root. I saw pieces fly off and coolant began to pour out. I broke away because of a cloud and then caught him on the other side when he emerged from the cloud. I fired two more long bursts and saw strikes on the fuselage and wings. The enemy fighter then burst into flames, went into a spin and crashed.

Mustangs from 5th Squadron spotted two Fw-190s 30 minutes later and First Lieutenant Rollag shot down both in flames. The 4th Squadron's Ralph Peterson scored the last victory of the mission, shooting down a Bf-109 30 miles northeast of Niš. The group returned to base without loss, though they reported another close call when "A flight of four P-51s with red tails made passes at us." Bob Curtis also commented that two P-38s made passes on his flight.

Colonel David S. Campbell arrived on July 10 to assume command of the 14th Fighter Group, accompanied by Lieutenant Colonel Thomas B. Whitehouse as deputy group commander. Both flew their first missions on July 14 as flight leaders. Seasoned veteran First Lieutenant John Schill led the group's 48 Lightnings as they escorted the bombers to Budapest, where 30–40 enemy aircraft were spotted preparing to attack the bombers. The 48th Squadron went after them and squadron leader Major Frank Robinson destroyed a Bf-110, while Michael Brezas found success, claiming two Fw-109s and a Bf-109 destroyed in a wild fight.

The 49th Squadron's First Lieutenant Larry O'Toole recalled, "A new pilot flying as John Schill's wingman collided with him in a huge ball of fire. These things make you feel awful when you witness them. Schill was such an outstanding professional. I hardly knew him, but we saw his performance in the air over and over and really admired him. It felt good when he led the group." In the fight, Lieutenant Ward McCombs was seen to get out of his Lightning after an enemy Bf-109 set the right engine on fire; he was quickly rounded up and made a prisoner of war.

That afternoon an unusual mission was flown by the 14th and 82nd Groups. A B-24 had been captured after it made a forced landing in Italy that left it in flyable condition. The enemy had taken it to Ghed airdrome, where it was sitting in a revetment. The 82nd's pilots had the dive-bombing skills from their training and mission to Ploești back in June, and the group was assigned to destroy the bomber while Lightnings from the 14th Group covered them. The bomb-carrying P-38s were led by Colonel Litton. Number four was Captain Dick Willsie, who recalled that each Lightning peeled off slightly to the left of the one previous, which resulted in the dive bombers coming down on the target from "all around the clock." "I was given my assigned position so I could get some good movie film of the target being destroyed, since my P-38 had a 35mm camera installed where the 16mm gun camera was normally carried, because I had been working with the 1st Combat Camera Unit which was doing a movie about our airplanes in action." When Willsie entered his dive, he saw that the first three planes – including Colonel Litton – had missed. "I dove down and luckily hit it right in the middle." The bombs used were 500-pound cluster units; the dive bombers scored four hits inside the revetment, setting the B-24 on fire. Unfortunately, the camera jammed during Willsie's attack:

> When I asked Colonel Litton if I could make another pass to try and get footage of the burning B-24, he said it was too dangerous. Returning to base, the Lightnings strafed targets of opportunity. When Willsie flew low to get footage, he ran into a cable strung between two towers. It didn't damage the props, but as it slid along the bottom of the nacelle it took off my VHF antenna and caught in the lower hinge of the right boom. I tore it loose with my momentum and brought nine feet of cable back with me.

A mission to Ploești to attack the Română Americana refinery on July 15 found poor weather with heavy cloud cover obscuring the target. Over Yugoslavia, headed for Ploești, the 52nd Group encountered dense clouds and the squadrons became scattered. The 2nd Squadron came out of the clouds north of the briefed route near Turnu Severin, to find themselves in the sights of a formation of 20 Romanian Air Force Bf-109s. The battle that followed saw three of the Bf-109s shot down – one each to Captain Curtis and Lieutenants Art Johnson and Willard Pretzer. Curtis reported:

> We were east of Turnu Severin, Romania, at 26,000 feet when I saw 20 Me-109s at 27,000 feet coming toward us from nine o'clock. We dropped tanks and climbed above them, turning to the left with

them and then diving on the last three in the group. I closed on one of them to about 200 yards astern and fired a two second burst. I saw numerous strikes all over the fuselage, engine and wing roots. The enemy aircraft then rolled over and started down, with small pieces flying off of it, and glycol and black smoke streaming from it. I was unable to follow it down to the deck because of the violent tail buffeting of my aircraft. Lieutenant Johnson, number three in my flight, saw the plane crash and burn.

Curtis was flying a P-51D-5 without the dorsal fin extension that was finally added to many early P-51Ds as a field modification to solve the control problem.

The early P-51Ds generated problems the way the early P-51Bs had, only different from the earlier fighters. Mechanical problems that resulted in the loss of aircraft included a wing weakness that could result in loss of a wing during a high-G high-speed pullout. The radiator under the fuselage depended on a small electric motor that automatically opened and closed shutters to regulate coolant temperature. Occasionally, oil dripped on the motor, which led to malfunction with the doors remaining closed, leading to overheating of the engine. The Mustang groups reported several losses that were listed as due to unknown causes that were ultimately tracked to this design defect.

One thing for which there was no cure was the physical problem for the pilots as the missions became longer and longer, with resulting stiffness of the hips and posterior. When some pilots resorted to using morphine to deaden the pain and eliminate the feelings of tiredness, it was found that while sensitivity was lost as desired, a critical muscle was also relaxed, with the result that "the pilot ended the mission sitting on more than he had bargained for" in the words of one flight surgeon who studied the problem.

The mission to Münchendorf airfield on July 16 resulted in the group scoring eight kills, two probables, and four damaged in a fight that began when several enemy fighters made a feint attack on the 5th Squadron's Mustangs. When the Mustangs challenged the attack, the Bf-109s dived away. Moments later, other Bf-109s were spotted after they shot down two B-24s under escort by the 1st Fighter Group's P-38s. One flight of Mustangs had to split-ess away when they came under attack from P-38s that turned on them and opened fire.

Ten minutes later, the Mustangs ran across a larger gaggle of 30 Bf-109s and Bf-110s. Four Checkertail Mustangs swooped on the gaggle and opened fire. As the Bf-110s attempted to dive away, the 5th Squadron's Lieutenant Dwayne Franklin dived down and fired at one that then turned to evade and collided with a second Bf-110, with both twin-engine fighters exploding. He then chased a Bf-109 to the deck; when the enemy pilot tried to split-ess away, he lost control and smashed into the ground in an explosion. Franklin pulled up from this victory and spotted another formation of Bf-110s. Leveling off at 13,000 feet, he made a pass on one just as it entered a cloud. Flying around the cloud, he caught the Bf-110 as it came out. Just as he was ready to fire on the fighter, it collided with a Ju-88 that suddenly appeared out of the clouds; both turned into a ball of flame that etched a path through the clouds to hit the ground. Franklin was credited with four – the two Bf-110s that collided in the first attack and the Bf-110 and Ju-88 in the second collision, though he had actually only fired at the first Bf-110.

Minutes later, the 4th Squadron's Lieutenants Bill Hanes and Frederick Straut spotted a gaggle of Bf-110s and attacked the rearmost fighter, which rolled into a second, with the first exploding and the airplane it swerved into snapping in half. Hanes then turned on a gaggle of five Ju-88s and shot down one while Straut was joined by Lieutenant Robert Deckman to attack another formation of Bf-110s. Deckman shot down one and damaged three others while Straut lost his target in the clouds.

While the 52nd Group was so engaged, the Checkertails flew a sweep ahead of the bombers that lasted from 1000 hours to 1105 hours, during which the Clan ran across a large formation of Bf-110s, half of which evaded the Mustangs by retreating into a large cloud bank. A gaggle of 15–20 of the twin-engine fighters were not so successful in evading the attacking Mustangs; in a fast-paced action of only a few minutes, two were destroyed by First Lieutenant Robert Black, while new deputy group commander Lieutenant Colonel Ernest Beverly and First Lieutenant Bruce Cobb scored one each. Lieutenants Stanley DeGrear, Horace Self Jr., and Edwin R. Williams managed one of the most oddball victory scores in Clan history when they dived on a formation of three more Bf-110s approaching the bombers. The leader of the three saw the three Mustangs heading toward them and panicked. His attempt to evade the Mustangs by

JULY 1944 – HIGH POINT OF THE CAMPAIGN

quickly banking over and diving between the other two resulted in his hitting both wingmen with his wingtips, sending all three fighters out of control to crash almost simultaneously. Williams later recalled, "His wingtips struck the others and all three crashed together. The air was suddenly filled with a mass of motors, wings and tails." The mission report credited the three victories as a "Group claim," rather than awarding individual credit to the three pilots who forced the midair collision.

The 14th Fighter Group escorted B-24s to Vienna and found the enemy up and aggressive. Several formations of enemy fighters were spotted preparing to attack the bombers, but the Lightnings broke up their attacks before they could hit the bombers. The final result saw Lieutenants Richard Pinter, William Church, and Cody Stout from the 48th Squadron claim one Bf-109 destroyed each.

After a stand down due to poor weather on July 17, the Clan took the B-24s to Friedrichshafen, Germany, the next day, to attack fuel facilities. There was no enemy response and the mission turned out to be a "milk run". The next day's escort to Munich only turned up minimal opposition by five Bf-109s, of which three were promptly destroyed by Lieutenants J.R. Oxner, S.E. Myers, and D.J. Schmerbeck. The next four missions, in which the Checkertails escorted B-24s to oil production facilities in Romania, saw no aerial opposition; the only action seen was from strafing targets of opportunity on the flights home.

Then-20-year-old First Lieutenant John D. Mullins of the 1st Fighter Group's 94th Fighter Squadron later wrote of the great fighter battles in the summer of 1944:

> The huge bomber escort raids had, in some ways, a terrible beauty about them from a fighter pilot's point of view. Arriving at our rendezvous point, we would circle anxiously, looking for the bomber formations. Suddenly, there they were, a few thousand feet below us in a column extending as far as the eye could see, each squadron in its own box formation boring ahead to the target, sometimes underlined by contrails. All of a sudden the flak would start, ugly black explosive puffs with an occasional red flash as something was hit. At that point, you're glad you're in a fighter and not sitting there plowing through those deadly explosions.

While the Checkertails experienced a "milk run" in their sector of the mission to Friedrichshafen on July 18, the biggest battle of the campaign involved the 52nd, 31st, 1st, and 332nd Groups. During the battle, American pilots claimed 40 enemy fighters destroyed.

The 99th Squadron's Captain Lee Rayford led 66 Mustangs from all four 332nd Group squadrons to their rendezvous point over southern Germany. The B-17s of the 5th Bomb Wing that they were supposed to escort to bomb the Luftwaffe base at Memmingen were nowhere to be found. The Mustangs orbited over Udine–Treviso, a hotbed of Luftwaffe activity. Sure enough, as the bombers finally appeared, a swarm of 30–35 Bf-109s were spotted to the right of the formation. The enemy fighters attacked in groups of two to four from "three o'clock high" and "five o'clock low," split-essing after their attacks. Rayford led 21 Mustangs to break up the attacks. In the fight that ensued, 11 enemy fighters were claimed destroyed. With the enemy departed, the formation continued on to Austria. Over the target, 30-40 enemy aircraft – identified as Bf-109s, Fw-190s, and Me-410s – were spotted. When four Fw-190s swooped in to attack, two were shot down.

Overall, the day's tally was impressive. Lieutenant Clarence "Lucky" Lester claimed three, Lieutenant Jack Holsclaw two, and Lieutenants Lee Archer, Charles Bailey, Walter Palmer, Roger Romine, Hugh Warner, and Captain Ed Toppins claimed one each.

In his second fight in as many days, Palmer hit his Bf-109 with several short bursts after he caught up with it following its pass at the bombers. He later wrote in his diary, "On the second or third burst I noticed his engine smoking heavily, so I broke it off because there were others to shoot down." As he closed on a second Bf-109, his guns jammed. As he considered chopping off the Messerschmitt's tail with his propeller, the enemy fighter disappeared into a cloud bank shrouding the Alps; Palmer wisely decided to break off the pursuit.

Ed Toppins dived on his Bf-109 at such a high speed that when he pulled out on the enemy fighter's tail, he warped his fuselage; the Mustang was scrapped after the mission. Two P-51s were lost in combat – Lieutenant Gene Browne was taken prisoner while Lieutenant Wellington G. Irving was killed. Oscar Hutton was forced to bail out when a drop tank jettisoned by another P-51 hit his Mustang.

The 52nd Group also covered the 5th Bomb Wing's B-17s on their withdrawal; as the bombers came out of the flak field, they were hit

JULY 1944 – HIGH POINT OF THE CAMPAIGN

by a formation of more than 60 enemy fighters. Before the Flying Fortresses had departed the target, they had lost 14 of their number. The 2nd Squadron's Lieutenants Art Johnson and Barry Lawler, and the 4th Squadron's Second Lieutenant William Parent each claimed a Bf-109 destroyed before the enemy fighters disappeared through a cloud deck below the bombers.

The 1st Fighter Group's 27th Squadron took top honors with claims for 14 destroyed while they defended the B-17s bombing the Manzell Dornier Works after failing to rendezvous with the 49th Bomb Wing's B-24s as planned. A huge gaggle estimated at nearly 90 enemy fighters was spotted attacking the bombers from their "six o'clock." The P-38s dived into the gaggles of Fw-190s that were intent on attacking the bombers, with the 27th Squadron leading the assault; unfortunately, the 94th Squadron was out of position to hit the enemy and the 71st went after other enemy fighters. Flight leader First Lieutenant Bill Caughlin recalled:

> I shot at least eight of them and two of them went down. All the Jerries I didn't get, my flight got; every man in my flight claimed at least one destroyed. We were badly outnumbered but had the advantage of speed and altitude. Fourteen of us attacked at least 75 enemy aircraft and shot down 14 of them, and the B-17s came out unscathed. The Bf-109s and Fw-190s would split-ess away from the Lightnings but rebound immediately and resume their assault on the bombers. We rarely saw an enemy fighter that wasn't going straight up or straight down. Going straight down in a P-38 was a considerable risk, something the Germans knew as well as we did.

The 31st Group was briefed to fly penetration, target, and withdrawal cover for B-24s bombing the oil refiners at Friedrichshafen. When the bombers failed to show up at the rendezvous point, the group's Mustangs flew on to Memmingen, where they arrived in the middle of the fight over the airfield. The 307th Squadron's Lieutenants Brooks and Dillard and Captain Buck and Flight Officer Elder each destroyed a Bf-109 in the initial clash when the Mustangs dived into the battle. The 308th Squadron engaged ten enemy fighters; Major Dorris and Lieutenants Voll, Goehausen, and Kennedy each shot down an Fw-190, while Flight Officer Martin claimed two Fw-190s.

Lieutenant Herman was hit by an Fw-190 and bailed out, but his chute never opened. The 309th's Major Warford shot down an Fw-190 while Lieutenants Dustrude and Dorsch shared a second. The 309th then returned to Friedrichshafen in time to pick up a flight of B-24s that had become separated from their wing and escort them safely out of the battle area.

On July 19, the 14th's Lightnings conducted a fighter sweep over Munich ahead of the attack by B-17s and B-24s against the Messerschmitt factory. The 48th Squadron's Lieutenants Michael Brezas, Henry Van Horn, and Bruce Langley scored a Bf-109 destroyed each, with Brezas "making ace" with his fifth victory. Sadly, the 37th Squadron's Lieutenants David Wilson and Aurelian Jekot collided over Munich, but both were able to escape their badly damaged fighters and bail out to become prisoners of war. Following their relief by P-51s, the Lightnings strafed targets of opportunity in southern Austria and northern Italy on their return home. The 49th Squadron's Lieutenant Richard Thompson and Cody Stout of the 48th Squadron then collided over San Giorgio, Italy, with both pilots killed in the midair explosion. A third midair collision saw Lieutenant Oliver Bryant's Lightning escape with light damage, but Lieutenant Walter McConnell's fighter was badly damaged. He recalled, "My right engine was damaged; the prop was bent so it wouldn't feather. The squadron commander assigned another Lightning to escort me home, but I was losing 500 feet a minute and told him to go on because I was going to have to bail out soon. But around 11,500 feet, the bad prop stopped windmilling and I found I could maintain that altitude using 50 inches of manifold pressure and 2,800 rpm on my good engine." As he crossed the Adriatic coast, McConnell spotted a single-engine fighter approaching and ducked into a cloud bank. Afraid to come out too quickly and be spotted, he stayed in the cloud on instruments for 90 minutes. When he came out, he found himself over Ancona Point, and turned toward Triolo to land. "As I started my approach, my landing gear refused to come down. I started pumping, but I ran out of gas before it came down, and I made a crash landing in a wheat field about five miles from the base."

Lieutenant Michael Brezas continued his run of luck on July 20 over Udine, where the group engaged small groups of enemy fighters trying to go after the bombers. Brezas shot down and destroyed the only enemy fighter claimed, a Bf-109. The group managed to break

JULY 1944 – HIGH POINT OF THE CAMPAIGN

up enemy fighter formations gathering for attacks on the bombers, resulting in no losses among the bombers.

On a follow-up mission to Memmingen, the 82nd Group ran across 30 Bf-109s while flying target and withdrawal support. The 95th and 97th Squadrons went after the enemy fighters to break up their formation. The 95th's First Lieutenant Elwood Howard claimed one of the Fw-109s destroyed. While that happened, the 96th Squadron spotted another formation and went after them with the 1st Group's 37th Squadron. Unfortunately, one of the Hungarian-flown fighters managed to shoot down Second Lieutenant Hughey. His element leader, First Lieutenant Walt Carper, reported, "eight Me-109s came around from 12 o'clock to six o'clock high, and the squadron broke into a 360. As we started to weave again, four 109s came in from the left, high. My wingman, Lieutenant Hughey, was apparently hit by their first shots. As tracers went over my canopy, I broke right and dived. I saw Hughey in a 60-degree dive with his right engine smoking. I lost sight of him at 15,000 feet; he had not recovered."

The following day, July 21, the 14th Group escorted B-24s to Brux, Germany. Some 40–50 enemy fighters were encountered, most in small groups trying to get through to the bombers, but again the Lightnings were able to prevent the attacks. The 48th's Second Lieutenant Dick Welch and First Lieutenant Walter White scored a Bf-109 destroyed each.

On July 22, 72 P-38s from the 14th and 82nd Groups, and 47 P-51s from the 31st Group flew Operation *Frantic III*. Due to the fact that the German bombing of Piryatin on the second *Frantic* mission had seen most of the American aviation gasoline on hand blown up, which the Russians did not allow the Americans to replace with increased flights from Iran, the third mission involved only the two Lightning groups and the 31st's Mustangs, flying a long-range strafing mission over Romania to attack Fliegerhorst (Military Airfield) Buzău and Fliegerhorst Zilistea as a way of keeping the *Frantic* project alive. The attacks were later described as "devastating," with the American fighters destroying 56 German and Romanian aircraft.

The 82nd's Lightnings joined up with those of the 14th 15 miles due north of Vincenzo; the two groups then joined with the 31st's Mustangs over Point Rossa. The huge formation climbed to 32,000 feet over the Adriatic as it crossed to Yugoslavia. XV Fighter Command's General

Strother led in a 31st Group Mustang. Four 82nd Group Lightnings aborted for mechanical problems, including Colonel Litton. The 95th Squadron's Major Phillips took over for Litton.

Two hours after takeoff, the Lightnings had crossed over the mountains separating Yugoslavia from Romania. When the formation passed the Danube, they dropped through the overcast and headed on at 7,000 feet, before descending and heading across the central Romanian plain at low altitude, with the Mustangs flying high cover while the 14th Group flew middle cover for the 82nd's strafers. The 82nd's three squadrons dropped to the deck 15 miles from Buzău and fanned out in "company front" for their strafing run over both fields.

Above the Lightnings, pilots of the 31st spotted four unidentified aircraft at "seven o'clock low." The 309th Squadron's Major Warford ordered his flight to drop tanks and went after the enemy formation. He recalled, "I signaled my flight to spread out. As we got closer, I identified an Me-109, an Me-210 and two Fw-190s." The enemy didn't see what hit them until it was too late. The action was brief and bloody as the Mustangs closed on them and they finally broke formation to evade. Warford shot down the Bf-109, while Lieutenants Thompson and Grose each destroyed an Fw-190. Warford then spotted the Me-210 and shot it down.

Willsie's Blue Flight and the rest of the 96th and 95th Squadrons followed Phillips' flight to hit Buzău while the 97th went after Zilistea. The results were fantastic, as 41 enemy aircraft at both fields and three smaller landing grounds went up in flames. Dick Willsie destroyed a Gotha Go-242, while Charlie Pinson destroyed an Fw-190 and damaged an He-111. Captain Sognier destroyed a Bf-109 and Captain Gangel an unidentified biplane. At Zilistea, the 97th's Major Ford blew up an Bf-109 and an Me-410; Major Green destroyed two Bf-109s; Lieutenant Griffith set two Fw-190s on fire and exploded an He-111; Lieutenant Lee Lette destroyed two Ju-88s; Lieutenant Dave Arndt lit up an Fw-190. The 96th's First Lieutenant Tom Rosier destroyed a Ju-88, a Bf-109, a Ju-87, and an Fi-156. Three additional landing grounds were hit by pilots of the 97th Squadron; Colonel Mason destroyed one of three Ju-52s, while Lieutenants Bob Biggs and O'Grady destroyed the other two; Biggs also destroyed two Ju-88s, while Lieutenant Vaughn destroyed a third Junkers bomber. The 95th's Lieutenant Hildebrandt set three He-111s on fire, with Lieutenant Mass scoring another and

JULY 1944 – HIGH POINT OF THE CAMPAIGN

Lieutenant Harmon two more. Three Ju-52s were shot down as they approached Zilistea by the 95th's Captain Joe Belton and Lieutenant Bob Haller, and the 97th's Lieutenant Bob Biggs. Lieutenant Paul Mass scored an aerial claim when he shot down an He-111 that had just lifted off. Lieutenants Lee Lette and Bob Griffith each destroyed an Fw-190 from a formation of three that attempted to attack the Lightnings.

While Willsie and the rest of the 82nd were carrying out their strafing attack, the 14th Group's P-38s got involved in a big dogfight while protecting the strafers and claimed 11 "Fw-190s" (most likely IAR-80s) destroyed for the loss of two P-38s. The 31st's Mustang high cover claimed three Fw-190s from II./SG 2 (II.Gruppe, Schlachtgeschwader 2), and a Bf-109 destroyed without loss. Lieutenant Henry Van Horn remembered:

> Over the target, we got into a hell of a fight. When enemy fighters jumped us, I was unfortunate to find myself alone after breaking into four 109s coming in from behind me. I saw I was in for it, so I hit the deck headed for Russia alone. My radio was out, so I couldn't call for help.
>
> Three 109s stayed on my tail close enough for me to see the white prop spinners. I dumped flaps and racked around to the right, and they missed me. I guess their gunnery wasn't so hot, or I would have had it then and there. I caught one as he chandelled up, and gave him a good burst. I saw hits, and he rolled over and started down from about 200 feet. I didn't see him hit, so it couldn't be confirmed.
>
> My gas was getting low, and I began to sweat getting over the front lines. When I saw the Dnieper River, I was more at ease, but I was running out of gas, so I landed on a wheat field 20 miles short of my destination.

Peasants in a nearby village came out, and Van Horn was able to convince them he was American and friendly. He was taken to the village and treated to a large dinner with lots of vodka, which he had never drunk before. "I stayed with the major that night and the next morning a mechanic arrived with some gasoline so I could fly on to Mirgorod."

Following their arrival in Ukraine, the 86th landed at Poltava, while the 14th went to Mirgorod and the 31st to Piryatin. Due to fears of another German bombing attack like that during *Frantic II*, aircraft were dispersed to satellite airfields at night and returned to the main base in the morning, and a four-plane alert flight was on standby during the day. The next two days saw poor weather that kept the Americans grounded. On July 25, the fighters flew a strafing mission to Mielec airdrome 70 miles northwest of Krakow in western Poland to provide support to the Red Army, with the 82nd strafing the airfield while the 14th and 31st Groups provided cover. The 82nd's formation was out of position when it attacked the airfield. The group did encounter some aircraft in the air and claimed three destroyed, including the 95th's First Lieutenant Roy Harman's claim for a Ju-87.

The 31st's Captain George G. Loving remembered that after the Lightnings strafed the field, the Mustangs were free to go after anything they found. "Within minutes, Yellow Flight's Lieutenant Carey spotted a Ju-52 that he and Flight Officer Shipley shot down in flames. I sighted two Ju-52s at 300 feet headed for the front lines. I eased down to a firing position off the rear one and opened fire at 100 yards. After a 10 second burst I broke away at 75 yards as it burst into flames and slammed into the ground. I watched Lieutenant Zierenberg finish off the other one." The 309th evaded a thunderstorm by going around to the right. "Four minutes later, our radios exploded with a torrent of excited voices from the 307th Squadron which had gone around to the left."

The 307th's Mustangs had run into a formation of 37 Ju-87s returning from a mission to the front. In the wild fight that followed the sighting, the squadron's pilots shot down 21 of the dive bombers, and claimed three more as probables and six damaged.

Back at Piryatin, the 31st's pilots claimed 21 Ju-87s, three Ju-52s, an He-11, an He-177, and an Fi-156s destroyed for no losses.

On July 26, the three fighter groups returned to Italy, making a sweep to Ploești. Over the oil refineries, the 31st's Mustangs broke formation, with the 307th dropping down to strafe Buzău airfield, where they claimed six aircraft left burning on the ground, after which they shot up a marshaling yard and claimed three locomotives destroyed and a number of trucks on flatcars set afire. The Mustangs were then jumped by enemy fighters and the 308th Squadron – which was covering the strafers – dived to help them fight their way out. Pilots from the two squadrons claimed six Bf-109s destroyed and two IAR-80s damaged. After five hours and 15 minutes in the air, all aircraft landed safely back at San Severo.

JULY 1944 – HIGH POINT OF THE CAMPAIGN

The 82nd Group also scored. The 96th's Major Ike Isaacson spotted an Me-410 and then shot it down. All but three of the 82nd's P-38s followed him and were jumped at low altitude by 24 Bf-109s and IAR-80s, leading to a 20-minute battle in which the 96th's Dick Willsie spotted a Ju-52 taking off from Manesti airfield moments after shooting down a Bf-109, and shot it down while the 95th's Major Gardner shot down the He-111 that had followed the tri-motor transport into the air. Lieutenant Ellis was credited with two Bf-109s that collided with each other as they attempted to get on his tail. The 96th's Captain Dick Gangel and First Lieutenant Ed Bodine each destroyed a Bf-109 while First Lieutenant Walt Carroll shot down an IAR-80.

The 97th's redoubtable Charlie Pinson had an engine knocked out and decided to return to Poltava. He was intercepted by four Romanian Bf-109s and forced to crash-land, where he was quickly captured. Leading strafer and aerial ace First Lieutenant Bob Griffith was shot down and killed by Bf-109 pilots of the Romanian Grupul 9, having engaged six and fought them alone before finally going down on fire, as reported by the Romanians. This was Griffith's 63rd mission. Major Hank Ford and First Lieutenant Bob Biggs each shot down a Bf-109 that gave each of them his fifth victory, to become the 23rd and 24th – and last – aerial aces in the 82nd Fighter Group during the war.

The 14th's Lightnings added two Ju-52s shot down by Lieutenant Colonel Tom Whitehouse and First Lieutenant James Mitchell, along with five aircraft destroyed by strafing as well as three locomotives.

The score for *Frantic III* was 69 enemy aircraft destroyed in the air and 60 on the ground. The mission was not as successful as hoped due to poor communications between the three bases and a lack of recent intelligence regarding possible targets.

The Checkertails flew a mission that day, escorting B-24s in an attack on Zwölfaxing airfield in Austria. The mission was memorable for the 317th Squadron. Ace Wayne Lowry later described what happened:

> Twelve pilots of the 317th took off for what was just another routine mission. For the past week or two we had only encountered scattered opposition. As Operations Officer, I was required to put up at least 12 P-51s daily. As I had only 13 pilots that meant that every 12th

mission one of us could be relieved. Fortunately, I had some real hunters and had little trouble with people aborting. The other two flights were led by Lieutenants Fiedler and Davis.

While they were en route to the target, Lowry picked up a distress call from a group of B-17s under attack. Lowry took his flight and Fiedler's to the rescue. "I could see they were in plenty of trouble as one after another was bursting into flames." As Lowry searched the sky to spot the enemy, Fiedler radioed that he had spotted them. "He was already gone and I followed with my flight of four. When I did catch sight of them a second later, I was appalled at their numbers."

The Checkertails had come across a formation of "at least 80" Bf-109s and Fw-190s. "I went on the air and informed the group of the serious nature of the situation."

Fiedler led his four in a dive through the middle of the huge gaggle, hoping to break them up. Lowry followed with his four. The attack broke up the formation for several minutes and diverted the enemy's attention from the bombers. Davis' flight of four soon joined the battle, followed quickly by the other two Checkertail squadrons, adding another 26 Mustangs to the defenders.

"I could see that Lieutenant Fiedler's flight had achieved instant popularity with the Luftwaffe and I was doing equally well." In the initial assault, Lowry fired at three different Fw-190s. As the Germans sought to evade the Mustangs' gunfire, the formation was now scattered all over the sky and individual dogfights were breaking out in all directions. "I followed one Fw-190 to the deck. I found myself locked in a tight turning circle at the bottom of a steep canyon. Our wingtips were just barely clearing the ground and it was certainly a fight to the finish for one of us. There was no way out, for the one attempting to leave would be slaughtered by the other." Lowry had expended most of his ammo and his gun barrels were burned out, which meant his fire was only accurate for a short distance. He closed on the enemy fighter to no more than 50 feet. "I fired again, aiming at a point over the cockpit. A tracer fell into the vicinity of the cockpit and the Fw-190 flipped over, crashing into the ground in a sheet of flame not more than thirty feet below me."

Lowry got out of the canyon as fast as possible and rejoined his flight and Fiedler's, and the Mustangs headed for home. "I then saw

JULY 1944 – HIGH POINT OF THE CAMPAIGN

a 109 trying to escape up a canyon and immediately gave chase. After overhauling him, I remembered that I had no guns, so I took a station well above him and waited for the rest of my flight to catch up with him." Fiedler was soon on the scene and dropped behind the fleeing fighter, knocking it down with three short bursts. It too exploded when it hit the ground.

Lowry's "Tail-end Charlie," First Lieutenant Henry "Hank" Greve, got separated with his wingman from the rest of the flight in the initial assault on the enemy. He managed to score hits on four or five of the enemy fighters and the two acted as rear guard for the B-17s, beating off repeated attempts by the enemy to get into the bomber formation. Eleven of the original 36 B-17s had been shot down by the time the Checkertails arrived on the scene, but Greve's effort prevented further losses. In the middle of the battle, a 20mm shell hit his leg and shattered it, knocking him unconscious. When he came to, his Mustang was in a spin. He managed to open the canopy and bail out over southern Bavaria. Unable to move with his shattered leg, he was captured and hospitalized.

Besides the Bf-109 that Lowry had cornered which Fiedler shot down, Fiedler also knocked down an Fw-190 that made him an ace as his fifth victory. As an indication of both Fiedler's skill as a fighter pilot in learning as fast as he had, and the tempo of action that summer, his ace-making kill came only five weeks after his first mission, three weeks after his first victory.

The 319th's Captain Richard Dunkin flamed an Fw-190 and exploded a Bf-109; these were his fifth and sixth victories, making him an ace. The 319th's commander, Major Jack Peery, and Lieutenants John F. Kenney, Jack Bond, W.R. Hinton, and Ernest T. Strauss each destroyed an Fw-190, while Captain S.W. Farnham and Lieutenants Paul Tatman and Victor A. Woodman each scored a Bf-109 destroyed.

July 27 saw the Clan score five more victories when Lieutenants Jack Houghton and Sam Brown scored an Fw-190 each while Lieutenants John P. Conant, Harry Parker, and Bob Brown added a Bf-109 each to their scores.

July ended with a bang, so to say, with two missions that saw lots of combat for the Checkertails.

In a mission flown to Ploești on June 28, the Clan again scored when they spotted 20 Bf-109s and ten Fw-190s waiting for the bombers to get out of the flak zone, and dived into the gaggle. Lieutenants Harry

Parker, Ben Emmert, and Paul Jensen each destroyed a Bf-109 while Lieutenant George B. Edwards scored an Fw-190 destroyed.

The 31st Fighter Group also flew the Ploeşti mission, the tenth time they had escorted bombers to this target. No enemy aircraft were spotted until the group was about to turn for home and was low on fuel. A huge gaggle of 60-plus Bf-109s appeared from out of the clouds. The group was engaged within minutes of the enemy's appearance. In the fight that followed, the 308th Squadron's Captain Leland P. Molland shot down two Bf-109s; Lieutenants Hardeman and Edge scored one apiece, while Lieutenants Smith and Vogt shared a Bf-109 between them. The 209th's Captain Freddie Dorsch engaged a formation of 20-plus, and shot down one of three Bf-109s that attacked him, damaging the other two. On arrival back at San Severo, Molland was mobbed by reporters and photographers after his victory was identified as the 306th Fighter Wing's 1,000th enemy aircraft destroyed.

The mission that the 82nd flew to Budapest on July 30 to escort B-24s encountered enemy fighters over the target. A formation of 15–20 Fw-190s and Bf-109s was intercepted by the 97th Squadron, which made a head-on attack. The enemy fighters evaded and then gathered again to attack the bombers, at which point they were attacked by the 96th Squadron, which forced them to break off their attack on the bombers; they disappeared into the haze at 10,000 feet before the Lightning pilots could score any shot down.

Meanwhile, the Checkertails escorted B-24s to bomb the Mogosaia oil storage depot in Bucharest on July 31. They encountered a gaggle of 40 Bf-109s and five Fw-190s at 26,000 feet. When the Mustangs hit the formation, the Germans went into a huge Lufbery circle, which they managed to maintain as the Clan's pilots kept diving into them and zooming. The high scorer was First Lieutenant Harry A. Parker, who destroyed four Bf-109s, bringing his score to eight and making him an ace. Lieutenants Phillip Sangermano and Ben Emmert scored three Bf-109s each, both becoming aces with six victories each. Lieutenants John W. Reynolds and Bill Pomerantz claimed a pair of Bf-109s each, while Victor A. Woodman shot down a Bf-109 and an Fw-190 and Lieutenant Harry E. Southern and Flight Officer Wes Terry each destroyed a Bf-109.

July 1944 was the most successful month of the war for the six groups in XV Fighter Command, with 379 enemy aircraft claimed destroyed.

JULY 1944 – HIGH POINT OF THE CAMPAIGN

It was also the worst month for bomber losses, with 319 bombers lost to fighters or flak.

The last of the major mid-summer missions saw the 82nd Fighter Group fly shuttle mission *Frantic IV* on August 4. This one was also an all-fighter affair, with the Lightnings covered by the 52nd Fighter Group's P-51s.

The early morning light glittered on the whirling propellers of 48 P-38 Lightnings of the 82nd Fighter Group as they taxied for takeoff at Vincenzo airfield. "Tail-end Charlie" in Group Commander Colonel Litton's flight was Flight Officer Dick Andrews, a 100-hour P-38 pilot who had celebrated his 20th birthday the day before and was looking forward to his first strafing mission. Right behind in the pack of Lightnings was Dick Willsie, the 96th Squadron's operations officer. Neither knew that today would find them flying the most memorable mission of their wartime careers.

En route to Russia, the 82nd strafed the Romanian fighter base at Focşani, where five aircraft were destroyed and four damaged, including an unidentified transport and an unidentified single-engine aircraft hit by Lieutenant Colonel Mason, who was flying with the 97th Fighter Squadron as usual.

Dick Andrews followed Colonel Litton over the airfields, "shooting at everything." They pulled off and swept down a railroad track where Andrews strafed two locomotives; just as he blew a switch control tower to pieces, he ran out of ammunition. "I went right over an armored train, crying and cursing because I didn't have a shot left." The defending flak was heavy and several other P-38s were shot down

As Willsie pulled out of his run:

> I got pretty well hit by flak in my right engine. As I feathered the prop, I spotted a 109 coming in on my right. I turned into the dead engine and came around on him. I was losing speed so fast he couldn't lead me, and he shot past beneath me. I came out of the turn on his tail and let him have it. At that moment, I took a hit in my left engine. It was still running, but it wasn't going to for long.

Andrews turned away from the armored train after he and Litton became separated in the smoke, "I saw Willsie's P-38 with one prop feathered and coolant pouring out of the other engine, which meant he wasn't going to stay up much longer. I pulled over, flying his left wing, and said 'Pick a good field and I'll come down and get you.'"

Willsie's first response was to say "no," but at the moment he was too busy with his emergency landing to reply. "I gave a call to the others about my intentions and asked for cover. I expended my last ammo trying to clear out any of them ahead as I glided in to a crash."

Andrews watched Willsie hit the ground, and saw he could land in the nearby field.

One of the other pilots yelled "Don't be a damned fool!" I had been called worse, so I went ahead. I suddenly realized the field was plowed and I was going to land across the furrows, so I poured on the power, pulled around and set up again to land with the furrows. I think the only reason I managed to do this successfully was everyone was so surprised to see me drop wheels and flaps, they didn't shoot at me. I was more afraid of making a poor landing than anything, since it doesn't take much to bust a nose gear on a P-38, which would have put both of us on the ground.

When Willsie opened his canopy, it didn't sound to him like the fighting had died down at all. "I managed to smack myself pretty good against the gunsight when I hit, and it knocked me out for a minute. I came to with blood in my eyes, and three P-38s were going overhead, firing at soldiers on the ground, then another flight came in. I saw Dick Andrews' plane across the way as he touched down. Bullets were flying everywhere when I jumped out and started running toward him." Overhead, Second Lieutenant Nick Pape bagged a Bf-109 lining up to strafe the two P-38s on the ground.

Willsie, who still had his parachute on, turned back to try to set his fighter on fire. When he saw Andrews turn his Lightning to taxi back to a takeoff position, "I forgot all about lighting the P-38 on fire, shucked my chute and took off after him." Andrews bumped slowly on the plowed ground. "Someone yelled over the radio that Willsie was running after me, so I hit the brakes, and saw him back there."

Willsie caught up with Andrews' slowly moving P-38 while Andrews climbed out of the cockpit and took off his parachute, then reached in and cleared out the seat pack and everything else he could to make room. "I was thinking so fast, I almost didn't realize that bullets were flying around till one grazed the canopy right beside me."

Andrews dropped the stirrup at the rear of the nacelle. Willsie made a running leap at the P-38, "I managed to haul myself onto the wing like I never had before." They were now faced with the prospect of cramming themselves into the tight single-seat cockpit in such a way that they could still operate the controls and fly their way to safety.

Andrews explained, "I was a low-time P-38 pilot and Willsie was the most experienced guy in the squadron, so I said, 'You fly.'" Andrews dropped into the cockpit, making himself as small as possible so Willsie could sit atop and in front of him.

Willsie recalled:

If the P-38 had had a control stick like a P-51, this would have been much easier, but it has a yoke that's on the right side of the cockpit and bends over to the center. I got in, and Dick's foot was in the way of the yoke and I was further forward than normal, so I couldn't work the yoke completely. I finally managed to pull his right leg up over my shoulder, and I could just work the yoke. His left foot was just enough in the way to make it hard to operate the throttles.

The next problem was to close the canopy for flight. "The P-38 canopy was very tight around you in normal conditions. After Andrews closed it, I had my head jammed right against the lid – I couldn't look behind me at all and could barely look from side to side."

As Willsie and Andrews worked to escape, the other Lightnings made repeated strafing runs on the field. Three truckloads of Romanian troops speeding toward the pasture were strafed by Lieutenant Campbell as they headed toward the P-38. Willsie remembered, "We didn't have time to taxi the full length of the field. I started to gun the engines for takeoff, but the nosewheel started digging in the ground. I had to throttle back to get her to move at all. I started rolling in up trim as I accelerated slowly, holding the yoke back and trying to get the weight off the nose as soon as I could." Ahead, there was a line of trees at the end of the field they were going to have to get over if they were to successfully escape. "I kept her on the ground as long as I could. I just had flying speed when I yanked her off. If I hadn't had all that up-trim, we'd never have made it because I couldn't pull the yoke back far enough to get her over the trees. I was sure glad they weren't ten feet higher."

The big P-38 made quite a sight to the Romanian troops on the ground as it mushed into the air through the line of trees, tearing limbs from the trees with the props. Willsie remembered, "I thought for a minute we were going to lose a prop and crash, but we pulled out of there and managed to stay in the air." Andrews checked his watch as they lifted off. "From my touchdown to our takeoff, the entire event took about two minutes."

Once airborne, Willsie put the nose down and gathered airspeed as they roared low over the heads of the troops who a moment before had been intent on catching them. "I held us as low as I could till we were out of range of the flak, then started getting some altitude." Willsie asked Andrews for a map, but he didn't have one. "I told him to get the map from his escape kit. He did and unfolded a cloth map of Southern France and we were headed for Russia."

The other squadron members formated on the now-two-seater P-38, providing close escort as they set off to fly to Poltava, two-and-a-half flying hours away. Soon, they ran into thunderstorms; Willsie had to fly through a blinding rainstorm that battered the P-38 with torrents of water. Still at low level, Willsie told Andrews to watch the ground while he leaned his head on the panel cover and flew instruments. "We didn't talk much on the way except a few warnings from him that we were approaching a hill and needed a little more altitude."

Once over Ukraine, Soviet Yak-9s intercepted them and guided them to Poltava. Willsie was going to have to land hot, without a lot of control, with no chance for a go-around because they were practically flying on fumes. He brought the P-38 in on a long straight approach and dropped it on its mains onto the runway. As he lowered the nosewheel, one engine started to sputter from fuel starvation. "Nobody thought too much of it when I climbed out, but they were pretty surprised when Andrews pulled himself out." Ground crews later found tree branches in the wheel wells when they checked the P-38.

The next morning, the 82nd's public relations officer wanted to take photos of Willsie and Andrews re-staging their escape. They attempted to climb into the cockpit as they had, but things didn't work. "We couldn't do it!" Andrews recalled. "Try as we might, we couldn't remember what we had done. It took us 30 minutes to finally give up – and it took us

30 seconds to do it the first time!" Willsie remembered, "I just sat on Dick's lap for the pictures, but we never could have flown it that way."

Unfortunately, the 82nd's group commander, Colonel Litton, was hit and his P-38J "Lucky Lady" was seen to crash and explode. While all assumed he had been killed, Litton survived, despite being badly injured, to become a prisoner of war. Three other P-38s were also lost to the flak. The 52nd's Mustangs claimed two aerial victories while losing four P-51s to the murderous flak.

The 82nd returned to Foggia on August 6, strafing targets of opportunity on the way and destroying one enemy aircraft on the ground. This brought to an end the most eventful and productive period in the group's history.

Word of the amazing rescue spread throughout the Fifteenth. When they arrived back in Italy, Andrews was met by General Twining, who awarded him the Silver Star and a promotion to second lieutenant on the spot. Over the next two months, Fifteenth Air Force pilots tried twice more to effect such rescues. "The second try ended up with them crashing into a haystack, and it was discovered they were actually in friendly territory only they didn't know it," Willsie recalled. "General Twining gave a direct order that nobody was to try it again."

In September 1944, Willsie took command of the 96th Fighter Squadron. "When Dick Andrews had the minimum time to be promoted to 1st Lieutenant, a lot of people thought I was prejudiced when I promoted him. They were right – I was prejudiced!"

9

AUGUST CRESCENDO

While July had been hot and heavy for air combat for all the Fifteenth's fighter groups, and August started out as a continuation of that, the month ended up very different for different groups. The Checkertails found air combat on about half their missions, while the 82nd's Lightnings found none that month and would not engage in air combat for the rest of the war. Pilots were soon asking "Where is the Luftwaffe?" as the enemy failed to appear to contest missions. This was due to the fact that the oil campaign had seen major blows struck by the Eighth Air Force against the German synthetic oil industry, while the Fifteenth's bombers completed the destruction of Ploești, which was in Soviet hands by the end of the month. With Romania surrendering and joining the Allies in the struggle against Germany, the Luftwaffe units in the country were forced to evacuate back into Hungary, Czechoslovakia, and Poland. Operation *Bagration*, the rolling Soviet offensive all along the Eastern Front, which began two weeks after the Normandy invasion, threw all German units into retreat. When this was coupled with the decrease in aviation gasoline available, the Luftwaffe's disappearance was the logical result.

The Checkertails maintained their momentum from July with a mission flown to Friedrichshafen on August 3, escorting B-24s to bomb the Manzell Dornier factory. As the bombers departed the target, three Bf-109s were spotted. One was shot down by First Lieutenant John Simmons, who reported: "I observed a Me 109 at 16,000 feet flying straight and level. Using the cloud cover for concealment, I was able to surprise the enemy aircraft, and I came in from the rear at six o'clock and began firing at 500 yards, closing to 50 yards. Hits were observed to enter the cockpit and the left wing, and shortly afterwards the enemy aircraft exploded and spun in." Simmons' victory was confirmed by Flight Officer Victor Ames.

At about the same time as Simmons claimed his victory, 14 Bf-109s and 20 Fw-190s appeared out of the clouds and attacked the trailing B-24 formation, shooting down five Liberators. Checkertail Mustangs attacked these enemy aircraft as they pulled away from their attack and a running battle over 50 miles duly broke out as the Clan endeavored to protect the surviving bombers. Nine more kills were claimed; First Lieutenant Harry Parker shot down a Bf-109 for his ninth victory in ten days. He later reported: "I attacked three Me-109s at 24,000 ft, singling out one of them, who saw me and dived away. I followed and fired from 300 yards to 150 yards, and saw many hits on the left wing and fuselage of the enemy aircraft. The Me-109 began burning and the pilot bailed out."

First Lieutenant Robert H. Brown shot down another Bf-109 for his fifth victory. Brown reported: "I attacked a Me-109 that was in a steep climb at 12,000 feet. The enemy pilot saw me and turned sharply, but I fired from 200 yards with 60 degrees deflection, before moving in directly astern of him. I closed to about 20 feet, fired a burst and saw hits on the tail and wing of the '109, which split-essed and crashed into the side of a mountain."

The battle's top scorer was Lieutenant Colonel J.V. Toner, who destroyed two Fw-190s, while four other Focke-Wulfs were destroyed by Lieutenant Colonel E.H. Beverly and Lieutenants J.R. Bond, E.T. Strauss, and H.R. Loftus, who destroyed one each; Lieutenant A.J. Fitch destroyed a Bf-109. All Checkertail Mustangs returned to base without loss or damage.

Following another "milk run" to southern France on August 6, the Clan escorted bombers once again to Blechhammer, where they encountered 13 Bf-109s that came up to fight, and an He-111 that blundered into the battle. In the first of two clashes that occurred at 1110 hours, five Bf-109s dived on the bombers as they withdrew from the target but then they spotted intercepting Mustangs and dived away. Lieutenant Paul Tatman followed and shot down one that caught fire.

Thirty minutes later another gaggle of eight Bf-109s made a pass at the bomber formation but were intercepted and split-essed away when they spotted the Mustangs. First Lieutenant Henry Wolfe and Captain Richard Dunkin went after them and each shot down one; for Dunkin it was his seventh victory. He later recalled:

> I saw a group of Me-109s getting ready to bounce the bombers. Diving from 28,000 feet, I came in behind one and started firing from six o'clock, I observed many hits on the fuselage and continued to fire in what became a turning fight. I closed to 150 feet, seeing parts come off of the enemy aircraft. Shortly afterwards I saw it emit smoke and the propeller began wind-milling. The pilot jettisoned his canopy, rolled over and bailed out, but his 'chute did not open.

Ten minutes later, Lieutenants Wayne Lowry and Barrie Davis spotted two Bf-109s and quickly shot them down. Lowry reported:

> I was a section leader on an escort mission to Blechhammer when I observed eight enemy aircraft preparing to attack the Allied bombers from five o'clock low. I executed a 90-degree turn and closed on the extreme right Me-109, closing to 800 feet and firing a short burst. I continued firing from 500 feet dead astern. I observed hits in the fuselage, around the cockpit and in the engine as the enemy aircraft went into a spin and the pilot bailed out.

Barrie Davis wrote in his report:

> Leading my section on an escort mission to Blechhammer, I saw eight Me-109s 5,000 feet below me preparing to attack our bombers. Executing a diving turn, I led my flight down to 20,000 feet and closed on the Number 2-positioned enemy aircraft in the leading flight. I fired a short burst from six o'clock with no apparent results. I continued firing short bursts as I closed in from dead astern, and from 100 yards I saw hits in the fuselage near the base of the wings. Coolant began pouring from the Me-109, followed by a stream of smoke as the enemy aircraft went into a steep dive and exploded as it hit the ground.

Lowry's victory was his 11th, and last, while Davis' Bf-109 was victory number four. Lieutenant John Simmons scored his fourth victory when he downed the He-111 that wandered into the fight as it headed toward the nearby airfield; it was the last victory of the day. The August 9 mission to southern France came up dry for enemy aircraft, and only one was spotted during the escort mission to Ploești the next day. Captain Richard Dunkin quickly scored victory number eight, later reporting:

> On an escort mission to Ploești, and after leaving the bombers, I noticed a lone Me-109 at 15,000 feet making a pass at a forward flight of P-51s. I dove after him and closed in, starting firing from six o'clock from 300 yards, closing to 225 yards and firing again. I saw many strikes on the fuselage and followed the Me-109 down to 1000 feet, where I watched the enemy aircraft split-ess and head for the ground. A faulty 'chute was seen trailing the Me-109, and I believe the enemy pilot, when jumping, fell out of his 'chute.

On August 17, the Checkertails flew the first of two missions to Ploești after having flown several support missions for Operation *Dragoon*, the invasion of southern France. No enemy aircraft were spotted on any of these missions, which were among the last flown to bomb Ploești before the refineries were captured by the Red Army. The enemy also failed to appear when the Clan escorted B-24s to bomb Hajduboszormeny airfield in Hungary on August 21. On this occasion, the Mustangs spotted enemy aircraft on the airfield and went down to strafe them. After several passes, the Mustangs departed the field with claims for 37 enemy aircraft destroyed on the ground, 13 probables, and 17 damaged. The only aerial victory came when Second Lieutenant Robert Brown spotted a Bf-109 at 11,000 feet south of the field; he dived on it before the enemy pilot knew he was there and shot it down.

The Luftwaffe finally put in an appearance the next day when the Clan escorted B-17s and B-24s to attack the oil refinery at Edertal, Germany. Enemy fighters were spotted attacking a group of straggling B-17s. The Mustangs claimed four destroyed, two of which were Barrie Davis' fifth and six victories. He later reported:

> I was escorting a B-24 straggler home when I heard a call for help from a B-17. I turned 180 degrees and headed north. About 15 miles west of Lake Balaton, I saw six Fw-190s attacking a B-17 at 17,000 feet. Just as I arrived at the scene the bomber went down in flames. I quickly bounced the enemy aircraft, firing several short bursts at two

of them and then tacking onto a third Fw-190. I fired short bursts from 300 yards down to 50 yards, dead astern, and saw many strikes around the cockpit area of the fuselage. The enemy pilot went into a spin at 12,000 feet and I followed him down to 1,000 feet, where I was forced to break off because of the Fw-190 that followed me down. Lieutenant John Conant saw the enemy aircraft crash and confirmed my claim.

I then heard bombers calling for help over Lake Balaton, and after turning north I saw six Me-109s making passes at a B-17 and a B-24, which were both straggling. As I approached, the Me-109s scattered. I followed one of them down to 3,000 feet before breaking off my attack and heading back to the bombers. At this time I saw another Me-109 on my tail so I broke left. After three or four turns I closed in on the enemy aircraft from six o'clock and opened fire from 300 yards. Hits were scored on the fuselage as the Me-109 rolled and headed for the deck. I followed him and fired short bursts from dead astern. Smoke began streaming from the Me-109 as a result of many hits in the fuselage and the pilot bailed out at 2,000 feet.

The last two victories – both Bf-109s – were credited to Lieutenants William Hinton and Larry Ritter. One Mustang was lost due to mechanical failure; however, pilot Lieutenant James Lintz was able to bail out successfully over enemy territory. He was captured after a few days on the run and became a prisoner of war.

The 52nd Group didn't experience the success of the Checkertails. August 1944 saw a definite downturn in the group's encounters with enemy aircraft. The 2nd Fighter Squadron had recorded 49 victories in nine encounters in June, reduced to 34 victories in 12 encounters in July, that became six victories in four encounters in August while the 5th Squadron scored only four victories. The 4th Squadron had been fortunate to be better located, with assignments that put them closer to those enemy fighters that did appear, which led to an August total of 14 victories.

Following the Russian shuttle at the beginning of the month that saw the majority of the August claims, group war diarist Captain Tom Thacker wrote:

> Overall, combat operations in August were on the level of the previous two months. Aerial victories were becoming more difficult to achieve

as the enemy was beginning to react from heavy losses from both the Mediterranean attack and from western Europe. Constant bombing of oil fields and refineries was helping to cause a fuel shortage and many more planes were located on the ground. Thus, the air battle was changing, with longer and more varied missions becoming commonplace. With the requirement for top cover for the bombers diminishing, the fighter planes were striking more frequently at ground targets. This was essential but dangerous work.

As with VIII Fighter Command in England, the majority of XV Fighter Command losses from late summer 1944 on through the end of the war would be to defending flak over ground targets.

The poor weather that had limited operations at the beginning of August gave way to better weather. During this time, the 52nd returned to their previous role of providing air support to ground troops. Operation *Anvil*, the invasion of southern France, was finally able to be carried out when invasion shipping that had been removed from the Mediterranean to Britain for the Normandy invasion was returned following the success of that operation. Air operations in support of *Anvil* began on August 12 when bombers of the Mediterranean Allied Air Forces hit targets in southern France and northern Italy in an attempt to confuse the enemy as to exactly where the invasion would take place.

The night of August 12–13 saw B-24s of the 885th Bomb Squadron (Special) drop 67,000 pounds of weapons, ammunition, and supplies to the French Forces of the Interior (FFI), along with Office of Strategic Services (OSS) agents whose job it would be to work with FFI units so that their efforts were coordinated with the events of the invasion.

On August 13 and 14, the bombers struck targets between Toulon and Cannes on the Riviera coast in which 35 artillery positions were knocked out, as well as bridges and other communication infrastructure. The 52nd Group escorted the bombers on August 14 and 15, following up the bombings with strafing attacks against radar installations along the coast in the area of Nice. Despite heavy defending antiaircraft fire, all the Mustangs returned safely from these missions.

Other XV Fighter Command units were not so fortunate. The 1st and 14th Groups flew low-level support missions to cover the landings; between August 13 and 20, they lost a total of 23 Lightnings to flak, though they also managed to destroy 100 enemy vehicles, 12 bridges, and several defending artillery positions.

With the invading troops safely ashore by August 16, the final two missions to Ploești were flown on August 17 and 19. No enemy aircraft rose to defend the bombed-out refineries. The Romanian Air Force had taken such heavy losses in June and July that the *Grupurile* were unable to rise to meet these attacks, while the Luftwaffe units had been withdrawn from Romania by the middle of the month in the face of Soviet advances into Romania that threatened their ability to use bases in the country; the German units were now to be found in Hungary.

Thus, when the 52nd Group escorted B-24s to Blechhammer, they found the enemy willing to engage the raiders. High winds delayed the rendezvous of the fighters and bombers over Lake Balaton; their prolonged approach and the difficulty of forming up was seen on German radar, which provided plenty of early warning to the Luftwaffe. The Yellow Tails of the 52nd ran across the first enemy formation at 1100 hours when they spotted a huge formation of "100+" Bf-109s north-northeast of Bratislava, at 28,000 feet, ten miles behind a B-24 formation as the Mustangs approached the rendezvous.

The Mustangs were at 29,000 feet. They turned up-sun of the enemy formation and approached from the rear. As they dived on the enemy, they were finally spotted and nearly all the Bf-109s split-essed to avoid the defending P-51s. First Lieutenant Frank Grey, who led the attack on the enemy fighters, wrote in his encounter report:

> Most of them split-essed for the deck but I was able to fire on several of them before they took this evasive action. After damaging one enemy aircraft, I saw a Me-109 at three o'clock. I turned and closed on him from dead astern. He rolled over and dived and I followed him to 10,000 feet where I had to break off because of another enemy aircraft that gained position behind me. I was able to level off and turn to attack this enemy fighter, and fire several bursts at it. I saw strikes on the left wing root, the left side of the cockpit and fuselage. The enemy fighter then went down from about 5,000 feet and crashed.

Grey's wingman, who had warned him about this fighter, then managed to jump one of the Bf-109s and shoot it down.

Unfortunately, Grey's flight got separated. Lieutenants James Hoffman and Harry West followed the enemy down and then got further separated from each other. Hoffman was last heard to radio, "I see a perfect bounce, I am going down alone." He was never seen again.

At the same time, 4th Squadron pilots spotted a gaggle of 50 enemy fighters northwest of Ostrava. Seven Mustangs broke away to intercept the enemy before they could form up for an attack. Climbing to 24,000 feet the P-51s dived into the mixed formation of Bf-109s and Fw-190s, concentrating on a group of 16 Bf-109s which split-essed for the deck when they spotted the Mustangs. First Lieutenant Don J. Stinchcombe closed in and shot down the two "Tail-end Charlies," who were slow in making their break. The four P-51s of Stinchcombe's flight then turned for home under the leadership of flight leader First Lieutenant Bill Hanes. Nearing an airdrome near Szombathely, Hungary, Hanes saw over 40 enemy aircraft packing the field. The Mustangs flew on, then dived and turned back to strafe the field. Making three passes against the lightly defended target, they set eight aircraft afire before departing.

The next day, August 23, the Luftwaffe appeared in force during a mission to Markersdorf airfield in Austria. The Checkertails – escorting B-24s of the 49th Bomb Wing – spotted a group of 45 Bf-109s and Fw-190s at "nine o'clock" to the bombers about 20 miles southwest of Wiener Neustadt. Herky Green immediately led the 317th Squadron in a diving attack on the enemy fighters and a major battle broke out as 31 Checkertail Mustangs engaged the defenders. Eighteen Mustangs stayed with the B-24s over the target. Four Fw-190s and a Bf-109 were destroyed during the encounter, with Green destroying one of the Focke-Wulfs for his 18th, and final, victory. He later reported:

> Upon hearing distress calls from the bombers I led my squadron in a diving turn to the right, passed under the bombers and attacked the enemy aircraft from six o'clock. I picked out a Fw-190 and opened fire from 300 yards down to 175 yards. The Fw-190 took a barrage of hits in the fuselage around the cockpit; a small explosion occurred. The enemy aircraft made a right turn at 22,000 feet, then split-essed and the pilot bailed out after a second explosion shook his fighter.

Second Lieutenant Harry Parker kept his fast-paced record, shooting down an Fw-190 for his tenth victory. He later reported, "I attacked a Fw-190 at 25,000 feet and the enemy aircraft dove into the clouds and I followed. I overtook the Fw-190 at 20,000 feet and opened fire from 300 yards and six degrees deflection and closed to 150 yards with no deflection. I got many hits in the tail and fuselage of the Fw-190 and the pilot bailed out as his airplane went down smoking badly."

First Lieutenant Phillip Sangermano destroyed two Fw-190s, which raised his total to eight. He later described the fight: "I attacked a Fw-190 that had just made a pass at the bombers. The enemy aircraft started spiraling down at a steep angle, and I overtook him at 15,000 feet and commenced firing from 250 yards with 15–45 degrees deflection. I then closed to within 50 yards dead astern and fired. I observed many hits in the wings, engine and cockpit of the Fw-190, which exploded and went down enveloped in flames." Moments after destroying his first victim, he spotted a second Focke-Wulf at 500 feet. "The enemy aircraft attempted to evade by turning sharply but I followed, firing from astern with 15–45 degrees deflection and closing to 75 feet with no deflection. I saw many hits in the cockpit of the Fw-190, which crashed into the ground and burned."

First Lieutenant John Simmons was also victor over two Fw-190s, raising his total to six to become the Clan's newest ace. Spotting 15 Fw-190s when they attacked the rearmost bomber box, he winged over and dived on the enemy formation to break it up, making a firing pass on the gaggle. Picking out one Focke-Wulf that was a little late in taking evasive action, he closed on the enemy fighter as it passed through 5,000 feet and shot it down. Climbing back to 10,000 feet, he looked down and saw a pair of Fw-190s on the deck. He dived on them, closing in on the trailing fighter until they spotted him and split-essed to get away. He continued to follow the leader, closing to within 50 feet before opening fire as the two fighters passed through 1,000 feet. The enemy fighter caught fire and crashed into a mountain hillside.

Another seven Fw-190s were destroyed by Major John E. Peery, Captain S.W. Farnham, Lieutenants J. Bond, W. Pomerantz, and L. Schacheur, and Flight Officers F.G. Johnson and W.D. Terry, all of whom scored one each. Additionally, Lieutenants Woodman and Bass each destroyed a Bf-109. A total of 15 enemy aircraft had been destroyed for the loss of Second Lieutenant Donald Hawkins.

The 52nd Group also participated in the Markersdorf mission, escorting the Liberators from the 55th Bomb Wing, flying high cover over the target during the bombers' withdrawal. They spotted a mixed force of Bf-109s and Fw-190s, just as a flight of Bf-109s shot down a B-24 and escaped into the clouds. This was the same formation that was attacked by the 325th Group. Shortly after the Checkertails dived away, the 52nd's Mustangs dived into a gaggle of 25 enemy fighters attempting to re-form after being hit by the Clan's fighters. As the group of enemy fighters approached the tail end of the bomber formation, several Fw-190s peeled off and dived on the stragglers. Spotting the approaching Mustangs, they attempted to break away and evade, but Lieutenants Richard Evans, Roy Frye, and George Nash caught them before they could disappear in the clouds and each destroyed one Fw-190.

Captain Bob Curtis spotted another group of Fw-190s and led his flight to attack them. He later reported:

> I saw five Fw-190s approaching the bombers on the far right from dead astern. As one attacked a B-24, I closed on him from six o'clock. He broke to the left. When he saw me he rolled over, diving toward the cloud tops. I followed, closing rapidly, and fired a burst from 100 yards, scoring strikes on the fuselage and wing roots. I closed to 50 yards and fired another burst as he went into a cloud. I overshot and pulled off to the side. The enemy aircraft appeared out of the bottom of the cloud and went straight into the ground.

This was Curtis' 14th, and last, victory.

Overall, the 52nd claimed 20 enemy aircraft destroyed in the battle, but nine B-24s were lost. The mission summary noted that the enemy pilots made a "spirited defense," and were "experienced and aggressive." They also noted that the bombers "could have and should have" flown further from the clouds; not doing so allowed the enemy to get close to the formation before being spotted, thus limiting the time to engage and disrupt their attacks.

The next day, August 24, the bombers attacked oil refineries in Pardubice, Czechoslovakia. Two P-51s were hit by the very heavy flak that opened up as the formation approached the target. Both P-51s successfully returned to base, along with a third that suffered mechanical failure. Captain Richard Dunkin spotted the only enemy aircraft seen, when a Bf-109 dived on the bombers. Dunkin went after it and later reported:

> I was leading my section over the target area when I observed a single Me-109 making a pass at the B-24s. I was at 29,000 feet when I made a diving turn and chased the enemy aircraft to the deck. The Me-109 made a gentle turn to the left, then straightened out as I closed from 275 yards to 150 yards and fired several short bursts from dead astern. I observed strikes in the cockpit as the pilot jettisoned the canopy and the airplane crashed into the ground.

This Bf-109 was Dunkin's ninth, and final, victory.

Moments later a huge gaggle of 20 Bf-109s and 20 Fw-190s was spotted as they bounced the bombers, shooting down seven before the Mustangs could intervene. Several Checkertails reported spotting a captured P-51, painted black with yellow wing stripes, among the German fighters. The Checkertails were able to down three of these enemy fighters, with First Lieutenant Harry Parker later reporting: "I attacked a Me-109 at 15,000 feet and fired a short burst from 300 yards, before turning away after my guns quit working. The pilot of the Me-109, however, rolled over and bailed out. My wingman, Lieutenant Gaston, observed the action and confirmed my victory." This victory tied Parker with Wayne Lowry as the second-highest scoring Checkertail, with 11 victories each.

First Lieutenant Robert H. Brown scored his seventh, and final, victory when he clobbered an Fw-190, reporting: "I attacked a Fw-190 at 15,000 feet and he dived away, but I caught up with him at 10,000 feet. I opened fire from 100 yards astern with 40 degrees deflection and closed to 20 feet with no deflection. Many hits were observed on the wings and fuselage of the Fw-190 and it burst into flames and crashed into the ground."

After the 82nd Group's last shuttle mission in early August, opportunities for the group's pilots to engage enemy aircraft declined dramatically. This was partly due to the heavy losses the Axis had suffered in June and July, but also due to the forced evacuation of Luftwaffe units from Romania. Over the course of the final eight months of the war in Europe, pilots of the 82nd would claim only four enemy aircraft destroyed in the air and 12 on the ground.

August also saw many of the 82nd's more successful pilots finish their tours. The 97th's Bob Biggs and squadron mate Lee Lette, along with Ed Bodine and Dick Gangel of the 96th Squadron, and Roy Harman, Jack Joley, and Paul Mass from the 95th, had all left the group for return to the United States by mid-August. Over the course of the rest of the month, the only claims in August were for two Ju-88s damaged on the ground on August 13 by Majors Gardner and Greene, and a C.202 damaged in the air by Gardner on August 26. Major Herb Phillips turned over command of the 95th Squadron to Warnie Gardner on August 12, while Major Ford handed command of the 97th Squadron to former American Volunteer Group (AVG, known as the "Flying Tigers") pilot Paul Greene an hour later that same day. On August 29 Major Ike Isaacson turned over command of the 96th Squadron to former squadron operations officer Captain Dick Willsie. By the fall, all the combat veterans of North Africa, Sicily, Italy, and the Fifteenth's campaign against Ploeşti had departed. Deputy group CO Lieutenant Colonel Ben Mason flew his last mission on October 17, while both Major Gardner – the last ace still in the group – and Lieutenant Colonel Greene left the group on October 26; Greene moved up to the newly established 305th Wing, which was now responsible for the three P-38 groups in XV Fighter Command. Dick Willsie was the last to go, promoted to major before he departed on December 15 after flying his 82nd mission on December 6.

The P-38J-25-LO Lightning finally began arriving in the 1st Fighter Group in August. The sub-type was equipped with dive brakes under the wing that were electrically operated and became wedge-shaped when extended, altering the airflow over the wing and preventing the airplane getting caught in the transonic range where it went out of control. It also had hydraulically boosted ailerons that vastly improved maneuverability. The dive brakes removed the greatest fear of pilots – that they would end up out of control and quickly dead – while the boosted ailerons gave the heavy twin the ability to out-turn both the Fw-190 or Bf-109. The dive brakes had been designed and approved for production in 1943, but by the time they finally showed up on the production line, more than half the Lightnings that would be built had already come off the line.

The 1st Fighter Group flew their new P-38s to Ploeşti on August 10, following their successful escort of the 14th Group's P-38s to dive-bomb the airfields at Plan de Dieu and Valence in southern France in preparation for the coming invasion. Unfortunately, the enemy declined to come up and defend the refineries. Only two enemy fighters were spotted attacking a straggling B-17, and they evaded by split-essing to the deck when they spotted the flight of P-38s that turned toward them.

The 1st Group began their move to Aghione airfield on the east coast of northern Corsica when advance units started moving to the island on August 10. They were joined there in following days by the 14th Group; both units were assigned to close air support of the coming invasion of southern France, which was only 100 miles from the new base. The 1st's Captain "Beans" Caldwell recalled a mission flown to the Riviera coat invasion area on August 15, two days after they began flying missions from the island. "I led a flight of four on an armed recce over southern France where we dive-bombed a bridge and then patrolled the coast. It got dark on the way home so I called for a D/F steer direct over the mountains to Aghione to save on fuel. They gave me a heading and sometime later we saw some lights below. We continued on, assuming we had seen lights on the West Coast of Corsica." What Caldwell didn't know at the time was that the steer was to the port of Bastia at the northern tip of the island. The four P-38s flow on out into the Tyrrhenian Sea, and were soon lost. "About that time, my wingman, Carroll Feather, checked in with 'Red Leader, I have about five minutes of fuel remaining.'" Caldwell called for another steer to the nearest base, and they were vectored to Borgo airfield. "I told Feather to leave formation and land immediately and get it right on the first pass. I watched his lights and saw him pull up just short of the runway and go around. I was sweating bullets while he did that, but he landed okay. His right engine shut down right after touchdown, and his left a minute later, leaving him on the runway. We three landed all right."

Missions from Corsica for both groups involved dive-bombing gun positions, transportation infrastructure, and airfields, followed by coastal patrols. Caldwell recalled "We had to be very careful overflying the Navy, because they would shoot at any plane that came in range."

On August 13, the 14th Group sent P-38s to attack the German airfield at Orange. The 49th Squadron was assigned as "strafers" while the 37th and 48th Squadrons flew top cover. Captain Don Luttrell, who led the 49th Squadron, recalled the mission:

> We were right on the deck all the way, and hit the target dead on. But there wasn't a single enemy aircraft on the field, or in any of the revetments. But the AA was waiting. They opened up on us like it was the fourth of July! It was intense and accurate. I saw Lieutenant Don Tracy pull up slightly, a big stream of fire coming from under the aircraft. He rolled over, the nose dropped, and he hit the ground inverted, rolling up into a ball of fire about half a mile long.
>
> We escorted the other two squadrons to Valence. They had the same kind of luck, no airplanes on the ground, but an alert anti-aircraft defense. I saw the explosion of Lieutenant Clarence Thompson from the 37th Squadron. On the way out I shot up two gun positions and a radar tower that I just happened to stumble across. We came out of France with two losses and nothing to show for it.

In fact, when the group returned to Corsica, they realized there had been a third loss, when the 37th Squadron's Second Lieutenant Elmer Torgeson failed to return.

When the Lightnings arrived back at Corsica, the first few aircraft to land had no problems. But their props stirred up the dust on the dirt strip into a cloud that became larger and thicker as others landed, which hung over the field, leaving the later arrivals with the problem of seeing the field to land. "One of our pilots, Lieutenant Lloyd Bro, put his landing lights down, mistook the top of the dust cloud for the runway, and landed about 15 feet in the air. When the P-38 stalled out, it came crashing down and pieces flew all over that end of Corsica. He was unharmed, but the plane was destroyed." Luttrell managed to land by setting up a slow constant rate of descent, landing on instruments. "When I entered the dust, I just held my heading and rate of descent and hit the runway between the runway lights. On the rollout, I could make out one or two runway lights ahead to maintain direction. Once down I had to kill my landing lights because the light shining back from the dust blinded me."

Between D-Day on August 15 and August 20 when beach patrols were no longer needed because the majority of troops were inland, the P-38 groups flew hundreds of sorties from Corsica, with pilots flying two and even three missions in a day.

The Luftwaffe was noticeably absent, though on D-Day itself two groups of Bf-109s were encountered. A 71st Squadron flight was forced to jettison its bombs when a gaggle of 11 Bf-109s showed up; Lieutenant Robert Longworth destroyed one while the rest fled. Minutes later, Major James Moorehead's 27th Squadron flight ran into another group of Bf-109s. He later recalled:

> Tom Maloney and I were on a dive-bombing mission. Tom had a flight of four P-38s with two 500-pound bombs each; I had a second flight also loaded with 500-pound bombs. Suddenly we spotted seven Me-109s diving on us! I had been searching for our target and hadn't seen them in time to toggle our bombs. We turned into them and fortunately no bombs were hit by German bullets. We then dumped our ordnance and joined the fight. I was chasing a 109 and gaining on him, when he suddenly bailed out though I had not fired a shot. That was because he knew he was no match for a P-38 at low altitude in terms of speed and maneuverability when we were so low he couldn't dive away.
>
> I quickly found another target and followed him up the Rhone River Gorge – Europe's Little Grand Canyon. Great towering walls rose up on either side and was 500 yards behind the 109 when three others popped out of a side canyon and flew right in front of me. I put the pipper on them and was about to open fire, I had them cold – full ammo, lots of gas and all I needed was a few seconds. I heard the old admonition "check your tail." I looked back and damn! There he was! I jerked on my yoke and with those hydraulic controls my P-38 shot straight up those cavernous walls just as he took his shot and missed.
>
> As I shot up into the sky out of the canyon, my wingman closed on the 109 and shot him down. I continued around in my loop – fortunately my alignment was true and I came out of between the canyon walls just in time to see the German smash against the canyon wall and explode in a fiery crash.

The invasion cost the 1st Fighter Group four pilots – the 71st's Lieutenant Harold Kline failed to return on August 18, while Lieutenant Lauren Erickson was lost to flak the next day. Lieutenants Robert Taylor and Walter St John of the 94th Squadron both went down in flames after being hit by flak on August 20.

Both groups returned to their Foggia bases on August 18.

August 19 was a bad day for the group. The 94th's Major Ed LaClare was leading a flight from the 94th and one from the 27th when they spotted a train heading for the front that turned out to be loaded with ammunition, which exploded when they strafed it. First Lieutenant Dick Arrowsmith's P-38 caught fire and he was forced to crash-land not far from the target. Lieutenant Walter Gonring made it back to Corsica in his heavily damaged fighter, which had one engine out, no hydraulics, one wheel locked down, and no radio. He managed to safely crash-land at Cape Calvi, thought the Lightning was a total loss. The 94th's eight-victory ace Tom Maloney was hit in both engines, forcing him to ditch off the coast. Major Francis J. Pope, flight leader of the 27th Squadron's flight, orbited to the limit of fuel, but it was too late in the day to get a Dumbo air rescue. When Pope led a flight to the crash area at dawn the next day, Maloney was nowhere to be found.

Fortunately, during the night Maloney had drifted ashore near the mouth of the Rhone River. He had walked about 40 feet when he stepped on something solid and heard a click. It was a landmine, and the explosion injured his feet and legs. After lying on the beach for three days, he began pulling himself backward in a sitting position. It took five days to reach a marshy area where he constructed a raft and drifted along the coast to a French village. Village men took him to the local hospital, which could do nothing for him, but they contacted a nearby American field hospital where he was taken by American medics. He was then flown to the Army hospital in Naples, where his legs were saved. He was finally sent back to the United States in November 1944.

Dick Arrowsmith was able to get out of his burning fighter after the crash before it exploded. He evaded for three days, then was found by a French farm hand. He stayed with the French family for five days, when the French resistance arrived to rescue him. He was taken through the lines and returned to Corsica at the end of August.

Overall, during the invasion the two P-38 groups lost 25 airplanes and 14 pilots between them. The invasion went so quickly and Allied troops advanced so fast that on August 21, Major Moorehead led a flight of P-38 dive bombers to attack a reported formation of tanks. When they got overhead, "One of my pilots yelled 'They're ours!' I stopped the attack just before we rolled into our dives."

The 14th Group lost a total of seven pilots during the invasion, all to the murderous light flak at low level over targets that were devoid of the Luftwaffe.

By late August, the scarcity of Luftwaffe defenders resulted in bombing missions being flown to attack German airfields in the hope of forcing the defenders to rise to the challenge.

On August 24, 52 332nd Fighter Group P-51s were assigned to escort the 5th Bomb Wing to bomb Pardubice airfield, in Czechoslovakia. While no enemy aircraft were encountered during the flight to the target, or over the target itself, First Lieutenant John Briggs' flight was bounced by a single Bf-109 on the way home. The enemy fighter was spotted making an attack run from "six o'clock" and the Mustangs turned sharply into the attack. Briggs managed to get on the tail, below the fleeing fighter as it climbed toward the cloud deck it had popped out of. Firing bursts from 250 yards, Briggs saw no results and pressed his pursuit to 25 yards, opening fire as the two fighters passed through 35,000 feet. The six .50-caliber machine guns knocked pieces off the Bf-109, which flew back toward Briggs; they were followed moments later by the pilot, who jettisoned his canopy and bailed out.

As Briggs was scoring his victory, First Lieutenant Charles McGee spotted an Fw-190 on an opposite course below him. He peeled off to attack but the German pilot saw his Mustang and abruptly split-essed for the deck. Despite the enemy's use of a series of evasive maneuvers, he failed to shake off the pursuing McGee. Finally, he rolled into a steep dive toward the Pardubice airfield. McGee later reported, "I recall as we flashed over the field proper in a right turn, there was a hangar and several aircraft fires brightly blazing." McGee closed behind the enemy fighter and fired a burst that hit the Focke-Wulf's control cables; the fighter made two erratic turns before it slammed into the ground and caught fire. Wingman Second Lieutenant Roger Romine saw the crash and confirmed McGee's victory.

McGee was now in trouble, as flak from the airfield's defending light antiaircraft guns flashed past. "I made a low-altitude dash out of the area to avoid ground fire [and] got a good burst off on a locomotive at a railroad stop" before he was able to rejoin the group.

At 1235 hours, First Lieutenant William Thomas spotted another Fw-190 at 24,000 feet; simultaneously, the German pilot spotted him, but instead of turning into Thomas and forcing him to break off, the enemy pilot split-essed and dived to escape. Thomas caught up at about 800 feet and fired six times as he closed from 100 to 75 yards. The final burst was a 30-degree deflection shot; the Fw-190 to hit the ground, crumpling into a pile of smoking wreckage.

On August 25, the Red Tails sent 60 Mustangs to escort B-17s of the 5th Bomb Wing to attack Brno airfield in Czechoslovakia. For once, the mission went exactly as briefed; however, this time no enemy defenders rose to challenge the bombers. All the P-51s were back at Ramitelli by 1315 hours.

The next day, the 332nd put up 56 P-51s to accompany the B-24s of the 304th Bomb Wing to attack barracks located near the Banasea airfield in Bulgaria. Unlike the "perfect" mission the day previous, the Liberators arrived at the rendezvous point ten minutes late. When they eventually attempted to hit the target, the Mustang pilots saw the bombs fall harmlessly in the nearby forest. The 99th Squadron's Second Lieutenant Henry Wise saw his oil pressure drop, forcing him to bail out when his Merlin engine began putting out heavy smoke, a warning it was about to blow up. Once on the ground, Wise was quickly captured and made a prisoner of war. His fortunes changed dramatically when Bulgaria severed ties with Germany. While the Germans marched a large number of prisoners of war out of the country, Wise was among several hundred others left behind. Eventually, they were evacuated through Turkey and Egypt, finally arriving back in Italy in September, when Wise returned to Ramitelli. After an immediate promotion to first lieutenant, he was issued orders sending him back to the United States.

The mission of August 27 saw the group's 57 Mustangs escort the Liberators of the 55th and 304th Bomb Wings to hit the synthetic oil refinery at Blechhammer, Germany, once again. After the fighters had completed their rendezvous and escort of the bombers, Captain Melvin Jackson spotted an enemy fighter as it lifted off an airfield near Prostejou, Czechoslovakia. Since they had not come across any opposition, the Mustangs were still fully armed; the group attacked the field, along with another airfield at nearby Kostoleo. With virtually no defending flak at either target, the 332nd's pilots were able to make several strafing passes, and hit a large number of aircraft. By the time the pilots exhausted their ammunition, the score was 13 Ju-52/3ms, four Ju-87s, and three He-111s destroyed, with another four Ju-87s, four He-111s, nine Ju-52/3ms, and an Me-323 "Gigant" damaged.

High scorers were Wendell Pruitt, with three Stukas and two He-111s destroyed; Spann Watson, credited with four of the Ju-52/3ms destroyed and one of the He-111s; and Luther Smith, who claimed three Ju-52/3ms and an He-111 destroyed. The airfield's barracks and the unlucky locomotive spotted near the airfield were also destroyed. Best of all, no Red Tails were shot down or damaged.

Maintaining their pace in light of good weather, 48 P-51s covered the 47th Bomb Wing's B-24s when they bombed the main railroad marshaling yard at Miskolc, Yugoslavia on August 28, with all Mustangs again returning safely to Ramitelli. The following day, 55 Mustangs escorted the 5th Bomb Wing's Flying Fortresses when they attacked the Bohumin and Privoser oil refineries and the Morvaska main railroad marshaling yard in Yugoslavia.

With the Luftwaffe still refusing to come up, on August 30 the 332nd's pilots spotted 150 aircraft at Grosswardein airfield in Romania, which were poorly camouflaged under stacks of hay. The moderate flak didn't deter the 302nd Squadron from making seven passes, while the 100th Squadron made five, and the 99th Squadron made three. After making their attacks, the biggest hazard the pilots faced was the rising smoke caused by burning hay and gasoline that blanketed the field.

Forty-six different pilots made claims from the attack with a list of destroyed aircraft that reads like a German wartime aircraft inventory: 30 Ju-88s, 12 He-111s, seven Fw-189s, six Ju-87s, six Do-217s, five Ju-52/3ms, four Fw-190s, three Bf-109s, three Go-242 gliders, two Me-323s, two Me-410s, two Bf-110s, and a single Ar-96. Top scorers were the 302nd's Captain Roger Romine with seven aircraft destroyed, while Lieutenants Alfonso Davis and Freddie Hutchins claimed four each destroyed. In all, the Red Tails claimed 83 aircraft destroyed and 31 more damaged; it was the most destructive day in the 332nd's history. The only casualty was First Lieutenant Charles Williams, who was a victim of flak in the target area that forced him to bail out, after which he was taken prisoner.

August ended with two escort missions on August 31. The first saw the 100th and 301st Squadrons send 32 Mustangs to cover the second wave of B-17s attacking Popesti-Leordeni airfield; a similar mission involving the 99th and 302nd squadrons sent 31 fighters to cover the third wave as they hit the airfield. There was no enemy aerial opposition. Another mission to bomb this field the next day was canceled when bad weather and poor navigation prevented the 301st and 302nd Squadrons from rendezvousing with the bombers.

August also saw a dramatic change in the overall war when the Romanian government surrendered and joined the Allied side as a co-belligerent; this "turning of arms" against Nazi Germany was one of the key actions of World War II in Europe, since Romania's turn away from the Nazi cause meant the denial of sorely needed foodstuffs from Romanian agriculture, and the end of German access to petroleum products from the Ploeşti refineries. The Romanian Army had been a major ally on the Eastern front from the opening of Operation *Barbarossa* in June 1941 to the defeat of the Axis forces at the Battle of Kursk in July 1943.

Importantly, the young Romanian king, Mihai I, had lost faith in the alliance with Nazi Germany following the defeat at Stalingrad in January 1943, and had increasingly started to challenge the dictator Antonescu, who had taken power in 1941 as prime minister. He also made moves to establish secret contact with the leaders of the outlawed historical parties and demanded that Antonescu keep him better informed regarding the military situation on the Eastern Front. During the first half of 1943, the king began gathering a small group of conspirators, primarily from the generals who had been previously purged by Antonescu for being too close to the king's father, King Carol II. His goal was to have a group of recognized leaders who were prepared to take action against the Antonescu regime if there were further defeats. Following the defeat at Kursk in July, the king contacted Iuliu Maniu, leader of the National Peasant Party – the largest part of the United Opposition – who had been working with the British Special Operations Executive (SOE) since Romania had joined Germany in attacking Russia three years earlier.

Beginning in September 1943, following the example of Fascist Italy, which had secretly negotiated an armistice with the Western Allies, representatives of the king made contact with American and British diplomatic representatives in neutral countries with the aim of discussing terms of a surrender. The Romanians were rebuffed by both Americans and British, who told them they must deal with the Soviet Union.

Both the Antonescu regime and the United Opposition wished to retain northern Bukovina and Bessarabia; both groups hoped that American and British forces would invade the Balkans and reach

Romania before the Soviets did. Their hope was reinforced by their knowledge that Churchill was at the time arguing with the Americans over the idea of an invasion of central Europe through the Ljubljana Gap in northern Yugoslavia, forestalling a Soviet occupation. In the end, Churchill failed to carry the day at the Quebec Conference, where the main strategy was fixed on the invasion of northern France in 1944. The Romanians discovered that September that all the signs of an Allied amphibious operation in the northern Adriatic to take the Gap were a feint created to distract the Germans from focusing on the intended cross-channel invasion. The king, an avowed anticommunist who had collaborated in the overthrow of his father and the imposition of Fascist rule in Romania ten years earlier, could not bring himself to negotiate with the Soviets, who he knew would demand he leave the throne as a condition of any surrender.

March 4, 1944 saw the commencement of an early spring Red Army offensive meant to split the Axis forces in two, pressing the German Northern Front and Central Front forces to retreat into southern Poland while the German Southern Front forces, the Romanians, and the Hungarian forces were pushed into eastern Romania.

The size and scope of the Red Army's offensive surprised both the German Army High Command (the Oberkommando des Heeres, or OKH) and the Romanian General Staff. On March 15, armored units of the Soviet 2nd Ukrainian Front seized Vapniarka – an important railroad junction in Transnistria only 30 miles from the Dniester River border with Romania.

With most of its troops in Crimea, the Romanian Army had few resources to throw into this battle. On March 18, Soviet troops from the east crossed the Dniester near Mogilev–Podolskii into northern Bessarabia, and eight days later crossed into northern Moldavia by crossing the Prut River before the Romanians could organize an effective defense. Simultaneously, the 1st Ukrainian Front broke through from the north, forcing the German Eighth Army into a disorderly withdrawal. On March 26, the Bukovina regional capital Cernăuți fell without a fight. On April 1, Soviet forces advancing from the north and east linked up near Hotin. While those events happened, the German Sixth Army and Romanian Third Army in southern Transnistria on the Black Sea coast were threatened with being isolated and destroyed by the 3rd Ukrainian Front.

AUGUST CRESCENDO

In the face of this, diplomats from the Antonescu regime in Sweden contacted their Soviet opposite numbers in Stockholm and attempted to start negotiations. These talks led to secret negotiations between Romania and the Soviet Union in Stockholm over the course of the summer. While the talks went on, the Red Army's planners developed a plan to advance into Romania and take Iași, the Moldavian regional capital, and Chișinău, the regional capital of Bessarabia. This would position the Soviet forces to advance into Yugoslavia and Bulgaria, where Stalin hoped to install pro-Soviet postwar governments. After these two objectives were taken, the Red Army would advance into Wallachia, where Bucharest and Ploești were located.

On April 8, the 2nd Ukrainian Front advanced between the Siret and Prut rivers south into Moldavia, heading for Iași. The same day, the 3rd Ukrainian Front attacked Axis forces in Crimea, taking Odessa on April 10. The fall of Odessa finally convinced Hitler to allow the troops in Crimea to retreat, which began on April 12. This retreat involved only Axis support troops, since OKH had ordered combat troops to hold a perimeter around Sevastopol. Those Axis forces that arrived at Constanța were demoralized and disorganized following an evacuation in which they were harassed by Soviet submarines and air attacks. The Axis forces that did escape Crimea were of little use for further operations in Romania defending Moldavia and Bessarabia.

German Army Group A was reorganized, becoming German Army Group South Ukraine, controlling the battered German Eighth and Sixth and Romanian Third Armies, reinforced by the Romanian Fourth Army. This force would make its stand in Romania.

What became the First Iași–Chișinău offensive was launched by the Red Army on April 15, 1944. After months of hard winter fighting, the 2nd and 3rd Ukrainian Fronts that comprised the offensive force were tired and overextended, while their Axis opponents were retreating into a solid logistical network; in addition, they had favorable defensive ground, since Moldavia and Bessarabia were hilly and forested, as opposed to the open steppe in Ukraine. The Romanian rail and road transport network had not yet been hit hard by the Fifteenth Air Force, though the bombers began flying missions against these targets in support of both the Soviet advance and the Transportation Plan supporting Operation *Overlord*.

The rainy spring hindered movement as rain turned roads into muddy rivers. The 2nd Ukrainian Front made little progress advancing into northern Moldavia and Bessarabia, while the 3rd Ukrainian Front stalled on the Dniester when they were unable to cross the river and advance into central and southern Bessarabia. By April 17, the German Army Group South Ukraine stabilized the front.

Throughout late April, May, and June, the battle raged, with the Axis defenders giving ground slowly. Crimea fell on May 13, three days after Odessa was taken. At the end of May, the Germans began local counterattacks at Iași, which lasted through June and July as the Soviets prepared their summer offensive. The Red Army's Operation *Bagration*, which began as Stalin had promised at the Tehran Conference in November 1943, would start two weeks after the Western Allies landed in Normandy, to keep the Wehrmacht from reinforcing the invasion area; it aimed to liberate Byelorussia, followed by an advance into eastern Poland.

After the Soviet Forces in Romania had paused to allow for replacements to be fed into the army, the Second Iași–Chișinău Offensive began with Soviet probes on August 19. This was also the day that saw the final Fifteenth Air Force mission against Ploești, which was more a mass of ruins than an operational refinery after the four-month air campaign.

The Axis forces were not strong enough to resist their reinforced Soviet opponents, and arguments developed between the German and Romanian commanders over the planned retreat to the fortified Focșani–Nămoloasa–Brăila (FNB) Line that blocked the 56-mile-wide Focșani Gap, the gateway to the Wallachia plains. After only a day of fighting on August 20, German Army Group South Ukraine showed worrying signs of a total collapse, particularly along the Romanian-held Iași front in Bessarabia. That night Marshal Antonescu held a meeting with the German commander, General Freissner, where the discussion devolved into an argument over whether to retreat to the FNB Line immediately or to delay doing so. Freissner had been suspected of involvement in the July 20 attempted assassination of Hitler, and was afraid of being thought a coward if he requested permission to retreat from Oberkommando der Wehrmacht (the Wehrmacht High Command, or OKW).

After receiving news of the Soviet offensive, the king traveled to Bucharest using the pretext of inspecting new military aircraft. At the villa in Bucharest that he used as a royal residence, he met with seven trusted intimates from the Army who were opponents of Antonescu. They determined that the Soviet offensive was the event they had been waiting for and made plans for a coup. The next day, the king met with the leaders of the United Opposition, and the coup was set for August 26.

The day after the meeting, August 21, the Axis counterattack on the Soviets was over almost before it began, when the Red Army pushed past the units on the front line, smashing the Romanian 3rd Infantry Division's forward elements, allowing the 3rd Ukrainian Front to break out south from Iași. By midday, the Soviets threatened to overrun the remains of the Romanian 7th and 3rd Infantry Divisions holding the main defensive positions in Bessarabia. Antonescu and his staff met again with General Freissner that afternoon, and came away believing the German had no idea of what was actually happening.

By then, the Red Army had split open a gap between the Romanian Third Army and the German Sixth Army. By nightfall, the Romanian VI Corps surrendered. There was no hope of holding the line. This was followed by the collapse of the German 76th Infantry Division as it attempted to retreat.

The Romanian Fourth Army in Moldavia collapsed as the Red Army spread its frontal assault. General Freissner finally contacted Field Marshal Heinz Guderian, acting head of OKH, and sought permission to retreat to the FNB Line. Guderian said he would consult Hitler.

At about the same time, the king met with the United Opposition leaders. He presented his plan for the coup, which was approved. The opposition leaders then began arguing over the make-up of the planned national unity government. The king told them to present a list of ministers on August 24 and dismissed the meeting.

At midnight, Hitler approved a limited retreat, but not to the FNB Line. When Freissner presented what was approved, the Romanians understood that the Germans were planning to sacrifice the Third and Fourth Romanian armies to save the German Sixth Army. When Antonescu learned of the decision, he concluded that the alliance of Germany and Romania was over.

The renewed Soviet attack on August 22 saw the Romanian Fourth Army and German Sixth Army badly cut up, while the Romanian Third Army had its route of retreat cut off. The Germans did not realize that at 0900 hours Antonescu had ordered the Fourth Army to retreat to the FNB Line, which left the German Sixth Army badly exposed to their opponents.

Antonescu had decided to abandon the Germans completely. He directed Vice Prime Minister Mihai Antonescu to send telegrams to Romanian diplomats in Sweden, Turkey, and Switzerland, ordering them to make contact with Allied representatives to get an armistice. He planned to make a last visit to Freissner's headquarters before making a final decision, then go to Bucharest. News of this reached the coup conspirators, and the king immediately determined to arrest Antonescu when he arrived in Bucharest that night. At the same time, the Romanian Fourth Army made surreptitious plans to commence its retreat that night.

That night, the entire southern front collapsed. The Romanian Third Army was surrounded, and the Romanian Fourth Army was attempting to move to the FNB Line; this left the German Sixth Army surrounded.

Having arrived in Bucharest, Antonescu met with Ion Mihalache from the National Peasant Party, followed by Gheorghe Brătianu from the Liberal Party. Both told him they had asked for the meeting at the king's request. They pressured Antonescu not to return to the front without first briefing the king about the situation. Both told him it was time for an armistice; they reported to the king that Antonescu seemed open to that idea. Antonescu scheduled a meeting for lunch with the king for August 23.

Dawn on August 23 saw the southern front implode as the retreat became a rout. The Sixth Army Headquarters had relocated but was not able to re-establish telephone communication, leaving the combat units without direction. The roads were jammed with broken-down vehicles. The Soviet 46th Army blocked the Romanian Third Army's attempted retreat from the coast; the Soviets now controlled the roads to the Danube bridges.

Antonescu planned to advise his government to keep fighting. The king and his advisors planned to arrest Antonescu and his staff at the lunch. Antonescu arrived promptly at 1500 hours. He and the vice prime minister waited in the drawing room with General Sănătescu for the arrival of the king, while just down the stairs three officers loyal to the king took position with three non-commissioned officers.

The king arrived; after greeting Antonescu he asked for a report on the situation. Antonescu admitted that the Soviets now controlled

Moldavia and Bessarabia, blaming the army for not fighting hard enough while accusing the political opposition of weakening morale by propaganda. The king asked, "Don't you think the moment has come to conclude an armistice either by you or by another government?" Antonescu replied that he had reached out to the Allies but would not agree to an armistice without warning Hitler first and obtaining guarantees from the Allies for time in which German troops would withdraw without harassment and for the continuation of Romanian civil administration, as well as an agreement that no border changes would be made before a post-war peace conference. The king and General Sănătescu said there was no time to obtain such concessions. The vice prime minister stated that the government needed a few days to hear back from the Allies. Sănătescu responded that Romania had only a few hours to decide. When the king asked Antonescu to step aside, he vehemently refused, saying he would fight on. The king replied, "If that's how things are, then there's nothing more for us to do." This was the code phrase to set the coup in action. The three officers and the NCOs entered. They saluted Antonescu and asked him to come with them as they grabbed his arms. Antonescu demanded, "What does this mean?" The king's adjutant yelled to the soldiers, "Carry out your orders!" Antonescu threatened them with execution for treachery, but he and the vice prime minister were taken upstairs and both were locked in a large wall safe in which King Carol II had kept his stamp collection.

The conspirators then asked Antonescu's staff to come in out of the heat, and arrested them. Messages were sent in Antonescu's name to the other government ministers, calling for a meeting. When they arrived, they too were arrested. The head of the police saw things in disarray when he arrived; he drove off and alerted the Germans that a coup had occurred.

As the royal coup happened in Bucharest, the German Army Group South Ukraine fell apart. Panic gripped German and Romanian soldiers desperate to escape capture. There was no retreat for the Sixth Army, while the Romanians were surrounded. The German soldiers became a mob desperate to escape.

Back in Bucharest, the royal coup grew stronger. The king appointed General Sănătescu as new prime minister; he had chosen generals to be his ministers. The king named the four leaders of the United Opposition

– now the National Democratic Bloc – ministers without portfolio. The Royal Palace was under guard by loyal soldiers.

At 1900 hours, Baron von Killinger, the German ambassador, was finally informed of the coup and went to see the king, who told him that the Antonescu regime had been deposed and that General Sănătescu's new government intended to cease hostilities and sign an armistice with the Allies. The king concluded by asking von Killinger to convince the German government to withdraw all German forces. Soon after, the new Romanian foreign minister officially broke diplomatic relations with Nazi Germany.

General Alfred Gerstenberg, head of the Luftwaffe Mission in Romania, informed OKW of what had happened and, without consulting anyone else, suggested launching a counter-coup. Unsurprisingly, Hitler enthusiastically agreed and ordered the king arrested.

News of the coup became public when the king gave a speech on radio at 2225 hours, saying, "Romanians, in this most difficult hour of our history I have decided, in full understanding with my people, that there is only one way to save the country from total catastrophe; our withdrawal from the alliance with the Axis powers and the immediate cessation of the war with the United Nations." He announced the creation of the national unity government, and agreed to accept an armistice, ending all hostile acts against Soviet forces, as well as US and British forces. The BBC monitoring service picked up the speech and Romania's defection became worldwide news 30 minutes later.

For now, the new government was on its own.

At the front, Red Army commanders continued to treat Romanian units as hostile. Most Romanian soldiers had not heard the news. The king had not trusted the officer corps, so the Romanian commanders were taken by surprise.

At 2245 hours, Baron von Killinger telephoned German Army Group South Ukraine Headquarters to inform General Freissner that Romania had abandoned the Axis. Freissner asked Romanian Generals Ilie Șteflea and Petre Dumitrescu to keep fighting. Both declined. General Dumitrescu said, "I cannot take another attitude than that which His Majesty the King and the new government have taken." The two generals tried to save what they could of the Romanian Fourth and Third Armies, but the Third Army surrendered within hours.

In Bucharest, General Gerstenberg moved to organize a counter-coup. There were 35,000 German troops in and around the capital, but most were not combat troops and were not capable of such an operation. Overnight, Gerstenberg assembled fewer than 3,000 men at the Otopeni airfield on the northern outskirts of Bucharest. General Erik Hansen, chief of the German Army Mission in Romania, warned Hitler they were underestimating the training, ability, and strength of Romanian reserves, but no one listened.

At 0300 hours on August 24, the king and his entourage departed Bucharest so that he would not be captured. The Sănătescu government cut the communications of German offices and began disarming German personnel. The Romanian Capital Military Command had 7,000 Romanian soldiers, with tank support, with more on the way. At 0830 hours Gerstenberg headed toward the capital with his motorized column of ragtag infantry. They took the Romanian fighter airfield at Băneasa but were then stopped at a bridge by a Romanian military group composed of cavalry and light tanks. At 1035 hours, Gerstenberg ordered air attacks on the city.

The relatively weak Luftwaffe attacks were ineffectual, failing to spread panic among a civilian population now accustomed to much stronger American air attacks. The Brandenburg Division, a special forces unit, landed two platoons of special forces at two Romanian airfields to immobilize Romanian aircraft; the two teams were quickly killed or captured by Romanian paratroopers and air force security troops. An SS parachute battalion led by Otto Skorzeny, who had rescued Mussolini, was on standby in Serbia to attempt a rescue of Antonescu, but he had been turned over to Romanian communists who kept him in a secret location, negating any possibility of a German rescue effort.

With Gerstenberg's force stalled outside Bucharest, the Romanian 2nd Călărași Regiment assaulted German Army and Luftwaffe offices downtown. At the front, the German–Romanian military divorce was cordial. When news of the royal coup reached Romanian units, they had three choices: continued resistance, surrender, or withdrawal. Most of the Romanian troops decided to retreat, often on roads which were also occupied by German units. Confusion about the unexpected political developments, loyalty to former allies, and a desire to escape the Red Army convinced most Germans and Romanians to avoid fighting each other for as long as possible in order to escape the advancing enemy.

By noon on August 24, the 1st and 2nd Ukrainian Fronts had joined up and were pressing the defeated Germans and Romanians. Following the surrender of the Romanian Third Army the day before, the Fourth Army surrendered that afternoon.

The Romanian government declared war on Nazi Germany on August 25. Everything had turned around in Romania over three days.

In the midst of all this, a daring plan was set in motion between the 1,200 American flyers held as prisoners of war in the Bucharest prison and officers of the Royal Romanian Air Force to inform the USAAF command in Italy of the position of the prisoners of war, and to organize a rescue.

On August 17, Lieutenant Colonel James A. Gunn III, commander of the 454th Bomb Group, had led one of the final missions to Ploești. Before "bombs away," eight B-24s from the 454th had been hit by flak and shot down, including Gunn's bomber. Gunn and all but one of his crew managed to get out of the blazing bomber. Once on the ground, the crew were quickly captured by the Romanian Army. After an initial interrogation, the colonel was transported to the officers' prison in Bucharest, where he became the senior Allied officer.

As news of the Romanian surrender spread, starting on August 22, the gates to the prison were left open as the Romanian prison guards vanished. Gunn's first responsibility was to convince the prisoners of war to remain in the prison and not vanish into the city and the surrounding countryside, while he found a way to organize their rescue and repatriation. Fortunately, Gunn was a charismatic, commanding personality, and despite the fact they had only known him for a week, the aircrews listened to what he said and stayed. The gates were closed to protect the men from the Romanian populace outside the prison. They were caught up in the attempted counter-coup organized by German General Gerstenberg. The Germans had started their reprisal bombing of the capital, which put the prison itself in danger of being hit. As the air raids continued, the Allied prisoners were released from the Timișul de Jos and Bucharest prisoner-of-war camps. They were given permission to hide in the trenches outside, and were also given a few rifles with which to defend themselves.

On August 24, Colonel Gunn met with Valeriu "Rică" Georgescu, who had connections to the British SOE. He managed to contact the Cairo SOE by radio to request an urgent airstrike on the German troops at Băneasa and Otopeni, but the British in Cairo were unsure if the Germans were in control of the communication. Georgescu also introduced Gunn to Prime Minister Sănătescu, War Minister General Racoviă, and Iuliu Maniu, now a minister without portfolio in the unity government.

A prisoner delegation asked the war minister to allow them to organize as a combat unit fighting the Germans under Romanian command. Some 900 prisoners of war from Bucharest were transported to the regimental barracks of the 4th Vânători Regiment, which was south of Ghencea, where they were issued carbines and pistols, and provided two trucks and two motorcycles with sidecars. They organized themselves as a battalion of four companies. However, the unit was short-lived; by the next day, the Romanian officers had determined that the Americans lacked the training and discipline to fight the Germans as an infantry unit. Still, the former prisoners of war were instructed to travel around Bucharest in open top cars whenever possible, in hopes that if the local population saw them, they would inform the Germans that American troops had arrived in Bucharest.

When Gunn met with General Racoviă, he proposed that the Romanians fly him to Italy to contact Fifteenth Air Force and arrange evacuation for the prisoners. He also agreed to convince General Twining to order attacks on the airfields that the Luftwaffe was using for its attacks on the city and to do what he could to convey their request that the British or the Americans occupy Romania. Rică Georgescu took Gunn to the Popesti-Leordeni airfield where they met Capitan Aviator Constantin "Bâzu" Cantacuzino, Romania's leading ace with 54 victories, who commanded the Grupul 9 Vânătoare. Cantacuzino proposed that Gunn fly to Italy in a Romanian SM 79 bomber. Twenty minutes after they took off, the aircraft returned; the pilot stated it had problems with its Jumo 211 engines. Cantacuzino then offered to fly him to Italy in his Bf-109G-6.

The radios were removed from their position in the rear fuselage to make room for Gunn. The Romanian insignia was painted over with large American flags on the fuselage and the US Air Corps pre-war national insignia on the wings. The original plan had been to take off the next morning, but while the final touches were being applied to the new markings, Cantacuzino learned that pro-German members of his squadron had informed the Germans what they were going to do.

Fearing that he Germans would try to intercept the flight and shoot them down, he told Gunn they had to take off immediately. There were no maps, so Gunn drew from memory a map of the southeast coast of Italy and an approach chart for his home base at San Giovanni airfield. Gunn told Cantacuzino they should make the trip on the deck to avoid being picked up by radar and intercepted by German or American fighters that might shoot first on spotting the Bf-109 and ask questions later. Cantacuzino replied that he was unsure of the reliability of his engine and that he would fly at 19,000 feet in order to give them a chance of making a successful forced landing. Cantacuzino provided a heavy flying suit for Gunn and the colonel managed to squeeze into the Messerschmitt's fuselage through the 18 x 18 inch radio access hatch, which was then screwed shut behind him. If anything happened during the flight, Gunn had no means of escape, and the altitude they were going to fly at would test his tolerance for cold and lack of oxygen.

The Messerschmitt took off at 1720 hours from Popesti-Leordeni airfield. The two-hour flight was completed without incident, though the engine began to run rough over the Adriatic. Over Italy, Cantacuzino flew at a lower altitude and when they arrived over San Giovanni airfield, the defending antiaircraft gunners gave the benefit of the doubt to a Messerschmitt painted with American markings. Once Gunn had been extracted from the fuselage and given the opportunity to warm up and recover from hypoxia, the two were immediately driven to Fifteenth Air Force Headquarters at Bari. Gunn made his report, and planning began that night for strikes on the German airfields that were flown the next day when 228 B-24 bombers escorted by 151 P-51 Mustangs struck Băneasa and Otopeni airfields at 1300 hours on August 28.

Later that afternoon, the German force in the Băneasa Forest was surrounded by the Romanian Capital Military Command and surrendered soon afterward. Gerstenberg and General Reiner Stahel, who had arrived with troops to put down the Romanians the way he had recently dealt with the Polish Home Army in the Warsaw Uprising, held on at Otopeni airfield. Romanian antiaircraft guns were brought up and positioned around the field. They shot down several German transport aircraft, which included several Me-232 Gigants bringing in men and materiel from Yugoslavia. General Julius Kuderna's Luftwaffe flak troops around Ploești were surrounded by a Romanian armored detachment using a hodgepodge of World War I-vintage French

Renault tanks and Czech ČKD LT vz. 38 tanks. With no likelihood of German reinforcements, Kuderna's force also surrendered that afternoon.

In Italy, plans were made for the rescue of the Allied prisoners in Bucharest. The initial plan was called Operation *Gunn*. First, Capitan Cantacuzino would return to Romania and confirm that the Popesti-Leordeni airfield was still controlled by the Romanians. Then two B-17 bombers would transport radio equipment and personnel to Romania. An American pilot had ground looped and written off Cantacuzino's Messerschmitt. He was offered a P-51 Mustang. The 31st Fighter Group's Captain Walter J. Goehausen was assigned to teach the basics of flying a P-51 to Cantacuzino. When he took off for a test flight, Cantacuzino started performing some basic aerobatic maneuvers and landed the fighter "as if he had always flown it."

On the return flight to Romania on August 29, Cantacuzino was escorted by three other Mustangs with orders to shoot him down if anything suspicious happened. He landed at Popesti-Leordeni, and after assessing the situation on the airfield he fired a double yellow flare, the signal all was safe. To keep the mission secret from both the Germans and the Soviets, the American pilots were to transmit "I have six zero six gallons of gas, repeat I have six zero six" if the airfield was safe, and "ceiling and visibility zero zero, repeat zero zero" if it was not.

With the news that the field was under Romanian control, the two B-17s, commanded by Colonel George Kraiger, transported the OSS personnel to Popesti-Leordeni, where they were greeted by Rică Georgescu, now State Secretary for the Economics Ministry. Unable to raise Bari to make their report, Capitan Cantacuzino flew his P-51 back to Italy the next day with the necessary information for starting Operation *Reunion* on August 31.

The B-17s used in the operation were reconfigured to carry 20 passengers in their bomb bays. Others were modified to carry ten stretcher patients. The bomber crews were reduced to six to make room for the passengers.

Since some ex-prisoners were now scattered around Romania, radio broadcasts were transmitted with instructions to report to the Hotel Ambassador, headquarters of the OSS mission, for evacuation. To transport the prisoners to the airfield, 57 buses from the capital were used. Some had to be driven as far as Brașov to collect prisoners.

Wounded prisoners of war were accompanied by Princess Catherine Caradja, who was assisted by two American medics.

As Soviet troops entered Bucharest on August 31, the first 38 B-17s from the 5th Bomb Wing flew to Popesti-Leordeni in four waves. Fighter cover for the evacuation was provided by P-38s from the 1st, 14th, and 82nd Fighter Groups. The first day, 740 evacuees were carried back to Italy, escorted by Romanian Bf-109s until P-38s took over as they crossed Yugoslavia. On September 1, 16 B-17s were escorted to Romania by the 332nd Fighter Group. On September 3, the last day of the operation, after a break for weather on September 2, three B-17s and a C-47 Skytrain picked up the last passengers. A total of 1,161 ex-prisoners – 1,127 American, 31 British, two Dutch, one French, and a Romanian who claimed to be an American citizen – were evacuated. No enemy opposition was encountered. One P-38 was lost to flak during the evacuations.

Following the end of the mission, Generals Ira Eaker and Nathan Twining flew to Bucharest to personally thank the king and Secretary Georgescu. By then, the Romanian armed forces were operating with the Red Army to push the surviving Germans into Hungary.

10

WHERE IS THE LUFTWAFFE?

Starting in August 1944, after the big battles of June and July, the Luftwaffe became harder and harder for the XV Fighter Command groups to find and bring to battle over Ploești, and targets in Hungary, Austria, and Germany.

In part, this was due to the success of the oil campaign – the strikes by Eighth and Fifteenth Air Forces against the synthetic fuel industry, and Fifteenth Air Force's unrelenting campaign against Ploești. That was the "proof in the pudding" of the claims made by planners in search of economic targets whose damage or destruction would have wide-ranging effects in the enemy's economy. Planners who had argued in favor of the oil campaign against the unbelievers in Eighth Air Force and RAF Bomber Command had said that the effects of the campaign would be noticeable within six weeks. In fact, it was more rapid than that, with the campaign only starting against Ploești in any sustained manner in May and involving the synthetic fuel industry in June. From September 1944 to the end of the war in 1945, the Luftwaffe would make only limited appearances over the Western Front and the industrial targets in Germany; the majority of the fighters produced in the Emergency Fighter Program that began in the fall of 1944 and maximized German aircraft production never took to the air because of lack of fuel.

The three P-38 groups found no contact with the enemy during September, despite all three participating in 14 escort missions; and only a few enemy aircraft were engaged by the P-51 groups. As a result the Lightning groups became strafing specialists, hitting long-range targets. With the additional range inherent in the P-38J-25 and in the P-38L, which became the ultimate Lightning to see combat when it was introduced on operations over the fall and winter of 1944–45, the Lightning could carry one 310-gallon drop tank and up to a 1,000-pound bomb. This made attacks on enemy airfields and other ground targets much more devastating than was possible with the P-51s, which assumed the primary air-air responsibility due to their even-longer range than the Lockheed twins. Many of the P-38 missions involved harassing and interfering with the retreat out of Romania by the Wehrmacht and hampering their efforts to develop a defensive line in Hungary that might delay the onrushing Red Army.

The 52nd Fighter Group also found no aerial opposition on any mission flown in September. Like the other groups, they engaged in ground-attack missions. October found the group becoming one of the most colorful in XV Fighter Command when their group marking changed from a 24-inch-wide yellow stripe around the rear fuselage to painting the entire rear fuselage and vertical and horizontal stabilizers yellow. With this, they became the "Yellow Tails" in the same way that the 332nd Group was the Red Tails. At around the same time, the 325th changed their marking by extending the black and yellow checkerboard pattern over the rear fuselage as well as the tail surfaces. The only one of XV Fighter Command's Mustang groups that kept their original marking was the 31st Group with their red striped "candy cane" marking.

October saw the commencement of winter weather, with the Fifteenth Air Force operating on only 16 days of the month due to poor weather. November was even worse, with only 13 days where the weather allowed operations. December saw 11 days of operational weather.

With the Luftwaffe remaining on the ground, it became the fighters' task to search out the airfields where aircraft were found and attack them by strafing. This changed the air war for Allied airmen from a contest of skill between individual pilots to a battle against the laws of probability and chance in attacking well-defended airfields where the defenders could literally "fill the sky" with shells that an attacking airplane had to fly through. The final eight months of the war saw both VIII Fighter Command and XV Fighter Command record their heaviest losses as P-38s and P-51s with liquid-cooled engines that could be fatally damaged with a single hit in the cooling system turned more and more to ground attack.

With the continued absence of the Axis air forces in the sky, the Checkertails were ordered to attack Debrecen airfield in Hungary on September 1. Eleven Mustangs flew cover for the strafing P-51s, which made runs on the airfield from three different directions. The first strafed from west to east, the second from north to south, and the third east to west. This three-way attack was a complete success, with 59 aircraft claimed destroyed, along with several railcars and four locomotives. The cost was two Mustangs and their pilots. Proving that even a skilled aerial combatant was as vulnerable as the newest squadron member, one of those lost was ace First Lieutenant Benjamin Emmert, downed by multiple flak hits after destroying five aircraft on the airfield, who managed to bail out and became a prisoner of war. The other was Second Lieutenant Lowell Steere, whose fighter exploded when it hit the ground.

The day's action wasn't limited to strafing. Lieutenant Colonel Ernest Beverly shot down an Me-410, while Lieutenants Bruce Cobb and David Schmerbeck destroyed three Ju-52/3ms, with two credited to Schmerbeck and the third to both pilots.

Following release from escort duties on September 2, the 325th went "train hunting" in Yugoslavia. Pilots gave the marshaling yards at Niš a thorough strafing that destroyed several locomotives. The Checkertails went back to Yugoslavia the next day, again targeting rail traffic between Niš and Belgrade. Over a little more than an hour between 1350 and 1500 hours, 37 Mustangs strafed rail targets and claimed 13 locomotives destroyed and 25 damaged; destruction of 12 cargo wagons destroyed with 73 damaged; ten oil wagons destroyed with 15 damaged; 12 trucks destroyed and six damaged; destruction of two armored vehicles being transported on one train; two coal wagons destroyed while 15 were damaged; eight flatcars carrying 15 motor vehicles damaged; damage to one house; and one railroad repair workshop damaged. Breaking off from his strafing run, First Lieutenant Don Terry spotted a Ju-52/3m in the air and shot it down.

While the 325th Group made their slashing strafing attacks, 61 red-tailed Mustangs were turned loose on an armed reconnaissance over Serbia, covering the road between Stalac, Cuprija, and Osipaonica.

The Red Tails strafed goods wagons at the Kruševac train station damaging a nearby truck, while two Mustangs attacked five wagons on a rail siding and damaged all of them. Later, a 30-truck convoy was spotted by a group pilot who took off late and was hurrying to join the group; he raked it from end to end, claiming three vehicles set on fire while damaging ten others.

The day saw Second Lieutenant John Ondocsin from the 52nd Group's 2nd Squadron learn the dangers of low-level flying. The group escorted B-24s to bomb Niš airfield in Yugoslavia, then dropped down to search for "targets of opportunity" on the way home. Ondocsin was following his element leader, First Lieutenant Willard Pretzer, as the two Mustangs flew through some forested valleys, with Ondocsin kept busy watching both the terrain ahead and his leader. Looking over to check his leader's position, he took a moment too long; when he looked back ahead, he discovered he was headed straight for a tall tree on the top of a ridge line. Pulling the stick back violently, Ondocsin's Mustang seemed to leap over the tree. Unfortunately, the P-51's air scoop went through the top of the trees. Minutes later, his temperature gauge leaped through the yellow arc and went into the red. Ondocsin dropped the air scoop shutter behind the radiator as far as it would go, which brought the temperature back to just below red line.

Having managed to nurse his crippled Mustang across the Adriatic successfully, Ondocsin requested a straight-in approach at Madna. Just before touchdown, the temperature gauge went into the red zone and the engine failed. Still, he was able to land successfully, though the fighter had to be towed off the runway. Once parked, the problem was easily seen: the radiator air scoop was full of broken tree branches and leaves, and the bottom of the Mustang was "painted green" from having taken the top off the tree back in Yugoslavia.

During the first weeks of September, the 31st Fighter Group flew several escort missions covering C-47s flying to Bucharest, Romania to pick up Allied aircrew who had become prisoners of war before Romania's surrender in late August. Despite Romania being now under Soviet control, it was feared that Luftwaffe fighter units now in Hungary would attempt to shoot down the C-47s as they returned with their loads of freed former prisoners. Fortunately, no interception attempts happened during these missions. The two major escort missions flown on September 2 and 7 for Fifteenth Air Force bombers saw no contact with the Luftwaffe. The Fifteenth Air Force had turned its attention to destroying railroad bridges in northern Italy and Hungary as part of an effort to prevent the Wehrmacht shifting troops out of Italy into northern Europe to oppose the Allied advance. On September 3, 59 Red Tail P-51s covered the 304th Bomb Wing's attack on bridges at Szolnok and Szeged in Hungary on September 3. The next day, Captain Erwin Lawrence led 45 P-51s covering the 304th Wing to Tagliamento–Casarsa and Latisana on a bridge-busting mission in Italy. On September 5, Captain Andrew "Jug" Turner led 54 Mustangs escorting the 5th Bomb Wing to bomb the same targets. No enemy fighters were spotted on any of the three missions.

With the weather favoring continued attacks, the Checkertails escorted bombers striking railroad infrastructure in Italy and Hungary on September 5, later destroying one enemy aircraft and damaging several others in a strafing attack on Bački Brestovac airfield in Yugoslavia. The next day, the 5th Wing bombed the main railroad marshaling yard at Oradea, Romania. The 63 332nd Group Mustangs escorting the wing again found no opposition.

One of the most important missions flown by the 52nd Fighter Group occurred on September 8. Orders were received from XV Fighter Command the afternoon before, ordering that two flights of Mustangs would depart that night and fly to the RAF base at Falconara, to fly a joint mission with RAF Beaufighters.

Fourth Fighter Squadron commander Major James O. "Tim" Tyler was assigned to lead the mission, which Group Commander Colonel Marion Malcolm considered important enough that he assigned himself to lead the second flight. Tyler later described their night takeoff: "The strip at Madna had no lights for night operations, so for our early departure, vehicles were lined up on either side of the runway with lights on to guide the takeoff. All eight left the strip without incident and landed at Falconara just at sun-up." They were then taken to the operations office, where they found out just what kind of mission they were flying.

British intelligence had learned that the Germans planned to sink the huge Italian ocean liner *Rex* in the entrance to Trieste harbor to prevent its use by the Allies once they captured the port. Increased activity around the *Rex* had been spotted by reconnaissance flights at the end of August; a British bomber crew had overflown the port on September 4 and saw that the *Rex* was being towed away from her pier.

At the mission briefing, the American pilots learned that they would fly a mission with 16 Beaufighters from RAF 272 Squadron. It was expected the *Rex* would be escorted by two destroyers with antiaircraft armament, and that the liner itself would have antiaircraft guns mounted. The first flight of Mustangs was to strafe the enemy ships before the rocket-carrying Beaufighters made their attack. First Lieutenant Charles Wilson recalled, "The briefing was typically British, crude and to the point. I did not expect to come back."

The attack force took off and headed up the Adriatic at wave-top level toward Trieste. Major Tyler later described the attack:

> The possibility that single engine fighters might be called upon to attack destroyers and perhaps other defenses as well was not a comforting thought. We took off as directed and followed the prescribed course at minimum altitude. Once in the target area, we climbed to 6,000 feet. Directly in front of us was one of the largest ships I had ever seen. It was moving, though slowly. Then came the best possible news: there were no destroyers or other craft in the area.

Tyler informed the British crews of the news and then told Colonel Malcolm to cover him while he took his four Mustangs down to strafe. "We peeled off and approached the vessel at a fairly steep angle and at right angle to her course. I had attacked ships before and so opened fire at what I thought was the proper distance. Curiously, I didn't see any hits. Then I discovered I was shooting into the ocean. The huge size of the target had created an illusion of proximity that was confusing." Tyler and the other three Mustangs raked the liner with machine-gun fire. As he passed over the ship, Tyler noted there were no defensive antiaircraft guns on her. He let the British know this, and pulled off the target.

The Beaufighters came in, covered by Colonel Malcolm's four P-51s. During the next 40 minutes, the attackers ripped the helpless ship apart. *Rex* took 59 rocket and 3,200 20mm cannon hits, which set her afire. Numerous rocket hits were below the waterline, and the liner came to a stop. With their ordnance fired off, the Beaufighters and their Mustang escorts returned to Falconara.

An hour later, Beaufighters from 29 Squadron RAF and 16 Squadron SAAF made a second attack, putting 64 rockets and 4,000 rounds of 20mm into the liner. As they pulled off their final attacks and disappeared into the distance, *Rex* rolled over and sank off Capodistria. Trieste remained open.

Also on September 8 Captain William Mattison led 42 Red Tails to the Luftwaffe airfield at Ilandza, Yugoslavia. Twenty enemy aircraft were spotted and 23 P-51s made a strafing attack while being covered by 14 others. The strafers destroyed five Ju-52/3ms, four Ju-88s, three Do-217s, three Fw-200s, an Fw-190, a Bf-109, and an He-111. First Lieutenant James A. Calhoun was hit by flak, and was killed in the crash. The Red Tails followed up with an attack on the airfield at Alibunar; 15 P-51s made the strafing attack while 26 Mustangs flew top cover in the belief the now-alerted Luftwaffe would show up. However, there was no response, despite the group destroying 15 Fw-190s, two Bf-109s, and an SM.84 transport, opposed by only moderate flak. A locomotive was spotted and destroyed on the flight back to Ramitelli.

At the same time, the 325th Group attacked Ecke airfield in Yugoslavia. Hitting the airfield at 1000 hours, 35 Checkertail Mustangs made five to eight passes from south to north, during which 22 Ju-52/3ms, seven Fw-190s, four Fi-156s, 19 Ju-88s, two Me-410s, a Bf-109, a Hs-126, a Bf-110, and a Hs-129 were claimed destroyed. One flight made a run on nearby Petrovgrad airfield, claiming three Ju-52/3ms destroyed. Flight Officer Thomas Rogers was lost, last seen during the first pass over Ecke when he pulled up trailing smoke. The destruction at Ecke was confirmed by a photo-recon sortie. Brigadier General Dean Strother, Commander of XV Fighter Command, stated, "This is the most thoroughly effective strafing attack I have ever known in terms of the completeness of the destruction accomplished."

The Luftwaffe was still ground-bound during the Clan's escort mission to the refineries at Lobau and Schwechat in Austria on September 10. Once released from escort, the 318th Fighter Squadron found Me-410s on the airfield at Papa; a single strafing run left nine in flames.

These airfield attacks dramatically raised the 325th's score of enemy aircraft destroyed, but – unlike the result for the Eighth Air Force – this destruction did not count toward acedom.

On September 12, the 322nd Group sent 71 Mustangs as escorts for the 5th Bomb Wing. Four spares turned for home an hour after takeoff. Returning to Ramitelli, two pilots spotted a twin-engine aircraft in the Udine South airfield's landing pattern. When they dropped down to investigate further, the Udine control tower fired two red flares; the unidentified airplane disappeared into the haze, but the two Mustangs spotted ten aircraft hidden in sandbag revetments under camouflage netting near the base perimeter. Circling to the right, the two made a single pass, damaging one single-engine and three twin-engine enemy aircraft; when one was hit in the rudder by defending flak, the two pilots determined that discretion was the better part of valor and abandoned the attack.

The next day, 57 Red Tails escorted the 304th Wing for another strike on the Blechhammer North oil refinery. Three German fighters were spotted in the distance, but did not attack the bombers, split-essing and evading before the Mustangs could catch them.

At Lesina, Lieutenant Colonel Sluder completed his tour as 325th Group commander on September 11, when Lieutenant Colonel Ernest Beverly assumed command. After two uneventful missions, the Checkertails flew a mission to Greece on September 15, where two Ju-52/3ms were actually spotted in the air. Lieutenants Art Fiedler and John Simmons wasted no time in shooting them down. Simmons reported:

> I was flying over Megara airdrome, in Greece, at 14,000 feet when I saw two Ju-52s in the traffic pattern at one o'clock. I executed a 180-degree turn and closed on the leading Ju-52 from seven o'clock. I opened fire with a series of short bursts from 1000 feet down to 50 feet and scored hits on the left wing base and front section of the fuselage. The enemy aircraft exploded as I broke away from my attack, then hit the ground enveloped in flames.

The "Tante Ju" was Simmons' seventh, and last, victory with the 325th. Art Fiedler then shot down the other Ju-52/3m for victory number six. While that was happening, two flights strafed Megara and Eleusis airfields, leaving eight aircraft destroyed and four damaged. The strafing attacks claimed First Lieutenant John Lynch's Mustang, which was hit by flak; he was killed in the crash on Eleusis airfield.

Over the rest of September no Luftwaffe aircraft were seen in the air or on the ground during the 12 missions the Checkertails flew. Two pilots, Lieutenants R.A. Trautt and G.N. Strait, went missing due to weather over Hungary during the mission of September 21. The Luftwaffe's absence continued into October, when First Lieutenant Wayne Lowry suffered engine problems and was forced to bail out to become a prisoner of war on the escort mission to Munich on October 4.

The Red Tails escorted the B-17s of the 5th Bomb Wing to Budapest on September 17, for a strike on the Rakos railroad marshaling yards. The next day, the 304th Wing's Liberators attacked the Shell oil refinery in Budapest and nearby railroad bridges. On both missions, pilots observed a solitary twin-engine righter identified as an RAF Mosquito fly through the target area.

The 332nd sent 65 Mustangs on September 20 to escort B-24s from the 304th Bomb Wing sent to pound Malacky airfield in Czechoslovakia. The Luftwaffe again failed to appear. The next day, 62 Mustangs escorted the 5th Bomb Wing's B-17s for an attack on the Debrecen railroad marshaling yards in Hungary; unfortunately, the P-51s were delayed by weather and were thus 18 minutes late, while the bombers were ten minutes ahead of schedule, thus ruining any chance of a successful rendezvous. The Red Tails managed to arrive over the target as the last two bomb groups were unloading on the target. Fortunately, the Luftwaffe again failed to appear, which meant the bombers were unscathed except for flak.

The mission flown on September 23 again failed to flush the Luftwaffe into action. As the Mustangs escorted the bombers away from Munich area, First Lieutenant Chris Newman's "Goodwiggle" took a flak hit. He nursed the crippled Mustang to the mid-Adriatic, but then the engine caught fire, forcing him to bail out. The air-rescue service quickly picked him up and he returned to Ramitelli that evening. Second Lieutenant Leonard Willette was not so lucky. When he was ten miles north of Lake Chiem, Germany, he began losing oil pressure and radioed that he would be forced to bail out; he was never seen again and was declared killed in action in January 1945.

Flying operations for the 52nd Fighter Group essentially ended for an extended period on September 23, when heavy rainstorms began. The torrential downpour turned the group's Mada base into a sea of mud. Aircraft movement was impossible and ground equipment movement was difficult. Captain Tom Thacker later recalled:

> Ground transportation became a problem. Since Palermo, our pipeline for vehicular spare parts had been very slim. The move in

May to Madna plus subsequent heavy activity since had just about worn out our trucks and jeeps. Most of our "liberated" fleet of trucks and cars from North Africa had long since been abandoned. Now the weather was just about the last straw. Brakes, particularly, became inoperative as the mud ruined the linings and drums. Luckily, in the mud we could operate without brakes; we simply had nothing that could be safely driven on paved roads.

The war diary of the 2nd Fighter Squadron for October revealed grumbling about morale:

> The morale of the squadron was at its lowest point this month, mainly because of the marked drop in mail. After receiving the best mail service since being overseas, this squadron is at a loss to discover what in hell has caused the scarcity of letters. The bad weather and the resultant operational inactivity has had its effect on morale. If there were a fair-sized town nearby, we would at least have the opportunity to go and get out of camp. We also take a very dim view of the announcement by 15th AF that stoves will not be available for tent quarters. Recreation is nil due to the bad weather.

With winter closing in, the lack of heating for the tents the men lived in was an important consideration.

Fifty Red Tail P-51s escorted the 5th Bomb Wing's Flying Fortresses on a mission to bomb a synthetic oil plant in Germany on September 24, during which there was no air opposition. The next day saw another "milk run" when 37 P-51s escorted the Liberators of the 304th Bomb Wing to hit Athens airfield. Despite the local flak batteries being reinforced by four warships offshore, all the Liberators and Mustangs returned safely to their bases. With the Luftwaffe having disappeared for nearly two weeks, escort missions like this were becoming nearly routine. The situation would be swiftly reversed in October.

The uneventful mission the Red Tails flew on the morning of October 4 was the start of what would turn out to be the group's toughest month. Four Mustangs escorted three C-47s to Sofia, where the P-51s orbited while the Skytrains landed, then shepherded them back to safety. The nature of the day underwent an abrupt change when 37 Mustangs took off at 1058 hours, led by 99th Fighter Squadron commander Major Erwin Lawrence – flying his final mission – with the aim of strafing the airfields at Tatoi, Kalamaki, and Eleusis in Greece. Each airfield was to be attacked by one of the three group squadrons – the 99th, 100th, and 301st, which split off to make their runs as the Mustang formation arrived over southern Greece.

The 99th's P-51s went to Tatoi, where 25–30 well-dispersed enemy aircraft were spotted as they closed in. Suddenly, Major Lawrence rolled over at low altitude and crashed, exploding in flames. It was believed that Lawrence struck a cable strung across the airfield. Second Lieutenant Kenneth I. Williams also crashed on the airfield, surviving to be taken prisoner. Major Ray Ware wrote in his mission report, "We left four fires burning on the field, but two were ours." Nearly all enemy aircraft on the airfield were damaged, with First Lieutenant Herman Lawson claiming destruction of a Ju-52/3m destroyed; it was small reward for the loss of a popular leader.

At the same time, the 100th Squadron attacked Kalamaki airfield, claiming three enemy aircraft destroyed and eight damaged. At Eleusis, the 301st Squadron claimed four Ju-52/3ms and an SM.79 destroyed. As this happened, the 302nd Squadron sent 14 P-51s to escort 12 C-47s to Bucharest in an uneventful mission.

The three Greek airfields were the target once again on October 7, with the Red Tails led this time by their commander, Colonel Benjamin O. Davis. There was a bad omen shortly after takeoff from Ramitelli when Second Lieutenant Elbert Hudson's sputtering fighter belly-landed on the Biferano forward airfield.

The 99th Squadron again attacked Tatoi, this time claiming two Ju-52/3ms, an Fw-200, and an He-111 destroyed. Kalamaki was again the target of the 100th Squadron, where Second Lieutenant George Rhodes claimed an He-111 destroyed, while two other enemy aircraft were damaged. However, the Mustang flown by First Lieutenant Carroll S. Woods was hit by flak that set its tail on fire. Woods crashed on the field and was immediately taken prisoner. When the 301st arrived at Eleusis, they found the enemy had evacuated all aircraft other than a derelict Ju-52/3m. Regardless, the Mustangs shot up the base, setting a fuel dump on fire. However, Second Lieutenant Andrew D. Marshall's P-51 was hit by flak. Nursing the fighter back to Italy, he was eventually forced to bail out. Contacting the resistance in Croatia, he returned to the 332nd with slight injuries on October 18. Unfortunately,

51-mission veteran Second Lieutenant Joe A. Lewis wasn't as lucky. His Mustang was last seen trailing smoke as it departed the target; he was forced to bail out, joining Carroll Woods as a guest of the Third Reich.

Megara airfield was also empty, but the 302nd Squadron worked it over just the same. As he made his run, First Lieutenant Freddie Hutchins fired on what turned out to be an ammunition dump that exploded violently, raking his fighter – "Little Freddie" – with flak that blew off the right wingtip while shredding the tail surfaces. Hearing small arms fire rattling against the fuselage, he pressed himself against the armor plate; a burst came through the cockpit floor, peppering his legs with fragments. In agony, Hutchins flew the badly damaged fighter to a spot three miles west of the airfield where he crashed. Touching down at 250 mph, he was knocked unconscious. Coming to, he found himself still strapped into the Mustang's cockpit, with the Merlin engine several hundred feet away with the wings and tail ripped off. His goggles were smashed and his legs hurt terribly. Greek civilians who rushed to the crash lifted him out of the cockpit and put him on a donkey. He was taken to the home of a doctor who rubbed him with olive oil and bandaged his wounds. Put to bed, Hutchins was bitten awake by the fleas that inhabited the blanket thrown over him. He crawled out and departed, having decided to make it back to friendly forces by himself. Managing to avoid capture, he connected with resisters who put him in touch with a British SOE team who arranged a pickup that allowed him to return to Ramitelli on October 23.

At the same time, the 52nd's yellow-tailed Mustangs managed to get airborne to escort B-24s to Czechoslovakia. Over the target, Lieutenant Colonel Charles Boedeker was leading a flight of 5th Squadron fighters when he looked down and spotted enemy fighters at 700 feet. The mission report told the story: "At 1405 hours, four brown-mottled Fw-190s were observed heading west at 700 feet, about four miles south of the target. The P-51s gave chase, causing one to crash and explode. This was credited to Colonel Boedeker. Two other Fw-190s got on the tail of one of the P-51s which successfully eluded the enemy by going up through a solid overcast at 1,000 feet. Miserable weather returned and canceled operations for another extended period."

Despite losing five Mustangs on the previous mission, on October 8 a total of 53 P-51s led by Captain Spanky Roberts escorted the 5th Bomb Wing's Fortresses to the Lobau oil refinery in Vienna.

WHERE IS THE LUFTWAFFE?

The group's hand-me-down P-51Bs and Cs were getting war-weary; on the outbound leg, First Lieutenant Robert Wiggins experienced engine failure, surviving a crash-landing at Vis. Flight Officer Carl J. Woods and Second Lieutenant Roosevelt Stiger went missing in the cloudy skies. The adverse weather led to fuel becoming a major issue, resulting in 23 pilots making forced landings at forward fields, to be picked up and returned to Ramitelli by a fleet of trucks.

After a three-day break to rest and re-equip that saw a few new P-51Ds finally arrive in the group, the Red Tails were sent on an interdiction mission, hunting rail and road traffic from Budapest to Bratislava, to cut off German troops retreating from the Eastern Front in the face of the relentless Red Army advance. Due to weather, 52 of the 72 P-51s that took off from Ramitelli were forced to abort, leaving only 20 Mustangs to find targets. Those who managed to find holes in the cloud over Esztergom, on the Danube River in Hungary, were able to claim the destruction of 17 enemy aircraft at three different airfields. The Red Tails also left behind two wrecked locomotives, an oil wagon, and a burning fuel dump, claiming six barges, a locomotive, and a goods wagon damaged.

The 99th's First Lieutenant George Gray was credited with destroying two Me-210s, an He-111, and a biplane trainer, while Second Lieutenant Richard S. Harder claimed two Me-210s and an He-111 destroyed. The only loss was Second Lieutenant George Rhodes, who was hit by defending flak but managed to nurse his P-51 back to a crash-landing at Ramitelli, which wrote off the Mustang but left Rhodes safe.

October 12 saw 63 Mustangs take off again for freelance hunting in the area between Budapest and Bratislava. Fourteen Mustangs from the 99th Squadron dived down to investigate a report of a biplane over Kaposvas airfield. Although 35–40 aircraft were spotted parked in revetments, they saw no biplane. Just the same, they attacked the airfield. They made the first pass from east to west, with each of the nine following passes being flown in a counterclockwise manner. The Mustangs left 18 enemy aircraft burning on the field, including four Bf-109s, five He-111s, five Ju-88s, an Fw-200, and an Fw-190. Five others were damaged. First Lieutenant George Gray was credited with five destroyed while First Lieutenant Hannibal Cox was credited with three others set afire.

The 302nd Squadron received a radio report of an He-111 spotted near another landing field. Captain Wendell Pruitt led his flight in a search for the Heinkel bomber, when the other half of "the Gruesome Twosome" – First Lieutenant Lee Archer – spotted a gaggle of enemy aircraft climbing at "two o'clock low." Pruitt ordered an attack, but before the Mustangs could turn after them, they were jumped by nine Bf-109s covering two He-111s. Archer later reported: "Two Messerschmitts were flying abreast. I tore the wing off one with a long burst. The other one slid in behind Pruitt. I pulled up, zeroed in, hit the gun button and watched him explode." Pruitt had already bagged an He-111 and a Bf-109 and was chasing another Bf-109 fighter when his guns jammed. Archer followed the enemy fighter to the deck, later recalling: "He appeared to be trying to land. I opened up at ground level, hit him with a long volley and he crashed." At that point, flak and small arms caused Archer to climb back to higher altitude. He ended the mission by landing on Vis, with his Mustang running off the perforated steel planking runway and sustaining damage to the propeller.

In 15 minutes, all three He-111s and six of the nine Bf-109s had been destroyed. Lieutenants Milton Brooks, William Green, Roger Romine, and Luther Smith scored one each, destroying the four enemy aircraft not accounted for by Pruitt and Archer. The fight had happened from 7,000 feet all the way to the deck. The pilots reported that their German opponents used "very poor" and – in some instances – no evasive tactics.

After encountering the enemy aircraft, the 302nd attacked the nearby airfield, claiming three He-111s, two Bf-109s, a Ju-88, a Bf-110, and an otherwise unidentified biplane trainer, with an additional four aircraft damaged.

While the 100th and 301st Squadrons flew on toward their assigned targets, they were disrupted by several yellow-tailed Mustangs from the 52nd Fighter Group that turned into the Red Tails as if to attack. Fortunately, when the 100th Squadron turned to counter the intruding Yellow Tails, the two sides avoided any fratricide. Once the "threat" had been dealt with, the 100th's P-51s strafed a railroad siding and a factory; they claimed three locomotives, three passenger carriages, 30 goods wagons, and 25 trucks on the nearby highway damaged, while destroying an additional 45 trucks in the parking lots surrounding the factory itself.

WHERE IS THE LUFTWAFFE?

The 301st set its sights on 50 oil barges spotted in the Danube. The 18 Mustangs claimed three sent to the bottom and 11 others shot up during the attack. First Lieutenant Walter L. McCreary was hit by flak and forced to bail out over Kaspovár, Hungary, where he was captured and became a prisoner of war.

The Checkertails flew a train-hunting mission to Budapest and Vienna on the same day that the 332nd had such success. This mission saw the Checkertails claim one electric locomotive, 33 steam locomotives, eight trucks, 20 tanker cars, two civilian vehicles, one oil barge, and a powerplant destroyed. Enemy aircraft were spotted on Csákvár by a flight of Mustangs whose pilots then attacked, claiming five Ju-52/3ms, one Ju-88, one He-111, and two unidentified twin-engine aircraft destroyed, with four Go-242 gliders and two Ju-52/3ms claimed damaged. Another flight spotted targets on Győr airfield and destroyed four Ju-52/3ms, a Fi-156, and a Ju-88 destroyed, with two Ju-52/3ms damaged.

Art Fiedler managed to find an airborne target. He reported:

While on a strafing mission between Budapest and Vienna I observed a He-111 at seven o'clock at approximately 1,000 feet. I closed to about 300 yards and decided to pull out to the side so that I could further identify the enemy aircraft. When the He-111 started firing I turned into it and fired from 75 yards. Many hits were seen to enter the wings, motors and cockpit of the enemy aircraft. At this time the He-111 began burning and started down in a left turn. As I followed it down I fired a few bursts and saw parts flying off of the enemy plane. The burning enemy aircraft continued on down and crashed and exploded.

The He-111 was Fiedler's seventh victory. First Lieutenant J.V. Heimback also found another He-111 and shot it down, while Lieutenants H.L. Long and C.C. Whitmire destroyed an Fi-156 and an unidentified twin-engine aircraft, respectively.

The 52nd Fighter Group finally got back to some scoring after three missions canceled for bad weather on October 12. A force of 54 Mustangs left Madna at 1157 hours to strafe enemy airfields. At Lake Balaton, the three squadrons began a gradual descent from 13,000 feet through the overcast layer and leveled off just above the deck. The haze at low level was so bad that the 2nd Squadron – flying high cover – climbed to 1,500 feet to be able to see far enough. The 4th and 5th Squadrons made the attacks, with the 5th Squadron making a line-abreast attack in their first pass on the field, while the 4th Squadron's formation became separated in the haze, with only six Mustangs making the initial attack. Major Wiley's 4th Squadron flight, which had become lost in the haze, happened upon a gaggle of 25 Bf-109s maneuvering to land.

Wiley's flight rolled in to attack the airborne Messerschmitts just before the strafing attack hit the airfield. Four Bf-109s were destroyed in the first attack, crashing onto the airfield in flames, with two credited to Wiley. Lieutenants Charles Hudson and Charles Wilson were credited with the other two. Wilson recalled his victory:

> We were approaching the target close to the ground when 25 enemy fighters were sighted, flying at 100 feet. My wingman and I veered to the right and became separated in the haze. I circled and was suddenly joined in formation by two Me-109s which flew beside me for a short time. I immediately made every effort to get behind them and as I did so, one of them broke away and disappeared. I chased the remaining one, firing short bursts and getting strikes on his fuselage from 300 yards to point blank range. Catching up with him on the other side of a hill, he pulled and attempted a loop, but the plane couldn't make it and crashed into the ground and burned.

As this was going on, Captain Fred Ohr, who was leading the 2nd Squadron, decided the wrong airfield had been attacked; he led six of his squadron a short distance, then made a 180-degree turn and approached the target from the northeast. His flight thoroughly strafed six trucks, a bus, and a strange-looking locomotive, then made repeated strafing attacks on the airfield. Ohr spotted "many Ju-88s in revetments, with several Fw-190s also observed." These were thoroughly shot up and many were on fire when the Mustangs departed, having run out of ammunition.

The mission turned out to be one of the 52nd's most successful: 53 enemy aircraft were destroyed by strafing, while five were shot down in air combat. Numerous highway and river transport vehicles were hit, with several set on fire. All Mustangs returned to base, and Fred Ohr was awarded the DFC for leadership.

WHERE IS THE LUFTWAFFE?

On the 13th, the 325th took B-17s back to attack the oil refineries at Blechhammer. Again, there was no aerial opposition. Following their release from escort duties, the Checkertails went looking for targets of opportunity on the ground. Aircraft were spotted on the ground at Csákvár airfield. Two Mustangs made a strafing attack, destroying two Ju-52/3ms, an Fw-189 and an unidentified twin-engine aircraft. All of the Mustangs returned safely to Lesina. The group returned to Blechhammer the next day. On the return flight, six locomotives and three oil tanker cars were destroyed, for the loss of Second Lieutenant J. Houghton.

The same day, the 332nd also experienced strafing success. After completing their escort of the 304th Bomb Wing's B-24's to the Blechhammer oil refineries, the 60 Red Tails went looking to repeat the strafing successes from the day before. Four P-51s from the 99th Squadron found a train headed east from Bratislava and strafed it, damaging the two locomotives and a flatcar carrying a full load of trucks. Three 100th Squadron Mustangs found and shot up six previously damaged goods wagons, while another flight from the 302nd spotted a train and strafed it, destroying the locomotive and damaging goods wagons and coal cars. When they strafed a small house next to the track, the violent explosion was proof that it had been turned into ammunition storage.

Two 302nd flights strafed Tapolcza airfield, claiming seven enemy aircraft destroyed, including three He-111s and two Ju-52/3ms, with six more aircraft damaged. Two Mustangs were shot down by the intense flak. First Lieutenant Walter Westmoreland was killed in the crash, while First Lieutenant William Green spent a week with Tito's partisans after he parachuted into a field near Sisak, returning to Ramitelli a weeks later.

First Lieutenant Luther Smith strafed what turned out to be an ammo dump in Hungary. His P-51B caught fire after being damaged in the explosion. He rolled over to bail out, but the Mustang snapped into an inverted flat spin; Smith was caught in the cockpit half-in and half-out. Attempting to get back in and free himself, he jammed his right foot between the floor and the rudder pedals. The slipstream tore his oxygen mask off, causing him to pass out. Somehow, he was thrown free and his parachute deployed. He came to and discovered he was hanging from a tree with his right hip and foot badly broken. After spending time in a series of German hospitals, where he suffered from bone infections and dysentery, he was finally sent to Stalag Luft VII-A, from which he emerged at the end of the war weighing only 70 pounds.

The morning of October 14 saw 52 Mustangs take off from Ramitelli to escort the 49th Bomb Wing's Liberators to bomb the Odertal oil refineries in Germany. The Luftwaffe again put up no opposition, but the 100th's First Lieutenant Rual Bell suffered mechanical problems with his Mustang when they were an hour from the target and bailed out, returning to Ramitelli in December. After this mission, the 332nd received a much-needed respite from the losses, with more P-51Ds delivered to replace the aging P-51Bs.

The 52nd Group flew missions to Blechhammer on October 13 and 14. The second mission was canceled after takeoff due to high winds, and the group was released to hunt ground targets. Captain Ohr led the 2nd Squadron to Hungary; over Yugoslavia, the weather improved. In the vicinity of Szekesfehevar, south of Lake Balaton in Hungary, they found a well-packed enemy airfield and mounted a strafing attack with all three squadrons. The results were 31 aircraft destroyed on the ground, 28 locomotives at a roundhouse destroyed with 14 damaged, three trucks, 47 freight cars, and four oil tanker cars. 2nd Squadron's Second Lieutenant Thomas C. Leary, who was hit by flak over the field, bailed out and was quickly captured, while 5th Squadron's First Lieutenant Raymond H. Man was seen to depart the field trailing coolant; he was never seen again. Escort missions were flown four times over the remainder of October without coming into contact with the enemy. When Ohr landed back at Madna and went to report their success, he found an infuriated Colonel Malcolm waiting for him. There had been no order to go "hunting" when the weather canceled the escort mission, and Malcolm was of the opinion that Ohr had gone off "scalp hunting" on his own, "risking the rest of your flight." Ohr got a dressing down for this, but cooler heads prevailed, and the colonel came to see that the report of a successful strafing mission would make up for the failure of the escort trip.

On October 16, the Checkertails provided fighter escort for an operation involving a PBY delivering British SOE agents to Greece, while the second mission involved a standard escort to Brux, in Czechoslovakia. In complete contrast to recent experience, the group encountered 48 enemy aircraft between Brux and Dresden forming to attack the bombers. Two Mustangs were led by First Lieutenant

WHERE IS THE LUFTWAFFE?

Sheldon K. Anderson, who had yet to meet the Luftwaffe in aerial combat despite the fact this was his 31st mission.

His story of what happened next was written up by the 325th's public relations officer:

> Anderson and his wingman, Lieutenant Vernon Kahl, swooped down for positive identification. About half of the enemy formation saw them, dropped their tanks and started to climb. Five minutes later, the youthful flyer who had not done too well in pilot training (by his own admission) had shot down five enemy airplanes. Number one – "My wingman and I hit the tail-end flight of the box. The one I went after blew up right in front of my prop." The speed of their dive carried them through to the next flight. Number two – "Again I thought I was going to hit him, but the explosion of his airplane came just in time. I flew right through the smoke of his explosion." Number three – "The formation was scattering out now, but we still had enough speed to keep going after them. The one I got this time seemed to fall apart, there was no explosion." Number four – "I went in and got on one's tail. I chased him around a couple of turns, firing all the time. He began to smoke and started going down." The second of two enemies who sought to ambush Anderson was now on his tail, "so I cut the throttle and slowed down." Number five – Anderson suddenly twisted his Mustang to the left and then he was on the enemy's tail. He started firing as soon as he came in range. "Only one gun was working. It sounded like a B-B. All of a sudden the Jerry airplane went limp, like a rag, as if it didn't have a pilot. It went into a stall and headed down." After that Anderson really did get started for home.

A review of his claims credited Anderson with three destroyed – two Bf-109s and one Fw-190 – and two probables. Wingman Second Lieutenant Kahl destroyed one Fw-190 and probably destroyed a Bf-109. Lieutenant L.D. Voss closed out the day's scoring by destroying two Bf-109s. The Checkertails had no losses.

Colonel Davis led the 332nd's mission of October 16 to escort 5th Bomb Wing B-17s to attack the Brux oil refineries. While there was no aerial opposition, one P-51 was holed by flak. The next day, 51 P-51s again escorted the 5th's Flying Fortresses to the Blechhammer South oil refinery. A second 51-Mustang mission four days later saw the group escort the 5th's B-17s to the Brux oil refineries, again with no resistance.

While flying escort missions to Brux and Blechhammer on October 16 and 17, respectively, the 52nd Group sent out a special armed reconnaissance mission to Budapest to check German troop movements in the area on October 17; the mission was composed of one four-plane flight each from the 2nd and 5th Squadrons, and they met unexpected opponents. On reaching Budapest, both flights encountered a thick overcast and got separated. Closing on the assigned target, things "went south." As recorded in the group's war diary:

> No enemy aircraft were encountered. However, both flights were prevented from carrying out their missions by interference from Russian planes. The 5th Squadron was attacked from behind at 5,000 feet by three Yak-9s. The P-51s immediately recognized the planes by their star emblem. Although the P-51s dropped their wings in the prescribed signal, the Yaks opened fire with machine guns and cannon. The P-51s went into a Lufbery, consistently avoiding combat, and finally decided to break away. P-51 pilots voiced the opinion they could have easily shot down the Russian planes, which were noticeably slow. The 2nd Squadron's flight decided to turn back when two aircraft believed from a large Russian Air Division took off from the field as though to come up and make an attack.

Despite all this, the Americans accomplished the mission assignment of spotting and noting the location of retreating German forces.

Looking to take the fight to the enemy again, on October 21 the 325th flew a long-range strafing mission covering the territory between Vienna and Budapest. The primary targets were Szombathely and Seregélyes airfields, with a secondary target being any rail traffic found in the area. The mission's results were spectacular: 37 enemy aircraft, six locomotives, and four oil tank wagons destroyed, with 20 aircraft, one locomotive, and two freight wagons damaged. Lieutenant John Gaia managed to run across a Ju-88 in the air. He reported:

> While on a strafing mission to Szombathely airdrome I observed a Ju-88 ten miles northeast of the target, coming head-on at me at nine o'clock at about 1,500 feet. I made a diving turn and came in dead

astern of the enemy aircraft. I opened fire at 400 yards and closed to 50 yards. Hits were seen in the cockpit, fuselage and left engine of the enemy aircraft. At this time the left engine caught fire and the enemy aircraft went into a shallow dive. Other members of the flight got hits on the fuselage and right engine. Shortly afterwards the enemy aircraft crashed and burst into flames.

Lieutenant Gaia received full credit for the victory.

The 52nd's Captain Fred Ohr marked his final mission with a special order to take eight P-51s to Naples, where he learned they would escort Prime Minister Winston Churchill back to London. The flight across France was uneventful, and the pilots were able to experience a rare opportunity to take part in London night life. Departing the next day to return to Italy, they ran into heavy clouds and were forced to divert for another overnight in Paris. Taking off again the next morning, they ran into more heavy clouds and bad weather. Lieutenant Clarence Carson and Captain Albert McGraw collided in the soup; both were killed. On return to Madna, Ohr found that his orders transferring him back to the "Zone of the Interior" were waiting for him and he caught a flight for home on November 3.

Between October 23 and November 4, the 325th flew four escort missions without coming across the Luftwaffe. Finally, during an escort mission to Vienna on November 5, a small formation of eight Bf-109s was spotted and engaged, with six destroyed. The enemy formation was spotted heading northeast just south of Lake Balaton on the deck. First Lieutenant Oscar Rau led his flight to bounce the enemy pilots, who failed to spot the Mustangs until it was too late. In a one-sided combat, Rau had destroyed four of the six Bf-19s claimed destroyed. He reported:

I saw three Me 109s flying on the deck and dived down to attack the rear enemy aircraft, opening fire at 250 yards with 20 degrees deflection. Closing to 200 yards, I saw many hits on the wings and fuselage. The Me 109 burst into flames and the right wing fell off, the fighter crashing to the ground. I then pulled up behind another Me 109 and opened fire at 250 yards, closing to 200 yards where I saw numerous hits on the fuselage. The Me 109 immediately pulled up to 800 ft, where the pilot bailed out. I next saw a Me 109 trying to pull in behind my wingman. I made a very tight turn and fired a short burst from 90 degrees deflection at the Me 109. My burst missed the enemy aircraft, but in his attempt to evade he tried making a very tight turn and spun into the ground and burst into flames. After this Me 109 crashed I was flying at 100 ft when I spotted two Me 109s attempting to land. I chose my target and told my wingman to attack the other enemy aircraft. I closed to 200 yards and opened fire, then closed to 150 yards and saw my gunfire score many hits on the fuselage and cockpit. The enemy aircraft immediately spun into the ground, where it burst into flames.

The second of these Bf-109s went down shortly thereafter, having been hit by gunfire from Lieutenant Robert Newell. The day's sixth victory was scored by Major Norman McDonald, who had recently transferred from the 52nd Fighter Group to the Checkertails to take command of the 318th Fighter Squadron. McDonald – already an ace with seven and a half victories – destroyed a Bf-109.

On November 3, Red Tails commander Colonel Benjamin O. Davis returned to the USA for a meeting at USAAF Headquarters in Washington. Once again, Major Spanky Roberts assumed command. The onset of winter weather slowed the operational pace, but on November 4 Captain Andrew Turner led 61 Mustangs to cover the 5th Bomb Wing's attack on the oil storage facility at Regensburg–Winterhafen. Remarkably, 20 minutes after the group took off from Ramitelli, a Mustang with a red tail and other 332nd Group markings – but lacking a side number – joined the formation for 45 minutes before it turned northeast when they got to Trieste and disappeared. It was most likely a captured aircraft; there had been two earlier events in which captured P-38s were used by the enemy.

Elsewhere, Lieutenants Louis Purnell and Milton Brooks each led four-Mustang fighter escorts for F-5 Lightnings to Austria and northern Italy respectively during the afternoon.

November 4 saw the 5th Wing's B-17s escorted by 48 Mustangs on a mission to bomb the Florisdorf oil refinery in Austria. The uneventful mission was led by Captain Lee Rayford, while another two F-5 escort flights were flown in the afternoon.

Another mission supporting the 5th Wing's B-17s on November 6 saw 63 P-51s escort the Flying Fortresses to Vienna's Moosbierbaum oil refinery in Vienna. During the mission, the P-51C flown by the 301st's Captain William J. Faulkner was seen falling in a tight spin near Reichenfels, Austria. The cause was an apparent oxygen system failure, but Faulkner was listed killed in action.

November 6 saw two missions flown by the Checkertails. The first involved an escort of B-24s by the 318th Squadron to attack troop locations in Yugoslavia. Once their escort responsibilities were over, the squadron turned their attention to ground targets. The Mustangs made four strafing passes again motor transport spotted on the road between Mitrovica and Donje Stanovce in which 19 trucks were destroyed. A train was also spotted and the locomotive was destroyed while four wagons were damaged.

All three squadrons participated in the second mission to escort B-24s to attack an ordnance plant in Vienna. En route, a single Fw-190 was spotted and shot down by First Lieutenant J.E. Fehsenfeld. Second Lieutenant A.K. Rebb failed to return for unknown reasons.

The approach of winter brought worsening weather which had an adverse effect on XV Fighter Command's effectiveness. For the 52nd Fighter Group, the almost continual rain in the middle of November led to a struggle with the legendary Italian mud. The group war diary recorded:

> Traffic often became bogged down in deep mud holes or in ruts and ditches off the sides of the slippery roads which link up several squadron areas with headquarters. Officers and men were obliged to slog through mud almost everywhere within the Group area and, besides causing depressed spirits, this condition brought an additional fatigue since it made more work for everyone and provided a definite handicap in maintaining daily schedules.

The one good thing that happened during the month was the completion of the steel-mat PSP runway, which enabled aircraft to take off in conditions that had previously grounded them.

By the end of the month, the foul weather that had continued for over two months was deepening the morale problems among the enlisted men and was spreading to the officers as well. The constant rain was limiting the missions, which extended the time in Italy for men coming to the end of their tours who were looking forward to going home. The 2nd Squadron's war diary clearly stated the problems encountered in November:

> The morale of the pilots, however, has reached its lowest level. With such bad weather and infrequent missions, the outlook for early completion of their tour is not promising. With the arrival of 27 new pilots, this prospect is worse than black. On days of stand down, the pilots are at a loss for something to do. Although living conditions on the base are relatively comfortable, there is no decent town within a short travel time where they could go for entertainment.

Captain William Campbell led 63 Red Tails Mustangs escorting the 55th Bomb Wing's Liberators to Trento and Bolzano on November 7. Four P-51s suffered slight flak damage during the course of the mission. The next three days saw the group grounded by weather. On November 11, 52 Red Tails escorted 5th Wing B-17s that hit the Brux oil refineries. Heavy flak was found over Salzburg. Second Lieutenant Elton H. Nightingale was an apparent flak victim while First Lieutenant Turner W. Payne's P-51 also took flak hits that forced him to crash-land at Lesina; the airplane was wiped out but he was unhurt. The adverse weather forced 14 of the 325th Group's Mustangs to land at various friendly bases in Itay while returning from the Brux mission. A week later, on November 18, Lieutenants R.A. Fischer and R.D. Dowiatt crashed near the group's Lesina base because of poor visibility caused by thick clouds.

November was the month when the Me-262 became a threat to XV Fighter Command. The Lightnings of the 1st Fighter Group experienced their first encounter with the German jet on November 26, when three P-38s led by First Lieutenant Royal Nyby were returning from a photo-recon escort mission to Munich. Over Innsbruck, Austria at 26,000 feet, Second Lieutenant Guy Thomas was lagging in a turn but was attempting to get back in position when the Me-262 – which was flown by Leutnant Rudolph Zinner – made a pass from the rear. Nyby called a break left. As the Lightnings turned through 90 degrees, the German jet chandelled over them and disappeared into the haze level it had popped out of. Thomas' Lightning was nowhere to be seen. Post-war, Zinner's report became available, confirming that he had shot down Thomas, who survived briefly in a German hospital after bailing out, before dying of his wounds on December 4. He was lost on his second mission. This was the first loss to the new German jets.

The Checkertails were able to fly seven bomber escorts in mid-November, regardless of the weather. Again, the Luftwaffe failed to put in an appearance. The group returned to strafing attacks on November 21 when the Mustangs were assigned to hunt road traffic between Prijepolje and Rogatica in Yugoslavia, along with the nearby rail facilities. During strafing attacks made over 45 minutes, the 325th destroyed 51 trucks, three staff cars, three ammunition trucks, a German jeep, and 12 horse-drawn carts as well as a locomotive. Six horse-drawn carts, another 23 trucks, and ten flatcars were damaged while 49 Wehrmacht soldiers were killed. Two Mustangs were victims of flak during the attacks; both pilots, Lieutenants D.C. Haertel and C.C. Whitmire, bailed out and landed safely, to become prisoners of war.

Owing to the increasingly bad winter weather, the 332nd was prevented from flying missions until November 16, when the Red Tails escorted the 304th's Liberators to bomb the Munich West railroad marshaling yard. During takeoff at Ramitelli, a neighboring farmer absentmindedly drove a herd of sheep across the end of the runway. Captain Roger Romine managed to hit the animals in his P-51D. He was in turn rammed by First Lieutenant William Hill's P-51C. Hill was badly burned in the immense explosion, but was rescued by First Lieutenant Woody Crockett, who – though not scheduled to fly – was watching the takeoff. Unfortunately, Romine was unable to get out of his Mustang's tangled wreckage and died in the flaming aircraft.

The Mustangs met up with the B-24s over Masseria. As they flew on, they encountered a pair of Bf-109Gs south of Latisana flown by Capitano Ugo Drago and Tenente Renato Mingozi of the ANR. The two Italians positioned themselves up-sun and at "six o'clock" to a formation of six P-51s and in a diving attack damaged Second Lieutenant George Haley's P-51 before four yellow-tailed Mustangs from the 52nd Fighter Group chased them off.

After the bombers dropped their loads, Lieutenants Melvin Jackson, Louis Purnell, and Luke Weathers spotted a crippled B-24 in the vicinity of Udine. As they flew escort for the Liberator, they were jumped by eight Bf-109s that attacked in a string, after which they broke into a Lufbery. Weathers dived into the formation, closing to within 100 yards of the last two enemy fighters. His short bursts fired with zero to

20 degrees of deflection quickly resulted in one of the Bf-109s smoking from fire in the engine as it dived away. Weathers followed it down to 1,000 feet, where he saw it hit the ground.

Tracers suddenly arcing past his canopy alerted him that the other Bf-109 had followed him. Weathers later recalled, "It looked like he had me, so I decided to follow the falling airplane. I made a dive, came out of it and looked back. He was still on my tail and I was headed back towards Germany, but I didn't want to go that way. I chopped my throttle and dropped my flaps to cut my speed quickly. The fellow overshot me, and this left me on his tail. He was in range, so I opened fire." After several bursts, the Bf-109 slammed into a mountainside.

The next day, Captain Ed Gleed led 44 Mustangs to escort the 5th Bomb Wing's B-17s in another attack on the Brux refineries. The Red Tails reached the escort rendezvous 40 minutes late due to unforecast headwinds, to find the bombers were a further ten minutes late due to running into the same headwind. Again, the enemy made no appearance, turning the mission into another "milk run."

On November 18, the weather cleared enough for a low-level strafing mission to be flown to Hungary, hunting trains and road and river traffic between Győr in Hungary and Vienna. The 99th Squadron was covered by the 302nd as top cover, while the Mustangs worked over a stretch between Győr and Veszprém, where they destroyed 15 horse-drawn vehicles and 20 goods wagons, leaving another 100 horse-drawn vehicles, two locomotives, 40 goods wagons, and ten trucks damaged. The 100th Squadron destroyed one tanker wagon and damaged 30 goods wagons. The squadron searched out river traffic between Esztergom and Győr, in the process damaging a tugboat and six barges. Flak caught First Lieutenant Roger B. Gaither's Mustang, forcing him to bail out and spend the rest of the war as a prisoner of war.

The 301st – which had provided top cover for the 100th for their strafing attacks – traded places after the 100th used up its ammunition and also wreaked havoc with the river traffic. The Mustangs shot up two 88mm guns on a German lighter, and damaged six barges. Returning to Ramitelli, a burst of flak hit the 100th's Second Lieutenant Quitman C. Walker, forcing him to bail out near Lake Balaton. Unfortunately, Walker was never seen again.

Captain Rayford led 50 Mustangs on November 20 to cover an attack by the 5th and 55th Bomb Wings on the Blechhammer South oil refinery. Again, the mission was a "milk run," with the enemy failing to appear. The Red Tails' activities over the rest of the month were limited by winter weather to a photo-recon escort to Grodenwoh and Nuremberg on November 26.

Finally, on December 2, Captain Red Jackson led 51 P-51s to escort Liberators from the 49th and 55th Bomb Wings back to Blechhammer's oil refineries. Just before they completed their escort, the coolant system on Second Lieutenant Cornelius P. Gould's war-weary P-51B belched white glycol vapor as it gave out, leaving Gould with little option but to bail out; he parachuted into imprisonment for the remainder of the war in Stalag Luft I.

That same day, the Checkertails were the first XV Fighter Command group to have one of their photo-recon escort missions encounter an Me-262. The Mustangs and the F-5 Lightning they were escorting were 50 miles north of Augsburg, Germany, when they were surprised by an Me-262 that flashed through the undercast and attempted to attack the formation. One pilot managed to hit it with a few rounds as it shot on past, heading for the F-5 they were protecting. The jet fired at the reconnaissance Lightning but missed. The pilot then turned and executed a head-on pass at leader First Lieutenant Billy Hinton, who scored a few more hits before the enemy pilot disengaged and broke to the east; Hinton received credit for damaging the enemy jet.

On the December 3 mission, 64 Mustangs covered the 49th Bomb Wing's Liberators to hit targets in the Udine area. The only enemy aircraft spotted were six shot-up German aircraft on the bombed-out field at Maniago.

The 31st Group followed the Checkertails as the second XV Fighter Command group to experience a run-in with the Me-262s the day following the Clan's jet encounter. Mustangs from the 309th Squadron were escorting an F-5 to Munich when two Me-262s were spotted while the P-51s were at 26,000 feet, with the F-5 a thousand feet below and slightly ahead of the escorts. The mission report stated:

> They came in, straight and level, from the six o'clock position, like bat out of hell, closing easily at 100mph-plus faster than we were going. One P-51 broke 250 yards in front of the two Me-262s, but they ignored him to concentrate on the F-5. The F-5 broke to the

left and down while the jets closing to 1,000 yards, but they were not seen to fire. The F-5 easily out-turned the two jets.

Lieutenant Rask fired several long bursts at one of the Me-262s. Although badly out of range, he forced the jets to break sufficiently for the F-5 to escape into the clouds at 10,000 feet. Lieutenant Rask continued to dive with the Me-262s without gaining, pulling up only when he reached compressibility.

On December 5, the 308th Squadron encountered the German jets while escorting another F-5 photo-recon mission. This time, three Me-262s were spotted in formation. The mission report stated:

> Due to their tremendous speed, neither contact nor combat could be achieved. The fighter escort had been vigilant on the mission, but these three Me-262s just whizzed beneath the F-5 and vanished, out of sight, with no further passes. The exchange of radio transmissions between the pilots would never clear the censors, except for the religious parts, those referring to the Holy Father, and the son, Jesus Christ. There were some really funny and obscene descriptions shouted into their microphones at the time, but nobody was laughing.

Further escort operations were closed down because of weather until December 9, when the Red Tails flew a memorable mission covering the 5th Bomb Wing's Flying Fortresses in a raid on Brux. As the B-17s and P-51s approached the target, a single twin-engine aircraft made a fast pass at the Mustangs before it split-essed into a cloud bank, then zoomed up through the formation. Thus were the Red Tails introduced to the Me-262. A second of the German jets then made a head-on pass at a flight of Mustangs minutes late over Mühldorf. Two three-plane formations of the jet fighters were spotted east of the bombers, but made no attempt to attack. On the way back to Ramitelli. First Lieutenant Robert Martin's P-51C suffered engine trouble, forcing him to make a wheels-down landing at the gunnery range at Cuetelo. The Mustang nosed over, damaging the propeller.

The 31st's jet contacts continued on December 12 when the 309th sent a flight of P-51s to accompany another F-5 to Nuremberg, Germany. Two Me-262s attacked the formation just south of the city, with the first chandelling upwards into the sun after making an initial unsuccessful firing pass, disappearing into the glare. The second made four separate passes from "nine-o'clock level," from which he would split-ess then climb back for another attempt, refusing to get closer than 1,500 yards. He opened fire on two runs, before split-essing into the clouds and disappearing.

Between December 9 and 18, the Red Tails flew several "milk run" escorts as the bombers continued to pummel the oil industry targets in Austria and southern Germany. The Luftwaffe made no attempts to intercept, since the *Jagdwaffe* was being saved for the coming Operation *Bodenplatte* in the German assault that began at the end of this time, later known as the Battle of the Bulge. The weather affected the Checkertails similarly. Between December 9 and 17, a further 12 uneventful missions were flown. The "milk runs" ended on December 17, when the Checkertails escorted B-17s to Blechhammer and encountered four Fw-190s during the approach to the target. Attempting to positively identify the "bogies," a flight of Mustangs overran the enemy fighters, but not before firing at them beforehand. The Focke-Wulfs evaded the Mustangs by split-essing and diving for the deck. Moments later two Bf-109s were spotted; they escaped by diving into the clouds. The group lost First Lieutenant L.E. Schackner, whose P-51 was last seen trailing smoke as it headed south across Lake Balaton.

The 31st Group had received a large number of replacement pilots in late November and early December, who finally got their chance to experience air combat on December 17 during an escort mission to bomb the Odertal and Blechhammer refineries. Nearing the target, the 308th Squadron spotted ten Fw-190s and 20 Bf-109s, which split in two, with 18 attacking the Mustangs while the other 12 went after the bombers. In the fight that ensued, Captain Jack R. Smith destroyed an Fw-190 and First Lieutenant Paul E. Malone destroyed two – an Fw-190 and a Bf-109.

The 309th Squadron came across 25 "aggressive" Bf-109s. First Lieutenant Mannie Rask destroyed two Bf-109s whose pilots managed to bail out. First Lieutenant Kenneth Campbell scored what turned out to be his only victory when he destroyed a Bf-109. First Lieutenant George E. Gibson Jr. also destroyed a single Bf-109 while Second Lieutenant James Cowin, flying his second mission, destroyed a Bf-109.

For the whole mission, the 31st's pilots were credited with destroying 11 enemy fighters, one probable and one damaged, for no losses.

Fifteen of the 325th's next 20 missions were escorts for reconnaissance aircraft, with the remaining five being in support of heavy bombers. In all, the Luftwaffe failed to appear due to its commitment to the German offensive in Belgium and Luxembourg.

The 52nd Group flew a few escort missions in December, during which there was no contact with the enemy. The continuing bad winter weather canceled several missions, with the cancellations held to the last minute in hopes of things changing. The 52nd wasn't the only group facing this drought of action amidst the deluge, since the 31st Group was dealing with the same situation.

On December 17, the Luftwaffe finally made an appearance. The bombers were up in several mass formations to attack oil refineries around Blechhammer and Odertal. The bomber force got the attention of German fighter controllers and all four groups became engaged in air combat during what was XV Fighter Command's biggest air battle in several weeks.

Just south of Blechhammer, the 52nd encountered 45 Bf-109s and 30 Fw-190s. The war diary recorded:

> These enemy aircraft turned 180 degrees and started an attack from six o'clock. The P-51s broke into the attacks. Some of the enemy fighters dived down to the top of the undercast at 9,000 feet. The P-51s were outnumbered, while the enemy aircraft appeared to be both aggressive and skillful. When the fight was over, four Bf-109s and two Fw-190s were claimed destroyed, three of which were credited to Captain Bob Karr, giving him a score of six to become the group's newest ace.

Karr later reported:

> I chased one to 18,000 feet and opened fire, getting hits on the fuselage, cockpit and engine. The pilot bailed out before I closed in. I picked up another and got hits in the engine. It started smoking and hit the undercast at 8,000 feet. My wingman saw large pieces fall off. Tagging onto another, I got into a circle with him. Finally I got inside him and scored some hits and saw the pilot bail out at 11,000 feet.

Lieutenants Charley McCloskey and Vincent Tranquillo found others. McCloskey later reported:

> A whole bunch came at me and made a pass. I called the flight to break and went into a diving spiral, pulling out at 15,000 feet. Approaching an Fw-190 from the rear, I didn't see any hits until I was almost on him, and then I got him good. As I passed by he exploded on my right. Climbing back to 25,000 feet, I spotted a P-15 with a '109 on his tail. I dropped in on him, clobbered him hard, and saw him spinning out of control through the undercast with his left wing on fire.

Tranquillo scored the final victory, diving on a straggling Fw-190 and opening fire. "On the second burst, I got a hit on the canopy and the ship went out of control and spun down burning."

In addition to those of the 52nd, fighters of the 332nd, 325th, and 31st Groups scored an additional 17 destroyed for a grand total of 23 for the day. The 52nd's victories gave the group a total 403 enemy aircraft destroyed.

The 332nd Group's reconnaissance escort missions were by now becoming commonplace. The mission on December 20 saw First Lieutenant Charles Dunne's flight cover an F-5 sent to photograph Prague. That on December 22 had First Lieutenant George Gray and five Mustangs protecting another F-5 that photographed Ingolstadt. It was Captain Andrew Turner's turn on December 23 to conduct another five-Mustang mission covering another Prague-bound F-5. On this flight, Captain Lawrence Dickson's P-51D suffered engine failure near the target area. Though he successfully bailed out over the Alps and his parachute was seen to open, it was later found that Dickson had frozen to death.

The 31st's Mustangs had another run-in with the Me-262s on December 22 when a flight from the 308th Squadron escorted an F-5 to Munich but had to divert to Regensburg due to bad weather. As they approached Regensburg, the Mustangs were attacked by an Me-262 that damaged one of the P-51s. First Lieutenant Eugene P. McGlauflin and Flight Officer Roy L. Scales chased after the jet. Amazingly, they managed to catch up after a 15-mile pursuit, northwest of Passau, and stay with the Me-262 when the pilot attempted to split-ess and evade.

The two pilots made a scissors attack on the jet, which crashed and exploded, becoming the first enemy jet fighter destroyed in the MTO.

Colonel Benjamin O. Davis returned from his visit to Washington on Christmas Eve and resumed command of the 332nd. The group received a present when he announced that he had convinced USAAF Headquarters to speed up re-equipment of the Red Tails with new P-51Ds based on their achievements in the summer and fall. The next morning, Captain Andrew Turner again led 42 Mustangs on an escort mission to Brux. Returning, four Bf-109s were spotted, chasing seven B-26s. Four P-51s peeled off to intercept. The enemy pilots spotted the Mustangs diving on them, quickly split-essing and fleeing the area.

The three missions flown by the 325th on December 25 were photo-recon escorts – to Pilsen, in Czechoslovakia, followed by two to Munich – that saw all aircraft return safe. On December 26, three more missions were flown, two being photo-recon escorts while the third was another bomber escort to the Blechhammer oil refineries. Approaching the target, one Mustang took a flak hit and was escorted back to Lesina. The bombers unloaded on the target at 1340 hours; 20 minutes later First Lieutenant David Ambrose spotted a single Bf-109 low:

> I was at 22,000 feet when I observed a Me 109 flying at 18,000 feet heading toward Linz and dived down to identify it. The enemy pilot firewalled his engine upon observing our P-51s and climbed to 24,000 feet. I closed in and fired a short burst at a ten-degree deflection and saw many hits on the wing. The enemy pilot then split-essed and executed violent turns toward the deck, before leveling off at 10,000 feet. I fired a long burst from dead astern, from 1,000 feet to 500 feet and observed many hits in the fuselage around the cockpit. The enemy pilot then executed another split-S, leveled out at 3000 feet, jettisoned his canopy and went into a dive, his fighter bursting into flames as it hit the ground. Confirmed by Lieutenant Hosford.

The 325th's pilots were able to make so many successful attacks at relatively long ranges because the Mustangs had been equipped with the K-14 lead-computing sight in September 1944. The "no missum" sight vastly improved fighter gunnery. As one pilot explained, "Put the pipper on the target and you've got him."

WHERE IS THE LUFTWAFFE?

Five minutes after Ambrose's success, First Lieutenant Fred Wulf claimed another victory:

> I was flying at 26,000 feet when I observed a Ju-88 ahead of me at about 24,000 feet. I attacked from 700 yards, at which point the enemy aircraft turned away and started to climb, firing back at me. I closed to 200 yards dead astern, fired again and observed many hits entering the wings, engines and fuselage. The Ju-88 rolled over, went into a spin and burst into flames. Lieutenants Woodson and Margetts observed and confirmed the destruction of this enemy aircraft.

The end of 1944 saw the Checkertails fly two missions on December 27 to cover two different groups of bombers in a strike against the railroad marshaling yards in Maribor, Yugoslavia. The bombing was successful, ripping the target apart, but again the Luftwaffe's fighters were nowhere in sight. The next day the group flew a penetration escort for B-24s from the 304th Bomb Wing to attack in Kolin and Pardubice, Czechoslovakia. The group was released from escort duty after the bomb run was completed, allowing 32 of the 325th's 51 Mustangs to carry out strafing attacks on two airfields and several road and rail targets. Over 45 minutes, the Checkertails destroyed four Me-323s, an He-111, a Ju-52/3m, and an Fw-190 on the airfields, with 26 locomotives, one freight wagon, and two vehicles also destroyed. First Lieutenant W.C. Margetts failed to return.

The momentous year of 1944 was brought to a close for the Checkertail Clan with an escort mission for the 47th Bomb Wing to northern Italy, where the bombers attacked bridges and rail targets in the Brenner Pass as part of Operation *Bingo*, the operation to destroy the railroad through the pass that provided supplies to the German Tenth and Fourteenth Armies in the Gothic Line.

The end of the year was also busy for the Red Tails. On December 26 they provided two separate escorts for the 5th and 55th Bomb Wings, which were sent to attack refinery targets in Odertal and Blechhammer. The 100th and 301st Squadrons sent 23 Mustangs on the mission, with the 99th and 302nd providing 21 Mustangs for withdrawal cover. The bombers' formations were tight, making them easy to cover. High winds on the next day found the 5th's B-17s strung out over several miles as they flew to Vienna. Fortunately, the

52 P-51s, led by Captain Ed Gleed, found no opposition as the enemy stayed on the ground and missed the opportunity to take advantage of the situation.

The next day, the 304th Wing's Liberators hit oil refineries at Kolin and Pardubice. The 50 Red Tails that covered the mission were able to split into two 25-Mustang formations when the bombers split into two groups.

A replay of that mission was planned for December 29, with the targets being Mühldorf and Landshut, in Germany. The 304th and 332nd rendezvoused successfully in the cloudy sky and then picked up the 49th Wing's Liberators. Soon after, 11 Mustangs were detached to cover a single 49th B-24 when it attacked Passau. While there was no enemy aerial opposition, the flak was heavy. Over the target, the 301st's Lieutenants Frederick D. Funderberg and Andrew Marshall fell victim to either flak or a midair collision, both being killed. The worsening weather on the return forced the pilots to depend on instruments and Second Lieutenant Robert Friend's P-51 went into a spin, forcing him to bail out over Larino, while similar difficulties forced Second Lieutenant Lewis Craig to bail out over Termoli. Both landed safely and returned to Ramitelli later that day. Weather moved in on December 30 and closed down operations for the remaining two days of 1944.

The 52nd Group's last casualty of 1944 happened during the strafing mission flown along the Vienna–Linz railroad on December 27. Searching for "targets of opportunity," the group hit various rail and industrial targets, including an aircraft junk pile that the 2nd Squadron's First Lieutenant Dave Emerson came across. Moments later, he spotted a locomotive and led his flight to attack it. Despite the Mustangs' blistering attack, German flak gunners nearby managed to line up on the flight's number four, Second Lieutenant Daniel Adams' P-51, and set it afire. The Mustang exploded when it hit the ground, killing Adams.

Captain Tom Thacker wrote that "The vile weather that became notorious for its duration extended from England down to the Med. Twenty heavies landed at our base on 24 December; thus our Christmas Turkey was sliced rather thin in order to be shared with 200 unexpected guests." The two missions flown on December 28–29 were canceled for weather. Second Squadron's Daniel Emerson recalled that the mission on December 29 was so bad that the group returned through rain with a ceiling down to 100 feet in places.

At New Year, Colonel Davis wrote a message to every group member, telling them he had learned in Washington that the Red Tails' escort record was not unnoticed. "Unofficially, you are known by an untold number of bomber crews as those who can be depended on, and whose appearance means certain protection from enemy fighters. The bomber crews have told others of your accomplishments, and your good reputation has preceded you in many parts where you may think you are unknown." The Red Tails' struggle for recognition through their achievements had been accomplished.

Everyone knew that 1945 would be the war's decisive year.

11

THE FINAL BATTLES

The first month of 1945 saw weather so rotten throughout the Mediterranean that the Fifteenth Air Force only attempted three major missions in the whole month. All the groups in XV Fighter Command reported the same story: miserable weather, lack of activity in the air and on the ground, and lowered morale. The 52nd Group's war diarist wrote, "Few months have been filled with more inclement weather and less activity than January 1945 with its almost constant wind, rain, snow, sleet, and mud. It was without a doubt the toughest month spent by the Group at Madna of the entire war. For the most part, January was a month to be endured with a lot of suffering and inconvenience." The war diarist for the 31st Fighter Group, writing at mid-month with little operational achievement in the face of repeated snowstorms around San Severo, observed, "Winter weather in Europe is great for skiing and bob-sledding, lousy for flying."

The other Mustang groups in XV Fighter Command experienced a similar lack of results. The Red Tails attempted 11 escort missions over the month, with only three not being canceled due to weather. On January 29, five 99th Squadron Mustangs who had flown one of the unsuccessful photo-recon escorts attempted that month ran into a snowstorm on the way home, being forced down to 300 feet to get below the clouds, where they were nearly blinded by the raging snowfall and all became separated. Fortunately, all were able to find Ramitelli in the storm and successfully land.

THE FINAL BATTLES

All the escort missions flown by the 31st Group over the first three weeks of January were listed in the war diary as "milk runs" since there was no contact with the Luftwaffe. With the P-51s essentially grounded, the armorers took the opportunity to fit all fighters with the K-14 gyroscopic sight. Great things were expected from the "no missum" sight, if only the weather would break and the Luftwaffe would decide to show up. No one liked hearing that one of the older residents of the village of San Severo had said this was the worst winter he could remember. After the squadrons had been snowed in for most of the month, some warmer weather toward the end of January led to the snow melting, with the result that the airfield was flooded to the point that flight operations were canceled. Some local clearing allowed the many newly arrived replacement pilots to get their final checkout in the Mustang. By the end of the month, the 31st had 63 pilots qualified for operations, a vast improvement over the end of December 1944, when the entire group consisted of 40 pilots, following the departures of many who had completed their tour.

After eight missions between January 3 and 18 in which no enemy aircraft were seen during bomber escorts to northern Italy, Germany, Yugoslavia, and Austria, the Checkertails finally found action on January 19 during a fighter sweep between Zagreb and Szombathely. Action began when First Lieutenant David Ambrose spotted a Ju-52/3m north of Zagreb at 1005 hours and shot it down. At 1015 hours, Second Lieutenant Robert Reid shot down another "Tante Ju" southeast of Vienna; he reported:

> While participating in a fighter sweep in the Zagreb and Szombathely areas I covered my leader as he made a pass on a Ju-52 flying due east at an altitude of 1,000 feet. Because of his excessive speed, my leader overshot, and I closed on the enemy aircraft, opened fire with short bursts at 1,000 feet and broke off at 500 feet. Direct hits were seen at the wing roots and in the front section of the fuselage as the enemy aircraft went into a spiral and crashed with the left wing enveloped in flames.

At 1025 hours, future ace First Lieutenant Gordon H. McDaniel scored his first victory. He reported: "I was leading a section of eight

P-51s at 1,000 feet and observed a Fw-190 at five o'clock at our altitude. I overtook the enemy aircraft, opened fire from 1,000 feet with ten degrees deflection and scored many hits on the fuselage and tail. The tail of the Fw-190 broke off and the enemy aircraft went straight down, crashing into the ground. Witnessed and confirmed by Lieutenants Wulf, Anodro and Raymond."

First Lieutenant Robert Reid claimed his second kill of the day at 1035 hours, reporting, "I was flying at 9,000 feet and observed a Me 109 at one o'clock, 8,000 feet below me. I executed a diving turn and closed on the Me 109. I closed throttle, dropped flaps and fired a series of short bursts from 1,500 feet to 800 feet from six o'clock high. Direct hits were seen in the fuselage around the cockpit and the Me 109 dropped a wing and went directly into the ground. Capt Burr observed and confirmed."

The sweep came to an end at 1105 hours when First Lieutenant Robert W. Bean scored the final victory, claiming an "Me-309" (likely an Fw-190D). The group's success was tempered by the loss of Second Lieutenant David Aiken, who bailed out successfully after his engine failed.

The next day, the 325th returned to escort duty on a mission to Regensburg, where three groups of B-17s targeted oil storage facilities. Again, the Checkertails ran across the Luftwaffe in the air when the 317th Squadron spotted 40 Fw-190s as they attempted an attack on the rearmost box of B-17s. Captain Art Fiedler led his flight into the enemy formation, breaking up the attempted attack and claiming destruction of four Fw-190s for one Mustang lost. Fiedler scored the first of the four victories, which was his eighth and final victory. He reported:

> While on an escort mission to Regensburg, I observed 40 Fw-190s just east of the target, approaching from a northeasterly direction at 34,000 ft. We were at 32,000 ft, and I led my flight in a climbing turn after them. I was able to get on the tail of two of the Fw-190s and closed on the rearmost enemy aircraft. I opened fire at 200 yards from seven o'clock. I continued closing to 50 yards and fired again. Many hits were seen to enter the bottom left side of the fuselage, and shortly thereafter the Fw-190 burst into flames and exploded in the air.

Second Lieutenant Edward L. Miller was top scorer in the fight, claiming three Fw-190s destroyed. He later reported:

> While escorting B-17s attacking Regensburg, my flight observed 40 enemy aircraft attempting to attack the B-17s and we intercepted them. The Germans went into a Lufbery at 33,000 ft and I closed on one and fired a long burst with 20 down to five degrees deflection, from 300 down to 150 yards. I saw many hits in the fuselage around the cockpit and base of the wings. The Fw-190 executed a snap roll and the pilot bailed out. After this encounter I observed another Fw-190 on the tail of a P-51. I dove after the Fw-190 and closed from seven o'clock high, firing a long burst from 300 yards, with 25 down to 10 degrees deflection. I saw hits on the base of the wings and the front section of the fuselage. The enemy aircraft executed a modified split-ess, then began burning and smoking profusely and was last seen spinning into an overcast at 10,000 ft. I then saw an enemy aircraft below the Lufbery and pursued it, opening fire at 400 yards, closing to 150 yards for my last burst. I observed hits on the wings and fuselage, and shortly afterwards the engine quit and the propeller started wind-milling. I followed the Fw-190 down and saw it crash-land. I noticed large pieces of it flying off as it crash-landed.

For two days, it appeared the Luftwaffe was back in action, but the 325th's Mustangs wouldn't see another enemy aircraft over the next 18 missions flown.

Escorting the 5th Bomb Wing's B-17s on a mission by all groups of the Fifteenth Air Force to bomb the Moosebierbaum refineries on February 1, the weather over the target was so bad that the bombers made three unsuccessful runs in an unsuccessful attempt to spot the target through the clouds before finally switching to Graz in the worsening weather and successfully dropping on the refinery there. The weather cleared sufficiently on February 8 to allow a second attack on Moosebierbaum, which saw the bombers successfully hit the target. On February 15 during an escort mission to Vienna the Red Tails finally spotted "attackers" in the air when two P-38 pilots confused by the weather made two unsuccessful attempts to attack the Mustangs before disappearing back into the clouds.

For the pilots of the 31st Group, the mere fact that they were able to fly an entire mission for the Moosebierbaum mission on January 31 was counted as an achievement, even though there was no enemy air opposition to be found. Following their scoreless return, the group war diarist wrote, "January 1945, which had started out full of hope, might best be forgotten. For the entire month, not one enemy plane fell to the guns of a single 31st Fighter Group P-51."

February wasn't much better, though the clouds lifted enough for the 52nd Group to mound several low-level strafing attacks. There was the additional problem for active fighter pilots that the Red Army had broken into eastern Europe, with targets disappearing in Hungary, Austria, and Czechoslovakia as the red tide flowed west.

Second Lieutenant Hugh Ottley of the 52nd's 4th Squadron later wrote about the missions in February, during which he flew his 13th through 19th missions, recording his thoughts about escort and strafing missions in this period of the war:

> Most of our missions were heavy bomber escorts, lasting most of the day. We would be going to the mess hall for breakfast as the bombers were overhead, formed up and heading north. After breakfast, we had our briefing, went out to the aircraft and took off. We would overtake the bombers over the north coast of the Adriatic, stay with them over the target, and come back with them to the coast. Usually our fuel was low at this point, so we'd return to base. After debriefing, we stepped outside and watched for the returning bombers. For us, it was about a five-hour trip, while the bombers logged about nine hours.
>
> Nearly all the targets on the bombing missions were over heavily defended areas and flak was so intense it had the appearance of a severe thunderstorm. We usually flew about 6,000 feet higher than the bombers and were luckily out of the flak. It was very unnerving to see the bombers fly into the thick cloud and either explode or descend trailing smoke. I didn't envy the bomber crews. They were a brave bunch.
>
> Occasionally, we participated in strafing missions. On one in particular, we spotted a freight train coming into a small town. The locomotive stopped on a rail crossing in the center of town, which made it difficult to get a shot at him. We dove down and flew straight

down the main street between the buildings. For a split second I glanced to my right and there, standing in a second story window, was a well-dressed elderly woman. I shall never forget how she looked. Then with a burst of my six guns, the locomotive blew sky high. This was my first locomotive kill.

The one mission the 31st was able to fly on February 2, after four weeks of stand downs and cancellations, was one the group would have preferred not to have flown. After the planned escort mission was canceled, a strafing mission to Kurilovac airfield in Yugoslavia was laid on. The mission was decided so late that pilots didn't even attend a briefing before manning their planes. Over the target, the group ran into heavy, accurate flak that wreaked havoc on the 308th and 309th Squadrons, which made strafing runs while the 307th maintained high cover. The 308th's commander, Major John Wagner, was shot down as he approached the target at low level. First Lieutenant George Gibson Jr. was hit in the fuselage and crashed beside the runway. Five other Mustangs were seriously damaged, but their pilots were able to bring them back to San Severo where two made crash-landings. Missions on February 7 and 8 to Moosebierbaum and Vienna, respectively, had the bombers dropping their loads using H2X to bomb through the clouds with unseen results.

On the afternoon of February 8, six 307th Squadron P-51s escorted a photo-reconnaissance Mosquito from 60 Squadron SAAF to Lake Constance. Just before reaching the target, two Me-262s flew overhead through the broken cumulus without spotting the Allied formation before they dived away and disappeared in the clouds. Another escort for a 60 Squadron Mosquito the next day to Schongau in Germany resulted in the Mustang pilots spotting an Me-262 just as it took off from the airfield they were over. Three pilots dived to investigate what it was first thought might be an Me-410, but they ended up chasing the jet for 20 minutes at low level. In post-mission reports, the Mustang pilots reported they were surprised by the jet's low-altitude maneuverability, particularly in turns, one stating, "It could turn so sharply that the P-51's nose blocked it completely, then it did a half roll in the opposite direction and came around on my tail."

The Checkertails' "drought" of enemy action ended during an escort mission to bomb Neuberg airfield and the Rosenheim railroad marshaling yard in Germany on February 16. At 1340 hours, while staying with the Liberators during the return leg of the mission, First Lieutenant Walter Selenger spotted a Liberator being attacked by an Fw-190. He reported: "I observed a lone B-24 being attacked by a Fw-190 and immediately dived after it. I opened fire at 300 yards directly astern and closed to 160 yards, firing with no deflection. I saw many hits entering the engine, fuselage, cockpit and wings of the Fw-190. Black smoke poured from the enemy aircraft, its wheels fell down and the pilot bailed out. The airplane and pilot, whose 'chute did not open, went into the sea."

On February 17, 44 Red Tail P-51s left Ramitelli, headed for the Linz–Vienna railroad line, where they looked for strafing targets. The squadrons took turns between strafing and providing top cover for each other while they attacked four trains. The 99th and 302nd made three passes on targets while the 100th and 301st each made two. The claimed result was two locomotives, two trucks on flatcars, three oil tanker wagons, and a power transformer destroyed, with three locomotives, seven tanks on flat cars, 15 trucks on flatcars, five oil tanker wagons, 15 goods wagons, five armored cars on flatcars, a railroad control tower, and a small factory damaged. There were no losses. Missions over the rest of the month were largely unsuccessful due to bad weather; half of those that actually took off before being canceled were aborted en route when the weather reconnaissance aircraft reported the targets socked in.

After three more uneventful missions, the Checkertails came across many strafing opportunities in the Vienna–Linz area of Austria on February 19. The mission report stated:

> Seventeen P-51s strafed from St Polten to Amstetten, destroying four locomotives, one tank car, 13 motor transports and 15 men. Eighteen P-51s strafed between Ybbs and Enns, destroying 18 locomotives, five tank cars and one motor transport, damaging 92 freight cars and three barges. Sixteen P-51s strafed between Vienna and St Polten, destroying 19 locomotives, two freight cars, ten tank cars and three motor transports and damaging three barges. All strafing was accomplished between 1130–1215 hours. Four P-51s strafed Markersdorf airdrome at 1145 hours, destroying one Do-217 and two Fw-190s. Two P-51s were lost due to flak in the target area. Forty-eight P-51s down at base at 1415 hours.

The next five missions – one bomber escort and four photo-recon escort – were listed in the group's war diary, "Mission completed without incident."

Finally, on February 22, 800 Mustangs of the Eighth, Twelfth, and Fifteenth Air Forces engaged in Operation *Clarion*, a mass strafing mission flown against the German transportation system, industrial targets, oil facilities, and communications. After being turned loose from escorting bombers to Bavaria, the P-51 groups found many targets and intense flak. Second Squadron's First Lieutenant Bill Eddins later recorded in his diary:

> The 2d FS provided target cover for the bombers and then went down through a hole in the clouds and strafed rail targets. By the time we began strafing, the Germans had been under attack for more than an hour and were ready for us. Mel Bryant fired a long burst at a locomotive without producing a boiler explosion. Apparently, the engineer had time to blow down the boiler or perhaps it had been hit by other planes earlier. Bryan's plane was hit by light flak, knocking out the engine. He bailed out and was captured.

The 325th was turned loose to attack "targets of opportunity and rail targets in the Munich area." The heavy cloud cover limited strafing to targets around Salzburg, Austria, where 12 Mustangs found a hole in the clouds; once in the clear below the overcast, they damaged an electric locomotive, 14 freight wagons, six passenger carriages, several trucks, and a power station. The group experienced two losses, one when Second Lieutenant M.J. Wasser was forced to bail out when his Mustang was hit by flak, and the other when Second Lieutenant W.H. Taylor's Mustang took hits in his radiator and crash-landed. Both were quickly taken prisoner on the ground.

The 31st's Mustangs provided escort for the 49th Bomb Wing as it hit oil storage tanks in Regensburg. Afterwards, the 307th Squadron strafed transportation targets spotted between Regensburg and Munich. In total, the 307th claimed eight locomotives destroyed, seven damaged, and 26 rail cars damaged. The 308th Squadron, which went after transportation targets near Ingolstadt, claimed six locomotives destroyed, two damaged, one electric engine destroyed, one oil car destroyed, and 40 freight cars damaged. The 309th found themselves attacking through low-level weather to hit rail targets between Regensburg and Freising, where they destroyed four locomotives and damaged nine, as well as damaging 24 rail cars and two electric power stations.

Among the 52nd's casualties during Operation *Clarion* was Second Lieutenant Robert F. "Rocky" Rhodes, who was flying his sixth mission in P-51B "Little Ambassador," which had formerly been flown by group ace Jim Empey before he returned to the States. Rhodes attacked what turned out to be a flak train being run as a trap for shooting down fighter pilots. He was lucky to escape with his life, but that luck ran out minutes later when he made a run against a nearby airfield. On his second pass, the flak was ready and waiting. "Little Ambassador" took hits in the engine and tail. As he pulled away, Rhodes realized he was losing power and had suffered a control loss of the elevators and rudder. In an attempt to find an escape route, he unknowingly flew over the Swiss border while attempting to reach an Allied airfield in France by following the Rhine River. When his engine seized, he put down on the riverbank at 100mph, which ripped off the radiator scoop and right flap. Climbing out, he discovered the water was only three feet deep and waded ashore to discover he was in Liechtenstein. The authorities there handed him over to the Swiss government. After three weeks there, he was passed to the Americans in France, from where he was sent to London and then onwards to New York City.

The Checkertails' next 14 missions – a mixture of escorts for photo-recon aircraft and bombers – failed to find the Luftwaffe and were flown without loss to the group. The last mission of the month was a strafing mission on February 28 that saw the group sent to search for rail targets between Innsbruck and Salzburg. Unfortunately, the mission was only partially successful, since only one locomotive was destroyed though two others were damaged, along with nine oil tank wagons and 13 box cars. The modest success cost the Clan a pilot and his fighter lost to flak.

In the 332nd Fighter Group, lack of replacement pilots for the 302nd Squadron as the original pilots in the unit came to the end of their tours had led to its virtual deactivation by late February. On March 6 this status became permanent when the group was formally deactivated and the remaining pilots and ground personnel were distributed among the other three squadrons in the group. With this, the Red Tails became a three-squadron group like the others in XV Fighter Command. As the harsh winter weather gradually thawed into spring, the Fifteenth Air

THE FINAL BATTLES

Force was able to fly missions on most days between February 23 and 28. On February 25, eight 307th Squadron P-51s were turned loose for strafing following an escort mission for the 49th Bomb Wing to hit the Linz Benzoil plant. After 15 minutes going after road, river, and rail traffic around Amstetten, Austria, the pilots claimed six locomotives destroyed, two damaged, two oil cars damaged, 31 rail cars damaged, two electric trains damaged, and one radar tower damaged. The big news for the 31st came that night when they learned they were finally leaving the malarial swamp at San Severo, to be based as of the end of February at Mondolfo, 170 miles north of San Severo near the large Italian town of Fano, just 50 miles south of Venice on the Adriatic.

The last 31st Group mission flown from San Severo on February 28 involved six 307th Squadron P-51s that escorted another 60 Squadron Mosquito to Munich, which found enemy aerial resistance for the first time since the new year. Just east of Munich, two Me-262s swooped on the formation, but split-essed when two Mustangs turned toward the jets and opened fire; the K-14 sights put the bullets uncomfortably close to the two jets.

Although it was clear by the beginning of March 1945 that the future life of the Third Reich was now measured in weeks, as the Allied forces on the Western, Southern, and Eastern Fronts continued to squeeze Axis forces into a smaller and smaller geographic area, there was no sign of any cracking in German resolve.

On March 1, the Checkertail Clan moved from Lesina airfield to Rimini airfield near Miramare, which placed them closer to the action. That day, the Clan escorted B-24s to Moosbierbaum, in Austria. After the bomb run was completed, the group left the Liberators near Lake Balaton to engage six enemy fighters at 22,000 feet. Before the "smoke had cleared," five of the German fighters were confirmed as destroyed and the sixth was listed as probably destroyed.

The first victory was claimed by Second Lieutenant Carl Morey, who reported: "I attacked a Me 109 from the rear and opened fire from 350 yards with 20 degrees deflection and closed to within 250 yards, firing with no deflection. I saw many hits enter the wings and fuselage of the enemy aircraft, which burst into flames and started spinning down." As that fight happened, First Lieutenant Robert Newell bounced an Fw-190, and reported: "At an altitude of 10,000 feet I attacked a Fw-190 from the rear and opened fire from 400 yards with 20 degrees deflection. I closed to 250 yards dead astern, opened fire and saw hits on the tail and fuselage of the Fw-190, which burst into flames and crashed into the ground."

These were followed by Flight Officer Bland M. Barnes Jr., who claimed another Fw-190, describing his victory:

> While participating in a bomber escort to Moosbierbaum oil refineries, I, a wingman in a flight of four P-51s, turned to attack four Me 109s and two Fw-190s coming in from the east at 0530 o'clock. A Lufbery then evolved and I got on the tail of a Fw-190 and closed to about 300 yards, firing short bursts. Many hits were seen entering the wings and fuselage of the enemy aircraft. The Fw-190 split-essed from about 1,500 feet, struck the ground and exploded.

Fifteen minutes later, Second Lieutenant Morey scored again, claiming a Bf-109 destroyed. The mission's final victory was the first for future ace Second Lieutenant William Aron, who reported: "I was pursuing a Fw-190 from an altitude of 400 ft and opened fire from 850 yards with 20 degrees deflection and closed to within 500 yards with no deflection. I saw a number of hits on the wing and the enemy aircraft chandelled up and the pilot bailed out. Lieutenant Newell photographed the bail out and crash of the enemy airplane." All Checkertails returned safely to base. Following this fight, the Luftwaffe again disappeared during the next 16 missions flown through March 12.

On March 2 the Red Tails sent a flight of Mustangs to protect an F-5 photo-reconnaissance mission to Prague, while also providing a 34-Mustang escort led by Captain Jack Holsclaw for the 304th Bomb Wing's Liberators to bomb the Linz, Austria railroad marshaling yard. The next day, the 100th and 301st Squadrons sent 23 P-51s for a strafing sweep between Bruck and Wiener Neustadt, looking for trains and rolling stock. A train was spotted on the Maribor–Graz line and four Mustangs from the 100th Squadron shot up the train, parked rolling stock, seven goods wagons, and a passenger carriage. Another flight from the 100th then turned south, finally finding parked wagons on a siding near Langenwang. Eight other of the 100th's P-51s searched in the Graz area. Lieutenants Robert Martin and Alphonso Simmons spotted aircraft on a field south, but as they came up on the target to make their strafing run, waiting defenders opened up with a heavy flak barrage and both were quickly shot down. Simmons was killed in the crash of his fighter, but Martin radioed "I will walk in from here" after his Mustang was hit and made good on that when he returned to the group after a month spent evading the enemy on the ground.

Missions flown between March 4 and 13 saw no enemy action and were recorded in the war diary as "milk runs."

The 31st Group completed the move to Mondolfo on March 3 after a two-day delay for weather. The runway at the new base was paved and all-weather, a considerable difference from the PSP the Mustangs had contended with at San Severo. Particular note was taken of the fact that there were public hot showers in the Fano base, in actual buildings. The men of the 31st hadn't had an indoor shower since they arrived in North Africa two and a half years earlier. They flew their first successful escort mission on March 8, taking B-24s to Hegyshalom, Hungary to bomb the marshaling yards in support of the attacking Red Army. A large-scale strafing mission flown to Yugoslavia on March 9 found heavy clouds and no opportunity for low-level strafing.

March 13 saw Checkertail Mustangs fly a mission to strafe railroad-related targets in the Munich–Regensburg and Linz areas. On arrival, an overcast prevented any strafing. Not content to abort, nine pilots searched for a hole in the cloud cover. Once in the clear below the overcast, they strafed railroad targets in the Munich, Landshut, and Ingolstadt areas. Railroad targets in Wiener Neustadt were strafed by 14 other Checkertail Mustangs. Total claims were 26 locomotives destroyed with 33 damaged, 29 freight wagons destroyed and 15 damaged, 26 oil tank wagons destroyed and 16 damaged, five passenger carriages damaged, one power-house destroyed, and one switch house damaged.

The next day the 325th took off at 1020 hours to escort B-24s attacking the railroad marshaling yards at Nové Zámky, in Hungary. On the return trip, a pilot was forced to drop to a lower altitude when his oxygen system failed. Dropping out of the overcast, he spotted four Fw-190s and called for help. The other three members of his flight came down to assist him and ran into a gaggle of "30-plus" Fw-190s from the Royal Hungarian Air Force's 102. Csatarepülő Osztály (Fighter-Bomber Squadron). In what would turn out to be the Clan's final large air battle of the war, First Lieutenant Robert Burns quickly destroyed an Fw-190 as a major dogfight broke out. First Lieutenant Gordon McDaniel latched on to a flight of eight Fw-190s in a trail formation. He opened fire on the rearmost fighter and before the unfortunate pilots realized they were under attack, McDaniel had destroyed five to become an ace with a total of six.

Captain Harry Parker, who was flying his first mission since returning from leave, dived on two other Fw-190s and destroyed both, reporting:

> When I attacked a Fw-190 at 6,000 feet, it dived for the deck. I followed it down and opened fire from 1500 feet at 60 degrees deflection and closed to 50 feet dead astern. Many hits entered the fuselage and wings of the enemy aircraft, pieces of which fell off. The enemy aircraft went out of control and the pilot bailed out, but his 'chute failed to open. After downing this Fw-190 I attacked another one at 5,000 feet. I opened fire from about 4,500 feet with 30 degrees deflection and closed to within 50 feet, using no deflection. I saw hits enter the wing roots and fuselage of the enemy aircraft, which went out of control and crashed to earth.

The 13 victories put Parker in second place on the 325th's aces' list.

Second Lieutenant William Aron raised his total to three when he destroyed two Fw-190s at almost the same time that Parker claimed his victories. Second Lieutenant T.M. Bevan destroyed three remaining Fw-190s for his first victories. Single Bf-109s were claimed destroyed by Captain D.L. Voss and Lieutenant J.S. Sutherland, with Lieutenants J.B. Henry, J.G. Pace, W.K. Selenger, R.C. Burns, P.J. Murphy, and J.W. Barton each claiming an Fw-190 destroyed. The total of 20 destroyed for two P-51s lost was a tremendous victory for the Checkertails; they would not meet the enemy again in large numbers over the remaining weeks of the war.

The Red Tails were busy on March 14, with four scheduled missions. Two photo-recon escorts for Mosquitoes to Munich took off in the morning an hour apart. The 100th and 301st Squadrons received the main assignment, shepherding the 47th Bomb Wing's Liberators to hit the Varazdin railroad bridge and marshaling yard. While all three missions were without incident, the 21 99th Mustangs given the task of strafing targets on the Bruck–Leoben–Steyr railroad line saw enough action for the group as a whole. In spite of finding moderate, accurate, light flak at Hieflau, the squadron claimed nine locomotives and nine goods wagons destroyed, with nine locomotives, 127 goods wagons,

37 flatcars, eight oil wagons, seven trucks on flatcars, three railroad stations, two railroad buildings, and a power station damaged, while a warehouse was left burning.

99th pilot First Lieutenant Harold Brown had a close call with a lynching after he was hit and forced to bail out. The other pilots saw him get out of the crashed fighter and run for cover on a snowy mountainside. They were gone 30 minutes later, when he was apprehended by two constables who marched him back to Hieflau, where an angry mob with a rope waited. They quickly dragged Brown over to a small tree and were preparing to lynch him when a third constable armed with a rifle arrived on the scene and forced the mob back. Brown was handed over to the military police in a nearby town and eventually interned in Stalag Luft I for the few weeks of war remaining.

On March 16, 31 Red Tails flew a strafing mission against rail targets in Austria and Germany. Eight 99th Squadron P-51s attacked targets on a stretch of track between Ebersberg and Neumarkt for over an hour, leaving three trucks on flatcars and five goods wagons destroyed while damaging 45 other goods wagons, five locomotives, and four trucks on flatcars.

The 100th Squadron attacked a stretch of railroad to the west. Three Mustangs claimed two locomotives destroyed and two others damaged, along with five goods wagons and a baggage car. At Plattling, 11 301st Squadron Mustangs destroyed three locomotives and a flak car, with 15 goods wagons, nine locomotives, six coal wagons, three passenger carriages, an oil wagon, and a railroad station damaged. Five 301st Squadron P-51s strafed grounded aircraft at Mettenheim airfield. As a Bf-109 attempted to take off, it collapsed back onto the runway when a Mustang sprayed it with machine-gun fire. The 301st claimed three Fw-190s and a Ju-52/3m destroyed, with nine Fw-190s, two Bf-109s, one Fw-200, an unidentified biplane trainer, two barracks buildings, and an operations building claimed damaged.

The Mustangs repeatedly strafed a large reinforced concrete structure known to the Germans as *Projekt Weingut* (Wine Estate). The massive building – intended as a factory for production of Me-262 BMW jet engines and parts – was being built by Russian prisoners of war and inmates from the nearby Dachau concentration camp. It was only half-finished when it was damaged and construction was stopped.

The 325th's First Lieutenant J.R. Dytrych managed to spot and shoot down an Me-410 on the 16th while escorting an F-5 Lightning to photograph the oil refinery in Ruhland. Later that day Captain George Smith and Second Lieutenant T.M. Bevan joined forces while on another photo-reconnaissance escort to destroy a Bf-109. Four days later, on March 20, Lieutenants J.C. Wilkens and C.W. Morby destroyed an Fw-190 and a Bf-109, respectively, that they spotted near Wels, Czechoslovakia, while escorting another F-5, for the Checkertails' final victories in March.

On March 19, Fifteenth Air Force went after the German jets on the ground, mounting an all-out attack on the airfields known to harbor jets in the Munich–Neuberg area and Neuberg airdrome. It was later reported that 19 Me-262s had been destroyed in the bombing, to which the 31st Group's war diarist noted, "That made everyone feel real good, because they sure couldn't get that near to them in the sky!"

The mission of March 22 saw Fifteenth Air Force bombers penetrate to Ruhland, Germany – their deepest penetration yet – where the 31st Fighter Group finally engaged German jets in combat. The group's assignment was to cover the Flying Fortresses of the 5th Bomb Wing, which had the Ruhland oil refinery as its target.

As the bombers approached their target, 27 Me-262s were spotted approaching from the north. These jets were from JG 7 "Nowotny," the only regular Luftwaffe fighter group equipped with the Me-262 to engage the Allies in air combat; they were led by Geschwaderkommodore Major Theodor Weissenberger, an *Experte* with 208 victories and holder of the *Ritterkreuz des Eisernen Kreuzes mit Eichenlaub, Schwertern und Brillanten* (Knight's Cross of the Iron Cross with Oak Leaves, Swords and Diamonds) who would claim a total of eight victories flying the Me-262.

JG 7 had finally attained operational capability in February and first entered combat against the Eighth Air Force on March 3, when 29 sorties were flown, with eight victories claimed for the loss of one jet. A second battle with the Eighth on March 18 saw III./JG 7 engage in the *Geschwader*'s biggest attack to date with 37 Me-262s engaging 1,200 B-17s and B-24s, and 600 P-51 escorts headed for Berlin. For the first time, the attacking jets used the new, unguided R4M rockets to attack the bombers outside the range of their defensive fire. The Luftwaffe pilots claimed the destruction of 12 bombers and one fighter in exchange for three Me-262s shot down by the defenders, including three B-17s claimed by Weissenberger when he fired his 24 rockets into a bomber box. The Eighth acknowledged the loss of eight bombers, the air force's largest number of bombers lost to jets on one mission. The day before the battle over Ruhland, III./JG 7 claimed 13 B-17s destroyed while losing four Me-262s.

On the March 22 mission, a total 27 JG 7 Me-262's of I. and II. Gruppen attacked the Fifteenth Air Force bombers over Ruhland and Leipzig.

The 12 Me-262s headed toward the 5th Bomb Wing were spotted by pilots of the 31st's 307th Squadron. Four P-51s were ordered to intercept the jets. First Lieutenant Bobby Bush managed to close on one group of four attackers by gaining sufficient speed in a steep dive. He opened fire on the fourth jet just as the enemy fighter pulled out of his firing pass and scored five solid hits as the other three Me-262s broke away with high-speed evasive tactics.

The 308th Squadron also spotted the jets. Squadron newcomer Captain William J. Dillard was nearly out of control in his dive when an enemy jet flew in front of him at close range and he raked it from nose to tail, knocking out one engine that caught fire. The jet fell away and was observed to explode when it hit the ground.

The battle against the jets continued for the next 30 minutes as the Mustangs sought to interpose themselves between the attacking jets and the bombers to break up the German attacks. The 308th's Captain Hugh D. Naumann and First Lieutenant Claude Greene each claimed a jet damaged during the battle. First Lieutenant Harold Holland dived on a jet from 28,000 feet. Bucking in compressibility as he closed on the enemy fighter, he damaged one of the jet engines before the enemy pilot was able to split-ess and evade. Holland reported that the recoil of his guns when he fired slowed the Mustang to the point that he could regain full control.

Major Weissenberger and Oberfeldwebel Heinz Arnold each claimed a B-17 of the 12 Flying Fortresses claimed destroyed. Fifteenth Air Force admitted the loss of ten bombers shot down by the jets. The 31st Group's success against the jets was the only recorded combat with the new opponents by the groups escorting the mission, with the jets managing high-speed attacks on the bomber formations that allowed them to evade the defending escorts.

A second mission to Ruhland on March 23 found none of the enemy resistance the 31st Group had experienced the day before, even though

JG 7 again opposed the bombers with attacks against units not covered by the 31st, with 14 pilots claiming two bombers destroyed and one probable victory over the course of 11 aerial combats over Chemnitz. I./JG 7's Major Heinrich Ehrler claimed the two B-24s destroyed, while Oberfeldwebel Reinhold claimed a B-17 probably destroyed that the Americans confirmed as victory along with Ehrler's pair. The bombing was so successful that fuel production at Ruhland ceased completely after this attack.

The battle against German jets continued on March 24 when 38 Red Tail Mustangs relieved the 1st Group's new P-38L Lightnings as they rendezvoused with the B-17s of the 5th Bomb Wings over Kaaden in southern Germany. The mission was the first Fifteenth Air Force attack on Berlin – at 1,600 miles round trip, the Fifteenth's longest mission of the war – where their target was the Daimler-Benz tank factory. The purpose of the mission was to divert the Luftwaffe from going after the C-47s and Waco gliders of Operation *Varsity*, the largest paratroop attack of the war, which was part of the Rhine River crossing that day.

A few minutes later, Colonel Davis' P-51 developed a vibration at high manifold pressure, forcing the colonel to relinquish the mission leadership to 301st Squadron CO Captain Armour McDaniel. Davis and his wingman turned back south, leaving 36 Mustangs covering the bombers.

Twenty minutes later, the Red Tails were scheduled to turn over their escort duties to the 31st Fighter Group as they approached the outskirts of Berlin. However, the 31st's Mustangs were late and the 332nd continued on toward the German capital. The formation was nearing the target area at 1208 hours, when 25 Me-262s from JG 7 appeared from the southwest and engaged the bombers.

The 301st's Mustangs immediately turned and intercepted the first pass, which was made by four Me-262s that attacked the lower right echelon of the lead group of B-17s from "five o'clock high." As the lead jet continued down after executing his firing pass, numbers two and three rolled to the right, diving away from the bomber stream while the fourth Me-262 broke high and to the left.

First Lieutenant Richard Harder attempted to follow numbers two and three and managed to fire several bursts from 1,000 yards down to 300 yards, claiming one damaged. At the same time, Captain Edwin M. Thomas spotted the same attackers, later reporting, "My entire section of eight aircraft broke after the jets." Thomas and Second Lieutenant Vincent I. Mitchell pursued the two jets as they dived away, reporting that they also managed to hit one of the fleeing jets.

Two minutes later, the 100th Squadron's First Lieutenant Reid E. Thompson spotted a fifth jet making a firing pass from "two o'clock high." When he peeled away to attack it, he was cut off by another flight, forcing him to break off pursuit. Thompson then saw another enemy jet, originally misidentifying it as an Me-163. When Thompson fired a short burst from long range, the Me-262 dived steeply to avoid Thompson, who later reported the jet "was almost vertical in his dive," with no exhaust smoke. Thompson pulled out of his pursuit at 6,000 feet, later claiming that while he did not see it, he saw smoke on the ground "where I estimated he had hit."

A sixth Me-262 executed another firing pass at the bombers in a 30-degree dive in which he flew right across the nose of First Lieutenant Earl R. "Squirrel" Lane, who later reported, "He appeared as if he was peeling off from an attack on the bombers. I came in for a 30-degree deflection shot from 2,000 feet away. He didn't quite fill my sight. I fired three short bursts and saw the jet emitting smoke. A piece of it, either the canopy or one of the jet orifices, then flew off."

Lane's attack completely surprised Oberleutnant Alfred Ambs, who had already made two successful passes against the bombers. Ambs later wrote, "As I flew away from the bomber stream, phosphorus shells suddenly struck my cockpit. My oxygen mask was riddled and splinters struck my face. I quickly jettisoned the canopy and pulled up the nose of my Me-262 to lose speed. I bailed out at approximately 350 kph at an altitude of about 6,000 meters."

Breaking off his attack at 17,000 feet, Lane pulled up and circled over the spot where Ambs' jet had gone into its final dive and was rewarded with the sight of "a crash and a puff of black smoke." That was followed by a second smaller impact two seconds later, which was Ambs landing in a tree where he tore ligaments and broke his kneecap, making this combat his last flight in the war.

At the same time, the seventh and eighth Me-262s zoomed through the Red Tails formation. Unfortunately for the enemy, First Lieutenant Robert Williams and his wingman, Second Lieutenant Samuel Watts Jr., were waiting for them. As the two pilots turned into the Me-262s, both fired on Watts, whose Mustang had a hung-up drop tank. The two

Me-262s then passed below the Mustangs and Williams split-essed after them. Managing to close on their tails to a range of about 1,500 feet, he fired at the trailing jet as both accelerated away from him, claiming it damaged.

Following his earlier unsuccessful chase, First Lieutenant Richard Harder climbed back to 26,000 feet, where he spotted three other Me-262s attacking the B-17s from "five o'clock high." He later reported, "They did not reach the bombers, as I turned my flight into them." The two jets made a right turn as Harder's Blue Flight managed to turn inside them. One dived away while the second pulled up in a steep climb while the third continued its turn. Harder managed to close the range and fired at the third enemy jet from 2,000 feet down to 900 feet. He made a second "damaged" claim after seeing hits on the fuselage.

At the same time, Flight Officer Joseph Chineworth managed to claim a probable when three other Me-262s turned into his flight, reporting: "We broke right and down on them, pursuing them through a series of turns while descending. When I got to within 1,500 feet, I started firing on the rearmost enemy aircraft. I fired three bursts and my guns stopped." Pieces came off the jet and it started trailing smoke as it entered a dive at 15,000 feet.

A few minutes later, as Oberleutnant Ernst Wörner, flying Me-262 *Gelbe Sieben* ("Yellow Seven"), lined up for another pass, he cut in front of the Mustang flown by Flight Officer Charles Brantley, who firewalled his Merlin to close the distance. He later reported: "He was well within range when I fired four bursts." Brantley then broke off his attack, but another 100th Squadron pilot witnessed Wörner's jet catch fire and go out of control. Wörner managed to bail out but suffered injuries in doing so that put him in the hospital for the rest of the war.

First Lieutenant Roscoe Brown peeled off to attack four jets he'd spotted flying north below the bombers. However, as he later reported, "Almost immediately I saw a lone Me-262 at 24,000 feet climbing 90 degrees to me some distance from me. I pulled up at him in a 15-degree climb and fired three long bursts from 2,000 feet at eight o'clock to him."

Oberleutnant Franz Kulp, flying *Gelbe Fünf* ("Yellow Five"), managed to bail out as Brown's shells set his right engine on fire, spouting flames over the stricken jet's wing. Despite being wounded, Kulp managed to parachute to safety, but the severity of his wounds also put him in the hospital to war's end.

The Red Tails did not escape unscathed in the battle. First Lieutenant Leon "Woodie" Spears had the outer right wing of his Mustang, "Kitten," blown off. "Looking at that wing and hearing how the engine was running, I knew there was no way I could get over the Alps to Italy." He turned east, heading for the Red Army's lines in Poland. Looking for a landing spot, he selected a field near a river, only to discover he was flying into the middle of a fight between Soviet and German troops, who each held opposite banks of the river. "Between the two of them, they shot my airplane to pieces. I could feel shells hitting my fighter while I was flying down this river."

Dropping his gear, Spears decided to raise it again to prevent his Mustang falling undamaged into enemy hands. After the badly damaged fighter finally slid to a stop, Spears was captured by the German troops who drove up to the fighter. "They seemed to be trying to be as nice as they could. If they had a name badge, they'd shove it right under my nose so I wouldn't miss it. They knew that the war was coming to an end, so they did not want to be involved in any war crimes or any cruelty." His captors half-heartedly interrogated Spears. "They knew full well that any information they got would be useless to them."

Three days later, Spears heard a commotion outside the building in which he was being held. "I pulled a board off a window and the first thing I saw was this huge Russian tank." Since the Soviet troops were firing into the surrounding buildings at random, Spears began shouting and waving to avoid being hit. Over the din of the shooting, one Soviet soldier heard him. "I had an A-2 flying jacket on with a large American flag on the back. I put my back to the window so he could see it and I heard him yell, 'American! American!' He rushed up and gave me a big bear hug!" Spears was able to return to Ramitelli on May 10, following the war's ending.

Other losses included Second Lieutenant James T. Mitchell, who stayed with Spears when he headed for Polish territory and managed to land on the Soviet side of the front line. First Lieutenant Arnett Starks was shot down and killed in action. 301st Squadron CO Captain Armour McDaniel, who took command of the mission when Colonel Davis was forced to abort, bailed out when his own P-51 experienced engine trouble. Captured after landing, he ended the war a prisoner of war.

The Red Tails' effort on this mission was recognized by 5th Bomb Wing commander Brigadier General Lawrence, whose telegram thanking the group for their extraordinary efforts resulted in the 332nd Fighter Group being awarded a Distinguished Unit Citation.

March 24 was recorded in the 31st's war diary as "The Group's finest day of the war." The group managed to finally rendezvous with the 5th Bomb Wing's B-17s over Freiberg at 30,000 feet and relieve the Red Tails. The three squadrons then provided 15 minutes' cover over the target, during which the 31st continued the fight with the defending JG 7 Me-262s.

The 307th Squadron spotted 12 Me-262s menacing the bombers under their protection. When seven jets broke toward the bomber stream in a firing pass, First Lieutenants John Wilson and William H. Bunn combined to get hits on one enemy jet. It was obvious that the Me-262s were trying to avoid all contact with the defending escorts in their high-speed attacks. Seven jets dived through the 309th Squadron's formation without the Mustangs being able to offer any opposition as the enemy pilots flashed past.

Fortunately, the 308th Squadron was perfectly situated to break up the attack. The Mustangs turned into the enemy, with the 31st's commander, Colonel William A. Daniel, who led the formation, raking an Me-262 that flew across his nose, setting it on fire as it nosed over and headed down. Captain Kenneth Smith opened fire on a second jet, knocking off pieces of the engine cowling; the engine caught fire and that Me-262 also headed down. First Lieutenant Raymond A. Leonard pounced on a jet from the rear and poured fire into the cockpit, killing the pilot and sending a third attacker down. Finally, Second Lieutenant William M. Wilder hit a fourth jet in its engines and watched it dive into the ground and explode on impact. Lieutenants Forrest J. Keene and Ralph Erichson each claimed a fifth and sixth Me-262 damaged.

Over the course of the remainder of March, the 31st Group was able to fly several photo-reconnaissance escorts, with no sign of the enemy on any of them. The only combat action in the week remaining of March came the day after the battle with the jets over Berlin, when the 307th Squadron escorted bombers to hit the Prostejov-Kostelec airfield in Czechoslovakia. Four P-51s flew over to Olomouc airfield north of Brno to see if there were any enemy aircraft there and discovered six Fw-190s taxiing for takeoff. The Mustangs held off until the enemy fighters were airborne, then hit them as they retracted their landing gear. First Lieutenant Norman E. Skogstad raced through the enemy aircraft as they were trying to form up and gain airspeed, shooting down three. He was followed by Lieutenants Van Winkle and Pelt, who each claimed one destroyed. Skogstad came around again and set the last one on fire as its pilot tried desperately to get on the tails of the other Mustangs. Adverse weather was the rule over what was left of March.

The Yellow Tails of the 52nd Fighter Group finally found an opportunity to engage in air combat on March 25 when they escorted four B-24 groups to bomb Bruck Leithe East and West marshaling yards in Austria. As the bombers were leaving the target, several 2nd Squadron pilots spotted two flights of Fw-190s heading north along a rail line. When four of the enemy fighters dived toward the ground and began a strafing attack against unseen Red Army units, two flights dived on the enemy and broke up the attack. In the ensuing fight, two Fw-190s were credited to Captain John J. Meyers, one to First Lieutenant Herbert Toombs Jr., and the fourth to Lieutenants Oscar Bushwar and Paul Westphal. For his actions, Lieutenant Toombs was later awarded the DFC. The citation read in part:

> As the bombers were being escorted on withdrawal, the leader of Toombs' flight called in a bogie at 10,000 feet and took the flight down to look it over. It was a B-24. Then Toombs saw four Fw-190s flying north in a loose "V" at 4,000 feet in the area east of Papa, Hungary.
>
> After calling his leader, Toombs dived on these aircraft. As he approached them he saw they were starting a strafing attack along the railroad that apparently was in the control of the Russians. He closed to about 600 yards and fired, but saw no strikes. The enemy aircraft split-essed, leveled off on the deck and started to fishtail and make occasional tight turns. Despite this evasive action, Toombs stayed with the 190, closed to about 200 yards, fired short bursts and saw hits on the wings. Then he fired a long burst and saw strikes on the fuselage and around the cockpit. Parts of the plane flew off and the pilot jettisoned the canopy and bailed out.
>
> After the enemy aircraft crashed and Toombs rejoined his flight, more Fw-190s were seen. He immediately turned and chased on, at about 2,000 feet, encountering light Flak as he did so. When the

enemy was in range, Toombs fired a short burst, only to find that just one gun was firing. He called for someone else to continue the attack and broke off his attack.

Captain Meyers reported his experience of the fight:

We each picked a plane and went after him with everything we had. I got my first at about 1,000 feet when he was trying to gain altitude. Smoke began pouring from his engine and he rolled over on his back and plunged in the ground. The second victory came harder. I latched onto him just after the first plane hit the ground, but we were all over the sky for about 30 miles in a northwesterly direction before I finally got him. The plane blew up in the air.

These Fw-190s were all Fw-190F-8 fighter-bombers from the Hungarian 102./2 Csatarepülő Osztály. The Americans all reported that the enemy pilots were very experienced. All six Mustangs returned safely. With weather closing in over the last week of March, this was the last combat the Yellow Tails engaged in for the month.

The Red Tails made their greatest score of the war on March 31. Colonel Davis led 43 Mustangs on a fighter sweep of the Munich area. After finding no enemy aircraft, the Mustangs went down on the deck in search of rail targets. Just after the group broke apart with the three squadrons looking for targets of opportunity, seven pilots of the 99th Squadron were momentarily surprised when they saw five Bf-109s and a single Fw-190 suddenly break out of the overcast just as they were lining up to strafe a marshaling yard. Breaking off that attack, Second Lieutenant Thomas Braswell quickly nailed the Fw-190, which exploded when it crashed. Squadron leader Major William Campbell, First Lieutenant Daniel Rich, and Second Lieutenants John Davis, James Hall, and Hugh White each claimed one of the Bf-109s.

Five minutes after that, pilots from the 100th Squadron spotted eight Fw-190s and three Bf-109s at 3,000 feet. The German pilots were aggressive, but failed to fight as a team. First Lieutenant Robert Williams reported:

I dived into a group of enemy aircraft and got on the tail of one of the Fw 190s. I shot off a few short bursts. My fire hit the mark and the enemy airplane fell off and tumbled to the ground. As I pulled away from my victim, I found another enemy on my tail. To evade his guns, I made a steep turn. Just as I turned, another enemy fighter shot across the nose of my airplane and I immediately began firing at him.

Williams was credited with the destruction of both Focke-Wulfs.

First Lieutenant Roscoe Brown and Second Lieutenants Bertram Wilson and Rual Bell were each credited with the destruction of a Bf-109, with First Lieutenant Earl Lane and Flight Officer John Lyle claiming an Fw-190 each.

With the enemy fighters dispatched, the Mustangs resumed their strafing mission. The 99th Squadron claimed two locomotives destroyed and a third one damaged, along with 15 passenger carriages shot up. However, flak took out Second Lieutenant Clarence Driver, who bailed out and was quickly captured.

The 301st claimed three locomotives, two goods wagons, and a house destroyed, with nine locomotives, 14 goods wagons, six passenger carriages, five oil wagons, five hopper cars, a factory, a railroad roundhouse, a railroad station, and a truck all damaged. The 100th claimed two locomotives, eight oil wagons, three passenger carriages, and a warehouse destroyed, with a locomotive, two tank cars, a truck, and ten goods wagons damaged. Second Lieutenant Ronald Reeves managed to turn so tightly that he went into a high-speed stall/spin and was killed when his fighter hit the ground and caught fire.

On April Fools' Day 1945, 45 red-tailed Mustangs rendezvoused with the Liberators of the 47th Bomb Wing to hit the railroad marshaling yards at St Polten, Austria. Eight 301st Squadron P-51s preceded the B-24s through the target area, then turned west to conduct a fighter sweep in the vicinity of Wels and Linz. Four Fw-190s were spotted below near Wels airfield and the Mustangs dived on them, to discover too late that these four were bait. Two other Fw-190s trailed those down on the deck, while ten other Fw-190s and Bf-109s flew high cover to spring the trap. In a series of swirling dogfights, the enemy pilots tried everything – head-on passes, Lufberys, turning attacks, deflection shots. Regardless, the 301st came out on top. Captain Harry Stewart claimed three Fw-190s destroyed while First Lieutenant Charles White claimed two Bf-109s. Lieutenants Carl Carey, John Edwards, and Walter Manning claimed a Bf-109 each, while Harold Morris and James Fischer claimed an Fw-190 each. Fischer's Mustang was shot up by light flak when he chased the Fw-190 across an airfield. He took another flak hit as he flew over a small Yugoslavian town on the sway home, forcing him to bail out. Fortunately, he landed among friendly partisans. Flak over the airfield took Manning moments after he scored his kill, along with Flight Officer William Armstrong. Both died in the crashes.

The March 31 mission flown by the 31st Fighter Group saw the Mustangs claim 21 enemy aircraft shot down in the last big aerial engagement of the war in the Mediterranean Theater, which put the 31st in first place as the leading fighter group in the MTO with 568.5 victories since they had first claimed a victory over a German fighter during the Dieppe Raid on August 19, 1942.

The group had launched the 308th Squadron on a fighter sweep to cover the area Pilsen, Czechoslovakia, and Zwiesel, Germany. Hunting targets of opportunity, the squadron claimed four locomotives destroyed and 11 damaged, along with 15 oil tank cars and one tender, as well as a railroad station shot up.

The 16 307th Squadron pilots sent to cover the area between Prague and Ingolstadt claimed 13 locomotives destroyed, and three damaged. Major Woodrow W. Ramsey, First Lieutenant Nelson T. Womack Jr., and Second Lieutenant Olen E. Vernon spotted four Fw-190s engaged in ground strafing northeast of Ingolstadt. Each pilot scored one Fw-190, two of whose pilots were seen to bail out, while the fourth managed to split-ess away, pulling out just above the ground and escaping.

The 309th Squadron sent 17 P-51s searching for targets of opportunity southeast of Prague. Just slightly west of the city, the Mustangs came across a formation of over 30 Bf-109s between 1,000 and 3,000 feet. Over the next 20 minutes, the 309th's pilots destroyed 18 of the enemy fighters, claiming two more damaged. Group flying exec Lieutenant Colonel Fred C. Stoffel claimed three, as did Major Julius D. Shivers. Lieutenants Rollin M. Barton, Robert R. Blank, Ernest D. Hackney, and John E. Moore claimed two destroyed each. Major Simon H. Johnson Jr., and Lieutenants Arcola Johnson, Horace J. Maze, and Phillip G. Wheeler claimed one each. As it turned out, this was the last aerial combat the 31st would engage in before the war ended.

The 52nd Group's 2nd Squadron diarist, Captain Tom Thacker, wrote that April 1945 saw the advent of a beautiful spring. "Perhaps we are getting a little war-weary as we rolled into April. However, with spring at hand, the mud dried up and the grass became green once more, flowers bloomed and there was a definite air of enthusiasm once again. The impending move northward plus reasonable assurance that the war in Europe was nearly over contributed to that feeling." The 52nd Group would fly 80 ground support missions and escort missions. However, the one aerial victory claimed on April 11 was significant. Second Squadron's First Lieutenant Ben Hall and his wingman Second Lieutenant Cecil E. Cooper Jr. were giving cover to a damaged B-24 over the Brenner Pass when Hall spotted the elusive Ar-234 jet reconnaissance aircraft that had been operating over Italy with impunity. The mission report recorded:

> Giving chase, Hall cut the Nazi plane off when it attempted to run and closed to within 800 yards when he saw strikes on the left engine. This slowed the enemy aircraft down and Hall was able to pull up to 300 yards where he scored more hits and the plane started to burn. As the Ar-234 went into a shallow dive, Cooper got some hits and the enemy aircraft was seen to hit the ground and roll over several times, burning fiercely.

The Ar-234 was "T9+DH" of Kommando Sommer, flown by Leutnant Gunther Gneismer. It was the only one of its kind shot down by XV Fighter Command pilots.

Four 99th Squadron P-51s led by First Lieutenant Hannibal Cox escorted an F-5 to Munich on April 2. The Mustangs had just arrived over the city when an Me-262 jumped the formation with a single pass from "seven o'clock high." While the P-51s turned into the enemy jet, the F-5 continued toward Regensburg. Without a photo plane to escort, Cox led the flight down to the deck, where they strafed six river barges on the way back to Ramitelli.

The day's escort mission saw the Red Tails cover the 304th Bomb Wing's B-24s when they hit the railroad marshaling yard at Krems,

Austria. The 99th made a sweep west of Vienna but found nothing to strafe. All 47 Mustangs returned safely.

The Checkertail Clan moved to its final base of the war on April 2, when the group shifted from Rimini to Mondolfo, where it would share the field with the 31st Fighter Group. The group was broken into A Force, which conducted a fighter sweep attacking targets of opportunity from Ljubljana to Celje to Zweiweg to Bruck, and B Force, which flew its sweep against targets from Celje to Maribor to Graz. The sweeps turned out to bring both triumph and tragedy for the group.

Strafing results were minimal, but in an encounter with 15 enemy aircraft near Klagenfurt, Major Norman McDonald claimed two Bf-109s destroyed, raising his score to ten and a half victories, while First Lieutenant G.E. Amedro destroyed a third. Sadly, these victories were no recompense for the loss of Captain Harry Parker, the Checkertails' second ranking ace with 13 victories. Wingman Second Lieutenant Sidney Rosenbloom reported the loss after landing at Mondolfo: "I was flying as Captain Harry A. Parker's wingman on April 2 on a strafing mission in the vicinity of Klagenfurt. Captain Parker observed a bogie below and called me, stating that he was going down to investigate. He ordered me to escort Lieutenant Clifford Hill back to home base." Nothing was ever learned of Parker's fate, and he was listed as missing in action.

On April 4, the 325th flew a strafing mission to the Regensburg–Munich–Linz area, where the Mustangs were quite successful against targets on the ground and airborne. The pilots claimed destruction of five locomotives and several other freight and oil tank wagons. As the P-51s pulled up from their attacks, they came across six Fw-190s, quickly shooting down five. The leading scorer was First Lieutenant W.K. Selenger, who claimed two destroyed. Lieutenants Bill Aron, J.G. Howell, and L.F. Seevers claimed the other three. Aron's claim was his fourth.

Forty-five minutes later, the group encountered two Me-262s. Second Lieutenant W.N. Clark shot up one enough to make a claim for a probable, while First Lieutenant W.K. Day got hits on the second enemy jet before it accelerated out of range and disappeared in the clouds.

The Checkertails split into A and B Groups on April 6 when they went to Germany, Austria, and Czechoslovakia. The Mustang

THE FINAL BATTLES

pilots claimed 15 aircraft on the ground destroyed, along with nine locomotives and several other railroad wagons, including four flatcars loaded with aircraft wing assemblies.

After a short weather break, the Red Tails flew escort for the B-17s of the 5th Bomb Wing when the Flying Fortresses bombed Udine airfield in the afternoon. This was the last major enemy fighter base in northern Italy, but by this time there were no Luftwaffe units in the country and the ANR pilots were unable to counter the bombers due to lack of fuel.

On April 10 while flying another strafing mission to the Regensburg–Munich–Passau railroad, the 325th claimed six locomotives destroyed and a radio station damaged. Turning for home, the Mustangs encountered nine enemy aircraft southeast of Linz. In the dogfight that followed, five Fw-190s were claimed destroyed. Ten minutes later, a Ju-88 was spotted and shot down in flames. Major Norman McDonald's claim of one Fw-190 destroyed raised his final score to 11.5 victories, while the remaining four Focke-Wulfs were claimed by Lieutenants R.D. Christian, W.W. Forsyth, J.E. Mason, and J.A. Leonard. Lieutenant Bill Aron spotted a Ju-88 and shot it down for his fifth, and final, victory, which made him the last Checkertail ace of the war. He reported, "I observed a Ju 88 flying at 8,000 feet, and when I began my attack, it went into a dive. I followed it down and opened fire from 1,000 feet with 30 degrees deflection. Closing to 600 feet dead astern, I again opened fire. Many strikes were seen in the wing roots before the pilot bellied the Ju-88 in and it burst into flames."

After several uneventful bomber and photo-recon plane escort missions, the Red Tails finally found some action on April 15, when Colonel Davis led 37 Mustangs on a strafing mission against rail targets in the Munich, Salzburg, Linz, Prague, and Regensburg areas. The three squadrons split up to hunt for targets. Two rail trains that were spotted were defended by flak wagons, which did not deter the Mustangs from attacking and destroying both locomotives, part of the score of four locomotives that the 99th Squadron claimed destroyed, along with four other locomotives, 14 goods wagons, four motor transports on flatcars, and two railroad buildings that the squadron claimed as damaged.

Twelve 100th Squadron P-51s strafed the rail line from Plattling to Passan to Klatovy, claiming destruction of five locomotives while damaging four others, along with five goods wagons, a passenger carriage, and a house.

The 301st had the best luck of the three. After strafing and damaging two river barges, a steam crane, and a house near the river, they attacked a rail line, destroying an oil wagon and damaging six others. Four other Mustangs found a nearby rail line and destroyed seven locomotives; nine others, along with 15 goods wagons and a passenger carriage, were damaged.

As they pulled up from their run, First Lieutenant Jimmy Lanham and his wingman spotted a Bf-109 and turned to attack it. The enemy fighter attempted to turn inside the Mustangs, but Lanham caught it with a series of deflection shots, scoring hits in the cowling. The Bf-109 burst into flames when it hit the ground.

The war in Italy came to a swift end following the commencement of the Allied spring offensive on April 15, 1945. After nine unsuccessful months of Allied attempts to break the Gothic Line defenses held by the German Tenth and Fourteenth Armies, the enemy succumbed to the effect of Operation *Bingo*, the six-month bombing campaign against the rail line through the Brenner Pass, which had cut the enemy's supplies by 80 percent from the end of fighting in October 1944 with the onset of winter. Everywhere, the enemy's armed forces reeled back in the face of the offensive, with Bologna – key to the Po River Valley – surrounded three days after the campaign's commencement.

On April 18, Major Ralph Johnson provided the excitement on a freelance fighter sweep in the Regensburg–Munich area that had been uneventful up to the moment when he caught and destroyed an Me-262 that managed to pop out of cloud nearly right in front of him, with the pilot suffering a fatal surprise when he discovered a Mustang on his tail. The next day, the Checkertails destroyed seven enemy aircraft when the 317th Squadron escorted B-25s from the 57th Bomb Wing's 340th Bomb Group. The Mitchells were going after the Ora bridge in the Po River Valley to block any attempted retreat of German forces from Bologna in the face of the British Eighth Army's breakthrough at the Argenta Gap – the decisive event of the Allies' spring offensive, which led to the end of the war in Italy ten days later. Returning from the attack, eight Mustangs ran across a gaggle of ANR-flown Bf-109s and sent six crashing into the hills below in flames. First Lieutenant

THE FINAL BATTLES

W.F. Baldwin claimed two Bf-109s destroyed, while the other four were credited to Lieutenants F.W. Schaefer, W.B. Bagley, J. Barrett, and F.M. Bolek, who each claimed one. These were in addition to an Fw-190 that Lieutenant Bill Gertin had come across while on a test hop to slow-time his engine when it made a pass at him as he flew near Florence. Chasing the enemy fighter to its base outside Verona, Gertin shot it down when the pilot attempted to land after he had damaged it with a burst of fire. These were the final victories that closed out two years of fighting the Luftwaffe and its allied air forces across the Mediterranean for the 325th Fighter Group.

The remainder of the last ten days of war in Italy passed uneventfully for the checkertailed Mustangs. The war took one final life on April 22 when Bill Aron, the group's final ace of the war, was forced to bail out after taking a flak hit and was captured on the ground by Fascist paramilitaries and murdered.

Over 542 missions flown since the 325th Fighter Group had entered combat in the final weeks of fighting in Tunisia in the spring of 1943, the checkertailed fighters had shot down 534 enemy aircraft in air combat, destroying an additional 281 on the ground. This came at a cost of 148 pilots lost during 567 missions.

After flying several "milk run" escorts in which the enemy made no response, the Red Tails scored their last victory of the war during an F-5 escort on April 26, which also saw the final aerial victories for XV Air Force Fighter Command. First Lieutenant Charles Wilson led six Mustangs escorting an F-5 to photograph Linz, Prague, and Amstetten. Fifteen miles east of Prague at 1205 hours, a Mosquito was spotted. Three Mustangs dropped down to investigate. Just as they rejoined the formation, they spotted five Bf-109s that rocked their wings to appear friendly. The six Mustangs broke into them, and two Bf-109s peeled up as if to dive. Second Lieutenant Thomas Jefferson fired two bursts at one of them; it exploded after spiraling into the ground and exploded. The other enemy fighters split-essed and dived toward the ground, but Lieutenants Jimmy Lanham and William Price caught up with and destroyed two of the Bf-109s, one of whose pilots bailed out. Richard Simmons caught up with the remaining Bf-109s after a short chase, and hit one solidly that crashed into the ground and exploded while he claimed the other as a probable.

In a year of combat, the pilots of the 332nd Fighter Group had completely disproven the claims of ignorant racists like William Momyer that African Americans could not be successful fighter pilots. The pilots of the Red Tails had performed as well as the other three Mustang groups of the Fifteenth Air Force against a determined enemy and established a reputation among bomber crews for providing excellent escorts. Their record has stood the test of time over 80 years since, with several of the men who remained in the Air Force after the war rising to high rank in the new independent Air Force; in 1955, Benjamin O. Davis became the first African American Brigadier General in the Air Force.

BIBLIOGRAPHY

Ambrose, Stephen E., *The Wild Blue: The Men and Boys Who Flew The B-24s Over Germany* (New York: Simon and Schuster, 2001)
Blake, Steve, with John Stanaway, *Up and At 'Em: A History of the 82nd Fighter Group in World War II* (Boise, ID: 82nd Fighter Group Association, 1992)
Bucholtz, Chris, *332nd Fighter Group – Tuskegee Airmen* (Oxford: Osprey Publishing, 2007)
Camp, Joe H., Jr., *Langdon Liberando: An Abbevillian's Fifty Missions Over Southern Europe* (North Charleston, SC: Kindle Direct Publishing Independent Publishing Platform, 2022)
Chamberlin, J.V., *Frantic Joe: American Air Bases in Russia World War II* (Washington DC: Chamberlin & Chamberlin LLC, 2012)
Cleaver, Thomas McKelvey, "The P-38's Blackest Day," *Flight Journal*, June 2008
Cleaver, Thomas McKelvey, "Piggyback in a P-38," *Flight Journal*, August 2008
Conversino, Mark J., *Fighting With the Soviets: The Failure of Operation Frantic 1944–45* (Lawrence, KS: University Press of Kansas, 1997)
Craven, Wesley Frank and James Lea Cate, *The Army Air Forces in World War II – Volume Two – Europe: Torch to Pointblank – August 1942 to December 1943* (Chicago, IL: The University of Chicago Press, 1949)
Davis, Richard G., *Carl A. Spaatz and the Air War in Europe* (Washington DC: Center for Air Force History, 1993)
Ehlers, Robert S., Jr., *The Mediterranean Air War: Airpower and Allied Victory in World War II* (Lawrence, KS: University Press of Kansas, 2015)
Ehrhart, Robert C., "Mediterranean Theater 1943–45," in John F. Kreis (ed.), *Piercing the Fog: Intelligence and Army Air Forces Operations in World

War II (Washington, DC: Air Force History and Museums Program, 1996)

Faulkner, Tom, *Flying With the Fifteenth Air Force* (Denton, TX: University of North Texas Press, 2018)

Green, Herschel H., *Herky! The Memoirs of a Checkertail Ace* (Atglen, PA: Schiffer Military History, 1996)

Hansell, Haywood S., Jr., *The Air Plan That Defeated Hitler* (New York: Arno Press, 1980)

Haulman, Daniel L., *Legend of the Black Ace* (Maxwell AFB: Air Force Historical Research Agency, 2008)

Haulman, Daniel L., *Nine Myths About the Tuskegee Airmen* (Maxwell AFB: Air Force Historical Research Agency, 2011)

Haulman, Daniel L., *A Short History of the Tuskegee Airmen* (Maxwell AFB: Air Force Historical Research Agency, 2015)

Haulman, Daniel L., *Misconceptions About the Tuskegee Airmen* (Maxwell AFB: Air Force Historical Research Agency, 2016)

Horn, John E., *Liberando: The Reflections of a Reluctant Warrior* (Hooskick Falls, NY: Merriam Press, 2019)

Ivie, Tom and Paul Ludwig, *Spitfires and Yellow Tail Mustangs: The 52nd Fighter Group in World War II* (Crowborough, UK: Hikoki Publications, 2005)

Kucera, Dennis C., *In A Now Forgotten Sky: The 31st Fighter Group in World War II* (Stratford, CT: Flying Machines Press, 1997)

Lambert, John W., *The 14th Fighter Group in World War II* (Atglen, PA: Schiffer Military History, 2008)

McDowell, Ernest R., *Checkertails: The 325th Fighter Group in the Second World War* (Carrollton, TX: Squadron/Signal Publications, Inc, 1994)

Miskimins, Sean M., *Operation Tidal Wave: Enlisted Airmen in the Attacks on Ploesti*, Airman Heritage Series (Washington, DC: The Airmen Memorial Museum, 1944)

Modrovsky, Robert J., "1 August 1943: Today's Target is Ploesti – A Departure From Doctrine," unpublished MA thesis (US Air Force Air University, 1999)

Mullins, John D., *An Escort of P-38s: The First Fighter Group in World War II* (St Paul, MN: Phalanx Publishing, 1995)

Murray, Williamson, *Strategy for Defeat: The Luftwaffe 1933–45* (Maxwell AFB: Air University Press, 1983)

Parramore, Lt Col Woody W., "The Combined Bomber Offensive's Destruction of Germany's Refined-Fuels Industry," *Air & Space Power Journal*, March–April 2012

BIBLIOGRAPHY

Perret, Geoffrey, *Winged Victory: The Army Air Forces in World War II* (New York: Random House, 1993)

Seyer, Sean H., "The Plan Put into Practice: USAAF Bombing Doctrine and the Ploesti Campaign," unpublished MA thesis (University of Missouri, 2009)

Spaatz, Carl A., *Strategic Air Power in the European War* (Maxwell AFB: Air War College Associate Programs, Vol. I, 1995)

Syrett, David, "Northwest Africa 1942–43," in Dr Benjamin Franklin Cooling (ed.), *Case Studies in Air Superiority* (Washington, DC: Air Force History and Museums Program, 1994)

Truxal, Luke W., "The Failed Bombing Offensive: A Reexamination of the Combined Bomber Offensive in 1943," unpublished MA thesis (University of North Texas, 2011)

Truxal, Luke W., *Uniting Against the Reich: The American Air War in Europe* (Lexington: University Press of Kentucky, 2023)

Stout, Jay A., *Fortress Ploesti: The Campaign to Destroy Hitler's Oil* (Havertown, PA: Casemate Publishers, 2003)

Tillman, Barrett, "The Forgotten Fifteenth," *Air & Space Forces Magazine*, September 1, 2012

Tillman, Barrett, *Forgotten Fifteenth: The Daring Airmen Who Crippled Hitler's War Machine* (Washington, DC: Regnery History, 2015)

USAAF, "Ploesti Operations Report, 1944," Army Air Force Operations Board Report, Vol. VI (Washington, DC, 1944)

GLOSSARY

The list below contains acronyms and non-English terms used in the text.

ACRONYMS

AA: antiaircraft
AAF: Army Air Force
ANR: Aeronautica Nazionale Repubblicana (Italian Fascist Air Force)
CO: commanding officer
DFC: Distinguished Flying Cross
DSC: Distinguished Service Cross
ETO: European Theater of Operations
FNB: Focşani–Nămoloasa–Brăila (the FNB Line was the German line of defense that blocked the Focşani Gap that led to the Wallachia plains)
HALPRO: Halverson Detachment
JG: *Jagdgeschwader* (Luftwaffe fighter wing)
MTO: Mediterranean Theater of Operations
NJG: *Nachtjagdgeschwader* (Luftwaffe night fighter wing)
OKH: Oberkommando des Heeres (German Army High Command)
OKW: Oberkommando der Wehrmacht (Wehrmacht High Command)
OSS: Office of Strategic Services
PSP: pierced-steel planking
RAF: Royal Air Force
RCAF: Royal Canadian Air Force
SAAF: South African Air Force

GLOSSARY

SG: *Schlachtgeschwader* (Luftwaffe dive bomber wing)
SHAEF: Supreme Headquarters Allied Expeditionary Force
SOE: Special Operations Executive
USAAF: US Army Air Force
USSTAF: United States Strategic Air Forces
ZG: *Zerstörergeschwader* (Luftwaffe heavy fighter wing)

NON-ENGLISH TERMS

German
Experte(n): German term for "ace"
Geschwader: wing(s)
Gruppe(n): group(s)
Gruppenkommandeur: group commander
Nachwuchs: lit. "new growth," a new recruit later in the war
Jabo: abbreviation for Jagdbomber, a German fighter-bomber
Jagdflieger(n): fighter pilot(s)
Jagdfliegerführer Rumänien: Romanian Fighter Command (Luftwaffe)
Jagdgeschwader(n): fighter wing(s)
Jagdwaffe: German Fighter Force
Luftwaffe: German Air Force
Panzer: tank
Staffel(n): squadron(s)
Staffelkapitän(e): squadron leader(s)

Italian
Gruppo/gruppi: group(s)
Gruppo Caccia/Gruppi Caccia: fighter group(s)
Stormo/Stormi: wing(s)

Romanian
Grupul/Grupurile: group(s)
Escadrila/Escadrile: squadron(s)
Vânătoare: fighter

INDEX

Abbott, Lt Carlyle 137
aborts 56, 61, 87, 119, 122, 133, 138, 146, 157, 159, 161, 167, 190, 194, 247, 276, 289
accidents 26, 34, 53, 55, 133, 157, 159, 160, 161, 215
ace pilots 51, 53, 69, 86, 99, 107, 108, 111, 118, 122, 123, 124, 128, 142, 145, 146, 170, 174, 180–181, 188, 193, 195, 196, 210, 212, 256, 282, 296, 297, 299; German *Experten* 54, 123, 172, 284
Adams, Lt Chuck 176
Adams, Lt 'Junior' 110, 132
Adams, Second Lt Daniel 268
Adelson, Lt Merrill 174, 176
African Americans in the USAAF 12, 150–168, 300
Aho, First Lt Arne E. 103
Aiello landing ground, Udine 97
Aiken, Second Lt David 272
Aiken, Second Lt John 83
Ainsley, First Lt John M. 98, 99, 101
air ingress 45
air maneuvers 65, 68, 108, 293; Lufbery circle 104, 135, 136, 196, 254, 259, 273, 280, 293; split-ess 69, 118, 129, 163, 164, 165, 166, 177, 183, 184, 186, 187, 203, 205, 208, 209, 210, 214, 218, 219, 242, 263, 265, 266, 273, 279, 288, 291, 294
Air Sea Rescue patrols 144, 157

air tactics 86, 248
air-to-air refueling 18
aircraft, Bulgaria: Avia B-534 27, 34, 35
aircraft, Germany: Arado Ar-96 220; Arado Ar-234 295; Dornier Do-24 80; Dornier Do-215 128; Dornier Do-217 68, 123–124, 220, 241, 276; Fieseler Fi-156 "Storch" 137, 190, 192, 241, 249; Focke-Wulf Fw-189 220, 251; Focke-Wulf Fw-190 54, 56, 60, 63, 64, 65, 69, 70, 72, 73, 78, 85–86, 88, 91, 98, 99, 101, 106, 109, 111, 118, 119, 120, 121, 124, 131, 132, 134, 138, 139, 141, 142, 143, 144, 149, 162–163, 186, 187, 188, 189, 190, 191, 194, 195, 196, 203, 205–206, 209, 210, 211, 212, 213, 218–219, 220, 241, 246, 247, 250, 253, 257, 263, 264, 265, 267, 272–273, 276, 279–280, 281, 282, 283, 292–293, 294, 296, 297, 299; Fw-190D 272; Fw-190F-8 290–291–292; Focke-Wulf Fw-200 241, 245, 247, 283; Gotha Go-242 59, 190, 220, 249; Heinkel He-111 59, 60, 80, 105, 128, 190, 191, 192, 203, 204, 219–220, 241, 245, 247, 248, 249, 251, 267; Heinkel He-177 192; Henschel Hs-126 67, 68, 241; Henschel Hs-129 241; Junkers Ju-52 58, 67, 68, 80, 105, 173, 190, 191, 192, 219, 220, 237, 241; Ju-52/3m

INDEX

242, 245, 249, 251, 267, 271, 283; Junkers Ju-87 "Stuka" 190, 192, 219, 220; Junkers Ju-88 80, 100, 110, 118, 131, 138, 145, 147, 154, 184, 190, 213, 220, 241, 247, 248, 249, 250, 254, 267, 297; Messerschmitt Bf-109 44, 49–51, 52, 53, 54–55, 58, 59, 60, 61–62, 63, 64, 66, 67, 68, 69, 70, 72, 73, 74, 75, 78, 79, 80, 83, 84, 85, 86–87, 88, 91, 97, 98, 99, 100, 101, 103, 104, 105, 106, 107, 108, 110–111, 112, 118, 120, 121, 122, 127, 128, 129, 130, 131, 132, 134, 135, 137, 138, 139, 140, 141, 142, 143, 144–145, 146, 147, 148–149, 155–156, 161–162, 163, 164, 165, 166, 167, 168, 169, 170, 171, 172–175, 176, 177, 178–179, 180, 181, 182, 183–184, 185, 186, 187, 188, 189, 190, 191, 192, 193, 194, 195–196, 198, 202–203, 204, 205, 206, 208, 209, 210, 211, 212, 213, 216, 218, 220, 232, 234, 241, 247, 248, 250, 253, 255–256, 259–260, 263, 264, 266, 272, 279, 280, 282, 283, 284, 293, 294, 296, 298–299; Bf-109G 11, 32, 33, 34, 123, 259; Bf-109G-2 25; Bf-109G-4 25; Bf-109G-6 25, 231; Messerschmitt Bf-110 35, 60, 69, 72, 74, 83, 87, 99, 121, 131, 145, 146, 170, 173, 181, 184, 220, 248; Bf-110C 25; Bf-110F 25; Messerschmitt Me-210 128, 137, 140, 141, 146, 156, 170, 190, 247; Messerschmitt Me-262 53, 258, 261–263, 265, 275, 279, 283, 284, 285, 286–288, 290, 295, 296, 298; Messerschmitt Me-323 "Gigant" 137, 219, 220, 232, 267; Messerschmitt Me-410 74, 121, 131, 138, 144, 145, 146, 147, 170, 173, 176–177, 186, 193, 220, 237, 241, 275
aircraft, Italy: Fiat G.55 167; Macchi C.202 "Folgore" 68, 78, 79, 84, 213; Macchi C.205 "Veltro" 59, 79, 80, 91, 106, 134, 143, 167, 173; Savoia-Marchetti SM.79 231, 245; Savoia-Marchetti SM.84 241
aircraft, Romania: IAR-80 29, 30, 32, 96, 98, 100, 101, 105, 106, 111, 112, 118, 123, 124–126, 128, 142, 144, 148, 162, 191, 192; IAR-80A 20, 25; IAR-80B 25, 35; IAR-80C 25
aircraft, Soviet Union: Ilyushin Il-2 Shturmovik 44; Petlyakov Pe-8 17; Yakovlev Yak 44; Yak-9 200, 254
aircraft, UK: Avro York 90; Bristol Beaufighter 70, 239, 240–241; de Havilland Mosquito 35, 243, 275, 279, 299; Supermarine Spitfire 44, 77, 89, 90, 101, 107; Spitfire V 57, 77; Vickers Wellington 49
aircraft, USA: Bell P-39 Airacobra 117, 154; Boeing B-17 Flying Fortress 21, 39, 40, 41, 42, 43, 48, 49, 54, 56, 58, 59, 64, 70, 72, 73, 74, 78, 83, 90, 92, 96, 105, 106, 107, 109, 114, 116, 117, 118, 119, 120, 141, 142, 153, 162, 173, 175, 186–187, 188, 194, 195, 205, 206, 214, 219, 220, 233, 234, 243, 246, 251, 253, 254, 256–257, 258, 260, 262, 263, 267, 272, 273, 284, 285, 286, 288, 290, 297; Boeing B-29 Superfortress 116; Consolidated B-24 Liberator 44, 45–46, 49, 52, 54, 61, 63, 69, 72, 73, 82–83, 84, 85, 86, 90, 91, 92, 96, 101, 102, 103, 104, 105, 120, 121, 130, 135, 140, 141, 142, 144, 145, 147, 148, 155, 162, 163, 164–165, 166, 167, 170, 171, 172, 173, 174, 175, 181–182, 183, 185, 188, 193, 196, 202, 203, 205, 206, 207, 208, 211, 212, 219, 220, 230, 232, 238, 243, 244, 246, 251, 252, 257, 258, 259, 261, 267, 268, 276, 279, 281, 282, 284, 286, 291, 293, 295; B-24D 17, 18, 20, 21, 22, 23, 25, 26, 27, 28, 29–32, 33–34, 35, 40–41, 43–45; B-24G 45; B-24H 45; B-24J 45; Model 32 prototype 41–42; as PB4Y-1 44; Consolidated PB2Y Coronado 41, 106; Curtiss P-36 Hawk 86; Curtiss P-40 Warhawk 57, 108, 120, 152; Douglas C-47 Skytrain 106, 166, 234, 238, 244, 245, 286; Douglas C-54 Skymaster 57; Lockheed P-38 Lightning 11, 12, 39, 48, 49, 50, 51, 54–55, 56, 59, 60–63, 64, 70, 73, 74, 76, 80, 122, 123, 124–126, 128, 129–130, 132, 135, 136, 137, 139–140, 146,

161–162, 170, 172, 174, 176, 177, 181,
182, 183, 185, 187, 188, 189, 190, 191,
192, 193, 197, 198–200, 207, 213–215,
216, 217, 234, 235, 237, 273; F-5 256,
261–262, 265, 280, 283–284, 295, 299;
P-38F 80, 113; P-38G 51, 52, 80;
P-38H 51, 52, 70, 80–81; P-38J 51,
52, 80, 81, 83, 84–85, 86, 87, 91, 92,
97, 99, 101–102, 103–104, 105, 106,
107, 112, 201; P-38J-25-LO 82, 213,
236; P-38L 81, 236, 286; Martin
B-26 Marauder 39, 52, 266; North
American B-25 Mitchell 50, 63, 298;
North American P-51 Mustang 11, 12,
88, 91, 97, 99, 100, 101, 104, 110, 112,
113, 114, 117, 119, 121, 131, 134–135,
138, 140, 141, 142, 144, 146–148, 149,
165, 167–168, 171, 172, 174, 176, 179,
181, 184–185, 186, 187, 188, 189, 190,
192, 193, 194, 195, 196, 197, 201, 203,
204, 205, 208, 209, 212, 218, 219, 220,
232, 233, 235, 236, 237, 238, 239, 240,
241–242, 243, 244–245, 246, 247, 248,
249–250, 251, 252–253–254, 255, 256,
258, 259, 260, 261, 262, 263, 264, 265,
268, 270, 271, 272, 273, 274, 275, 276,
277, 279, 280, 281, 283, 285, 286–288,
289, 290–291, 292, 293, 294, 295–298,
299, 300; P-51B 12, 13, 76, 77, 89–90,
108–109, 133, 154, 160, 161–164,
247, 251–252, 261, 278; P-51C 92,
132–133, 160, 166, 247, 257, 259, 262;
P-51D 12–13, 120, 141, 143, 170,
247, 252, 259, 265, 266; P-51D-5 183;
Republic P-47 Thunderbolt 39, 56–58,
65–66, 67–68, 69, 76, 77, 79, 84, 87, 92,
97, 102, 103, 107, 108, 154, 155–158,
159; P-47D 159
airfields 17, 19, 24, 26, 57, 58, 74, 80,
112, 115, 117, 119, 123, 131, 144, 161,
187, 189, 191, 197, 214, 219, 229, 232,
236, 239, 241, 243, 244–245, 248, 249,
250, 251, 254, 267, 275, 279, 284, 290;
Avignon, France 138–139; Borgo
Poreta, Corsica 77; Capodichino,
Italy 154; Debrecen, Hungary 237;
Eleusis, Greece 52, 54, 242, 245;
Foggia, Italy 38, 47, 57, 58, 59,
61, 77, 79; Gioia del Colle 52–53;
Ramitelli 154, 241; San Severo 88,
271; Vincenzo 60, 83, 197;
Hajduboszormeny, Hungary 205;
Kecskemet, Hungary 137–138;
La Jasse, France 138; Madna, Italy 105,
249; Megara, Greece 242, 246; Mielec,
Poland 192; Montecorvino, Italy 154;
Münchendorf, Austria 161, 183;
Orange Plan de Dieu, Corsica 138;
Otopeni, Romania 229, 232; Piryatin,
Ukraine 114, 115, 117–118, 119,
189; Popesti-Leordeni, Romania 123,
124, 128, 220, 231, 232, 233;
Udine, Italy 80, 91, 297; Veszprém,
Hungary 139–140; Villaorba,
Italy 66–67; Zwölfaxing, Austria 174,
193–194
Alexander, Lt "Dixie" 109, 110, 111
Allen, Second Lt Calvin 130, 131, 175
Allen, Second Lt John 126, 127
Allied strategy 17, 21, 40, 93–96, 207,
231, 298 *see also* US strategy
altitudes 22, 43–44, 67, 91, 123 *see also*
low-level flying
Ambrose, First Lt David 266, 271
ammunition feeds 89, 163
Andersen, First Lt Leslie "Andy" 52, 53
Anderson, First Lt Sheldon K. 253
Anderson, Gen Frederick 95, 115–116
Andrews, Second Lt Dick 197–201
ANR (Aeronautica Nazionale
Repubblicana) 59, 80, 167, 173, 259,
297, 298; 1° Gruppo Caccia (Fighter
Group) 85
antiaircraft flak 48, 63, 83, 86, 88, 97,
102, 104, 112, 126, 128, 129, 130, 133,
137, 138, 156, 164, 165, 166, 171, 172,
185, 186, 197, 201, 207, 211, 215, 216,
218, 219, 220, 230, 232, 234, 237, 241,
242, 243, 245, 246, 249, 252, 253, 258,
259, 260, 268, 274, 275, 276, 277, 278,
280–281, 282, 291, 294, 299
Antonescu, Ion 16, 221, 225, 226–227, 229
Antonescu, Mihai 226
Anzio landings 82, 89, 154
Archer, Lt Lee 156, 186, 248
Arndt, Lt Dave 190

INDEX

Arnold, Gen Henry H. "Hap"   12, 18, 22, 23, 37, 40, 41, 70–71, 95, 150, 152–153
Arnold, Oberfeldwebel Heinz   285
Aron, Second Lt William   280, 282, 296, 297, 299
AVG (American Volunteer Group) ("Flying Tigers")   213

bail outs   10, 29–30, 60, 62, 63, 64, 73, 79, 84–85, 90, 104, 108–109, 111, 112, 121, 130, 135, 140, 147, 148, 155, 159, 163, 166, 171, 172, 175, 178–179, 186, 188, 195, 203, 204, 206, 237, 243, 245, 249, 258–259, 260, 261, 268, 272, 283, 287, 288, 289, 293, 294, 299
Bailey, Lt Charles   186
Baker, Lt Col Addison   28, 29–30
Baldwin, First Lt W.F.   298–299
Barkey, First Lt Robert   66, 79, 107, 118
Barnes, FO Bland M., Jr.   280
Barnes, Lt Samuel   139
barrage balloons   25, 31
Baseler, Lt Col Bob   57, 66, 68, 84, 86
Bass, Lt Robert S.   108, 118, 173, 210
Bell, First Lt Rual   252, 293
belly landings   63, 84, 88, 129, 245
Belton, Capt Joe   174, 191
Benne, First Lt Louis   135, 136–137
Bevan, Second Lt T.M.   282, 284
Beverly, Lt Col Ernest H.   184, 203, 237, 242
Biggs, First Lt Bob   190, 191, 193, 213
Bodine, First Lt Ed   193, 213
Boedeker, Lt Col Charles   246
Bohl, First Lt Frederick L.   98, 144
bomb loads   24, 33, 41, 236
bombing missions   53, 55–56, 61–62, 64, 76, 78–79, 85, 91, 94, 114, 118, 120–121, 140–141, 154–155, 156–157, 159, 163, 165, 166, 173, 174–175, 178, 185, 205, 207, 213–214, 215, 218, 219, 220–221, 223, 238, 239, 243, 244, 246–247, 252, 256, 258, 259, 263, 267, 268, 272, 273, 275–276, 277, 279, 280, 281, 282, 284, 285–286, 291, 293, 295–296; aircraft factories, Brunswick–Leipzig region   72; aircraft factory, Vienna   109; airfields, Munich   165, 284; airfields, Rome   62, 64;

Almasfuzito oil refinery, Budapest   170–171; Benedictine Abbey, Monte Cassino   72; "Big Week" (February 20–25, 1944)   72–75, 76; Blechhammer, Germany   148–149, 173, 176, 203, 204, 208, 219–220, 242, 251, 252, 253–254, 260–261, 263, 264, 266, 267; Brux oil refineries, Czechoslovakia   165, 189, 252, 253–254, 258, 260, 262, 266; Bucharest, Romania   91, 100, 147–148, 196; Budapest, Hungary   146–147, 156, 159, 167, 181, 243; Constanța, Romania   130–131; Eleusis airfield, Greece   52, 54; Friedrichshafen, Germany   165, 187, 188, 202; Lobau oil blending plant, Vienna   139–140, 241, 246–247; Markersdorf airfield, Austria   209–211; marshaling yards, Avignon   144, 164; marshaling yards, Debrecen   114, 117, 145, 243; marshaling yards, Turnu Severin   90, 102; Messerschmitt factory, Wiener Neustadt   47–49, 60, 99–100, 103, 110; Münchendorf airfield, Austria   161–162, 183; Odertal refineries, Germany   263, 264, 267; Pardubice, Czechoslovakia   211–212, 218–219, 267, 268; Ploești oilfields, Romania   13–14, 19–20, 21, 23, 24–25, 27–37, 96, 97, 100, 101–102, 105–107, 111, 112, 113, 122, 128–129, 130, 141, 142–143, 162, 163, 165, 167, 168, 196, 202, 205, 213, 235; Sofia, Bulgaria   53, 59, 60–61, 63, 85; Steyr, Austria   86–88; Szony oil refinery, Budapest   135–136; Udine, Italy   54, 56, 69, 80, 91, 261, 297; Verona, Italy   55, 58, 78, 82–83, 84; Wöllersdorf airfield, Austria   107, 114; Zwölfaxing airfield, Austria   193–194
Bond, Second Lt Jack H.   173, 195, 210
Boris III, Tsar (Bulgaria)   34
Botvidson, First Lt Charles   175, 179
bouncing   56, 107, 109, 140, 146, 174, 204, 205, 209, 212, 218, 255, 279
Brereton, Gen Lewis H.   23, 24, 36
Brezas, Lt Michael   174, 181, 188
British Eighth Army   19, 298

Brooks, First Lt James L. 105, 141, 187, 256
Brown, First Lt Robert H. 148, 195, 203, 205, 212
Brown, First Lt Roscoe 288, 293
Brown, FO Robert H. 148
Brown, Lt Sam 195
Brown, Maj George S. 30
Brown, Maj Samuel J. 120, 137, 138, 144, 145
Bullock, First Frederick "Ted" 112, 121, 142–143, 145
Burnett III, First Lt Robert L. 121, 132
Burns, First Lt Robert 281, 282
Butler, Lt Barry 137, 140
Byrnes, Capt Thomas W. 97, 141, 145

Cairo Conference 21, 71
Campbell, Lt Warren "Beans" 132, 199
Campbell, Maj William 258, 292
canopy 50, 62, 63, 70, 90, 108–109, 118, 121, 125, 136, 143, 146, 171–172, 175, 178, 180, 195, 198, 199, 265, 287, 291
Cantacuzino, Capitan Aviator Constantin "Bâzu" 231–232, 233
Caradja, Princess Catherine 234
Cardimona, Lt Joe 102
Carey, Lt Carl 294
Carey, Second Lt Albert J. 120
Carnie, First Lt Jim 121
Carnie, Lt Bob 172, 175
Carol II, King (Romania) 16, 221, 227
Carroll, First Lt Walt 173, 176, 193
Casablanca Conference 71, 119
CBO (Combined Bomber Offensive) missions 58, 76 *see also* bombing missions
Chatfield, First Lt Gene H. 52, 74, 83, 137, 139
Chick, Maj Lewis W. "Bill" 57, 58, 64, 66, 69, 80, 108
Church, Second Lt William 99, 185
Churchill, Winston 17, 21, 23, 43, 90, 95, 222, 255
Clark, Lt W.N. 296
Clarke, Lt John 141, 180
close air support 153, 214
Cobb, First Lt Bruce C. 173, 184, 237
Collins, Capt "Spot" 58, 64, 68, 69

Columbia Aquila refinery, Ploeşti 25, 28, 30, 31–32, 35
Compton, Col Keith 26, 27, 28, 30, 36
Conant, Lt John P. 195, 206
Congressional committee on the 99th Fighter Squadron 151, 152
Consolidated Aircraft Corporation 41, 44–45, 46
cooling systems and radiators 80–81, 237
Cooper, Second Lt Cecil E., Jr. 295
Cowan, Lt William 172, 175–176
Cox, First Lt Hannibal 247, 295
crash-landings 29, 42, 111, 128, 139, 177, 188, 193, 217, 247, 258, 273, 275, 277
Creditul Minier refinery, Ploeşti 35
crew 43, 46
Curtis, Capt Bob 109, 110, 130, 142, 143, 147–148, 175, 178, 180, 181, 182–183, 211

Dachau concentration camp 283
Davis, First Lt Alfonso 159, 220
Davis, First Lt Barrie 118–119, 171, 194, 204, 205–206
Davis, Lt Col Benjamin O. 151–152, 153–154, 158, 160, 161, 163, 245, 253, 256, 266, 269, 286, 289, 292, 297, 300
Davis, Second Lt Barrie 148
Davis, Second Lt John 292
Day, First Lt W.K. 296
Deakins, Lt Richard S. 119
Dean, FO Cecil 67, 68
Dean, Second Lt Cecil 103
deaths 20, 30, 32, 35, 60, 69, 97, 103, 125, 127, 130, 136–137, 138, 139, 143, 149, 157, 161, 174, 175, 176, 186, 188, 193, 216, 217, 218, 241, 242, 243, 251, 257, 258–259, 263, 268, 281, 289, 293, 294, 299; and civilian deaths 94, 95
designs 41–42, 45
Dickson, Capt Lawrence 265
Die Raupe (flak train) 31
Dieppe Raid 294
Dillard, Capt William J. 105, 187, 285
dive-bombing 122, 129, 181–182, 213–214, 216, 217
dive brakes 213
dogfights 85, 86–87, 98, 103, 104, 106, 118, 121, 124–125, 131, 139, 141, 142,

INDEX

143, 145, 146, 155–156, 166, 167, 170, 173, 177, 178, 184, 191, 194, 209, 210, 211, 218–219, 248, 250, 252–253, 259–260, 264–265, 266, 279–280, 281–282, 286–289, 291–293, 294, 297, 299
Doolittle, Lt Gen James H. "Jimmy" 39, 40, 57, 71, 81; *I Could Never Be So Lucky Again* (memoir) 49
Doolittle Raid 115
Dorris, Maj Harry 187
dorsal fin extension 143, 183
Dorsch, Capt Freddie 196
Douglas Aircraft Company 45
Drago, Capitano Ugo 259
Dreyer, Unteroffizier Willi 123
Dumitrescu, General Petre 228
Dunkin, Capt Richard 195, 204, 205, 211–212
Dunne, Lt Charles 158, 162, 265

Eaker, Gen Ira 18, 40, 234
Eberty, Lt Charles 137
Eddins, First Lt James 48, 277
Edge, Lt Jack 196
Edwards, Lt George B. 196
Edwards, Lt John 294
Ehrler, Maj Heinrich 286
Eisenhower, Gen Dwight 40, 76, 93, 94, 95, 96
Ellington, Lt Spurgeon 157
Elliott, Lt William 64–65, 66
Ellis, Lt Pelton 176, 193
Elsberry, Lt Joseph 158, 162–163, 165
Emerson, First Lt Dave 268–269
Emmert, First Lt Benjamin H. 119, 196, 237
Emmons, First Lt Eugene H. 103, 108, 134
Empey, First Lt James 110, 130, 131, 148, 278
engines 24, 43, 76, 77, 80–81, 129, 133, 139, 167, 186, 219, 231, 232, 237, 238, 243, 262, 288
Ent, Brig Gen Uzal Girard 23, 28, 36
Erchen, Unteroffizier Herman 130
Erichson, Lt Ralph 290
Erickson, Lt Lauren 216

Esters, First Lt Maurice V. 159
Evans, Second Lt Richard N. 110, 175, 211

Fairhurst, Lt Jim 139
Farnham, Capt S.W. 195, 210
Faulkner, Capt William J. 257
Feather, Second Lt Carroll 214
Fehsenfeld, First Lt J.E. 257
Felton, FO John A. 98
FFI (French Forces of the Interior) 207
Fiedler, First Lt Art 119, 132–134, 144, 148, 179–180, 194, 195, 242, 249, 272
fighter escort missions 48, 50, 51, 52, 54, 56, 57, 58, 59, 60, 61–62, 63–64, 69, 70, 76, 77, 78, 82–83, 85, 88, 90, 91, 96, 101, 102–103, 105, 107, 110, 111, 113, 114, 118, 119–120, 130–134, 135, 137, 140, 141, 146, 147, 148–149, 154–155, 156–157, 159, 161, 163–164, 165, 166–168, 169, 173, 174, 175, 178, 181, 185, 189, 193–194, 196, 202–204, 207, 208–209, 219, 220–221, 238–239, 241–242, 244, 246, 252, 255, 256–257, 259, 260, 261, 262, 264, 266, 267, 272, 277, 280, 281, 282, 286, 290, 295, 297, 299
fighter sweeps 64–65, 66–68, 77, 103, 143, 173, 174, 176, 179, 184, 188, 192, 271–272, 292, 293, 294, 296, 298
First Iași–Chișinău offensive 223
Fleet, Reuben 41
flying conditions 45–46, 51
FNB (Focșani–Nămoloasa–Brăila) Line 224, 225, 226
Ford, Maj "Hank" 170, 190, 193, 213
Ford Motor Company 45
foreign ownership of the Romanian oil industry 16–17
Forrest, Lt John M. 64, 103
Franklin, Lt Dwaine 172, 184
Free French Air Force 77
Freissner, Gen Johannes 224, 225, 228
French railroad infrastructure 94
Friend, Second Lt Robert 162, 268
"friendly fire" 90, 106, 180
fuel consumption 24, 34, 44, 131, 144
fuel supplies 13, 161, 207, 247, 297
Fuller, Maj Edwin W. 110, 112, 179
Funderberg, Lt Frederick D. 155–156, 268

Gangel, Capt Dick   173, 176, 190, 193, 213
Gardner, Maj Warner "Warnie"   170, 176, 193, 213
George VI, King (Britain)   36
Georgescu, Valeriu "Rică"   230–231, 233, 234
German aircraft factories   47–49, 60, 72, 73, 74–75, 99–100, 103, 110
German Heer   72, 222, 232; Afrika Korps   19; Armies: Eighth Army   222, 223; Fourteenth Army   298; Sixth Army   222, 223, 225, 226, 227; Tenth Army   298; Army Group South Ukraine   223, 224, 227; Divisions: 76th Infantry   225; Brandenburg   229
German oil requirements   15, 16–17, 21, 94, 137
German railroad infrastructure   94
German–Romanian relations   16, 221, 224, 228–229
German strategy   16, 25, 114, 115, 137, 208, 212, 223, 224, 225, 229, 230, 236, 263, 264
German synthetic oil industry   15, 93, 94, 95, 137, 139, 148–149, 165, 202, 219, 235, 244
Gerstenberg, Gen Alfred   25, 31, 228, 229, 230, 232
Gibson, First Lt George E., Jr.   263, 275
Gilbert, Second Lt Reginald C.   98, 100
Giuseppe Missori (Italian destroyer)   158
Gleed, Capt Ed   167, 260, 268
Gneismer, Leutnant Gunther   295
Goebel, Capt Robert J.   142, 147
Goehausen, First Lt Walter J.   138, 147, 187, 233
Gray, First Lt George   247, 265
Green, First Lt William   155, 166, 248, 251
Green, Maj Herschel "Herky"   58, 59, 64, 66–68, 69, 77–79, 80, 88, 102, 103, 108–109, 114, 117, 118, 119, 134, 135, 138, 143, 145, 146, 159–160, 173, 174, 179, 180, 209, 213
Greene, First Lt Claude   285
Greene, Lt Col Paul   213
Greenley, Lt Don   138

Greve, First Lt Henry "Hank"   195
Greve, Second Lt Clarence   58
Grey, First Lt Frank   120, 147, 175–176, 178, 208–209
Griffith, Lt Bob   170, 176, 190, 191, 193
Grose, First Lt Richard L.   99, 141, 190
ground crew   42, 130, 200
ground support missions   295
Groves, Lt Weldon   166
Gubler, Second Lt Edmund   175
Guderian, Field Marshal Heinz   225
gun cameras   182
Gunn, Lt Col James A. III   230–232
Gustav Line   72, 82

Haller, Lt Bob   176, 191
Halverson, Col Harry A.   18, 20, 21
Hancock, Second Lt Wesley   104
Hanes, First Lt William   110, 184, 209
Harder, First Lt Richard   286, 288
Harder, Maj Jürgen   123
Harman, Lt Roy   137, 191, 192, 213
Harmeyer, First Lt Raymond F.   98, 101, 104
Harriman, W. Averell   115
Harris, Second Lt Maceo   164–165
Hartley, Capt Raymond E., Jr.   64–65, 138
Hartmann, Major Erich   172
Hatch, Second Lt Herbert "Stub," Jr.   124–128
heating systems   51, 61
Hicks, First Lt Charles   51, 53
Hill, Gladwin   151
Hinton, First Lt W.R.   195, 206, 261
Hitler, Adolf   15, 17, 223, 224, 225, 227, 228
Hively, Maj Deacon   146, 170, 172
Hoenshell, First Lt Carl   126, 127, 128
Hoffman, First Lt Cullen J.   118, 134
Hoffman, First Lt James   110, 122, 130, 147, 180, 209
Hogg, Capt Roy   118
Holloway, Lt James   137, 139, 140, 146, 170
Holsclaw, Capt Jack   186, 280
Houghton, Second Lt Jack   173, 195, 251
House, Brig Gen Edwin   151

INDEX

"House Memorandum" 151, 153
Hungarian Army 136
Hutchins, First Lt Freddie 158, 166, 220, 246

I.G. Farben 15
IJA (Imperial Japanese Army) 18
insignia and markings 129, 154, 231, 232, 236, 256
intelligence 66, 72, 137, 239
interdictions 247
Isaacson, Maj Clayton M. "Ike" 63, 193, 213
Italian Co-Belligerent Air Force: 51° Stormo 108

Jackson, Capt Ray E. "Red" 155, 261
Jared, Maj Garth "Jug" 97
Jay, FO Edward 144, 170
"Jim Crow" 151
Jodl, Gen Alfred 17
Johnson, Col Leon W. 30, 31, 32
Johnson, Lt Art 141, 182, 187
Johnson, Lt James H. 110, 121–122
Joley, Lt Jack 137, 140, 174, 176, 213
Jones, Second Lt Clyde 135, 136, 137

K-14 lead-computing sight 266, 271, 279
Kahl, Second Lt Vernon 252, 253
Kane, Col John R. 23–24, 26, 27, 30, 31, 32
Karr, Capt Bob 121, 176, 264
Kellam, First Lt Bruce 111, 121, 122
Kessler, Gen Alfred 115
Kidder, First Lt Art 133, 173
kill claims and credits 35–36, 50, 52, 53, 58, 60–61, 62, 63, 64, 68, 78, 80, 83, 84, 86, 88, 90, 91, 92, 97, 98–99, 100, 101, 102, 103, 104, 105, 107, 109, 110, 118, 119, 128, 130, 131, 137–138, 140, 141, 142, 143, 145, 147, 148, 149, 160, 167, 170, 172, 174, 175, 176, 177, 178, 182, 184, 185, 186, 187, 189, 190, 192, 195, 196, 204–205, 206, 212, 213, 219–220, 237, 245, 247, 248, 249, 250, 251, 253, 254–255, 263–264, 267, 272, 276, 279, 280, 282–283, 284–285, 286, 288, 291, 293–294, 296–297, 298–299

Killinger, Baron von 228
Kriegsmarine 158–159
Kuderna, General Julius 232–233

Lampe, Lt Richard 109, 141, 142, 172
landing gear 42, 85, 89, 112, 188, 291
 see also belly landings
Lane, First Lt Earl R. "Squirrel" 287, 293
Lanham, First Lt Jimmy 298, 299
Lawler, Second Lt Barry 110, 111, 120–121, 131, 141, 172, 187
Lawrence, Maj Erwin 239, 245
Leeman, Lt Roland "Tuffy" 102, 112–113, 139, 140
LeMay, Gen Curtis 73
Lemon, First Lt Enoch 62, 87, 91, 104
Lette, Lt Lee 173, 176, 190, 191, 213
Lewis, Second Lt Joseph A. 158, 246
Litchfield, Maj John 80, 83, 84–85
Litton, Lt Col William 51, 53, 122, 182, 190, 197, 201
living conditions 52–53, 61, 88, 244, 258, 281
Ljubljana Gap 222
Lockheed Corporation 82, 92
long-range bombing missions 17, 18–20, 21–22
Loving, Capt George G., Jr. 97, 145, 192
low-level flying 22, 23–24, 33, 122–123, 128, 138, 157, 207–208, 238, 260, 274, 275, 278–279, 281
Lowry, First Lt Wayne 118, 134–135, 144, 148, 174, 193–195, 204, 212, 243
Luftwaffe 11, 13, 36, 71, 72, 91, 93, 94, 115, 116, 156, 202, 208, 212, 216, 218, 220, 229, 231, 235, 238, 241, 242–243, 252, 255, 259, 263, 264, 267, 271, 272, 278, 280, 297; Flak-Division 5 25; Flak-Division 15 25; Jagdfliegerführer Rumänien 27; JG (*Jagdgeschwader*): JG 4 25, 29; JG 7 "Nowotny" 284–289, 290; I./JG 7 285, 286; II./JG 7 285; III./JG 7 284–285; JG 27 34, 50, 61, 173, 174; IV./JG 27 51; JG 52 172; II./JG 52 173; JG 53: I./JG 53 123, 128; JG 77: III./JG 77 123, 128; NJG (*Nachtjagdgeschwader*): NJG 6 25; II./

NJG 6   25; SG (*Schlachtgeschwader*):
   SG 2: II./SG 2   191; *Staffeln*: 5./
   JG 301   130; 6./JG 51   54; ZG
   (*Zerstörergeschwader*): ZG 1   173;
   ZG 76: I./ZG 76   173
Luttrell, Capt Don   135, 136–137, 215

maintenance and repairs   19, 35, 47, 52,
   58, 71, 161
malaria and malarial swamps   47, 77–78,
   88, 279
Malcolm, Col Marion   239, 240, 253
Maniu, Iuliu   221
Maquis   139
Marshall, Second Lt Andrew D.   245, 268
Martin, First Lt Robert   262, 280–281
Mason, Lt Col Ben   190, 197, 213
Mass, Lt Paul   139–140, 146, 190,
   191, 213
materiel losses   29, 30, 32, 34–35, 49, 51,
   53, 69, 72, 73–74, 79, 88, 92, 104, 108,
   113, 116, 119, 124, 128, 130, 145, 158,
   163, 165, 186, 197, 207–208, 211, 212,
   217, 236–237, 246, 276, 285
Mattison, Capt William   241
McCampbell, Lt Bob   142, 143
McCorkle, Col Charles M.   86, 90, 99, 144
McDaniel, Capt Armour   165, 286, 289
McDaniel, First Lt Gordon H.   271–272,
   281–282
McDonald, Maj Norman   256, 296, 297
McLaughlin, Capt Murray D.   101, 131, 147
McLoughlin, Second Lt John A.   34, 137
mechanical issues   52, 81–82, 89, 108,
   122, 139, 146, 159, 163, 166, 167,
   183, 206, 252
Meyers, Capt John J.   291, 292
MI6   21
Miclescu, Capitan Comandor Aviator
   Gheorghe   123
mid-air collisions   34, 62, 84, 91, 124, 181,
   184, 185, 188, 193, 255, 268
Mihai I, King (Romania)   221, 222,
   224–225, 226, 227, 228
Mihalache, Ion   226
military honors and medals   21, 30, 32, 34,
   35, 69, 70, 83, 107, 110, 122, 128, 153,
   172, 178, 201, 250, 284, 290, 291

military strengths and complements   25,
   39, 51, 56, 60, 85, 92, 149, 152
"milk runs"   58, 64, 85, 135, 144, 174,
   175, 185, 203, 261, 263, 271, 281, 299
misidentification of Romanian IAR-80
   aircraft   98, 100, 101, 106, 111, 124,
   142, 144
missing in action   35, 59, 60, 66, 70,
   179, 296
mission reports   53, 185, 245, 246,
   261–262, 275, 276, 295
modifications   43, 45, 81–82, 183, 233
Mohawk, First Lt Hiawatha   107, 138
Molland, Capt Leland P.   98, 196
Molotov, Vyacheslav   115
Momyer, Lt Col William   150–151,
   152, 300
Moorehead, Maj James   216, 217
morale   244, 257–258, 270
Morey, Second Lt Carl   279, 280
Morrison, Second Lt Joe   125,
   126–127, 128
Moscow Conference   115
Mount Vesuvius eruption   79
Mussolini, Benito   229
Myers, Lt S.E.   173, 185

Nachwuchs (late recruits)   11
National Peasant Party (Romania)   221, 226
navigation errors   28–29, 33, 98
Newell, Lt Robert   256, 279–280
night missions   20
North African Theater   19, 23, 39,
   54, 101
North American Aviation   45, 92
nose turrets   45
Novotny, First Lt George   67, 68, 108

Ohr, Capt Fred   112, 141, 180–181, 250,
   252, 255
oil coolers   82
OKH (Oberkommando des Heeres)   222,
   223, 224
OKW (Oberkommando der
   Wehrmacht)   224, 228
Operations: *Argument* (February 1944)
   71–75; *Bagration* (June–August
   1944)   202, 224; *Bingo* (December

INDEX

1944) 267, 298; *Bodenplatte* (January 1945) 263; *Clarion* (February 1945) 277–278; *Dragoon (Anvil)* (Aug–Sept 1944) 139, 205, 207; *Frantic* (June–Sept 1944) 114–115, 116, 148; *Frantic II* 191; *Frantic III* 189, 193; *Frantic IV* 197; *Husky* (July–Aug 1943) 23; *Overlord* (June 1944) 40, 120, 149, 223; *Pointblank* (June 1943–April 1944) 71, 93, 94; *Strangle* (March–May 1944) 82–83; *Tidal Wave* (August 1943) 23–25, 26–35, 36–37; *Torch* (November 1942) 113; *Varsity* (March 1945) 286
OSS (Office of Strategic Services) 207, 233
oxygen deprivation 46, 56, 85, 161, 232, 257, 281

Palmer, First Lt Walter 165, 186
Parker, Capt Harry A. 195–196, 203, 210, 212, 282, 296
Paulk, First Lt Edsel 64, 67, 68, 108
Peery, Maj John E. (Jack) 195, 210
Peirson, Lt Gwynne 157, 158
penetration support 103, 107, 109, 120, 130, 267
performance and speed 42–43, 44, 89–90, 143, 156
Phillips, Maj Herb 137, 190, 213
pilot fatigue 183
pilot replacement 13, 52, 120, 263, 271, 278
Pinson, First Lt Charlie 86–87, 176–177, 190
Pitts, Second Lt Hiram 53, 54
Ploești oil refineries, Romania 12, 17, 75, 93, 94, 96–97, 192, 202, 221 *see also* bombing missions
Polish Home Army 232
Pomerantz, Lt Bill 196, 210
Portal, Air Marshal Sir Charles 95, 96
POWs 29, 48, 55, 116, 137, 159, 166, 186, 188, 201, 206, 219, 220, 230, 231, 233–234, 237, 238, 245, 246, 249, 252, 259, 260, 261, 283, 289, 293
Pretzer, First Lt Willard 141, 142, 182, 238
production 44–45, 49, 51, 56–57, 75, 77, 80–81, 92, 213, 235, 283

Projekt Weingut (Wine Estate) 283
Pruitt, Capt Wendell 155, 156, 158, 220, 248
PSP (pierced-steel) planking taxiways 61, 257, 281
Purnell, Lt Louis 256, 259

Quebec Conference 222

RAAF (Royal Australian Air Force) 44
racial prejudice 12, 150, 152, 300
radar 27, 32, 122, 123, 208; H2X 53, 72, 275
radiator air scoop 238
RAF (Royal Air Force) 18, 20, 43, 44, 49, 76; 29 Squadron 240–241; 272 Squadron 240; Bomber Command 71, 94, 95, 235; Second Tactical Air Force 94, 96
railroad infrastructure attacks 94, 237, 239, 249, 251, 267 *see also* bombing missions
ranges 43, 76, 81, 89
Rayford, Capt Lee 161, 186, 256, 260–261
RCAF (Royal Canadian Air Force) 44, 57
rear limit and center of gravity 108–109
reconnaissance 25, 35, 137, 214, 237–238, 239, 241, 254, 258, 261, 262, 264, 265, 266, 270, 275, 276, 278, 280, 282, 283–284, 290
Red Air Force 17, 116, 119
Red Army 11, 116, 192, 205, 223, 225, 228, 229–230, 234, 236, 274, 281, 289, 291; 1st Ukrainian Front 222, 230; 2nd Ukrainian Front 222, 223, 224, 230; 3rd Ukrainian Front 222, 223, 224, 225; 46th Army 226
Reid, First Lt Robert 271, 272
replacement matèriel/aircraft 60, 70, 81, 89, 92
Rex (Italian ocean liner) 239–241
Rhodes, Second Lt George 163, 245
Riddle, Lt Dennis 141, 142, 172
Roberts, Maj George "Spanky" 152, 246, 256
Robinson, Maj Franklin 169, 175, 181
Rollag, First Lt Stan 110–111, 112, 181

Romanian Army 221, 222, 225, 228, 232–233; Armies: Fourth Army 225–226, 228; Third Army 222, 223, 225, 226, 228, 230; Capital Military Command 229, 232; Divisions: 3rd Infantry 225; 7th Infantry 225; Regiments: 2nd Calarasi 229; 4th Vânători 231; Regimentul 7 Artilerie Antiaerian 25
Romanian oil reserves 12, 13, 15–16, 38
Romanian strategy and surrender 221–222, 223, 224–230
Romine, Capt Roger 186, 220, 248, 259
Rommel, Field Marshal Erwin 19
Roosevelt, President F.D.R. 23, 36, 57, 115, 153
Royal Bulgarian Air Force 11, 27, 34, 51, 60
royal coup in Romania 226–228, 229
Royal Hungarian Air Force 11, 137, 189; 101 "Puma" Group 140, 173, 174; 102. Csatarepülő Osztály 281, 292
Royal Romanian Air Force 11, 20, 32–33, 35, 91, 124, 128, 149, 182–183, 208, 230; Grupul 6 Vânătoare 29, 123; Grupul 7 Vânătoare 123, 128; Grupul 9 Vânătoare 193, 231
Rube Goldberg stoves 61

SAAF (South African Air Force) 35; 16 Squadron 240–241
Sănătescu, General Constantin 227, 228, 231
Sangermano, First Lt Phillip 148, 196, 210
Schanning, First Lt William H. 144, 145
Schill, First Lt John 138, 181
Schilling, Col David 86
Schmerbeck, Lt David J. 185, 237
Schneider, First Lt Jack 109, 120, 141, 142
Schultz, Oberleutnant Otto 54
Schumacher, First Lt John 112, 179
Schweinfurt mission ("Black Thursday") 51
Sebring, Second Lt Ralph 60, 62
Second Battle of Cassino 71–72
Second Iași–Chișinău offensive 224
Seevers, Lt L.F. 296
Selenger, First Lt Walter K. 276, 282, 296
Self, Lt Horace, Jr. 184
Semple, Lt Warren 139

SHAEF (Supreme Headquarters Allied Expeditionary Force) 93, 95, 96
Sheehan, First Lt Joseph B. 146–147
Sherrard, First Lt Earl S. 157, 161–162
Shipley, FO Eugene 192
Shipman, First Lt Ernest 101, 170
Shivers, Maj Julius D. 294
Short, Second Lt Swanson 137
Shropshire, Lt John W. 145
Simmons, First Lt John M. 148, 202–203, 204–205, 210, 242
Simmons, Lt Alphonso 280–281
Simpson, First Lt Harold 60
Skinner, Lt Darrel 83
Skinner, Second Lt Claude 69
Skogstad, First Lt Norman E. 291
Skorzeny, Otto 229
Sluder, Lt Col Chester L. 84, 86, 88, 116–117, 118, 242
Smart, Col Jacob E. 22
Smith, Capt George 284
Smith, Capt Jack R. 263
Smith, Capt Kenneth 290
Smith, Lt Arnold 175
Smith, Lt Bradley 110
Smith, Lt Fielder 64
Smith, Lt Luther "Quibbling" 164, 248, 251–252
Smith, Lt Philip 139
Smith, Lt Robert "Dissipatin" 164
Smith, Lt Tom "Dub" 62–63
Smith, Second Lt James 120
smoke generators 122, 129
SOE (Special Operations Executive) 221, 230–231, 246, 252
Sognier, Capt John 176, 190
Southern, Lt Harry E. 196
southern Democrats in the U.S. Congress 151
Soviet–Japanese Non-Aggression Pact 115
Soviet strategy 115, 116, 119, 202, 222, 223–224
Soviet Union 114–115
Spaatz, Gen Carl A. "Tooey" 18, 22, 37, 40, 70–71, 93, 94–95, 96, 97, 151, 154
Spears, First Lt Leon "Woodie" 289
Spencer, Maj Charles 53, 69
Spitler, Lt Robert 138

INDEX

St John, Lt Walter 216
Stacy, Lt Leland J. 173
Stacy, Second Lt J.J. 148
Stahel, General Reiner 232
Stalin, Josef 115, 116, 223, 224
Starks, First Lt Arnett 289
Steaua Română refinery, Ploești 33–34, 35
Steere, Second Lt Lowell 237
Șteflea, Gen Ilie 228
Steinmann, Hauptmann Wilhelm 29
Sternfels, First Lt Robert 26, 31
Stewart, Capt Harry 293
Stiger, Second Lt Roosevelt 247
Stinchcombe, First Lt Don J. 209
Stitt, Capt Jim 81–82
Stoffel, Lt Col Fred C. 294
Stout, Lt Cody 185, 188
strafing missions 80, 91, 94, 97, 105, 112–113, 129, 137–139, 154, 157, 158, 189, 192, 197, 214–215, 217, 219, 236, 237–238, 241, 242, 245, 249–250, 251, 252–253, 254, 259, 260, 267, 268, 274–275, 276, 277–278, 279, 280, 281, 282–283, 292, 293, 296, 297–298
Strait, Lt G.N. 242
Strauss, Lt Ernest T. 195, 203
Straut, Lt Frederick 184
Strother, Brig Gen Dean C. "Doc" 83–84, 117, 189–190, 241
sub-contractor delays 80, 92
Suehle, Lt Ferdinand E. 119
supply drops 207
Surratt, First Lt Maurice D. 141
Sutherland, Lt J.S. 282
Sweeney, First Lt George 148

tanks 233, 289
target cover 103, 120, 131, 132, 142, 170, 189, 207, 290
target navigation 22
targets of opportunity 28, 30, 48, 73, 182, 185, 188, 201, 238, 251, 268, 277, 292, 294, 296
Tarrant, Lt Col Yancy E. 144
Tatman, Lt Paul P. 134, 195, 203
Tatum, Second Lt Cleveland 60
Taylor, Lt Col Oliver 54–55, 60, 98, 103–104

Taylor, Lt Robert 216
Taylor, Second Lt W.H. 277
Tedder, Air Marshal Sir Arthur 93, 96–97, 101
Tehran Conference 57, 115, 224
Terry, First Lt Don 237
Terry, FO Wes T. 196, 210
tests and trials 41, 42–43
Thacker, Capt Tom 206–207, 243–244, 268, 295
Thiessen, Capt Ralph 86
Thomas, Capt Edwin M. 286–287
Thomas, First Lt William 218–219
Thomas, Second Lt Guy 258–259
Thomas, Second Lt John 137
Thompson, Capt Lee 69–70, 85
Thompson, Capt Ralph 28
Thompson, First Lt Floyd 159
Thompson, First Lt Reid E. 287
Thompson, First Lt Robert D. 170
Thompson, Lt Clarence 215
Thompson, Lt Richard 188, 190
Thorsen, Maj James D. 97, 98, 101
Tick, Lt Col 79
Time (magazine) 151
Toner, Lt Col James V. 64, 203
Toombs, First Lt Herbert, Jr. 291–292
Toppins, Capt Ed 165, 166, 186
Torgeson, Second Lt Elmer 215
Toth, Lt Lajos 174
tours of duty 213
Tracy, Lt Don 215
Trafton, First Lt Frederick O. 97, 98, 100
training 18, 23, 33, 57, 77, 86, 89, 100, 120, 151, 154, 161, 233
Tranquillo, Lt Vincent 265
Transportation Plan 94, 95, 96, 101
Trautt, Lt R.A. 242
Treaty of Brest-Litovsk 16
Tresville, Capt Robert 157–158
Trevsik, Lt Victor 131
Tribbett, Lt Frank 142, 143
tricycle landing gear 42
Trident Conference 23
Trombley, Second Lt Ray 48
Turner, Capt Andrew "Jug" 158, 239, 256, 265, 266
Tuskegee Program 151, 154, 160

317

Twining, Capt Robert B.   40
Twining, Gen Merrill B.   40
Twining, Maj Gen Nathan F.   11, 40, 77, 83, 99, 201, 231, 234
Twining, Rear Adm Nathan Crook   40
Tyler, Maj James O. "Tim"   110, 121, 142, 143, 239, 240

United Opposition   221, 225, 227–228
US Army: Fifth Army   82; VI Corps   154
US Navy   44
US strategy   17–19, 21–25, 36, 39, 66, 70–71, 82, 93, 114, 115–116, 119, 239
USAAC (US Army Air Corps)   41
USAAF (US Army Air Force)   114, 115, 230, 256; 1st Combat Camera Unit   182; 305th Wing   213; Air Forces: Eighth   11, 12, 13, 21, 36, 38, 39–40, 44, 47, 53, 57, 59, 61, 70, 71, 73, 76, 83, 93, 94, 95, 115, 145, 146, 148, 235, 277, 284; VIII Bomber Command   71, 95; VIII Fighter Command   51, 57, 76, 81, 83, 207, 236–237; VIII Technical Command   82; Eleventh   40; Far East   153; Fifteenth   11, 12, 13, 36, 37–38, 39–40, 42, 44, 47, 49, 52, 56, 57, 58, 59, 61, 66, 70, 71–72, 73, 75, 77, 81, 82, 83, 88, 92, 93, 94, 95, 105, 111, 149, 153, 231, 232, 235, 239, 244, 270, 277, 278–279, 300; XV Fighter Command   11, 12, 77, 113, 160, 168, 169, 170, 180, 189–190, 196, 207, 213, 235, 236–237, 239, 241, 257, 258, 261, 264, 270, 278; Ninth   21, 27, 36, 39, 76, 94, 96; IX Bomber Command   36, 39; North African Strategic Air Forces   39; Northwest African Tactical Air Force   151; Tenth   17; Thirteenth   40; Twelfth   12, 39, 41, 57, 77, 88, 92, 277; XII Air Support Command   151; XII Bomber Command   39; Army Air Forces Evaluation Board   96; Bomb Groups: 2nd   74; 9th   86; 44th   24, 25, 28, 30, 31–32, 33, 36; 93rd   24, 27, 28, 29, 30, 31, 32, 33, 36; 98th   18, 24, 30, 36; 301st   74; 321st   50, 63; 340th   50, 298; 376th   21, 24, 26, 27, 28, 29, 30, 33, 36, 47; 389th   24, 25, 27, 33, 34, 36; 449th   73; 454th   230; 459th   46; 463rd   107; 477th Medium   160; Bomb Squadrons: 14th   153; 513th   47–48; 885th (Special)   207; Bomb Wings   41; 5th   41, 109, 131, 137, 141, 155, 156, 159, 161, 163, 165, 167, 175, 186–187, 218, 219, 220, 234, 239, 241, 243, 244, 246, 253–254, 256, 258, 260–261, 262, 267–268, 284, 285, 286, 290, 297; 47th   130, 140, 142, 159, 161, 162, 165, 166–167, 168, 220, 267, 282, 293; 49th   41, 53, 144, 155, 156, 162, 165, 187, 209, 252, 261, 268, 277, 279; 55th   119–120, 144, 147, 155, 156, 163, 165, 166, 167, 211, 219, 258, 260–261, 267; 57th   155, 298; 304th   145, 155, 156, 159, 161, 165, 219, 239, 242, 243, 244, 251, 259, 267, 268, 280, 295; 306th   164; Fighter Groups: 1st   39, 49, 52–53, 55–56, 60, 61–62, 80, 82, 86, 87, 91–92, 97, 104, 106, 107, 113, 122–130, 132, 138, 139, 140–141, 172, 183, 185, 186, 187, 189, 207–208, 213–214, 216–217, 234, 258, 286; 4th   57, 100, 146, 148, 170–172; 14th   39, 48, 52, 53, 54, 55, 59, 60, 61–62, 70, 80, 81, 87, 88, 96, 97, 98, 102, 103–104, 105, 113, 135–137, 138–139, 169, 172, 174, 181–182, 185, 188, 189–190, 191–192, 193, 207–208, 213–214, 217–218, 234; 20th   51; 31st   12–13, 77, 86, 88–90, 91, 92, 97–99, 100, 101, 103, 105, 107, 112–113, 119–120, 131, 137, 138, 141, 143–144, 146–149, 159, 162, 170, 187–188, 189–192, 196, 233, 236, 238–239, 261–266, 270, 271–274, 275, 277–278, 279, 280–281, 284, 285–286, 289–291, 293–295, 296; 33rd   150; 52nd "Yellow Tails"   13, 77, 92, 101, 105, 107, 109, 110, 111–112, 113, 120–122, 130–131, 135, 140, 142–143, 144, 145, 147–149, 172, 175, 176, 178–179, 180–181, 182–183, 184, 186–187, 206, 207, 208, 211, 236, 237–238, 239, 243–244, 246, 248, 249–250, 252, 254–256, 257–258,

INDEX

259, 264–265, 268–269, 270, 274, 278, 291–292, 295; 55th 51; 56th 86; 79th 56, 154; 82nd 39, 48–50, 51, 52, 53–54, 59, 60, 63, 69, 70, 74, 80, 82–83, 84–85, 86–87, 91, 92, 96, 97, 101–102, 103, 105, 107, 112–113, 122–130, 132, 137, 138, 139–140, 146, 161, 170, 173–174, 176, 178, 181–182, 189–191, 192, 193, 196, 197–201, 202, 212–213, 234; 86th 191; 322nd 158, 241–242; 325th "Checkertail Clan" 13, 39, 56, 57–58, 59, 64, 65–69, 77, 78–79, 84, 86, 87, 91, 92, 97, 101, 102–103, 107–109, 113, 114, 116–119, 132–135, 138, 140, 143, 144, 145–146, 148, 149, 154, 159–160, 168, 170–171, 173, 174, 179–181, 184, 185, 193–196, 202–203, 205–206, 209–211, 212, 236, 237, 239, 241, 242, 249, 251, 252–253, 254–256, 257, 258, 259, 261, 263, 264, 265, 266–267, 271–273, 275–276, 277, 278, 279–280, 281–282, 283–284, 296–297, 298–299; 332nd "Red Tails" 11–12, 154–157, 159–163, 165–168, 186, 218–220, 234, 236, 237–238, 239, 241, 242–243, 244–245, 247, 248, 249, 251, 252, 253–254, 256, 258, 259, 260, 261, 262–263, 265, 266, 267–268, 269, 270, 273, 278–279, 280–281, 282–283, 286–290, 292–294, 295–296, 297–298, 299–300; 354th "Pioneer Mustang" 76, 77; 357th 76; Fighter Squadrons: 2nd 107, 109, 110, 111–112, 120–121, 130, 131, 140, 141, 142, 143, 145, 147, 172, 175, 178–179, 182–183, 187, 206, 238, 244, 250, 252, 254, 258, 268–269, 277, 291, 295; 4th 110, 112, 121, 131–132, 141, 142–143, 145, 175, 181, 184, 187, 206, 209, 239, 250, 274–275; 5th 110–111, 112, 121–122, 130, 131, 143, 145, 149, 172, 175, 176, 178, 181, 183, 184, 206, 246, 250, 252, 254; 27th 56, 113, 122, 123–127, 129, 138, 187, 216, 217; 37th 60, 62, 81–82, 87, 91, 99, 103–104, 138–139, 188, 189, 215; 48th 48, 55, 60, 87, 99, 102, 104, 105, 174, 181, 185, 188–189, 215; 49th 54–55, 59, 61, 102, 104, 135, 136–137, 139, 181, 188, 214–215; 71st 56, 60, 122, 124–128, 138, 187, 216; 94th 56, 60, 86, 104, 107, 122, 126, 128, 138, 139, 185, 187, 216–217; 95th 52, 54, 69, 80, 83, 85, 96, 102, 105, 122, 137–138, 139, 140–141, 146–147, 170, 174, 176–177, 189, 190–191, 192, 193, 213; 96th 52, 54, 63, 84, 85, 101–102, 122, 129, 137, 146, 170, 173, 174, 176–177, 189, 190, 193, 196, 197, 201, 213; 97th 50–51, 52, 53, 59–60, 69, 80, 83, 84, 102, 122, 137, 138, 139, 146, 170, 173, 176–177, 189, 190–191, 193, 196, 197, 213; 99th 150–154, 160–161, 163, 186, 219, 220, 244–246, 247, 251, 260, 267, 270, 276, 282–283, 292, 293, 295, 296, 297; 100th 154, 157–158, 220, 245, 248, 251, 252, 260, 267, 276, 280–281, 282–283, 287–288, 292–293, 297–298; 209th 196; 301st 154, 155, 156, 157, 159, 161, 220–221, 245, 248–249, 257, 260, 267–268, 276, 282, 283, 286, 293–294, 298; 302nd 154, 155, 156, 157, 159, 220–221, 245, 246, 248, 251–252, 260, 267, 276, 278; 307th 90, 91, 97, 98, 100, 101, 105, 112, 120, 137, 138, 141, 143–145, 147, 170, 187–188, 192, 275, 277, 279, 285, 290–291, 294; 308th 91, 97, 98, 100, 101, 105, 112, 120, 138, 141–142, 145, 146, 147, 170, 187–188, 192, 196, 262, 263, 265, 275, 277, 285, 290, 294; 309th 90, 91, 97, 98, 99, 100, 101, 104, 105, 112, 120, 131, 138, 141, 142, 144, 145, 147, 148, 170, 188, 190, 192, 261–263, 275, 277–278, 290, 294–295; 317th 57, 64, 66–68, 80, 103, 119, 132–134, 179, 193–194, 209, 298–299; 318th 79, 241, 256, 257; 319th 58, 64, 195; 334th 146, 170–172; 414th Night 70; Fighter Wings: 306th 83, 196; HALPRO (Halverson Project 63) 17, 18–20, 21, 22, 25 USSTAF (US Strategic Air Forces) 39–40, 72, 93, 94, 115

Van Horn, Lt Henry   188, 191
Van Sice, Lt Bob   139
Van Winkle, Lt Donald   291
Varnell, First Lt Sully   110, 112, 121, 122, 141, 147, 180
Vashina, Lt Stanley J.   147
Vaughan, Lt Tommy   177
Vernon, Second Lt Olen E.   294
Villa, Pancho   22
Vitale, Lt Thomas   139
Vizante, Capitan Aviator Dan   123
Vogt, Second Lt Tom   196
Voll, First Lt John J.   142, 145, 147, 170, 187
Voss, Capt L.D.   253, 282
Vrilakas, Capt Bob "Smokey"   49–50, 56

Wagner, First Lt Michael   102
Wagner, Lt Col Boyd "Buzz"   86
Wagner, Maj John   275
Walker, First Lt Jack   50, 51, 53
Walker, Lt Jimmy   165–166
Walker, Second Lt Quitman C.   260
war diaries   13, 48, 49, 52–53, 56, 62, 91, 107, 111, 121, 130–131, 138, 142–143, 145, 147–148, 152, 186, 206–207, 244, 254, 257, 258, 264, 270, 271, 274, 277, 281, 284, 290, 295
Warford, Maj Victor E.   120, 141, 147, 188, 190
Warsaw Uprising   116, 232
Wasser, Second Lt M.J.   277
Watson, Lt Spann   220
Watson, Maj Ralph "Doc"   172, 178
Watts, Second Lt Samuel, Jr.   287
weaponry   22, 28; 20mm cannon (US)   124, 135; .30-caliber Browning M1919 machine gun (US)   43; .50-caliber machine gun (US)   43, 89, 124, 177, 218; antiaircraft guns   31, 32, 36, 48; 88mm AA gun (Germany)   25, 28, 63, 260; R4M rocket (Germany)   284

weather conditions   38, 50, 55, 56, 58, 59, 61, 70, 71, 72, 73, 91, 97, 100, 103, 105, 118, 138, 141, 142, 146, 148, 167, 169, 182, 192, 207, 236, 243–244, 247, 252, 255, 257–258, 259, 264, 268, 270, 273, 276
Weathers, Lt Luke   259–260
Wehrman, First Lt Bob   100
Weissenberger, Maj Theodor   284–285
White, First Lt Walter   102, 104, 189
Whitehouse, Lt Col Thomas B.   181, 193
Whitmire, Lt C.C.   249, 259
Wicklund, Capt Harold   21, 26, 28
Wiggins, First Lt Robert   156, 247
Wilder, Second Lt William M.   290
Wiley, Maj James   250
Wilhelm, Lt David C.   101
Williams, First Lt Robert   287, 292–293
Williams, Lt Edwin R.   184–185
Willow Run Reference Book   44
Willsie, First Lt Dick   70, 122–123, 128, 129, 130, 182, 190, 191, 193, 197–201, 213
Wilson, First Lt Charles   240, 250, 299
windshield defroster   179, 180
Winston, Second Lt Paul   104
Wise, First Lt Henry   219
Wisner, Second Lt Allen   146
withdrawal support   87, 96, 99, 101, 103, 104, 105, 107, 113, 120, 149, 172, 189, 291
Wood, Col Jack   33
Woodman, Lt Victor A.   195, 196, 210
Woods, First Lt Carroll S.   245, 246
Woods, Second Lt Willard L.   157–158
World War I   16, 22
Wörner, Oberleutnant Ernst   288

Zelinski, First Lt Walter   110, 172
Zoerb, First Lt Dan   109, 112, 141, 142
Zuckerman, Prof Zolly   93–94